Predators and Prizes

William N. Still, Jr., Series Editor

Classics in Maritime History

What Finer Tradition:
The Memoirs of Thomas O. Selfridge, Jr., Rear Admiral, U.S.N.
by Thomas O. Selfridge, Jr.
A Year on a Monitor and the Destruction of Fort Sumter
by Alvah F. Hunter
Confederate Navy Chief: Stephen R. Mallory
by Joseph T. Durkin
Admiral of the New Empire: The Life and Career of George Dewey
by Ronald Spector
Sloops & Shallops
by William A. Baker
The Panama Route, 1848–1869
by John Haskell Kemble
The Confederate Privateers
by William Morrison Robinson, Jr.

Studies in Maritime History

Stoddert's War: Naval Operations
During the Quasi-War with France, 1798–1801
by Michael A. Palmer
The British Navy and the American Revolution
by John A. Tilley
Iron Afloat: The Story of the Confederate Armorclads
by William N. Still, Jr.
A Maritime History of the United States:
The Role of America's Seas and Waterways
by K. Jack Bauer
Confederate Shipbuilding
by William N. Still, Jr.
Raid on America: The Dutch Naval Campaign of 1672–1674
by Donald G. Shomette and Robert D. Haslach
Lifeline of the Confederacy:
Blockade Running During the Civil War
by Stephen R. Wise
Admiral Harold R. Stark: Architect of Victory, 1939–1945
by B. Mitchell Simpson, III
History and the Sea: Essays on Maritime Strategies
by Clark G. Reynolds
Predators and Prizes: American Privateering
and Imperial Warfare, 1739–1748
by Carl E. Swanson
"We Will Stand by You": Serving in the Pawnee, *1942–1945*
by Theodore C. Mason

PREDATORS AND PRIZES
AMERICAN PRIVATEERING
AND IMPERIAL WARFARE, 1739–1748

Carl E. Swanson

University of South Carolina Press

Portions of chapter 1 appeared in the *International Journal of Maritime History,* I (1989), 253–78; portions of chapter 4 appeared in Roger L. Emerson *et al.,* eds., *Man and Nature: Proceedings of the Canadian Society for Eighteenth-Century Studies* (London, Ont.: Althouse Press, Faculty of Education, The University of Western Ontario, 1982), 119–29; portions of chapter 5 appeared in the *William and Mary Quarterly,* 3d Ser., XLII (1985), 357–82; and portions of chapter 7 appeared in the *American Neptune,* XLII (1982), 36–56. All are reprinted here with permission.

Published in Columbia, South Carolina, by the University of South Carolina Press

Manufactured in the United States of America

Library of Congress Cataloging-in-Publication Data

Swanson, Carl E.
    Predators and prizes : American privateering and imperial warfare,
1739–1748 / Carl E. Swanson.
        p.   cm.—(Studies in maritime history)
    "[At] the Department of History of the University of Western
Ontario . . . this study began as a doctoral thesis"—P.
    Includes bibliographical references (p.   )
    Includes index.
    ISBN 0-87249-720-8
    1. United States—History—King George's War, 1744–1748—Naval
operations.   2. Anglo-Spanish War, 1739–1748—Naval operations.
3. Privateering—America—History—18th century.   4. Great Britian—
—Colonies—America—History—18th century.   I. Title.   II. Series.
E198.S83   1990
973.2'6—dc20   90-12917

FOR JAN

Contents

Tables

viii

Illustrations

Figures

Maps

ACKNOWLEDGMENTS

I HAVE INCURRED MANY DEBTS IN THE PREPARATION OF THIS BOOK. IT WOULD take many more pages than are available to acknowledge everyone who has helped me complete the voyage and bring this prize to port. I have been especially fortunate to receive generous financial support. I am indebted to my colleagues in the Department of History at East Carolina University for selecting me as the Lawrence F. Brewster Scholar for 1987–1989. This award, named in honor of an esteemed professor emeritus in the department, provided a stipend as well as a much-needed reduction in my teaching load, which enabled me to complete the manuscript much sooner than would otherwise have been the case.

All the research and much of the writing of this book took place during the many years I lived in Canada. Canadians are justly proud of their universities, and I have many fond memories of academia in the "true north." The Department of History of the University of Western Ontario, where this study began as a doctoral thesis, provided grants and scholarships without which the book would never have been started, much less completed. I also received timely support from the Canada Council, the Social Sciences and Humanities Research Council of Canada, and the Faculty of Arts of York University.

Numerous libraries, archives, and computer centers have assisted me. The staff of the D.B. Weldon Library of the University of Western Ontario was especially helpful. Pat Guyette of the Inter-

Library Loan Department at East Carolina University's J.Y. Joyner Library provided important assistance. The staffs of the Manuscripts Division of the Library of Congress; the Suffolk County, Massachusetts, Courthouse; the Massachusetts Archives; the Rhode Island State Archives; the Historical Society of Pennsylvania; and the Newport, Rhode Island, and Massachusetts Historical Societies all helped me find the widely scattered scraps of evidence concerning privateering. I received invaluable assistance from the Social Science Computing Laboratory of the University of Western Ontario, the Newfoundland and Labrador Computer Services at Memorial University of Newfoundland, the Institute for Social Research at York University, and the Computing and Information Systems of East Carolina University.

Many scholars have offered valuable criticisms, ideas, and suggestions over the years. I appreciate their advice, even though I did not always follow it. I was especially fortunate to be a member of the American Historians' Seminar at the University of Western Ontario and profited from the ideas of Jack Blocker, Bob Hohner, Jean Matthews, and Peter Russell, among others. I owe a major debt to Dick Alcorn, formerly of the University of Western Ontario, who first introduced me to computing and quantitative methodology. Skip Fischer of Memorial University of Newfoundland has been involved with the study almost from its inception; it has benefited from his advice over the years. Joe Ernst of York University read an earlier version of the manuscript and offered numerous valuable suggestions. Paul Lovejoy, former Chairman of York's History Department, provided needed encouragement and a convenient teaching schedule at a critical juncture, for which I am especially grateful. My colleagues at East Carolina, particularly Todd Savitt, Bill Still, Don Parkerson, and Ken Wilburn, have been very supportive.

Large debts are owed to four good friends from Ontario. I first considered a career in history after enrolling in Craig Simpson's course in nineteenth-century American history at the University of Western Ontario. In this regard, I was only the first of many students who have been inspired by his teaching excellence. David Flaherty supervised the thesis on which this book is based. His encouragement, suggestions, and guidance have been instrumental to this study. My biggest intellectual debt is owed to Ian Steele. His seminar in the First British Empire as well as his numerous books and articles have largely influenced my perception of the English

Atlantic in the seventeenth and eighteenth centuries. He also read the penultimate draft of the book and improved it with his challenging criticism. Don Sutherland of the University of Maryland, College Park, has helped in many ways, not the least of which was reading an earlier version of the manuscript. Don offered encouragement (and a place to stay) during lean years when positions for American historians in Canada were nearly nonexistent, and Americanists wandered like migrant laborers.

My biggest obligations are due to my family. My mother, my older brother, and my cousins, aunts, and uncles from Virginia introduced me to many of the historic sites in Virginia and Washington, D.C., and nurtured an abiding interest in American history. As usual, I owe more to my wife, Jan, than I can ever repay. Her advice, criticism, suggestions, and encouragement were invaluable. I could not have written this without her. That is why she has a page to herself, though it is hardly fair compensation.

Predators and Prizes

INTRODUCTION

PRIVATEERING AND PIRACY HAVE FASCINATED THE POPULAR IMAGINATION
since at least the seventeenth century. Numerous memoirs of
Caribbean buccaneers entertained the reading public of the
seventeenth and eighteenth centuries.[1] Nineteenth-century
romantic novels such as Robert Louis Stevenson's *Treasure Island*
have delighted subsequent generations with tales of buried
treasure, bloodthirsty pirates, and an endless supply of bottles of
rum. In the twentieth century, Hollywood has largely replaced
memoirs and novels. Rousing adventure pictures have achieved
enduring popularity, and the swashbuckler has become a standard
film genre. This interest in buccaneering is not limited to popular
art forms. Much recent work by colonial American historians
reveals that serious scholars are intrigued by pirates and their role
in Europe's development of the New World.[2] The struggle for prizes
on the high seas remains a subject of general interest.

During the intercolonial wars of the seventeenth and eighteenth
centuries the imperial governments of Great Britain, Spain, and
France encouraged businessmen to man and equip their own
private warships to intercept enemy commerce. As a result,
thousands of private men-of-war attacked rival merchantmen in the
North Atlantic. Capturing enemy vessels and cargoes (which were
referred to as prizes) weakened the enemy's ability to wage war
while profiting their owners at the same time. Privately financed, as
their name implies, privateers did not drain the national treasury, a
point appreciated by government officials nurtured in the political

1

economy of mercantilism. Private men-of-war also added to
national sea power at a time when states were simply too weak to
maintain navies that could control the seas. This book examines the
important role that privateering played in the British colonies
during the War of Jenkins' Ear and King George's War, the wars of
1739–1748.

Marshalling support for a nation's war effort by appealing to the
base desire for plunder, privateering looks like a curious and
disreputable enterprise from the perspective of the twentieth
century. Privateering seems but one small step away from the
infamous activity of piracy. Indeed, the difference between piracy
and privateering is not often made clear, and the legal activity blurs
into the illegal until there is no difference at all. Aside from
questions of notoriety, privateers took mariners and maritime
resources away from the Royal Navy, undermining the effectiveness
of the nation's fleet. Also, as private men-of-war were individually
owned and privately operated for profit, government coordination
of their activities was all but impossible. For just such reasons
scholars have often dismissed privateering as an unimportant aspect
of eighteenth-century warfare.

This book takes a different tack. It argues that far from being an
insignificant activity of borderline legality, privateering
represented a major and popular form of wartime endeavor.
Officials in London and the colonies encouraged privateering
ventures, and well-respected merchants responded by investing
heavily in private men-of-war. Hundreds of stout colonial vessels
worth thousands of pounds sterling were active in the maritime
prize war, and thousands of jack tars put their lives on the line.
Since hundreds of Spanish and French privateers also plied the seas
during wartime, even those merchants and mariners who shunned
personal involvement in privateering voyages were inextricably
caught up in the international scramble for prizes.

Privateering thus had a marked impact on Atlantic commerce in
the 1740s, just as it did in earlier wars and would continue to do in
the subsequent conflicts of the eighteenth and early nineteenth
centuries. Despite increasing economic growth and development in
the Old World and the New and the "rise of the state," Europe's
most important colonial powers could not dispense with
privateering. Instead of the increasing security and heightened
productivity which some economic historians have claimed for
ocean shipping during the eighteenth century,[3] the Atlantic was a

dangerous highway during the era's frequent colonial conflicts. The "military revolution" notwithstanding,[4] Europe's most powerful navies could not control the seas. The importance of privateering in the wars of 1739–1748 also reveals the commercial nature of the First British Empire. This colonial conflict was waged for trade, not conquest.[5] Not every private man-of-war was successful, of course, but the capture of a single merchantman of average value yielded windfall profits to the privateer's owners and substantial prize money to the crew. With such rewards in the offing, it is understandable that large numbers of colonial Americans were attracted to an enterprise that accounted for prizes worth millions of pounds sterling, and that for many colonists privateering and warfare were synonymous.

The book is arranged topically. Chapter 1 begins with a discussion of privateering's popularity and its relationship to the mercantilist world view of the eighteenth century. With its emphasis on seizing enemy commerce, but not drawing from the beleaguered exchequer, privateering augmented British sea power and enjoyed strong support among government officials and the merchant community. Chapters 2–4 discuss the organization of privateering. Chater 2 examines the British government's attempts to control private men-of-war through various statutes, instructions, and vice-admiralty court proceedings. Chapter 3 analyzes the shipping employed in the prize war and comments on the insecurity of Atlantic sea-lanes. Chapter 4 addresses the extensive competition for seamen to man the naval and merchant fleets as well as private men-of-war. The next two chapters explore the colonial privateers' extensive theaters of operations and demonstrate that insecurity, not increasing productivity, characterized ocean shipping during imperial conflicts. Chapter 5 examines the actions of British colonial private men-of-war, and suggests that privateering operations played the leading role in America's war effort. Chapter 6 discusses the disruptive influence that Spanish and French private men-of-war exerted on Anglo-American commerce. Chapter 7 investigates the predators' impact on transatlantic trade and speculates about the profitability of privateering. The Afterword returns to the general argument of privateering's relationship to mercantilism and the weakness of the eighteenth-century state.

I have tried as much as possible to retain the original spelling, punctuation, and grammar in all quotations. This includes the names of vessels. Captain Lahaye, a French privateer commander from Saint-Domingue, for example, probably captured British prizes on board the *Maréchal Vaudreuil,* not the *Marshal Vaudroy*; Captain de Lopez's Havana private man-of-war was probably the *San Miguel,* not the *St. Michael.* I have used the original spellings as they appeared in British colonial newspapers. Eighteenth-century American editors took great liberties when spelling non-English names, and I often determined that several spelling variations referred to the same individual. The *Pennsylvania Gazette,* for example, reported on 20 May 1742 that "Captain Don Juan de Laon Handinio" captured the *St. Andrew,* William Grigg master. The *New-York Weekly Journal*'s edition for 31 May 1742 stated that "Don Juan de Leon Handino" seized the *St. Andrew.* Three weeks later on 20 June the *Boston News-Letter* informed its readers that Captain Grigg surrendered to "Captain John Vandego." The *South-Carolina Gazette* added yet another spelling when it announced that "Captain Fandino" intercepted the *St. Andrew.* These spelling practices confused twentieth-century computers, which regarded four different spellings as four different commanders. I have assiduously tried to eliminate such duplicates. All dates are presented in Old Style, but I have refrained from using 1745/46, 1746/47, etc., for days falling between 1 January and 25 March.

Chapter 1

THE POPULARITY OF PRIVATEERING

T HE CONFUSION OF PRIVATEERING AND PIRACY IS A CURIOUS ASPECT OF THE fascination with predators and prizes. Novels and movies draw few distinctions between the two, and historians have followed suit. Perhaps J. Franklin Jameson set the tone for modern scholars when he coupled these two forms of endeavor in his extremely valuable collection of sources, *Privateering and Piracy in the Colonial Period: Illustrative Documents*.[1] At any rate, other historians have likewise associated privateering with piracy.[2] Thus, the biographer of Isaac Sears, the New York Revolutionary patriot and privateer, blurred the differences between the actions of pirates and privateers. "The work of privateers resembled . . . that of pirates. . . . Privateers existed on the margins of legality and respectability. Between them and piracy lay their commissions or letters of marque, but when the authority of those commissions was questioned, or when the privateersmen acted outside the limits of their commissions, they easily slipped into the pirates' ranks."[3] The picture that emerges is one of a shadowy activity of borderline legality that attracted only marginal elements of colonial society.

Although this view may be appropriate for seventeenth-century privateering and piracy,[4] it fails to describe privateering in the eighteenth century. Piracy declined at the end of the 1600s and was stamped out of its strongholds in the Caribbean and the Indian Ocean shortly thereafter.[5] Privateering, however, expanded and became an increasingly important enterprise in each of the

5

subsequent conflicts between Europe's colonial powers. In America, private men-of-war cruised during King William's War (1689–1697) and Queen Anne's War (1702–1713). As sparsely settled and weakly developed outposts of empire, however, colonial participation was limited. This would change when the European powers resumed their intercolonial wars during the 1740s.

The wars of 1739–1748 afford an opportunity to examine the important role that British colonial privateering played in imperial warfare at midcentury. (These dates span two wars commonly called the War of Jenkins' Ear and King George's War.) The long period of relative peace beginning in 1713 witnessed tremendous growth in Britain's New World possessions. By 1739 an unbroken string of colonies extended along the Atlantic seaboard from Newfoundland to the Annapolis Valley to Georgia. The British West Indies had also prospered. Britain's provinces had grown from crude settlements into considerable cities, towns, and agricultural communities. British North America's population, political institutions, and economy expanded greatly. Pennsylvania, for example, which had been founded just before the wars of King William and Queen Anne, grew dramatically, and Philadelphia rivaled Boston as the leading colonial port. New York, whose English title was relatively new during the conflicts of 1689–1713, also challenged Boston in the colonial urban hierarchy. Shipping between Britain and America became much more frequent and regular, aided by the eradication of piracy as well as economic growth. America's ability to aid the mother country in intercolonial conflict was much enhanced. Despite these increases in economic growth, imperial political institutions, and naval and military strength, privateering retained its important position in the colonies' contributions to Britain's war effort when hostilities broke out between Britain and Spain.

Encouraged by imperial and colonial governmental officials at every level, privateering attracted some of the most affluent and respected members of British North American society. This was clearly not a borderline enterprise limited to marginal elements in American society. In fact, the desire to launch privateering voyages served as a principal cause of the War of Jenkins' Ear and added to the conflict's popularity in England and the colonies.

Historians generally agree that war between Britain and Spain erupted in 1739 because of colonial trade.[6] Britain wanted to

Map 1. North America during the wars of 1739–1748. Drawn by G. Aaron Russell.

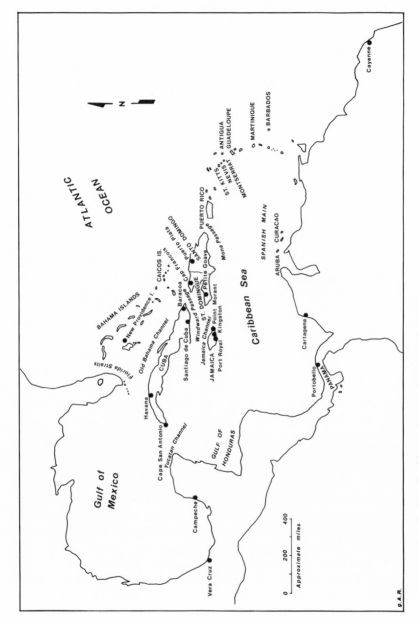

Map 2. The Caribbean during the wars of 1739–1748. Drawn by G. Aaron Russell.

expand its West Indian commerce, and Spanish colonial markets were especially appealing. The Treaty of Utrecht, however, virtually prohibited British merchants from trading with the Spanish colonies. The South Seas Company participated in Spanish West Indian trade fairs, but was limited to a single vessel of five hundred tons. That "annual ship" was the entering wedge of a sizable illicit commerce.[7] Cheap British goods were in great demand, so Spanish colonial merchants ignored the laws proscribing British trade.

Not surprisingly, officials in Old Spain disapproved and took steps to stamp out this illegal trade. *Guarda-costas,* Spanish coast guard vessels, patrolled the Caribbean to prevent British smugglers from reaching Spanish colonial ports. Ranging far from coastal waters, the *guarda-costas* stopped every British vessel they encountered. Legal niceties were often ignored, and anything the Spaniards regarded as Spanish produce, from logwood or cacao to goods produced in British as well as Spanish colonies, or even pieces of eight, which were legel tender throughout the Caribbean, could result in the forfeiture of vessel and cargo.[8] These provocative actions eventually became a major precipitant of the hostilities.

British subjects on both sides of the Atlantic were furious with the *guarda-costas.* The seemingly indiscriminate captures of British merchantmen prompted numerous indignant stories of Spanish "depredations" in British and American newspapers throughout the 1730s. The *Boston News-Letter,* for example, reported on 5 March 1730 that the Spanish had captured fourteen English vessels in the Bay of Honduras. Two weeks later the *News-Letter* related that a *guarda-costa* had seized the sloop *Olive Branch,* bound for Philadelphia from Jamaica, even though the Spaniards could find no evidence to condemn this sloop. After two months' detention in Mexico, the *Olive Branch* was finally released after the captain paid a bribe of seven hundred pieces of eight.[9] The numerous stories with English datelines that appeared in American newspapers indicate that British periodicals published similar accounts of Spanish captures.[10]

In addition to the questionable legality of these seizures, the rough treatment British tars received from the *guarda-costas* outraged the press. After taking a large sloop belonging to Boston merchant Peter Faneuil, for example, a Spanish boarding party "in cold Blood cut the Master and all his Men to pieces, saving only the Cabbin-Boy."[11] The most famous of these bloody encounters with the *guarda-costas* occurred in 1731 when the *Rebecca,* commanded by Capt. Robert Jenkins, was seized on its way from Jamaica to London. After a sound beating and repeated hangings (by his neck, but he was cut down each time before he died), Jenkins's captors finally believed that he was telling the truth when he said there was no hidden cash on the *Rebecca.* The Spanish commander "took hold of his [Jenkins's] Left Ear and with his Cutlass slit it down, and then another of the Spaniards took hold of it and tore it off, but gave him the Piece of his Ear again, bidding him to carry it to his Majesty King George."[12] Years later Jenkins supposedly displayed this "Piece of his Ear" before Parliament, providing historians with the colorful name for the Anglo-Spanish conflict of 1739–1743. Figure 1.1 shows a press account of the severing of Jenkins's ear.

While British subjects clamored for action against the *guarda-costas,* the Dutch colonists from Curaçao seemed to provide a model for dealing with the Spaniards. After a series of allegedly illegal seizures, Dutch officials fitted out four sloops to pursue four *guarda-costas.* Off the coast of New Granada, the Dutch captured three of the Spanish predators. The moral of the story was not lost on the *Boston Evening-Post*'s editor: "If the English were permitted to act with the like Resolution with these gallant Dutchmen, News of our Vessels being taken and plundered by the Spaniards, would not be so often heard as it has been of late years."[13]

Alarmed by the deteriorating relations, British and Spanish diplomats held a series of talks to maintain peace between the two nations. These delicate negotiations focused on the *guarda-costas,* illicit trade, and the tangled affairs of the South Seas Company in the Spanish Indies. Finally, an accommodation was concluded in the winter of 1738–1739. The Convention of El Pardo required Spain to pay £95,000 sterling as compensation for British losses. Because of Spanish grievances against the South Seas Company, this sum was never paid. This nonpayment became the proximate cause of the ensuing war.[14]

While diplomats tried to avert hostilities, English merchants called for retaliation against Spain. British businessmen wanted to increase their commerce with the Spanish colonies, and by 1738 many of them believed the best way to obtain Spanish goods (and redress grievances against the *guarda-costas*) was simply to go out and take Spanish ships on the high seas. The time for illicit trade

The *Rebecca*, *Robert Jenkins*, Mafter, failed from *Jamaica*, with a Lading of Sugar, &c. for *London*; but on the 9th of *April* laſt, being becalmed and near the *Havana*, a *Spaniſh Guarda Cofta*, which came out of that Harbour, came up with her by rowing with 16 Oars, when ſhe fired ſeveral Shot at the *Rebecca*, and ordered her Boat to be hoiſted out and ſent on board of her, which accordingly was done, and in it, with ſome others, went the Mate, with her Clearance from *Jamaica*, expecting that would give ſufficient ſatisfaction, it being a Time of profound Peace with *Spain*; but on the contrary, the People were detained by the *Spaniards*, who ſent the Boat back full of armed Men, who told Capt. *Jenkins*, that they were come to viſit his Ship for Money, Logwood, Hides, or Tallow, the Product of the *Spaniſh Settlements* in *America*. To which he anſwered, That the King of *Spain*'s Officers were welcome, and might do their Duty, for that there was nothing on board but what was the Growth and Produce of *Jamaica*. By that Time their Number amounted to about 50 Men. They broke open all her Hatches, Lockers and Chefts, in which

finding nothing to their Purpoſe, their Lieutenant ordered Capt. *Jenkins*'s Hands to be tied, as alſo his Mate's, and ſeized them to the Foremaſt, and then cut and violently beat a Mulatto Boy (his Servant) to extort a Confeſſion of there being Money in the Ship; but he confeſſing nothing, they began with Capt. *Jenkins*, putting a Rope about his Neck, and another about the Boy's, which they faſtned to him, and hoiſted them up to the Fore-Yard; the Boy being light, ſlipt through the Noofe, to the Captain's great Eaſe; and after keeping him hanging for a ſhort ſpace, they let him fall down amain on the Deck, and aſked him if he would not then confeſs where his Money was. But he ſtill told them he had none; on which he was hoiſted up a ſecond time, and ſwiftly let down again, and being then asked the ſame Queftion, he replied as before, adding that they might torture him to Death, but he could not make any other Anſwer: They threatned to burn the Ship, and him and his People in it, for that they were obſtinate Hereticks; but after giving him about half an hour's Reſpite, while they conſulted together about him, he having the Rope

all the while about his Neck, the Man who firſt put it on, told him he muſt go up again, ſearched his Pockets, took his ſilver Buckle-out of his Shoes, and then hoiſted him up and kept him hanging until he was quite ſtrangled, and then let him fall down the Fore-Hatch upon the Casks, which bruiſed him very much, from thence he was dragged by the Neck upon Deck again, and there lay to appearance dead for near a quarter of an Hour: When he recovered, their Lieutenant came to him with Piſtols and a Cutlaſs in his Hands, went to him, crying, Confeſs, Confeſs, or die: He told him he had no more Money than he had ſhewed him at firſt, being four Guineas, one Piſtole, and four double Doubloons, which he had already taken: The Lieutenant then took hold of his left Ear, and with his Cutlaſs ſlit it down; and then another of the *Spaniards* took hold of it and tore it off, but gave him the Piece of his Ear again, bidding him carry it to his Majeſty King *George*. Orders were then given for ſcalping of him, but finding his Head cloſe ſhaved, they forbore executing that part of his Sentence. His Mate, and Beatſwain were alfo umerciſully beat, but underwent no other Puniſhment. They ſtripped the whole

Crew of their Cloaths, Beds, Bedding, &c. The Captain's own Lofs, of his Watch, Gold, Cloaths, Linnen, &c. on a moderate Valuation, amounted to 112l. *Sterling* And in order to deſtroy the Ship, they took away all his Inſtruments of Navigation, and all the Candles they had, for want of which in the Night they burned Oil and Butter in the Benacle to ſteer by. Their Sloop appeared to have been built in *Bermuda*, and had *San Antonio* wrote in her Stern. Their Commander they called *Juan Francifco*, and their Lieutenant *Doree*; but theſe Names are ſuppoſed to be fictitious.

Having done tormenting the unhappy Capt. *Jenkins*, after keeping his Ship the beſt part of the Day, they difmiffed her, and the Captain bore away for the *Havana*, hoping to find there ſome *Britiſh Ships*, from whom he might procure ſufficient Neceſſaries to enable him to proceed on his Voyage; but thoſe in the Sloop perceiving it, ſtood after him, and declared that if he did not go immediately for the Gulph, they would ſet the Ship on Fire; and rather than have a ſecond Viſit from them, they recommended themſelves to the Mercy of the Seas; and after very many great Hardſhips and Perils, they happily in the River *Thames*

Figure 1.1. This report concerning the severing of Capt. Robert Jenkins's ear by a Spanish *guarda-costa* appeared in the *Pennsylvania Gazette* on 7 October 1731. This incident provided the colorful name of the Anglo-Spanish war of 1739–1743.

and diplomacy was over. The City of London petitioned both houses of parliament against the Convention of El Pardo.[15] Meanwhile, the numerous small London merchants and tradesmen who composed the "privateering interest" pressured the government to issue letters of marque and reprisal so British subjects would have a free hand to seize Spanish vessels.[16] For decades British businessmen had coveted Spanish commerce; for nearly ten years they had longed for revenge against the *guarda-costas*. Finally, Whitehall legalized both pursuits by authorizing letters of marque in June 1739.[17]

The War of Jenkins' Ear was popular in America mainly because it permitted privateering. Like their English counterparts, many colonial merchants and mariners were eager to fit out private men-of-war and get rich while they settled scores with the *guarda-costas*. American newspapers reflected the enthusiastic reactions to Britain's aggressive new policy. In Newport, Rhode Island, soon to be a center of colonial privateering, there was jubilation.

> Upon receiving the so long wish'd for News, that Liberty is granted us to make Reprisals upon the Spaniards, the Merchants of this Place are fitting out their Sloops for that Purpose, and will sail next week at farthest, they having already each of them several Voluntiers inlisted. This good News, and the Small Pox seeming intirely stop'd, causes universal Joy among the inhabitants here.[18]

West Indian colonists were also anxious to begin privateering voyages. " 'Tis said, that upon the first Advice of a War, all Business will be laid aside in Jamaica, but that of Privateering, the Men waiting with Impatience to have their Hands untied."[19]

Bostonians shared the excitement concerning the prospects of privateering. The *Boston Evening-Post* devoted most of its front page on 13 August to the duke of Newcastle's proclamation permitting Massachusetts Governor Jonathan Belcher to issue letters of marque. Two weeks later the *Evening-Post* again devoted page-one coverage to news about privateering because "there being of late much talk among us of fitting out Vessels to cruise upon the Spaniards, and great Hopes conceived of their Success; it is thought proper for the Information of Those concerned, to publish the following extracts from the Act of Parliament relating to Privateers."[20] At a time when American newspapers normally reserved the front page for European political news and essays, it was extremely unusual to see two issues in the same month devote page one to Massachusetts events. When Belcher subsequently proclaimed England's declaration of war against Spain, numerous spectators responded "with huzzahs & three volleys from the Regiment and Troop of

Guards and the discharge of the cannon at Castle William and the batteries."[21]

New Yorkers were no less exuberant than their New England neighbors. The newspapers devoted much space to the prize laws and published the proclamations authorizing letters of marque issued by Belcher and New York Lieutenant Governor George Clarke. By the end of August the city's merchants were busily equipping private men-of-war, and within two weeks of Clarke's proclamation the first New York privateers sailed out of port. In the last week of September New Yorkers learned that Capt. John Lush was sighted off the South Carolina coast on his way to the Spanish shipping lanes.[22]

Newspapers in Philadelphia, Williamsburg, and Charles Town also devoted their front pages to their governors' proclamations authorizing privateering, though the response was less positive than in the other British colonies.[23] Philadelphia's Quaker establishment shunned privateering because of religious scruples, thus greatly reducing the interest of the city's mercantile community in the prize war.[24] The press, however, covered privateering activities extensively, and eventually Philadelphians of other religious persuasions dispatched private men-of-war. The plantation colonies of the Chesapeake and the Carolinas, with fewer vessels to equip as privateers, were understandably less interested than their northern and West Indian neighbors. In addition, South Carolinians, separated from Spanish Florida by sparsely settled Georgia, were apprehensive about enemy actions. Even in the plantation colonies, however, Spanish prizes lured merchants and mariners to send out privateers from Norfolk and Charles Town.

The enthusiasm for privateering did not wane after the War of Jenkins' Ear began. In fact, Americans hoped the conflict would expand to include France. Newport merchant John Bannister was ready to begin privateering operations against the French in 1741: "Our Sloope the New Revenge 116 Tons Capt Allen We have in Such Readiness that upon advice of a french warr [I] can send her to Sea In 48 hours."[25] After France entered the war in 1744 privateering became even more popular in British North America. "Never did the privateering Spirit prevail here [Boston] as at this Time," the *Pennsylvania Gazette* reported during the summer of 1744.[26] The *New-York Weekly Post-Boy* agreed, " 'Tis certain the Spirit of Privateering has prevailed greatly in this City [New York], and but few of those fitted out here, have returned home empty."[27] When the privateer brigantine *Greyhound* was launched in Manhattan in 1744, two thousand New Yorkers (nearly 20 percent of the city's population) turned out to celebrate the occasion.[28] Letters to colonial editors also attested to the popularity of privateering. A letter to Benjamin Franklin, editor of the *Pennsylvania Gazette,* began, "As Privateering is now so much in Fashion, the printing of the following Question may be an Amusement." A mathematical puzzle followed concerning the number of hours required for a privateer to overtake a merchantman when they sailed at different speeds.[29] Numerous items from British periodicals that strongly supported privateering appeared in American newspapers: "Extract of a Letter from Bristol. . . . Nothing is to be seen here but the Rejoicing for the great Number of French Prizes brought into this Port; our Sailors are in the highest Spirits, and full of Money."[30] An article from Liverpool announced that "most of the large ships soon expected Home that are prime Sailors, are determin'd for Privateers, Men entering with great Alacrity."[31]

Throughout the war numerous press accounts praised privateersmen for their exploits against the enemy. The *Pennsylvania Gazette* reported that "the Barbados Gazette speaks in very handsome Terms of the Gallant Behaviour of Capt. Peter Marshal in the Prince Frederick Privateer of Rhodeisland."[32] Stories reprinted from London newspapers indicated that Captain Phillips, commander of the privateer *Alexander,* would receive "a considerable Pension . . . for his Bravery in taking the Solebay Man of War."[33] After capturing six French privateers that had menaced the sea-lanes around St. Kitts, Newport's Captain John Dennis was especially popular. "Capt. Dennis was highly caressed by the General, and other Gentlemen of the Island, who, as an Acknowledgement of his eminent Services, presented him with a Golden Oar, and a purse of 500 Pistoles."[34] Capt. John Burges, commander of the New York privateer snow *Royal Catharine,* also received a valuable gift when he returned home after taking an enemy privateer in 1748. "Immediately upon Capt. Burges's Arrival here, the principal Merchants of this City set Foot a Subscription for two Pieces of Plate, to be presented to him and his Lieutenant, as an Acknowledgement of the signal Service done in taking the above Privateer."[35] Commanders who were killed in action received eulogies praising their heroism and patriotism: "Captain [Thomas] Tucker was a Person of an excellent Disposition, and behaved with undaunted Courage and Resolution to his last Moment; he was justly beloved by his Men, and died much regretted by them all, as well as by every one who had the Pleasure of his Acquaintance."[36]

Privateering also received government support. Throughout the conflict officials in London and the colonies assisted the owners and mariners of private men-of-war. First, Parliament passed a new statute regulating private men-of-war designed to increase the profitability of privateering.[37] Informing colonial governors of this new law, the duke of Newcastle emphasized that private men-of-war would receive "the entire property of all Prizes;" that is, neither the Crown nor the Admiralty would take a percentage of the prize as perquisites of office. "This I am persuaded," Newcastle declared, "will be a great Inducement to His Majesty's Subjects to fit out rival Ships against the Spaniards, which you will encourage Those under your Government to do, as soon and as effectually as possible."[38] Responding to similar instructions in 1744 after France had become Spain's ally, Pennsylvania Lieutenant Governor George Thomas urged Philadelphians to fit out privateers and promised that he would "most readily give all the Encouragement and Assistance that in me lies, to every such Undertaking."[39] Rhode Island's legislature offered privateer owners much more tangible support when it loaned Godfrey Malbone, John Brown, and George Wanton "so many of the colony's small arms, pistols, cutlasses, and great shot, as they have occasion of, for fitting out their private men-of-war."[40]

New York privateers received support from the province's vice-admiralty court and chief executive. Royal customs collectors in Manhattan tried to exact the Molasses Act's enormous levy on French produce captured by New York predators, but admiralty judge Lewis Morris intervened. Morris decreed that "no Prize Sugars are Lyable to Pay the Duty laid upon Foreign Sugars etc."[41] Gov. George Clinton supported Morris by petitioning the Board of Trade "to interpose (in behalf of this City) with the Commissioners of the Customs to drop their pretensions to said Dutys, which will greatly encourage His Majesty's subjects to annoy the Enemy."[42] Similar action occurred in Massachusetts on 13 October 1744 when the House of Representatives resolved that "all Prize Goods which shall be brought in and condemned within this Province during the present war with France and Spain, shall be exempt from all Duties."[43]

British privateers were not alone in receiving government support as other belligerents encouraged their citizens to send out private men-of-war. In 1743 Philadelphia read the ominous news that "The French have made a new Regulation with Regard to their Privateers, which is so Advantageous, that Bretagne alone engages to fit out 500 Ships in Case of a War with England."[44] Spain also encouraged its privateers by awarding captors the prize shares that viceroys, captains-general, and governors had formerly claimed. Prize cargoes were also spared from port and sales taxes.[45] As Franco-Dutch relations deteriorated in 1748, the Dutch government supported its privateersmen by exempting them from naval impressment and by offering bounty money if they engaged French predators. In addition, the Dutch legislature, the States General, stopped deductions from the sales of prize vessels.[46]

The extensive colonial newspaper coverage and various government actions reveal the importance and widespread popularity of privateering. These press reports allowed colonists to learn about successes (and failures) in the prize war. By changing laws, altering customs regulations, and loaning supplies, officials successfully tried to increase the number of cruisers by making privateering more profitable. Merchants in every major colonial port dispatched private men-of-war to capture enemy merchantmen while thousands of men hoped to earn their fortunes serving on privateers. Privateering was clearly an extensive, popular, and possibly profitable enterprise.

The imperial government's official endorsement of private men-of-war and the popularity of privateering in America reveal much about the mercantilist world of the 1700s and the power of the eighteenth-century state. With its emphasis on destroying a rival's commerce but not adding to the government's financial burdens, privateering was perfectly attuned to the mercantilists' world view. Mercantilism has, of course, attracted considerable attention from economists and historians since Adam Smith's critique of England's "mercantile system" in *The Wealth of Nations*. Scholars have disagreed over the ultimate purpose of mercantilist policies. Did politicians and merchants attempt to increase the power of the state or did they merely facilitate private aggrandizement? The debate has thus centered on "power" versus "plenty."[47] Eli Heckscher, for example, emphasized that power was the ultimate end of mercantilist policies, while Jacob Viner, among others, contended that since wealth was essential to power, plenty was a major goal. Other scholars joined the debate.[48] More recently, some historians have suggested that mercantilism never existed. W.A. Speck has argued that Britain's "imperial authorities did not proceed from theoretical concepts when formulating views of colonial questions. . . . Above all, they were not implementing a body of doctrines that can be called mercantilism. Indeed, the notion that such a concept existed can no longer be seriously maintained."[49] D.C. Coleman has gone even further to expunge mercantilism as an analytical conception for the First British Empire: "As for mercantilism, in the end, though we may never succeed in disposing of the word we should at least understand that mercantilism is one of those non-existent entities that had to be invented in order to prevent the study of history from falling into the abyss of antiquarianism."[50] Surely such statements go too far. Arguing that mercantilism never existed because governments strayed from theoretical concepts when enacting or enforcing legislation is similar to suggesting that the United States, Great Britain, and Canada are not capitalist societies because governments play a powerful role in the economy, or that the Soviet Union and the People's Republic of China are not socialist states because of recent economic innovations based on profit and market mechanisms. Economists understand that perfect competition is a model that only exists in economics texts; historians should realize that "perfect mercantilism" is a similar concept. A mercantilistic world view clearly existed in the seventeenth and eighteenth centuries, and this outlook shaped the interactions of the British, Spanish, and French Empires in the 1740s.

Four basic beliefs formed the core of mercantilist policies. First, nations should strive for a favorable balance of trade. This idea, perhaps first stated in England by Edward Misselden in *The Circle of Commerce* (1618) and later popularized by Thomas Mun in *Englands Treasure by Frorraign Trade* (written in the 1620s but not published until the mid–1660s), became the mercantilists' central tenet. To achieve a favorable balance, nations enacted measures designed to encourage exports and limit imports, especially of manufactured goods.[51] Second, nations were vitally concerned about the flow of precious metals and tried to increase their holdings of gold and silver. Mercantilists were not prompted by the mistaken notion that only specie constituted wealth. Rather, precious metals were essential in certain markets, especially Asia and the Baltic, and were useful in clearing multilateral trading relations at a time when bills of exchange and other financial instruments were not fully developed.[52] Bullion was also preferred in times of international tensions; as Charles Wilson has observed, "Violence and the threat of violence in this turbulent age may help to explain why men put more trust in treasure than I.O.U.'s."[53] Third, mercantilists thought the volume of world trade and wealth were finite. The economic historian Kristof Glamann has written, "It was a widely held opinion in those days that the sum of prosperity in the world was constant, and the aim of commercial policy, as expressed in such features as the customs and navigation laws, was to secure for each individual nation the largest possible slice of the cake."[54] As a result, economic nationalism flourished, and nations created exclusive trading arrangements to bolster their own trade while restricting their rivals' commerce.[55] Fourth, the state should play an active role in the nation's economic life to ensure that mercantilist objectives were realized. This role included implementing legislation like the English Navigation Acts to restrict colonial commerce and promote a favorable balance of trade, establishing protective tariffs, regulating specie, maintaining navies to safeguard the sea-lanes, and even waging war to penetrate a rival's restricted market.[56] "Looking back," Jan De Vries has commented, "one cannot help but be struck by the seemingly symbiotic relationship existing between the state, military power, and the private economy's efficiency."[57]

These basic tenets of mercantilism dominated the capitals of Europe in the seventeenth and eighteenth centuries. Policies pursued in London, Paris, Madrid, Amsterdam, Berlin, Vienna, and elsewhere were predicated on similar assumptions. The basic tracts of English mercantilism were translated and published in French, Italian, and German editions, while the works of Continental mercantilists appeared in English, French, Dutch, and other languages as well.[58]

Not surprisingly, this emphasis on economic nationalism, exclusive trading areas, and a fixed amount of wealth created an explosive environment. This was especially true since the state was expected to use its resources, including the military, to aid in the battle for world trade. England fought three wars with the Netherlands during the late seventeenth century in an attempt to wrest control of colonial and European commerce. George Monck, the duke of Albermarle, succinctly stated the cause of these Anglo-Dutch wars, and of future imperial conflicts, when commenting on the war of 1664–1667: "What matters this or that reason? What we want is more of the trade the Dutch now have."[59] France joined this assault on Dutch commercial "hegemony" in 1672.[60] As a result of these wars, Britain and France supplanted the Netherlands as the dominant commercial power in western Europe and the New World. The elimination of Dutch mercantile ascendancy ushered in a century of Anglo-French conflict for domination of European and American commerce.[61] The wars of 1739–1748, "England's purest trade war," were, of course, part of this struggle.[62]

The prosecution of these commercial conflicts coincided with a "revolution" in European warfare.[63] Military and naval establishments escalated dramatically. Before 1600 armies seldom deployed over thirty thousand men in the field; by the end of the century the French army, Europe's most powerful, mustered four hundred thousand. The Swedish, Prussian, and Austrian armed forces witnessed similar growth, especially in relation to population.[64] Naval forces also expanded and became increasingly specialized. Because of changes in vessel construction, the practice of recruiting and arming merchantmen for naval service waned. Instead, vessels constructed specifically as warships became common. Britain's Royal Navy increased from 42 ships in 1603 to 334 in 1748, while the number of ships of the line (the large, specialized warships) grew from zero to 126. This escalation, of course, required tremendous expansion of the navy's shipbuilding facilities.[65] Clothing, feeding, arming, and transporting these armies and navies obviously entailed enormous financial and administrative effort. Whole new cities and towns such as Plymouth, England, and Brest and Rochefort, France, emerged to service the expanded military forces.

These changes in military requirements dramatically enhanced the power of the state. To pay for their larger armies and navies, governments increasingly focused on revenue collection. Access to capital became more important, and the state played a much larger role in the economy. Governments also needed a professional officer corps. Members of the upper classes in England, France, Prussia, and elsewhere earned rewards and prestige from leading the armed forces. This promoted a sense of national consciousness that also augmented the power of the state. As Betty Behrens has suggested, "As a result of this combination of circumstances the distinguished noble families, with the monarch's approval, integrated themselves into the machinery of the state."[66] The government also recruited thousands of soldiers and sailors and coordinated the movement of ships and supplies, which greatly increased government bureaucracies. All these requirements expanded the role and power of the state. "There was a major growth in state bureaucracy, state finance, and state intervention in the economy and society," Michael Duffy has concluded. "The net result was a great increase in the power of the state in early modern Europe."[67]

Yet there were limits to what an eighteenth-century state could achieve, and this is why privateering played an important role during wartime. Nations were unable to build and maintain fleets sufficiently strong to control the sea-lanes during imperial conflict. The costs were prohibitive. Although the financial strain was more severe in France and Spain, it was also felt in Great Britain, the preeminent naval power of the era. To augment the state's sea power, Britain, Spain, and France mobilized the private sector by authorizing merchants to equip and man private warships. These predators assisted the war effort, but did not add to the government's financial burdens. In addition, privateering possessed strong appeal for mercantilist policymakers. Intercepting an adversary's merchantmen increased national wealth while depriving the enemy of valuable resources. This was certainly attractive to officials steeped in the importance of the balance of trade and the finite nature of wealth. If the prizes happened to be laden with gold or silver, privateering would also augment the nation's bullion supply. Moreover, since the expansion of trade was the major cause of hostilities in 1739, privateering afforded the belligerents an opportunity to enrich themselves while waging war. The ends of the conflict became the means.

Britain's emerging professional navy was less of a departure from the nation's privateering traditions than it first appears. Like the private men-of-war, the king's service stressed personal financial gain to motivate its sailors. Although officers like Adm. Edward Vernon repeatedly criticized privateers because of the difficulties of coordinating private warships, their potential for friction with neutral nations, and their adverse impact on naval recruiting, such charges hardly represented a disinterested, patriotic outlook.[68] The navy competed with the privateers in capturing Spanish and French merchantmen. Naval officers stood to pocket enormous sums from seizing the enemy's vessels. Indeed, prize money, which received generous parliamentary support, was probably the navy's chief incentive and provided the basis for the private fortunes of successful officers.[69] Thus even the more modern, professional services shared a similar outlook with private ships of war.

Privateering also reveals the commercial nature of the First British Empire. Although scholars have debated the relative importance of military versus commercial expansion as the primary goals of empire during the reigns of the later Stuarts,[70] there can be little doubt that trade was the primary focus of the mideighteenth century. Certainly the lack of strategic planning on the part of Great Britain indicates the overwhelmingly commercial nature of the wars of 1739–1748. Neither the Privy Council nor the Admiralty formulated any objectives beyond attacking enemy shipping. The same was true for Spain and France. As British naval historian Daniel A. Baugh has written, "Once the war was begun, it was not clear what should be done besides giving a free hand to English privateers and protecting trade from those of Spain. The strategic aims of the war's proponents did not extend much beyond profit and plunder."[71] Charles II and James II may have sought conquests, but George II did not. Expanding British commerce in Spanish America caused the conflict; privateering provided the basic maritime strategy.

This emphasis on capturing enemy prizes and defending American merchantmen remained the primary focus of American naval policy until the publication of Alfred Thayer Mahan's enormously influential works in the late nineteenth century.[72] Mahan emphasized the importance of naval fleets and offered a devastating critique of strategy based on privateering. Mahan's persuasiveness may account for the dearth of scholarly attention paid to private men-of-war. Most naval historians have echoed Mahan, dealing almost exclusively with fleet actions and largely ignoring privateering.[73]

Despite its popularity, British colonial privateering is difficult to examine because the documentary sources concerning privateers are extremely sparse. This is true for the colonial period generally, and for the wars of 1739–1748 in particular. Many key materials— vice-admiralty court records, ships' journals, correspondence of privateer owners and captains—are no longer extant. Surprisingly, sources for Elizabethan privateering are far richer than those for

American private men-of-war in this later period.[74] The surviving court records, journals, and letters provide detailed information about privateer and prize shipping, ordnance, personnel, engagements, and cargoes. Because these sources are so sparse, however, they offer few insights into the scope and importance of privateering. Indeed, relying on them alone conveys the impression that privateering was only a modest business involving a few merchants, mariners, and vessels, instead of the expansive enterprise that played the leading role in America's war effort during the 1740s.

British vice-admiralty court records would constitute the ideal source for studying privateering if they were more complete. British statutes required every vessel captured by British predators to be condemned in an admiralty court before the captors were permitted to sell the prize vessel and cargo and pocket the proceeds. The court records usually provide extensive information on each prize case. Unfortunately, most of these materials have been lost. Although the West Indies were hotbeds of privateering activity, and Jamaica provided a convenient vice-admiralty court, virtually no prize litigation is extant before the 1770s.[75] Boston was a leading colonial port, but most of the Massachusetts admiralty papers were destroyed during the Stamp Act riots in 1765.[76] Altogether, the records for Massachusetts, Rhode Island, New York, Pennsylvania, and South Carolina, the colonies possessing America's major seaports, include just over two hundred cases. As a result, these legal sources offer numerous insights about a very limited number of cases but provide almost no sense of the number of vessels and men or the amount of capital involved in British colonial privateering.[77]

Ships' journals and correspondence of the privateer owners and captains are even more limited than the court records. King George II instructed all privateer commanders to keep a log of their activities, but only the journal of the Newport privateer sloop *Revenge,* commanded by Benjamin Norton, has survived. Even this record is incomplete. It covers the five-month period from 5 April to 5 September 1741 and ends before the completion of the *Revenge*'s cruise.[78] Privateers from Great Britain were also required to maintain a daily log of their actions. Regrettably, all these journals seem to have disappeared.[79] The correspondence of privateer owners and commanders is an extremely valuable source, but again, not much has survived. A few captains' letters were reprinted in the colonial press. The papers of John Bannister, Robert Pringle, Godfrey Malbone, Gerard Beekman, William and Samuel Vernon, among others, discuss the problems and profits owners encountered, but these letters provide only a glimpse of eighteenth-century privateering because the correspondence is so sparse.

The American press provides the best surviving evidence of British colonial privateering during the wars of 1739–1748, and this study of American private men-of-war is based primarily on colonial newspaper accounts of the maritime prize war. Newspapers from Boston to Charles Town carried numerous reports of engagements and captures involving American privateers and merchantmen. In addition, British colonial editors devoted much attention to the exploits of Spanish and French private men-of-war and the activities of the British, Spanish, and French navies. In fact, very few issues of colonial newspapers published during the conflict failed to carry a news report concerning the struggle for prizes.

The press accounts include much of the same historically valuable information that appears in the vice-admiralty court records. The name of the privateer commander and vessel, the home port, the type of vessel (schooner, sloop, ship, etc.), the number of crew members, and the amount of ordnance were frequently reported. Colonial editors often mentioned the name of the prize, its nationality and home port, its destination, the composition of its cargo, the place of action, and a narrative of the engagement. Americans read, for example, how Capt. Richard Jefferies in the New York brig *Greyhound* had captured a French ship (*La Fleury*) and how Thomas Gruchy, commander of the Boston privateer *Queen of Hungary,* had seized the French ship *Valliant.*[80] (See Figures 1.2 through 1.6.) The vice-admiralty court records normally contain more details for each case than appeared in the press, but the newspapers covered many more cases.

The newspapers are extant for the whole period of the conflict while the other privateering sources are not. Virtually complete runs of issues from 1739–1749 exist for the major North American ports of Boston, New York, Philadelphia, and Charles Town. Thus, the colonial press presents a more accurate picture of the maritime prize war than the other sources. There are still some gaps, however. The privateering center of Newport did not establish its own newspaper until 1758. West Indian newspapers are largely

N E W-Y O R K, April 29.

On *Wednesday last arrived here the Privateer Queen of Hungary, belonging to Boston, commanded by Capt. Gruchy, with a large French Prize Ship, which he took in Concert with Capt. Potter of Rhode-Island, the* 14th *April last, in Lat.* 33. *There were two Ships in Company, but in the beginning of the Engagement Capt. Potter lost the Head of his Main-mast; which obliged him to bear away to refit; in the mean Time Capt. Gruchy engag'd them both for three Glasses, when one of the Ships told his Consort, that he had receiv'd a Shot in his Stern, that had rak'd him fore and aft, and damaged him so much that he would make the best of his Way off. Capt. Gruchy then engaged the other very smartly, and the last* 3 *Glasses Yard-arm and Yard-arm, before she would strike. She is a Letter of Marque Ship of* 320 *Tons, called the Valliant, with* 12 *Guns, and* 50 *Men, completely fitted with Warlike Stores, and laden with* 320 *Hogsheads of Sugar, and* 35,000 *Weight of Indigo, and was bound from St. Domingo for Bourdeaux. Just after she struck, Capt. Potter having refitted, gave Chase to the other Ship, who was still in Sight, and at Dark came up with and engaged her; but we hear since, that he lost her in the Night, in a Squall. Capt. Gruchy had* 2 *Men killed, one lost his Thigh, one his Arm, and several wounded. Capt. Gruchy had but* 49 *Men, and but* 8 *of his Carriage Guns upon Deck, and in all Probability they had taken both, if Capt. Potter's Mast had not broke; for this was the largest. The French lost three Men, and sundry wounded.*

The above Privateers are those who lay Claim to part of the Prize lately taken by Capt. Richards and Capt. Jeffery; and we have certain Advice from St. Kitts, that a few Hours after Capt. Jeffery had sail'd with the Prize for this Port, Commodore Knowles at the Request of Captain Potter, sent Capt. Sommers, in a 20 *Gun Ship out after them, who carried them to Antigua. By the same Intelligence we are assured, that Capt Jeffery will soon have his Prize releafed, and may be expected here in a short Time, notwithstanding those Gentlemen chose to have their Pretensions decided at such a Distance from their Owners, and at a Time and Place of such imminent Danger, as St. Kitts did then and still does appear to be.*

Figure 1.2. Throughout the wars of 1739–1748 colonial newspapers from Boston to Barbados informed the colonists about the maritime prize war. These press accounts concerning Capt. Simon Potter, commander of the Newport privateer *Prince Charles of Lorraine,* and Capt. Thomas Gruchy, commander of the Boston Privateer *Queen of Hungary,* appeared in the 9 May 1745 issue of the *Pennsylvania Gazette.* Thousands of such accounts, included in the privateer data file, provide the major evidential base for this study.

missing for 1739–1748. In addition, no issues of the *Virginia Gazette* have survived for 1741–1744 and 1747–1748, and many issues are missing for 1740, 1745, and 1746. The absence of a

Figure 1.3. "A DRAUGHT of an ENGAGEMENT.—between Guardaloupe & Grandterre on the 12ᵗʰ. Novʳ. 1746. between. yᵉ Brig. GREYHOUND of New-York Rich. Jeffery. Comʳ. of 14 Guns & 92 Men & yᵉ La Fleury a FRENCH-SHIP of 22 Guns. & 84 Men. & a FRENCH Privateer. SLOOP. of 14 Guns & 130 Men. Wherein Captⁿ. Jeffery. & Company. Behav,d Gallantly & after an Engagement of 5 hours oblidg,d the Privateer. to Sheer off & took yᵉ Ship." This is a very rare engraving of a prize action from the 1740s. Captain Jeffery is the commander mentioned in Figure 1.2 who claimed the same prize as Captains Potter and Gruchy.

Figure 1.4. Capt. Thomas Gruchy, commander of the Boston privateer *Queen of Hungary,* captured these four beautifully carved wooden figures of cherubim in Boston's Old North Church from a French prize during the wars of 1739–1748.

Figure 1.5. This close-up of one of the four figures of cherubim captured by Captain Gruchy reveals the statues' exquisite craftsmanship.

Newport newspaper and missing issues elsewhere may result in understating the activities of Rhode Island and West Indian privateers. This is not a serious problem because papers in different cities printed essentially the same news items. Colonial (and British) periodicals were circulated widely along the Atlantic seaboard, and editors usually reprinted each other's stories. Numerous accounts with West Indian and Newport datelines appeared in Boston, New York, Philadelphia, and Charles Town newspapers; reports of prize actions frequently appeared verbatim in the *Boston News-Letter,* the *New-York Weekly Post-Boy,* the *Pennsylvania Gazette,* and the *South-Carolina Gazette.* The widespread circulation of newspapers throughout the English Atlantic provided an extensive information network and prevented the isolation of major ports.[81]

A systematic examination of American newspapers reveals the importance of privateering during the imperial wars of the mideighteenth century.[82] Thousands of vessels belonging to Britain, Spain, and France and their American colonies were involved. More than twenty-five hundred craft worth hundreds of thousands of

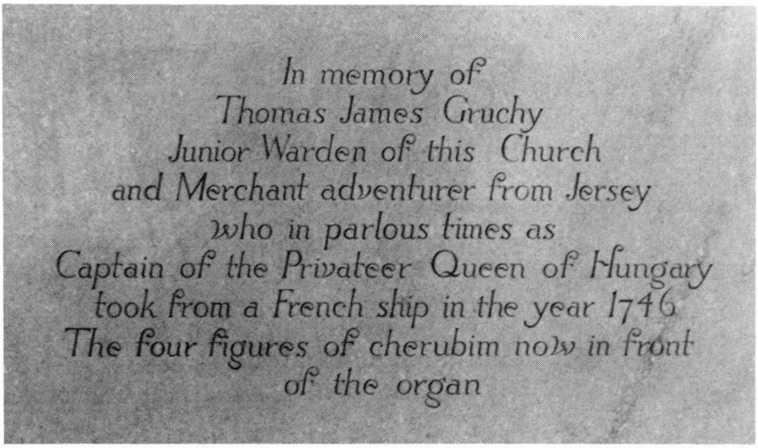

In memory of
Thomas James Gruchy
Junior Warden of this Church
and Merchant adventurer from Jersey
who in parlous times as
Captain of the Privateer Queen of Hungary
took from a French ship in the year 1746
The four figures of cherubim now in front
of the organ

Figure 1.6. This plaque in Boston's Old North Church commemorates Capt. Thomas Gruchy's privateering exploits against the French during the wars of 1739–1748.

pounds sterling were seized in prize actions. Privateers played the largest role in the scramble for prizes in American sea-lanes. These private warships embarked from all major British colonial ports throughout the decade of hostilities. Unfortunately for British shipowners, Spanish and French privateers also sought their fortune on the high seas, and Havana, St. Augustine, Martinique, and Cap François dispatched numerous private men-of-war. The privateers' cruising areas were as extensive and widespread as their home ports. In the New World private men-of-war plied the Atlantic from Newfoundland to Florida, from the east coast of Mexico to French Cayenne. A few American cruisers chased prizes in the privateer-infested waters off the shores of Britain and the continent of Europe. Merchantmen risked capture throughout the 1740s since all the leading sea-lanes attracted privateers and naval frigates. Security did not return to Atlantic commerce until the Peace of Aix-la-Chapelle ended the conflict and the predators stopped cruising.

Privateering was a popular way to wage war in a world dominated by a mercantilist *mentalité*. The belligerents' sea power was augmented, yet national treasuries did not have to pay the costs. Intercepting enemy commerce brought in valuable commodities while simultaneously weakening the adversary's commercial lifelines. Private vice (grasping the main chance by capturing enemy vessels) *was* public virtue. Privateering also reflected the weakness of the state. Despite increases in governmental power during the seventeenth and early eighteenth centuries, European monarchs still resorted to private warships during wartime. The most powerful European navies could not safeguard colonial commerce. Even absolutist states had to rely on the cooperation of their subjects. American colonists responded exuberantly to the opportunity to prey upon Spanish and, later, French commerce. To their dismay, the Spanish and French subjects reciprocated in kind. Privateering played a key role in imperial conflict and exerted a major influence on the economic life of Britain's American colonies. To understand the nature and impact of imperial warfare on colonial America, an examination of privateering is essential.

Chapter 2

THE RULES OF PRIVATEERING

Between 1689 and 1763, Great Britain, France, and Spain waged four major wars for control of North America. Each conflict expanded in scale and scope of operations. As the European powers' New World possessions grew and developed, colonial participation in these imperial struggles escalated. This was especially true of British colonial privateering. More American private men-of-war cruised the Atlantic in the 1740s and 1750s than in the earlier wars of King William and Queen Anne. As privateering expanded, successive British governments attempted to exert more control over this area of wartime enterprise. The Crown, for example, issued numerous instructions to promote privateering and govern the actions of private warships. Similarly, Parliament enacted a series of statutes laying down rules of conduct for privateers. These regulations outlined the eligibility of privateers, stipulated which vessels could be sought as prizes, and articulated a complicated procedure for ensuring compliance with basic rules. In effect, London endeavored to control American privateering in much the same way it attempted to regulate colonial trade; it even relied on the same courts for both purposes.

An examination of these rules of conduct and their implementation in America during the wars of 1739–1748 reveals much about privateering, a business that enjoyed considerable popularity and political influence in both England and America. It also reveals the difficulties Britain encountered in trying to control the mainland colonies. Following the mercantilistic principles of the day, England relied on private capital to augment the empire's sea power. Not surprisingly, the owners of private men-of-war sought to maximize profits. Despite detailed parliamentary statutes and royal instructions, the colonists persisted in operating private men-of-war in their own interest. Colonial courts recognized that interest and enforced the various prize laws and regulations to increase condemnations, even if that meant bending the rules and regulations.

I

The Crown regulated privateering by issuing letters of marque. The possession of a letter of marque (sometimes called a privateering commission) separated the privateer from a pirate. Both captured merchant vessels and sold the cargoes for profit, but the privateer's letter of marque legalized this activity; the pirate committed a capital crime. Responding to pressure for allowing privateering against Spanish commerce, the British Privy Council authorized the issuing of letters of marque in the early summer of 1739. "Owing to the many and repeated depredations of Spanish guarda costas in the West Indies and elsewhere, and to the non-payment by Spain of the sum agreed on as reparation by the convention of 14 January last [the Convention of El Pardo], his Majesty, by and with the advice of his Privy Council, orders general reprisals against Spanish ships, and the issue of letters of marque."[1] The duke of Newcastle, secretary of state in charge of the colonies, so informed the colonial governors instructing them to issue letters of marque such as the one in Figure 2.1.[2]

Although the mother country had authorized privateering commissions, the government established virtually no criteria for assessing applicants. Newcastle's letter offered little assistance. Governors were to issue letters of marque to "any of Our loving Subjects, or others, who shall apply to You for the same, and whom you shall deem fitly qualified in that behalf." Those receiving commissions had only to post security, "as hath been usual."[3]

Given that privateers had been out of business since 1713, these requirements provided few guidelines for uniformity throughout the colonies. Thus in Rhode Island, the procedures for issuing letters of marque were fairly straightforward. The owners and commander filed a bond for one thousand pounds sterling before a notary public listing their names, residence, and the name of the vessel. The bond stipulated that the commander would only pursue George II's enemies and would observe the instructions that were attached to the bond. If the commander obeyed these regulations, the bond would be voided; if not, the commander and owners forfeited one thousand pounds. (See Figure 2.2.) The instructions required that "Swearing Drunkenness and Prophaness be avoided" on board the privateer. Commanders were also required to dispatch all prizes to Rhode Island, if possible, without breaking bulk (i.e., without unlading any of the cargo) for vice-admiralty court proceedings and to prevent crews from embezzling or purloining any of the cargo. Additional instructions concerned taking prisoners and their treatment (i.e., no torture or cruelty) and keeping a detailed journal of prize actions. They also contained a catchall clause requiring the observance of all the king's laws. After signing a statement that he had received his instructions, the commander obtained his letter of marque.[4]

Procedures in other colonies were less orderly. Privateering commissions could be difficult to obtain in the West Indies because island governors sometimes demanded substantial bribes in exchange for letters of marque.[5] In New York, vessel owners applied to the governor for letters of marque. If he judged them and their captain to be responsible, the governor authorized the vice-admiralty judge to issue a commission and set of instructions. Thus, the owners and captain needed the approval of both the governor and the vice-admiralty judge. Given New York's factious politics in the 1740s, this was not always possible. Judge Lewis Morris, Jr., was often at odds with Lieutenant Governor Clarke and his successor, Gov. George Clinton. The admiralty court was caught in the middle. Morris issued letters of marque to persons who had not received the governor's approval. Clinton reported this conduct to the Lords Commissioners of the Admiralty, and they appointed a new judge. Morris, however, refused to step down and continued to act as New York's admiralty judge.[6]

Recognizing that "there have been formerly great Irregularitys in the manner of Granting Commissions in the Plantations to private Ships of War," the Privy Council released new, comprehensive instructions on 26 November 1739 for all governors to follow when issuing letters of marque.[7] The new instructions contained sixteen separate clauses to regulate privateering. They stipulated which vessels could be taken as prizes, and required all captures to be brought, without breaking bulk, to England or any English

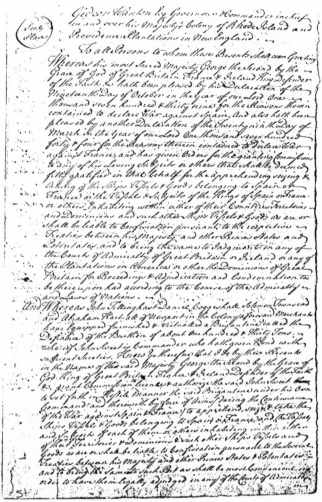

Figure 2.1. Letters of marque issued by colonial governments authorized merchants to fit out vessels to intercept enemy merchantmen. This authorization separated the legal enterprise of privateering from the notorious crime of piracy. This is the first page of a Rhode Island letter of marque issued by Gov. Gideon Wanton in 1747 authorizing the Newport brigantine *Defiance,* commanded by Capt. John Sweet, to capture Spanish and French commerce.

colony to be tried in an admiralty court. Commanders were ordered to bring three or four prisoners (two of whom had to be the master and pilot) to give evidence. The instructions required privateers to help any British ship engaged, or captured, by the enemy. Private

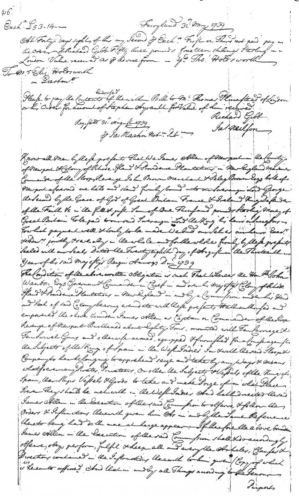

Figure 2.2. To insure that privateer owners, captains, and crews complied with British prize laws and regulations, the owners and commanders were required to file bonds of one thousand to three thousand pounds sterling with admiralty officials. If the privateer violated the statutes or rules, the stipulated sums were forfeited to the Crown. This bond insured that Capt. James Allen, commander of the Newport privateer sloop *Revenge,* complied with British prize law and royal instructions governing the conduct of private men-of-war.

men-of-war had to keep a journal of all prize activities. Before receiving their commissions, owners had to provide detailed information concerning their privateering voyage. The admiralty courts required the name of the vessel and its tonnage, the names of the owners and ship's officers, the size of the crew, the ordnance, and the number of months for which the craft was victualed. To ensure compliance with these regulations, private men-of-war with complements exceeding 150 men were required to post securities of three thousand pounds sterling; this was reduced to fifteen hundred pounds for privateers carrying smaller crews. Further instructions stipulated the types and colors of flags to be flown and, in an effort to increase manpower, required that one-third of every privateer crew be composed of "land men." In sum, these instructions represented an attempt by London at a comprehensive regulation of colonial privateers.[8] The numerous rules and requirements that accompanied letters of marque also indicate the marked difference in behavior expected of privateers in contradistinction to pirates.

II

In addition to royal instructions, Parliament enacted legislation to govern privateering. During seventeenth-century imperial conflicts no comprehensive statute existed to control private men-of-war. This allowed England's monarch great latitude to influence the outcome of prize cases and created an atmosphere of uncertainty for privateer owners.[9] The lack of supervision in America prevented the development of a uniform system of prize adjudication. Colonies condemned captures as they saw fit.[10] After the turn of the century, however, this fluid situation changed.

In 1708 Parliament passed "an act for the encouragement of the trade to America," which laid down specific procedures for all privateers in England and America.[11] The law ended much of the uncertainty that privateer owners had faced in the 1600s. Because this statute was still in force when letters of marque were authorized in 1739, an examination of its provisions is warranted.

Sections II, III, and IV were probably the most important parts of the Prize Act for British predators. The first two stated that all captures, upon condemnation in a British admiralty court, became the sole property of the captor. Section II guaranteed this right for the Royal Navy, section III for privateers. This was an important change. Previously, one-tenth of the value of all prizes automatically belonged to England's Lord High Admiral. The elimination of this perquisite significantly increased the profitability of privateering. Section III streamlined procedures for obtaining letters of marque. The owners of any British vessel could now acquire a commission simply by filing a request and posting security. This eliminated the ability of the Crown and the colonial governors to influence the issuing of letters of marque. This section also permitted privateer owners to distribute the proceeds of their prizes as they chose. (The Royal Navy was required to abide by royal proclamations governing the sharing of prizes.)[12]

Parliament created a uniform system of prize adjudication by spelling out admiralty court procedure in section IV. Litigation began when the captors of a vessel filed a legal document called a libel with the court asking for a condemnation of the capture as a lawful prize. Within five days, judges had to complete examinations of witnesses and the ship's papers. Next, documents called monitions were to be posted to inform the public that a vessel had been taken and was being proceeded against in court. To prevent condemnation by default, parties interested in the captured vessel or its cargo were to file a claim within twenty days of the libel. Claimants were required to provide sufficient security to pay double the court costs if the capture should be judged a lawful prize. If no claim was filed, the judge was required to "immediately, and without further delay, proceed to sentence"; if filed and all necessary witnesses were available, the sentence was to be determined within ten days. Provision was also made for examining witnesses who resided at great distances from the court. When this occurred, the judge would have the vessel appraised and require the claimants to post security equal to this amount in case the capture should be subsequently condemned. An interlocutory order releasing the vessel to the claimant's custody would then be issued. Within two weeks of the claim this process was to be completed.[13]

Sections VI and VII attempted to prevent abuses that had previously plagued prize cases. Captors were required to deliver their prospective prizes to the city's naval officer, without breaking bulk, immediately upon entering port. Section VI sought to end long, drawn-out litigation by forcing judges to follow the time limits stipulated in the act. They faced fines of fifteen hundred pounds sterling for unnecessary delays. The statute also regulated the cost of vice-admiralty justice by establishing maximum fees for all admiralty officials. For vessels under one hundred tons burden, the fees for all officers of the court (judge, marshal, and register) could not exceed ten pounds. This total could not exceed fifteen pounds for cases involving larger vessels.[14]

Section VIII spelled out the appeal process. Either party could appeal a decision to the Privy Council in England within fourteen days of the decree if security was posted to cover costs. If the Privy Council affirmed the decision, the appellant would have to pay treble costs. The lower court's decree would not be suspended during a pending appeal, and the successful party was not required to post security in case of a reversal in England. This clearly favored the winner in the lower court as it was conceivable that all proceeds from the original decision could be expended before a lengthy appeal was concluded.[15]

The remaining sections of the statute concerned the relationship among privateers, the Royal Navy, and the Navigation Acts' restrictions on foreign sailors and vessels. Privateersmen received an important benefit by being exempted from naval impressment. They were forbidden, however, from harboring or aiding deserters from the king's ships. To enforce this provision, the act created an elaborate system of maintaining and monitoring lists of privateer crews. Finally, Parliament increased the number of seamen and ships available for privateering by relaxing the restrictions against employing foreign mariners and vessels.[16]

These were the major provisions of the 1708 Prize Act. The statute represented the privateering interest's increasing political strength as well as a serious parliamentary attempt to regulate private men-of-war. Privateer owners and crews realized greater security and profit potential from sections granting them the sole interest in their prizes, limiting the fees of admiralty officials, and exempting privateersmen from impressment. The system of adjudication became more amenable to control by provisions that stipulated uniform procedure, attacked embezzlement and unnecessary delays, and regularized the appeal process. Moreover, recruiting foreign seamen and ships augmented Britain's potential sea power.

Parliament enacted a new prize statute soon after the Spanish war began. Virtually all procedural and property rights clauses of the earlier act remained intact. New provisions, however, increased government control of privateering. First, and most important for the crews, privateersmen were no longer exempt from impressment.[17] Parliament also provided smaller rewards for salvage—the recapturing of British vessels from the enemy. Since the 1708 law did not mention salvage, an admiralty judge could award the privateer a recaptured British vessel as a lawful prize.

The 1740 statute stated otherwise: the legal ownership of a British vessel was not altered by capture or condemnation in an enemy's admiralty court. The original owners were therefore entitled to the restoration of their property. Privateers recapturing British vessels received a salvage payment based upon the amount of time the prize was in enemy hands. One-half the value of the vessel and cargo was the maximum payment.[18]

Another 1740 innovation limited potential losses to litigants successful in appeal cases before the Privy Council. The 1708 Prize Act had required only the appellant to post securities. The new law stipulated that the winning party in the lower court should also furnish security to cover restoration of the value of the vessel and cargo in case the appellant was successful. This important change increased government control over prize adjudication.[19] Parliament also tried to curb fraudulent captures by threatening to confiscate all goods and vessels, including the private men-of-war, if prizes were taken by collusion."[20]

One new clause in the 1740 statute might have benefited privateers. To encourage the Royal Navy and privateers to attack enemy warships, Parliament offered bounty money. The treasurer of the navy would pay the crews of any British predator five pounds sterling for each seaman on board an enemy warship at the beginning of an engagement."[21]

When France became Spain's ally in 1744, Westminster drew up yet another new prize statute. Because the act's major purpose was to apply the various bounties, encouragements, and procedures against France as well as Spain, there were few innovations.[22] One change placed tighter control on private men-of-war. Previously, only the claimant needed to post security in case a capture was judged a lawful prize. Now, the captor was required to furnish security in the event that an alleged prize was acquitted. A sizable financial loss might deter privateers from making questionable seizures.[23] Other clauses tightened discipline on private men-of-war. All offenses committed by any officers or men on a privateer would be punished in the same manner as like offenses in the Royal Navy.[24]

The British government designed the royal instructions and prize statutes to regulate privateering and institute a systematic procedure for prize adjudication as the century progressed. These regulations escalated in number and complexity, mirroring colonial growth and development and the expanding scale of intercolonial warfare. As the colonies matured, they played larger roles in imperial conflict. This was certainly true of privateering. More American private men-of-war cruised during the 1740s than in earlier wars, and this trend continued throughout the colonial period.[25] Before the eighteenth century, prize adjudication was relatively unimportant in the northern mainland colonies. As this situation changed, Whitehall and Westminster attempted to alter the rules to fit the new conditions. Were the new orders obeyed in the colonies? Parliament enacted vice-admiralty procedure, but did the American courts follow it?

<h1 style="text-align:center">III</h1>

Colonial vice-admiralty courts adjudicated maritime disputes in America. Like their English counterparts, colonial courts decided disagreements between crews and masters. In addition, they enforced the Navigation Acts, a jurisdiction handled by exchequer courts in Great Britain. Finally, American vice-admiralty courts heard matters of prize adjudication. Because of their wide-ranging interests, these courts exercised considerable influence over the lives of many colonists residing in the major seaports. On the whole, most Americans thought these tribunals were useful and popular institutions.[26] Prize adjudication was a major reason for the courts' popularity. Vessels and cargoes condemned as prizes brought money into the community, and the courts in the major mainland ports seldom did anything but issue condemnations when they heard prize cases.

The following discussion of prize adjudication concerns only the major British North American mainland ports. Two reasons dictate this selection. First, virtually no records exist for the British West Indian admiralty courts, the busiest prize tribunals, for the period before the American Revolution.[27] Second, mainland privateering was primarily limited to Boston, Newport, New York, Philadelphia, and Charles Town.

Colonial admiralty judges were officially appointed at Whitehall by admiralty warrants.[28] In practice, colonial governors and assemblies preferred to have local people ruling on prize matters. Rhode Island offers a case in point. In 1743 Richard Partridge, the colony's London agent, announced that Leonard Lockman had been appointed judge of the Newport Admiralty Court.[29] Before learning of this appointment, the Rhode Island Assembly had selected a local man for the job, Newport resident John Gidley.[30] The assembly continued to support Gidley even after Lockman arrived in the colony. The legislators harassed the English appointee by refusing to swear in his deputy and by lowering all of the admiralty judge's fees and commissions. To stop this interference, Lockman informed the Lords of the Admiralty that provincial politicians were obstructing his duly appointed deputy marshal of the court. He also accused Rhode Islanders of following highly irregular procedures in taking bonds for letters of marque. Will Strahan, advocate to the Lords of the Admiralty, believed Rhode Island was abusing London's authority. "It is evident that the Judge and other Officers of the said Vice Admiralty Court of Rhode Island, have been interrupted in the execution of their respective Offices, to which they have been properly appointed by the Lords Comm.ʳˢ of the Admiralty," Strahan informed Thomas Corbett, secretary of the Admiralty. Strahan favored royal assistance to curb this colonial interference. "It must be submitted to their Lordships, whether it may not be proper to represent the Case to His Majesty, that he may give proper Directions that the Judge and Officers of the said Vice Admiralty Court may not be obstructed in the execution of their respective Offices."[31] Eventually Lockman took his seat on the Rhode Island court, but the incident indicates the colony did not readily acquiesce to London's controls.

The Rhode Island court's official status was as confusing as the procedures for appointing its judges. Actually, from 1700 until 1758 Rhode Island did not have its own admiralty court. It was part of the Massachusetts court. Most officials who decided cases in Newport were either Massachusetts judges or their deputies. Gidley's appointment, however, indicates that Rhode Islanders appreciated the importance of the court and of having their own judges. Newport privateers would probably benefit from a local resident deciding prize cases. Certainly this was the feeling in 1758 when colony officials sought to obtain a separate court. Great Britain was again at war, and Newport merchants invested in privateering. This enterprise might be more profitable if Rhode Island had its own admiralty court. Accordingly, the assembly instructed colonial agent Partridge to ask the Admiralty to establish a Rhode Island court with a Providence resident, Col. John Andrews—a privateer investor during King George's War—as judge. Partridge's petitions were successful, and court was held in Old Colony House in Newport, shown in Figure 2.3.[32]

What type of man sat on the admiralty benches in America?

Richard Pares's view was hardly favorable: "About the learning and discretion of the colonial judges, the less said the better."[33] Judges were often selected on the basis of patronage politics so it would have been unusual to find many who were learned in the law. Some were probably appointed because of their inclination to favor privateers. This seems to have been John Gidley's principal qualification. As the owner of substantial shares in the privateer sloops *Virgin Queen, St. Andrew*, and *Prince Frederick*, Gidley would hardly have been impartial.[34] The character of another Rhode Island judge also seems less than impressive. William Greene, the colony's governor, described Judge Samuel Pemberton as "an ignorant or indigent person," who was forced off the Newport court because he was "now a prisoner for debt."[35]

Many colonial judges, however, were admirably suited for the bench. They were not uneducated, unfamiliar with the law, or interested financially in privateering ventures. Pennsylvania Judge Andrew Hamilton, a graduate of Scotland's St. Andrews and Glasgow universities, had attended Gray's Inn before being called to the English bar in 1714. He also practiced law in Virginia and Maryland as well as Pennsylvania. In 1735 he gained widespread fame for his successful defense in the celebrated New York libel trial of John Peter Zenger.[36] Robert Auchmuty of the Massachusetts and Rhode Island courts was another experienced lawyer who had received an English legal education at the Middle Temple.[37] One of the Bay Colony's leading attorneys, Auchmuty practiced law from 1716 to 1750 and also acted as the colony's attorney general. South Carolina Judge James Graeme was an influential Charles Town lawyer who also presided as the colony's chief justice.[38]

In addition to legal experience, many colonial judges were influential provincial legislators before sitting on the admiralty benches. New York's Lewis Morris, Jr., was a member of the provincial council from 1721 to 1729, a representative from Westchester from 1728 to 1750, and Speaker of the New York Assembly from 1737 to 1738.[39] Andrew Hamilton and James Graeme were also leaders in the assemblies of their colonies.[40]

The records of the Massachusetts, Rhode Island, New York, Pennsylvania, and South Carolina vice-admiralty courts reveal that privateers were spectacularly successful before the bench. The vessels they libeled were condemned more than 90 percent of the time. (See Table 2.1). This condemnation rate prevailed in virtually every colony. Moreover, there were few individual differences

Figure 2.3. Old Colony House in Newport, Rhode Island, built in 1742 (the second oldest capitol building in the United States), was the site of one of the busiest colonial vice-admiralty courts during the 1740s.

among specific judges.[41] Only the Massachusetts court exhibited a significantly lower rate, and this was probably because of the paucity of records. Most of the Boston court papers were destroyed when a mob attacked the office of William Story, register of the Massachusetts Admiralty, during the Stamp Act riots of 1765.[42]

Undoubtedly, the major reason for the high condemnation rates is that most privateers captured vessels that were legitimate prizes—merchantmen belonging to Spanish and French subjects. Colonial judges were not adverse to bending (or ignoring) the rules in order to facilitate the condemnation of prizes, however. Table 2.2 actually underestimates the degree to which colonial judges evaded the law, since it is based only on compliance with the clause (section IV) requiring judges to allow interested parties twenty days to claim prizes. This provision was ignored in more than half of all cases. Rhode Island Judge Leonard Lockman condemned three vessels on the same day they were libeled.[43] On two occasions claimants appeared in the New York court within twenty days of the libel only to learn that Judge Morris had already condemned their vessels as lawful prizes. In both cases the claimants eventually received half the value of their vessels according to the Prize Act's provisions for salvage.[44]

TABLE 2.1

Vice-Admiralty Court Decisions for Massachusetts, Rhode Island,
New York, Pennsylvania, and South Carolina
1739–1748

No. of Cases	Pvtr. Won	Pvtr. Lost	Not Clear	Salvage	Pvtr. Ave. (%)[a]
192[b]	148	13	8	25	91.9

Sources: Massachusetts Vice-Admiralty Court Records, V, Suffolk County Courthouse, Boston; Rhode Island Vice-Admiralty Court Records, Rhode Island Admiralty Papers, I-VIII, Rhode Island State Archives, Providence; Minutes of the Vice-Admiralty Court of the Province of New York, I–II (photostats), Library of Congress; Pennsylvania Vice-Admiralty Court Records, Boxes 1 and 2 (photostats), Lib. Cong.; South Carolina Minutes of the Vice-Admiralty Court at Charles Town, Boxes 4 and 5 (photostats), Lib. Cong.

[a]The percentage of cases that privateers won was derived from dividing column 2 (cases won by privateers) by the total of columns 2 and 3 (cases lost by privateers).

[b]The discrepancy between column 1 (total number of cases involving privateers) and the sum of columns 2 through 5 results from some double counting. In one case, the privateers involved failed to avoid sharing their prize with a naval vessel. In another, the privateers involved won a contested salvage case.

When Philadelphia merchant John Reynell claimed salvage on a schooner recaptured from the French, he urged the vessel's owner to send proof of ownership without delay. "Send a Copy or rather a Certificate of her Register from the Office where she is registered under the proper Seals. Likewise you must send the Master of her if you can but if you can't then the Mate or one of the Sailors that was in her when she was taken to prove that she is the same Vessell and both this must be done as soon as possible[;] I can't tell how long time the court will give us, but I hope you will not loose any time in sending both as soon as ever you can."[45] Quick condemnations added to the urgency of admiralty litigation. Moreover, if the privateers had already expended their prize proceeds, the claimants faced difficulties receiving their salvage because the 1744 prize law only required the petitioner to post security in the event of an unsuccessful libel. In these cases, the vessels had all been condemned, raising the possibility of justice being denied because it was not delayed.

Judges probably also ignored the Prize Act's provisions requiring them to decide cases within ten days of claim when no witnesses were remote from the court. The stipulation that prizes be appraised and interlocutory orders issued within fourteen days of claim was also likely violated. Pennsylvania Judge Thomas Hopkinson waited nearly eight weeks before finally awarding salvage to the owners of the schooner claimed by John Reynell.[46] In any event, the length of vice-admiralty suits measured from the date of libel to date of decree was not excessive. The average case lasted less than five weeks, which compares favorably with the West Indian average duration of seven weeks or more for prize litigation during the American Revolution.[47] (See Table 2.3.) The vice-admiralty courts' performance certainly qualified as speedy justice by eighteenth-century, not to mention twentieth-century, standards. The length of time could be dramatically increased, however, if a case were appealed to England.

Colonial courts also ignored the prize laws' ceilings on legal fees. Normally, the petitioners paid all charges for condemnation out of the proceeds of their prize. Because privateers won more than 90 percent of the cases, they paid most costs. When the captors lost,

TABLE 2.2

Compliance with Admiralty Procedure (Section IV) of 1740 and 1744 Prize Acts

Colony	No. of Cases	Complied	Percent Complied
Massachusetts	3	3	100.0
Rhode Island	45	28	62.2
New York	89	32	35.9
Pennsylvania	15	3	20.0
South Carolina	22	18	81.8
All Colonies	174[a]	84	48.3

Source: Colonial vice-admiralty court records cited in Table 2.1.

[a]The total number of cases presented here differs from Table 2.1 because of missing libels or decrees in various cases.

TABLE 2.3
Duration of Vice-Admiralty Litigation, 1739–1748
(in Days from Date of Libel to Date of Decree)

Colony	No. of Cases	Average (Days)	Average (Weeks)	Shortest Case (Days)	Longest Case (Days)
Massachusetts	3	44.3	6.3	32	69
Rhode Island	45	35.9	5.1	0[a]	921
New York	89	35.6	5.1	2	868
Pennsylvania	15	13.1	1.9	1	88
South Carolina	22	24.8	3.5	2	159
All Colonies	174[b]	32.4	4.6		

Source: Colonial vice-admiralty court records cited in Table 2.1.

[a]The decision was handed down the same day the libel was filed.

[b]The total number of cases presented here differs from Table 2.1 because of missing libels or decrees in various cases.

they frequently, but not always, remitted the fees. Costs in salvage cases were clear-cut: captors were entitled to half the value of the prize without deductions, so the claimants paid all fees. The high cost of admiralty justice was criticized throughout the war.

Early in the Spanish conflict, Massachusetts Judge Robert Auchmuty defended the New England courts from attack on their legal fees by placing an advertisement in a Boston newspaper:

> Whereas it is insinuated (without any colour of Truth) in order to discourage the bringing in Prizes into the Court of Vice Admiralty for the Provinces of the Massachusetts-Bay, New Hampshire, and the Colony of Rhode Island and Providence Plantations in New England: that the Fees of that Court for Condemnation were excessive, and more than in other Courts of Vice-Admiralty within His Majesty's Dominions. These are therefore to advertise the Publick, that the Fees of that Court in such Cases are considerably less than in any other of His Majesty's Plantations, and always were so intended.[48]

The tone of this advertisement suggests that American courts ignored the Prize Act's provisions pertaining to fees. Instead of defending his court's costs by claiming to charge only the legal maximum, Auchmuty asserted that his fees were lower (but perhaps in excess of the statute's ceiling?) than in the other colonies. The Massachusetts judge also revealed the entrepreneurial spirit of vice-admiralty justice. Because his own financial remuneration depended largely on fees per case and not on salary, Auchmuty attempted to drum up business at the expense of his New York and Philadelphia counterparts. The ad announced, in effect, that admiralty justice was "on sale" in New England; but just how low were these fees? A few prize cases provide a glimpse of the cost of admiralty proceedings.

On 13 September 1742 Massachusetts Judge George Craddock acquitted the French sloop *St. John* because it was neutral property. Despite the acquittal, John Baudry, the sloop's master, faced rather substantial court costs:

To the Costs of Court on the first Petition	£20.10
To Ditto. . . . on the Second Petition	18. 8. 8
To the Register for Receiving and paying £2172.14.8 @ 2 1/2 p Cent	54. 6. 3
To a Warrant to Unlade the Sloop	1.16.—
Warrant to Survey and Appraizement and Copys	4——
Warrant for Sale Drawing Conditions and Copys	2——
To John Savell Jun.ʳ Dep.ʸ Marshall for Attending on Board the Sloop 38 Days and Nights and for Provisions and p acct.	57.12—
To M.ʳ Paxton for [Storage]	3.4—
To sundry Copys ddᵉ Capᵗ Baudry to go to Rhode Island and other Copy	5.15—
To M.ʳ Paxton the Marshall for charge of the Vessel and Cargo from 6th July to Sep.ᵗ 8.ᵗʰ is 63 Days and 15/p Day	47.5—

The total of nearly £215 in Massachusetts currency (about £39 sterling) was more than two and a half times the legal maximum of £15 sterling. Moreover, these costs did not include an additional £182 (Mass.) charged by lawyers, appraisers, vendue masters, and others. Some fees were incurred because Captain Baudry was forced to sell part of his cargo to refit the vessel before leaving Boston. Given that the *St. John* had been unlawfully seized, the cost of justice must have seemed exorbitant to Baudry. The greatest injustice in this case was Judge Craddock's insistence that the *St. John* was responsible for the costs, not the privateer. Because the captor was a Newport private man-of-war, Craddock told Baudry to seek damages in Rhode Island. There, Baudry would, of course, encounter additional legal fees.[49] It was unlikely that admiralty proceedings would be less expensive in Newport than in Boston. Rhode Island merchant John Bannister, who dealt extensively with the court, characterized vice-admiralty fees as "extravagant."[50] Perhaps Captain Baudry decided against risking further expenses in American courts; there is no mention of him or the *St. John* in the Rhode Island admiralty records.

Pennsylvania also provides some clear examples of violations of the parliamentary ceiling on fees. In 1745 Obadiah Bowne, commander of the Philadelphia privateer *Le Trembleur*, received salvage for recapturing the ships *Victory* and *Apollo*. Judge Thomas Hopkinson assessed the following fees for the sale of the *Victory*:

Officers fees for restitution		
Judge	£20	
Register	5	
Marshall	2	27——
Fees subsequent to decree		
Judge	5	
Register	6. 3	
Marshall	19.19.6	31. 2. 6

Hopkinson awarded similar fees for the sale of the *Apollo*:

Officers fees (£15 stg.)		
Judge	£20	
Register	5	
Marshall	2	27. 0. 0
Fees subsequent to decree		
Judge	5	
Register	11.17.2	
Marshall	18.17.5	35. 4. 7[51]

The notation in parentheses in the *Apollo* case reveals that Hopkinson was aware of the legal maximum. Yet he deliberately charged almost double the ceiling anyway. Since the statute clearly stated the costs of condemnations, adding fees "subsequent to decree" violated the intent if not the letter of the law.

Even in cases where the court complied with the legally prescribed fees, admiralty justice was expensive. Charles Town merchant Robert Pringle informed Richard Bennett of Queen's County, Maryland, of the high costs of South Carolina admiralty justice: "You'll please to observe that the Charges of the Court of

Admiralty and Lawyers Fees in Claiming the Schooner has Run very high and Comes to a Considerable Sume, but there is no help for it."[52] Capt. Thomas Frankland, commander of HMS *Rose*, recaptured Bennett's schooner *Hopewell* after it had been taken by a Spanish privateer. Pringle claimed the vessel on Bennett's behalf after it arrived in Charles Town.[53]

The amounts payable to admiralty officials did not include the advocates' fees, the costs of appraising vessels, the vendue masters' commissions for auctioning cargoes, the customs waiters' expenses for tending vessels awaiting adjudication, or a myriad of other miscellaneous charges. An examination of six salvage cases decided by New York's vice-admiralty court reveals that the claimants incurred costs averaging £117.14.6 (N.Y.), about £59 sterling. Yet, Judge Morris scrupulously observed the fee ceiling in each case.[54] Rhode Island litigation was also expensive. Charges exclusive of judge, register, and marshal amounted to £329 in local currency (about £35.11.0 sterling) in a 1747 salvage case.[55] The cost of appraising the snow *True Briton* in 1748 exceeded £28.10.0 sterling.[56]

A 1743 Rhode Island decision provides a dramatic example of the multiplicity of costs encountered in admiralty proceedings. The account of "Sundry Charges" in *Griffith* v. *Snow Caulker* contains thirty-seven separate debits. Among the entries were £60 "to the Appraisors for Appraising s.ᵈ Snow and Cargo"; £21.11.6 "to the Butchers Bill"; £17 "to the [customs] Collectors Bill"; £22 "to Judge Gidley"; £55 "to Fees of the Court for Condemnation"; £92.19.2 "to the Venduemaster's Charge for Sale of half of s.ᵈ Snow and Cargo"; and, to ensure comfort at the prize's auction, £3 "to Jacob Hassey for Liquor at the Vendue of s.ᵈ Snow." The total bill was £712.8.8, local currency, about £129 sterling.[57] All in all, vice-admiralty court proceedings were expensive throughout the colonies.

IV

As the New World colonies developed in the eighteenth century they were better able to participate in the intercolonial conflicts that characterized the era. The increasing volume and value of American commerce meant more potential prizes for private men-of-war, and privateering expanded. The seventeenth century had produced little interest in London in the creation of an effective, uniform system of control over American privateering. The number of privateers and prizes did not motivate imperial politicians to take action; the steady commercial and maritime expansion of America during the reign of Queen Anne did. Britain wanted to control privateering, so detailed instructions and statutes were implemented.

The colonies had become accustomed to pursuing independent policies in most economic and political activities. Privateering was no exception. Prize adjudication had been allowed to develop haphazardly and independently in the mainland colonies. As privateering grew in popularity and potential profitability, the colonists were unwilling to submit completely to imperial controls. The adjudication of prizes in the mainland vice-admiralty courts demonstrated this reluctance.

The vice-admiralty court records indicate that privateers enjoyed remarkable success in obtaining condemnations. Prize acquittals were extremely rare occurrences, and, when trying prizes, colonial judges did not shrink from bending, or even breaking, the instructions and statutes formulated in London. Legal fees were high, and some judges even owned shares in the private men-of-war that came before their courts. Like privateer owners, admiralty judges sought to earn as much as possible from privateering.

Private men-of-war and vice-admiralty courts operated in a world dominated by the political economy of mercantilism. Both complied with mercantilism's basic tenets: The state's power was augmented without draining the national treasury, and the profit motive played the key role. Privateers added to Britain's sea power by preying on Spanish and French commerce, while colonial admiralty judges, seeking fees, dispensed the king's justice. Neither added to the taxpayers' burden. Like today's lotteries—which also increase the state's power without raising taxes—privateering promised windfall profits. No one, either in Britain or America, wanted to be without a ticket.

Chapter 3

SHIPPING IN THE PRIZE WAR

THE WARS OF 1739–1748 UNLEASHED HUNDREDS OF VESSELS TO PREY UPON British, Spanish, and French commerce. These predators hunted the Atlantic from Europe to North America to the Spanish Main for rich merchantmen. Believing that foreign trade increased national wealth, Britain had tried to expand its commerce with the Spanish Caribbean, and Spain resisted the attempt. The desire to appropriate foreign resources was so strong that it accounted not only for the ends of the conflict but also for means by which it was fought. Instead of acquiring Spanish goods through barter and purchase, British captains now relied on gunpowder and boarding parties. The belligerents marshaled their forces, and the British, Spanish, and French navies accounted for a large share of both the predators and prizes. Royal ships did not operate alone, however; private capital, in the form of private men-of-war, was also mobilized to weaken the enemy, defend the empire, and increase national wealth, while earning income for investors. Even the royal navies kept an eye on the bottom line as they attempted to profit by capturing enemy merchantmen.

This chapter examines the shipping, ordnance, and manpower employed by the predators to prey on Atlantic commerce and by merchantmen to elude capture. The variety of types of captors illustrates the importance of private property in the prosecution of this conflict. A description of the predators' and prizes' vessels also demonstrates the rather substantial amounts of capital and labor ventured and lost in prize actions. Maritime commerce in the 1740s was a risky business; it was not characterized by security and increasing productivity. Curiously, economic historians have emphasized the growing safety and improved efficiency of Atlantic sea-lanes.[1] The chapter concludes with an evaluation of this view.

I

Merchantmen faced capture from several types of predators during the wars of 1739–1748. There were, of course, privateers from Britain, Spain, France, and their American colonies. In addition, naval warships, colonial coast guard vessels, and letter of marque ships attacked maritime commerce. Capturing merchantmen was probably uppermost in the minds of many naval commanders, as collecting prize money was the most attractive aspect of naval service. Indeed, the Royal Navy's effectiveness undoubtedly suffered as vessels left their stations in hot pursuit, not of enemy men-of-war, but of rich merchantmen. Some commanders even avoided contact with enemy warships to prevent damaging their vessels and thereby missing their opportunity to capture prizes.[2] Adm. Sir Peter Warren's career provides a classic example of the profitability of prize actions. Warren's prize money from the wars of 1739–1748 financed large landholdings in North America, Ireland, and England, in addition to substantial investments in English joint-stock companies.[3] This financial incentive prompted the Royal Navy to play an active role in the prize war.

Colonial coast guard vessels were armed craft publicly owned and fitted out by the various British colonial governments.[4] The colonial legislatures appropriated funds for their purchase or construction, their provisions and ordnance, and the wages of their crews, just as Parliament performed these functions for the Royal Navy. The guard vessels' primary purpose was to patrol the coasts of their respective provinces to prevent enemy warships from intercepting British merchantmen. In May 1741, for example, Massachusetts Governor Jonathan Belcher sent Capt. Edward Tyng, commander of the province snow *Prince of Orange,* "on a Cruize betwixt Cape Sables on the East, and Southward as far as Nantucket Shoales, for his Majesty's Service and the better Securing of Navigation and supressing of any Ships or Vessels of the Enemy." Intelligence concerning "divers Spanish Privateers that are hovering on the Coast between this Province and the Capes of Virginia" prompted Belcher's actions.[5] William Shirley, Belcher's successor, continued this vigilance of the coasts throughout the war.[6] Similarly, the Rhode Island and Connecticut provincial sloops often sailed together, patrolling the coastline from Rhode Island Sound to New York Harbor. The defensive nature of these operations is revealed in the correspondence of the colonies' governors. "I have given Orders for the fitting of our Sloop Defence for the Seas," Connecticut Governor Jonathan Law wrote to Gideon Wanton, his Rhode Island counterpart, "and should be exceeding glad if yours and ours might Cruise in Consort as in times past, if any Privateer should come on our Coast 'tis likely they will come pretty strong[.]"[7] In 1747 the New York General Assembly appropriated £130 to purchase provisions for the Rhode Island and Connecticut sloops "as a publik Acknowledgement for their generous Intentions in Guarding our Coasts, and protecting our Trade; knowing that this Province has not yet provided a private Vessel of War to answer these Purposes."[8]

Other British colonies—New York, Virginia, South Carolina, Georgia, Jamaica, and Antigua—also fitted out coast guard vessels. In Barbados, where British commerce faced especially high risks from the numerous French privateers of nearby Martinique and Guadeloupe, Bridgetown residents hired privateers to guard the coast. In 1746 Captain Fielding, commander of the *Leostaff* of Bristol, England, personally escorted three enemy privateers into Carlisle Bay. The islanders engaged Captain Grantham, commander of a Bermuda privateer, the following year.[9]

Pennsylvania was one of the few colonies that did not maintain a guard vessel. The Quaker-dominated assembly refused to appropriate funds, thus fueling a political controversy among Philadelphians who wanted protection for the colony's commerce. After France entered the war, Pennsylvania Lieutenant Governor George Thomas became increasingly strident and exasperated about the assembly's lack of concern.[10] The intensity of this squabble increased as French and Spanish privateers operated freely in Delaware Bay and even in Delaware River in 1747 and 1748. Finally, some Philadelphia merchants hired a privateer to cruise between the Delaware and Virginia capes. The assembly, however, turned down the merchants' request for reimbursement.[11]

Since the colonial coast guard's activities were largely limited to patrolling their home coastlines, they were unable to seek prizes in the enemy's busiest sea-lanes. Because they made the occasional capture, the coast guard comprised one of the captor categories.

Letter of marque ships resembled privateers since they were privately owned and legally authorized to take prizes because they carried letters of marque. But unlike private men-of-war, capturing enemy merchantmen was only a subsidiary activity; hauling goods and passengers from port to port, not chasing French and Spanish vessels, was their primary purpose. Privateers simply headed for the enemy's busiest shipping lanes; letter of marque ships set sail laden with cargoes cleared for specific ports. The *Blessing,* for example, was a London ship bound from Boston to Charles Town in 1741. From Carolina, it would return to Great Britain. While in Boston, Robert Rand, the *Blessing*'s master, applied for a letter of marque in case he encountered any Spanish vessels during his voyage.[12] John Sutcliffe, captain of another London ship, the *Friendship*, cleared Boston for London via Jamaica in 1741, after obtaining a letter of marque to take advantage of any prize opportunities that might arise during his trading voyage.[13] Newport merchant John Bannister, who owned several privateers, also dabbled in letter of marque ventures. In 1742 he planned a commercial voyage from Newport to Cape Fear, North Carolina, for his sloop *Victory*. After delivering its cargo and securing another, the *Victory* would proceed to England. Bannister, who intended to go as a passenger, wanted to combine commerce with commerce-raiding: "We shall fit her [the *Victory*] out in a War like Manner with Cargoe for Cape Fear where Shes to Cruise untill the Ships are Loaded and her Cargoe Provided and then for England[.]"[14] None of these vessels depended upon prize actions for profitable voyages, but if they encountered an enemy vessel, they could legally seize it and augment the voyage's profits.

Unlike privateersmen whose only remuneration resulted from prize shares, the crews on letter of marque ships worked mainly for wages and did not depend on successful prize actions for their livelihood. Should an enemy merchantman lower its colors, letter of marque sailors added money to their monthly earnings. The articles of the New York letter of marque ship *James Frigat* spelled out these financial arrangements: "Whatever shall be taken during the said voyage, one half thereof (besides the wages agreed on) shall belong to the said ship's crew, and the other half for account of the owners."[15]

The rewards for successful letter of marque ships could be quite substantial as the 1748 voyage of the *Bethel* illustrates. Capt. Isaac Freeman commanded this Boston ship on a passage from New

England to London. About midnight on 19 April the *Bethel* (shown in Figure 3.1) came alongside a large ship off the island of Santa Maria in the Azores. After evading Freeman's demands to identify himself, the ship's captain finally "answer'd she was from the Havannah for Cadiz, at which we gave them a Chear, and order'd her Boat and Captain on board immediately," Freeman later recounted. The Spaniard wanted to wait until morning "as his Boat was large and leaky, but we threatening him with a Broad-side (which he much feared) he comply'd." Capt. Don Antonio de Borges deeply regretted his compliance the next morning when he could see the *Bethel's* lack of firepower. "At Day-light we had the last of the Prisoners secured, who were ready to hang themselves for submitting, when they saw our Strength, having only fourteen Guns, besides six wooden Ones."[16] Captain Freeman's audacious actions allowed him to capture the *Jesus, Maria, and Joseph*, a 400-ton Spanish register ship mounting twenty-six guns with a crew of four hundred men. The prize was laden with a chest of gold and 160 chests of silver in addition to a cargo of snuff, hides, and cochineal, worth more than 300,000 pieces of eight, about £48,700 sterling.[17] The loss of such a rich prize so nettled the Spanish that they stalled the peace negotiations then underway at Aix-la-Chapelle.[18]

Figure 3.1. The Boston letter of marque ship *Bethel*, commanded by Isaac Freeman, was one of the most successful predators during the wars of 1739–1748. Just before the hostilities ended, the *Bethel* captured the *Jesus, Maria, and Joseph*, a 400-ton Spanish register ship worth nearly forty-nine thousand pounds sterling.

Although merchantmen risked capture from the coast guard and letter of marque ships as well as from naval and private men-of-war, Table 3.1, which presents the distribution of predator status for all belligerents during the wars of 1739–1748, clearly demonstrates that naval warships and privateers played the leading roles in the prize war, comprising more than 93 percent of all cases involving predators. The provincial guard vessels and letter of marque ships accounted for less than one case in twenty-five. Most captors were specialists putting to sea specifically to pursue enemy craft. Because naval vessels and privateers were not restricted to coastal defense as was the colonial coast guard, nor constrained by commerce like the letter of marque ships, they enjoyed greater opportunities to hunt enemy vessels. The small part played by letter of marque ships also indicates that the combination of trading and buccaneering, so popular in the sixteenth and seventeenth centuries, was largely replaced by full-time cruisers in the mideighteenth century.[19]

Great Britain dominated the prize war; more than two-thirds of the captors were British nationals from either Great Britain or its American colonies, as shown in Table 3.2.[20] Because these statistics were derived from British sources, it is likely that British warships are overrepresented. Ironically, this bias in favor of reporting British cases also compensates for underreporting of enemy warships. Although the American press devoted greater coverage to British cruisers than it did to the enemy's, colonial newspapers paid particular attention to British vessels captured by the Spanish and French. Britain's dominant role in the prize war is confirmed by an examination of the nationalities of the vessels actually taken as

TABLE 3.1
Distribution of Predator Status for All Belligerents, 1739–1748

Status	N	%
Privateer	2,828	72.2
Naval Vessel	878	22.1
Colony Vessel	67	1.7
Letter of Marque	75	1.9
Other[a]	125	3.1
Totals	3,973	100.0

[a]Includes predators lacking sufficient data for inclusion in one of the four status classifications.

TABLE 3.2
Distribution of Predator Nationality, 1739–1748

Nationality	N	%
British	2,598	65.4
Spanish	598	15.1
French	546	13.7
Enemy of Great Britain[a]	221	5.6
Dutch	2	.1
Other	8	.2
Totals	3,973	100.0

[a]Includes predators that captured British vessels for which the American press provided no specific nationality.

prizes. British warships captured the largest share of the prizes, nearly two-thirds of the total. (See Table 3.3.) The owners of British and American vessels were not unscathed by the prize war, however. Nearly eight hundred vessels lowered their colors to King George's enemies.

While a British bias in the sources is not a serious problem, the data for predators and prizes contain some weaknesses. They are probably incomplete, as there must have been some British colonial privateering successes that missed the attention of the American press. Moreover, the captures of some British merchantmen likely went unrecorded while some press reports were too vague to allow the entry of merchantmen and warships into the data file. If the exact number of predators and prizes remains elusive, the overall picture of privateering is clear; hundreds of armed vessels from both sides captured thousands of prizes in the maritime war, but Britain enjoyed the most success.

British colonial private men-of-war comprised the largest number of British predator cases reported in the American press. Of the total of 2,598, American privateers accounted for nearly one-half. The Royal Navy ranked second with more than one-fourth. Privateers from Great Britain were third with one-seventh. The remaining British captors, which included coast guard vessels, letter of marque ships, customs vessels, and British cruisers of indeterminable status, accounted for about one-eighth. The privateers' dominance indicates the extensive involvement of private capital in the maritime struggle.

TABLE 3.3
Distribution of Prize Nationality, 1739–1748

Nationality	N	%
British[a]	798	31.9
French[b]	892	35.6
Spanish[c]	423	16.9
Enemy of Great Britain[d]	332	13.3
Other[e]	59	2.4
Totals	2,504	100.0

[a]Includes prizes from Great Britain, Ireland, and the British colonies.

[b]Includes prizes from France, the French colonies, and neutral vessels carrying contraband goods to and from French ports.

[c]Includes prizes from Spain, the Spanish colonies, and neutral vessels carrying contraband goods to and from Spanish ports.

[d]Includes prizes captured by British predators for which the nationality was unknown. The American press usually referred to these captures as "enemy prizes" or simply as "prizes." Also included are 112 recaptured British prizes.

[e]Includes neutral vessels captured by the belligerents as well as a "Biscayan" vessel, some craft belonging to the 1745 Scottish rebels, and one pirate ship.

II

An examination of the shipping, manpower, and ordnance of British colonial privateering requires refinement of the data. The 1,153 cases involving American privateers include all instances of private men-of-war embarking on cruises, attacking enemy merchantmen, and engaging opposing warships. Thus many privateers were counted more than once. Successful private men-of-war like the New York brig *Hester,* commanded by Samuel Bayard, or Newport's *Prince Frederick,* with John Dennis as commander, accounted for nearly a dozen cases each. The following analysis focuses on individual British colonial privateers.

The most common types of vessels in the British colonies during the mideighteenth century were sloops, schooners, brigs, ships, and snows.[21] Not surprisingly, these craft were most commonly used as private men-of-war during the wars of 1739–1748. Sloops were the most popular and were employed most often as privateers because they were readily available and possessed highly desirable sailing characteristics.[22] Availability was important because although some vessels were constructed specifically for privateering, most private men-of-war were converted merchantmen.[23] These single-masted vessels were among the most nimble craft of the era and sailed faster than the square-rigged ships, snows, and brigs. In addition, the fore-and-aft rigged sloop was more weatherly; that is, sloops could sail close to the wind with little leeway. This was essential for safety and maneuverability in narrow waters, as well as for fast voyages.[24] This greater speed and seaworthiness allowed sloops to overtake slower, square-rigged merchantmen and to elude heavily armed but less maneuverable naval vessels. Colonial sloops varied widely in size during the 1700s. For local coastal shipping, merchants normally engaged small sloops averaging twenty to forty tons. On longer voyages, especially from the northern colonies to the Caribbean, sloops over fifty tons carried the cargoes.[25] Privateer sloops tended to be from this larger category and averaged eighty-seven tons. Mirroring their peacetime popularity, sloops accounted for nearly half the vessels fitted out as privateers, as Table 3.4 indicates.

Schooners were introduced in American waters during the second decade of the eighteenth century and soon rivaled sloops in popularity. These two-masted craft possessed many of the sloop's sailing characteristics plus some important qualities of their own.

TABLE 3.4
Distribution of Types of Vessels Employed by British Colonists as Privateers, 1739–1748

Type of Vessel	N	%	Valid %
Sloop	108	35.4	44.6
Brig	52	17.0	21.5
Ship	27	8.9	11.2
Snow	24	7.9	9.9
Schooner	22	7.2	9.1
Other[a]	9	2.9	3.7
Missing	63	20.7	MISSING
Totals	305	100.0	

[a]Includes galleys, bilanders, boats, and pettyaugers.

Like the sloops, schooners were fore-and-aft rigged vessels, which meant they were also good sailors. They were fast and handled well in narrow waters.[26] Schooners were also about the same size as sloops. Coasting schooners averaged twenty to forty tons while those engaged in the West Indian trade ranged from fifty to ninety tons.[27] Although they were about the same size and shared similar sailing attributes, schooners were easier to handle than sloops because their additional mast allowed the use of smaller sails and lighter spars, thus requiring smaller crews.[28] The need for fewer hands was an obvious attraction for merchants eager to reduce labor costs. As a result, schooners gradually overtook sloops in popularity, becoming the most numerous carriers of American cargoes on the eve of the Revolution.[29]

Despite their growing popularity as merchantmen, few schooners were employed as privateers in the 1740s. The greater availability of sloops was one reason for the failure to use schooners. Though their employment declined in the last quarter of the century, sloops were still the most popular craft when the War of Jenkins' Ear erupted. In addition, the employment of sloops and schooners varied from colony to colony. Sloops were favored in Rhode Island and the West Indies, two centers of privateering. Schooners were preferred in Boston and Charles Town, but residents in these ports dispatched fewer privateers.[30] Sailing characteristics also favored sloops because they were more weatherly than schooners and sailed faster when the wind was dead astern.[31] The schooner's primary advantage over the sloop, its lower manpower requirements, was irrelevant to privateer owners. Private men-of-war carried huge complements, much larger than the crews on merchant vessels. It made little difference that a sloop's sails were bigger, its rigging heavier, and its minimum complement larger than a schooner's. Privateers always carried more than enough men to work the vessel. The few schooners that did pursue enemy merchantmen were of the larger West Indian category and averaged eighty tons.

Although privateers relied on the larger sloops and schooners, some owners sent smaller vessels to the West Indies on privateering cruises. In 1740, Newport Captain Charles Hall sailed the thirty-three-ton sloop *Virgin Queen* to the Caribbean. Hall captured three Spanish vessels off the coast of Cuba and raided the town of Puerto Plata on the island of Hispaniola.[32] Captain Prew's forty-ton sloop *Sea-Nymph* took a Spanish sloop laden with sugar off Hispaniola and escorted it home to Charles Town. The *Sea-Nymph*'s small size caused Prew trouble, however, because he was too weak to capture the "richly laden" vessel that sailed in consort with his prize.[33] Another forty-ton sloop, the *Stephen and Elizabeth* of New York, commanded by John Lush, enjoyed similar success in the Caribbean. Sailing off the coast of New Granada between Portobello and Cartagena, Lush captured two Spanish sloops and seized twenty-two thousand pieces of eight belonging to Spanish subjects sailing on a neutral vessel.[34] The *Pennsylvania Gazette* characterized the schooner *Fame* as one of Newport's "Lilliputian Privateers." Yet the *Fame,* commanded by John Griffith in 1743 and Clement Lempiere in 1744, captured Spanish prizes in the West Indies and off the Florida coast.[35] Small sloops and schooners seldom cruised between North America and the West Indies during peacetime, but their size did not prevent them from disrupting Spanish Caribbean commerce during the 1740s.

Brigs, ships, and snows accounted for nearly half of the British colonial privateers whose type is known. These square-rigged vessels were larger and slower than sloops and schooners. During peacetime, they were usually employed on transoceanic voyages. Brigs and snows carried two masts with similar rigs; different spars used in setting some of the sails set them apart. Brigs were smaller than snows and averaged about one and a half to two times the tonnage of coasting sloops, approximately 60 to 100 tons. Snows averaged about 10 to 30 tons larger than brigs, ranging from 70 to 120 tons.[36] Ships carried three masts and were generally the largest craft afloat in the eighteenth century. Approximately twice the burden of brigs, colonial ships averaged about 120 to 160 tons, which was about the same as their English counterparts.[37] The square-rigged privateers, like the sloops and schooners similarly employed, tended to be larger than average. The smallest ship, Newport's *Duke of Cumberland,* was 180 tons burden. Charles Palmer commanded the largest American private ship-of-war, the 400-ton *Hercules* of St. Kitts. The average burden for colonial privateer ships was 267 tons. Privateer brigs and snows also exceeded normal peacetime tonnages with brigs averaging 132 tons while snows were larger still at 161 tons.

Eighteenth-century warships carried three major types of ordnance: carriage guns, swivel guns, and small arms. Carriage guns were the privateers' heavy artillery. Loaded with solid shot, these weapons could seriously damage an adversary's vessel; primed with chain or small shot and trained on an enemy's rigging, they could disable a prize vessel and inflict casualties on enemy sailors. Carriage guns varied in size from three- to nine-pounders, but it is difficult to say which sizes were most commonly used. Occasionally sources indicated the weight of the guns: On 11 July 1744 the Massachusetts House of Representatives voted to acquire a "suitable vessel" to patrol the coasts that would carry "eight Carriage Guns four pounders."[38] The owners of the Philadelphia privateer ship *Pandour* advertised in 1747 that the vessel mounted eighteen carriage guns, fourteen nine-pounders and four six-pounders.[39] Normally, the sources did not specify the carriage guns' size. A recruiting advertisement for the Virginia privateer brig *Raleigh,* commanded by Walter Coode, for example, only mentioned that the vessel carried thirty-two "Guns."[40] The same was true for the Philadelphia privateers *Wilmington* and *Tartar.*[41] Press reports of engagements between American privateers and enemy merchantmen, privateers, or naval vessels proved equally vague. Similarly, bonds for letters of marque and admiralty court records remained silent about the size of carriage guns.

Swivel guns were antipersonnel weapons that caused little damage to prize vessels but were deadly to the opponent's men. Swivels were used to repel boarding parties or reduce an adversary's crew before launching a boarding attack. Boarding parties used the small arms such as muskets, pistols, and cutlasses.[42]

The number of crewmen, carriage guns, and swivels varied directly with vessel size. The larger privateer ships and snows carried more men and armament than sloops and schooners. This was true for Spanish and French privateers as well as for British colonial private men-of-war.[43] The mean tonnage, crew size, and ordnance for the various types of vessels appear in Tables 3.5 and 3.6.

Although availability played an important role in determining the craft fitted out as private men-of-war, American privateer owners adapted to changing wartime conditions. The distribution of British colonial vessel types presented in Table 3.4 was not constant throughout the conflict. Privateering fell into two distinct periods: 1739–1743 when Great Britain opposed only Spain, and 1744–1748 when Britain faced France as well as Spain. In the first period, Americans fitted out small vessels as privateers, and sloops accounted for nearly three-quarters of the colonial private men-of-war (for which the type is known). This situation changed after 1743. Sloops declined in popularity and comprised fewer than one in five American privateers. At the same time, larger, more heavily

TABLE 3.5

Mean Tonnage, Crew Size, and Ordnance for all Individual Predators, 1739–1748

Type of Vessel	Tonnage		Size of Crew		Number of Carriage Guns		Number of Swivel Guns	
Ship	279	(52)	142	(68)	32	(137)	18	(20)
Snow	149	(14)	108	(28)	16	(37)	18	(16)
Brig	125	(11)	109	(25)	15	(41)	17	(23)
Sloop	85	(54)	79	(99)	10	(117)	13	(70)
Schooner	87	(6)	61	(22)	10	(19)	13	(8)
Other[a]	95	(4)	76	(15)	13	(11)	15	(6)
Grand Mean	166	(141)	100	(258)	20	(362)	15	(143)

Note: The figures in parentheses indicate the number of cases upon which the means are based. An analysis of variance revealed that the differences in the means were statistically significant at the .01 level.

[a]Includes galleys, bilanders, boats, and pettyaugers.

manned and armed vessels, especially brigs, became more common. French entry in the conflict probably caused this change. British colonists were pleased that French merchant shipping was liable for seizure, but the risks of privateering also increased.

TABLE 3.6

Mean Tonnage, Crew Size, and Ordnance for Individual British Colonial Privateers, 1739–1748

Type of Vessel	Tonnage		Size of Crew		Number of Carriage Guns		Number of Swivel Guns	
Ship	267	(19)	131	(17)	21	(18)	25	(12)
Snow	161	(11)	116	(11)	16	(13)	19	(8)
Brig	132	(9)	109	(16)	15	(27)	17	(21)
Sloop	87	(47)	72	(48)	11	(56)	13	(41)
Schooner	80	(4)	54	(12)	9	(9)	11	(6)
Other[a]	250	(2)	72	(4)	10	(3)	16	(4)
Grand Mean	138	(91)	89	(109)	14	(126)	16	(92)

Note: The figures in parentheses indicate the number of cases upon which the means are based. An analysis of variance revealed that the differences in the means were statistically significant at the .01 level.

[a]Includes galleys, bilanders, boats, and pettyaugers.

Americans faced French privateers, naval vessels, and letter of marque ships in addition to Spanish cruisers. French predators were larger than British North American warships. French cruisers averaged 198 tons and carried twenty-three carriage guns, thirteen swivels, and a crew of 149 men.[44] Americans needed larger vessels to face this new opposition.

The types of vessel, ordnance, and crew size illustrate much about the nature of prize actions. Private men of war were the only warships solely concerned with capturing enemy merchantmen. They required craft that sailed well enough to overtake commercial vessels or to elude pursuing naval frigates; they did not need floating fortresses. Consequently, larger than average sloops and brigs were most popular among privateer owners. These vessels sailed well and were readily available. Together, they captured nearly half of the prizes taken by British colonial privateers. (See Table 3.7.) Sloops and brigs were also responsible for the large number of vessels seized by American private men-of-war sailing in consort.

Although the carriage and swivel guns were important components of a privateer's armament, the crew was the most important offensive weapon. Obviously, a private man-of-war normally required more weaponry than a prospective prize, but privateer commanders did not want to fire broadsides that might

TABLE 3.7

Distribution of British Colonial Privateer Vessel Types that Captured Enemy Prizes, 1739–1748

Type of Vessel	N	%	Valid %
Sloop	129	15.6	28.0
Brig	88	10.6	19.1
Ship	45	5.4	9.8
Schooner	29	3.5	6.3
Snow	20	2.4	4.3
Consorts[a]	112	13.5	24.3
Other[b]	38	4.8	8.2
Missing	368	44.4	MISSING
Totals	829	100.0	

[a]Includes privateers of varying vessel types cruising together.

[b]Includes galleys, bilanders, boats, and pettyaugers.

wreck or even sink a prize. There was no money in it. Privateersmen had no desire to look on helplessly while a rich prize went to the bottom. Moreover, heavily damaged prize vessels fetched lower prices, and that meant smaller prize shares for the owners and crew. Privateers were better off if prizes eluded destruction. If they were sunk, there was no possibility of capture on a future voyage.

Since predators hoped to seize merchantmen intact, they mounted boarding parties to overpower enemy craft. After capturing a vessel, part of the privateer's crew would then sail the prize to a British port for vice-admiralty proceedings. Thus large crews dictated the success and duration of privateering voyages. Because complements were diminished when some of the men were assigned to prize crews (not to mention casualties, disease, accidental death, etc.), a privateer could remain on the hunt only while it was well manned. The Charles Town private sloop-of-war *Sea-Nymph,* mentioned earlier, lost a prospective prize because Captain Prew's complement was too small to launch an effective boarding party.[45] Captain Furnell, commander of the Bristol, England, privateer *Sheerness,* allowed five French merchantmen to sail away unmolested because he had insufficient crewmen to mount boarding parties. When the *Sheerness* returned to port, only seven men were fit for duty; the rest had departed as prize crews or had sustained casualties during the voyage.[46] New York merchant Gerard Beekman believed Capt. Samuel Bayard's successful 1746 cruise would have been even more profitable if Bayard had sailed with a larger crew: "I am of oppinion he'll make a great Voiage and Could have brought 3 more [prizes] had he ahad officers and men to man them."[47] Clearly a privateer's complement was a key variable in determining a voyage's length and success.

Carrying cargo was the principal function of letter of marque ships; pursuing prizes was only a sideline. For this reason their owners favored large vessels. Ships accounted for three-quarters of these captors while sloops and schooners comprised only about 5 percent. Large crews were not as important for letter of marque ships as they were for private men-of-war because the cargo's destination, not the complement, determined the duration of the voyage. Large crews also increased the owners' labor costs since their sailors earned wages, unlike privateersmen. The anonymous chronicler of the exploits of George Walker, a successful Bristol, England, captain, discussed the preparations for a letter of marque voyage from London to Charles Town via Gibraltar in 1740: "The war now declared, and Mr. Walker chusing to reap what advantages might accrue in the aforesaid passage, determined to put himself in the best posture of defence, and took out letters of marque for the said ship, not with an intent to cruise as a privateer, but to proceed with her on a trading voyage." Walker wanted to hold the line on wages. "Accordingly he fitted her out with twenty guns; but did not encumber his trade with a greater expence than that of taking thirty-two men, his business being only to secure his voyage."[48] The average complement of forty-one men on letter of marque ships reflected these different manpower requirements. Letter of marque ships carried an average of sixteen carriage guns, only two more than the privateers. This was probably because the vessels were larger and the requirements of both captors were similar; letter of marque ships needed to overawe any merchantman they encountered and to defend themselves against an enemy privateer or letter of marque ship.

Naval vessels were the largest warships in King George's War. Although naval commanders eagerly sought prize money, capturing merchantmen was not the navies' only wartime activity. The belligerents' naval vessels fought in fleet actions, convoyed merchantmen, blockaded ports, bombarded fortifications, and pursued enemy privateers. All of these functions required vessels, ordnance, and manpower that surpassed the needs of private men-of-war. Even the smallest naval vessels, the sixth-rate frigates and sloops-of-war, were much larger than the typical privateer. Royal Navy frigates averaged nearly 450 tons, normally mounted twenty-four carriage guns, and carried a standard complement of 130 men. They were clearly larger and more powerful adversaries than any American privateer, yet the frigates were dwarfed by leviathan ships of the line, as Table 3.8 demonstrates.

These vessel types and crew sizes afford an opportunity to speculate about the living conditions on board colonial privateers. Unfortunately, this important aspect of eighteenth-century privateering remains largely elusive because little evidence pertaining to shipboard life has survived. Sources shedding light on privateers' daily routine—the journals and logs captains were required to keep—have nearly all vanished. Only scattered clues provide a glimpse of the privateers' service at sea.

Extremely crowded conditions were probably the most striking feature of life on a colonial privateer. The data from Table 3.6

TABLE 3.8

Mean Tonnage, Ordnance, and Standard Complements for the Royal Navy,
1739–1748

Rate	Tonnage		Complement		Number of Guns	
Second	1,375	(3)	600	(3)	80	(3)
Third	1,172	(8)	420	(8)	65	(8)
Fourth	960	(40)	348	(40)	55	(40)
Fifth	703	(17)	250	(17)	44	(17)
Sixth	448	(35)	130	(35)	24	(34)
Sloop	248	(23)	70	(23)	14	(23)
Bomb Ketch	274	(2)	----		14	(2)
Grand Mean	670	128)	234	(126)	38	(127)

Note: The figures in parentheses indicate the number of cases upon which the means are based. An analysis of variance revealed that the differences in the means were statistically significant at the .01 level. Although the colonial press frequently reported prize actions involving the Royal Navy, information concerning tonnage, ordnance, and complements was seldom provided. This table was compiled using the tonnage and ordnance data supplied in J.J. Colledge, *Ships of the Royal Navy: An Historical Index,* vol. I, *Major Vessels* (New York, 1969) for each naval vessel in the data file. The standard complements are from Daniel A. Baugh, *British Naval Administration in the Age of Walpole* (Princeton, N.J., 1965), 164. Because naval vessels often sailed without full complements, the figures in this table should be viewed as the official crew size and not necessarily the actual number of men on board.

reveal that men were practically sandwiched into their vessels. Sloops and brigs carrying complements exceeding one hundred men were common. This was four to six times the number of hands needed to sail the vessel. Peacetime crews of fifteen to twenty men could easily handle craft of comparable size.[49] Privateersmen endured these close quarters for long periods of time, as privateering cruises often lasted the better part of a year.[50] During these long voyages the men could expect little help from the galley to break the tedium that must have existed between prize actions. Provisions on private men-of-war consisted of one pound of barreled pork or beef and one pound of bread per man per day, washed down with ample allocations of rum and beer.[51] Such culinary fare became monotonous, if not unhealthy, over a period of months. A similar diet on the New York privateer *Duke of Cumberland,* cruising during the French and Indian War, caused an outbreak of scurvy, a disease plaguing ships sailing on long voyages throughout the eighteenth century.[52]

Cramped quarters, long voyages, unchanging diet, and idle time were a volatile mixture, and violent outbreaks of temper on board private men-of-war were not unknown. In 1744, for example, Francis Dodsworth, a sailor on the Philadelphia privateer brig *Le Trembleur,* "had a large Piece of his Ear bit off in a very barbarous Manner" during a scuffle with a drunken joiner.[53] The following year a member of *Le Trembleur*'s crew died in a fight arising from a disputed card game.[54] Violence also erupted on board the Bristol, England, privateer ship *Duke,* where one hand died from knife wounds received in an argument with a fellow crew member.[55]

The uncertain nature of a privateer captain's authority probably posed a more serious problem aboard ship then isolated incidents of violence. Privateer captains did not have the Royal Navy's tradition of rigid discipline to back up unpopular orders. Because royal marines did not sail on privateers to uphold the captain's authority, commanders employed tact and diplomacy when issuing orders. The owners of the Boston privateer *Despatch* made this clear in their instructions to Capt. Nathaniel Ingersoll:

> We are Sencible the Minds of Weak people require the nicest judg^t. in Managing them where a Command is not altogether Absolute[,] and as the Success of our Enterprize depends very much on preserving a good Hermony between . . . the Officers and people. . . . That task we must Submit to y^r Skill and Shallonly Say that the most judicious way of Governing is always to preserve the Dignity of Command[,] and at a proper Season a Mild and Somewhat Familiar tho: distant behaviour will win Harts and Steal the affections of those in Subjection[.]

Ingersoll was even advised to cruise in waters recommended by his crew if the *Despatch* were unsuccessful in the banks off Newfoundland.[56] It is inconceivable to imagine the Lords of the Admiralty issuing similar instructions to the captain of one of the king's ships.

Privateer commanders also experienced difficulties having their orders obeyed. In 1739 Capt. Philip Dumaresque of the Boston privateer sloop *Young Eagle* forced John Rouse, his lieutenant, to leave the vessel during a cruise in the Wine Islands because of insubordination.[57] Apparently Rouse issued orders better than he obeyed them, because he subsequently commanded the *Young Eagle* and other private men-of-war and captured numerous enemy merchantmen. After commanding the Massachusetts coast guard ship *Shirley Galley* during the 1745 Louisbourg expedition, Rouse received a captain's commission in the Royal Navy.[58] New York privateer Captain John Lush faced a mutiny when he ordered the release of a neutral vessel that he and his crew had captured. Lush successfully thwarted the mutineers and replaced them when his vessel put in at Jamaica.[59] Newport's John Dennis, one of the most popular and successful privateer commanders in King George's War, was also forced to suppress a mutiny. Dennis placed a large number of his crew on "nomans key" in the West Indies in 1744 after they had unsuccessfully attempted to take over the *Prince Frederick*.[60] Captain Colt, commander of a St. Kitts privateer, narrowly averted a mutiny near St. Ann's, Jamaica, and was fortunate to receive timely assistance from the Royal Navy after his crew threatened to murder him and run off with a prize. Adm. Edward Vernon informed his superiors in London of this incident, expressing fears that privateers might lapse into piracy. "[I] do believe if this [i.e., the attempted mutiny] had not been prevented, this would have been the first English pirate in these seas. And it may not be amiss, previous to any peace to have the Governor abroad armed with an authority for timely disarming these privateers, for if they have first notice, I fear it is to be apprehended many of them will turn pirates."[61]

Perhaps Parliament had these situations in mind when it strengthened the authority of privateer commanders in 1744. Section XXV of the new Prize Act applied the Royal Navy's discipline to British and colonial private men-of-war: "All offenses committed by any officer or seaman on board any privateer or merchant ship taking letter of marque, during the present war with Spain and France, shall be punished in such manner as the like offences are punishable on board his Majesty's ships of war."[62] This statute's impact is undeterminable, but privateer commanders likely never exercised authority comparable to their naval counterparts. An incident from the 1747 cruise of the Bristol, England, Royal Family Privateers is instructive. This "squadron" of four English private men-of-war completed one of the most successful privateering voyages of the war. In eight months "Commodore" Walker's cruisers captured prizes worth approximately £220,000 sterling without the loss of a single man. Despite this success, Walker was forced to put down a mutiny. Although each mutineer was convicted by a court-martial composed of the squadron's captains and lieutenants, all were forgiven. One of the convicted men, a lieutenant, even retained his commission. Walker hoped to end the cruise "without having one dissatisfied man in the fleet."[63] He would soon be recruiting for another voyage and wanted to reenlist as many of his men as possible. Enforcing the twenty-fifth section of the 1744 Prize Act was obviously difficult; yet most privateer commanders maintained "good Hermony" between the quarterdeck and the fo'c'sle. Mutinies were uncommon, and after the hostilities ended, few privateers became pirates.

This absence of piracy was an important development since many privateersmen had earlier turned to piracy and gone "upon the account" at the conclusion of imperial conflicts. Hugh F. Rankin, a historian of piracy, has reported that numerous privateers illegally captured merchantmen after the wars of King William and Queen Anne.[64] Marcus Rediker partially concurs with Rankin and has concluded that the expiration of letters of marque and the navy's demobilization "contributed significantly to the rise of piracy" after imperial warfare. Peacetime unemployment is only a small part of Rediker's explanation for Anglo-American piracy, however. Instead, he sees pirates as social bandits. Alienated by the various means of social control operating in the First British Empire, the sea robbers constructed their own social world in an Atlantic community of pirates.[65] This did not happen in 1748, as American privateersmen demonstrated little of this collectivist behavior. Despite Admiral Vernon's fears, there was no epidemic of piracy after the Peace of Aix-la-Chapelle.

III

Because merchantmen generated revenue by transporting cargoes and passengers and not by intercepting enemy commerce, merchants' shipping requirements differed from those of privateer owners. Businessmen were more interested in a vessel's carrying capacity than its speed, and they were more concerned with the crew's productivity than its fighting ability. As a result, the vessels taken as prizes were usually larger and less heavily armed than their captors' ships. The risks to commerce posed by privateers and other warships, however, limited a merchant's ability to minimize costs by reducing ordnance and crew size. Thus one of the major costs resulting from privateering was that most merchantmen mounted carriage guns and carried sufficient mariners to man them.

Most colonial goods exported to Europe were agricultural staples. Sugar, molasses, tobacco, rice, indigo, and cocoa were all bulk items of low unit value. This fact, plus the length of voyages between Europe and America, required the employment of large vessels.

Vessels engaging in the tobacco trade from the Chesapeake to Britain were among the largest of the colonial period. English tobacco ships averaging 200 to 250 tons were larger than the craft employed in other trades. Tobacco bottoms of over 400 tons had occasionally been seen in the Chesapeake since the seventeenth century.[66] American-built tobacco vessels were also substantial as most bottoms built in Maryland and Virginia ranged from 100 to 200 tons.[67]

The West India trade also engaged large craft. London ships sailing to the Caribbean were typically between 100 and 150 tons, though English outport vessels averaged about 100 tons. West India merchantmen increased in size as the eighteenth century progressed. Ships of 300 and 400 tons, once very rare, appeared more frequently in Barbados and Jamaica. By midcentury, the average tonnage rose sharply, and 300-ton ships sailed into harbors throughout the islands.[68]

Large ships also dominated South Carolina's rice trade. Charles Town merchant Robert Pringle complained when Guernsey businessmen Henry and John Brock sent their ship *Anne Galley* to him to secure a cargo of rice and other Carolina produce for a voyage to London. "I am to take Notice to you that your Ship *Ann* is not a proper Ship for this Trade as she does not Burthen Well enough nor Carry neer the Quantity of Goods would be Imagined, having only 492 barrells of Rice, 14 hhds. Deer Skins, & some plant & wood for Dunnidge & Stowage." With such limited capacity, Pringle thought the Brocks would lose money. "She is not a profitable Ship for freight, yett She is very well stowed and Chock full as Mr. Bonamy [the *Anne Galley*'s mate] Can inform you."[69] Pringle recommended to Manhattan merchant John Livingston that a vessel of "about 150 or 160 tons would be a good size for this place."[70]

TABLE 3.9

Distribution of Types of Vessels Captured by Belligerent Predators,
1739–1748

Type of Vessel	N	%	Valid %
Ship	762	30.4	46.0
Sloop	378	15.1	22.8
Brig	147	5.9	8.9
Snow	135	5.4	8.2
Schooner	128	5.1	7.7
Other[a]	106	4.2	6.4
Missing	848	33.9	MISSING
Totals	2,504	100.0	

[a]Includes galleys, bilanders, boats, pettyaugers, ketches, doggers, and other craft.

The distribution of vessel types captured by British, Spanish, and French warships presented in Table 3.9 reflects the demand for large ships in most colonial staple trades. The pattern of prize shipping differed from that of the captors. The largest vessels, ships, snows, and brigs, comprised more than three-fifths of the prizes. Ships, the eighteenth century's largest craft, accounted for nearly half of the total; sloops, the most popular craft among privateer owners, yielded only about one prize in five. This distribution reveals the widespread employment of square-rigged bottoms in Atlantic commerce as well as the predators' preference for attacking larger vessels.

The prizes captured by British colonial privateers and the American merchantmen seized by enemy cruisers differed little from the pattern presented in Table 3.8. Ships were the most frequently captured vessel type, accounting for 35 percent of the prizes escorted into port by American privateers. Snows and brigs provided another 16 percent, bringing the proportion of square-rigged craft to over half of the prizes taken. British colonial vessels taken by Spanish and French warships were smaller than the prizes dispatched to British colonial ports, but ships, snows, and brigs still accounted for half the captures.[71]

The countervailing pressures of trade and defense are revealed in the data for prize tonnage, ordnance, and crew size. During peacetime, merchants desired little or no ordnance, small crews, and vessels designed for maximum cargo capacity. Carriage guns and other armament, after all, contributed little if anything to commerce and represented additional costs in fitting out vessels. The ability to withstand enemy gunfire required sturdier ship construction than would have been otherwise necessary. Moreover, larger crews were required to man the guns and repel boarding parties in addition to sailing the vessel. Robert Pringle emphasized the importance of additional manpower when he informed Boston merchant John Erving that Carolina businessmen refused to pay higher freight rates to ship rice on Erving's vessel, *Emma Susannah,* merely because it was heavily armed. The ship needed a larger crew, "guns being of no service without a sufficient number of men answerable."[72] Extra men increased the wage bill, and since maritime wages were double their peacetime level, this was a major added expense. Larger crews also required more provisions, which were more expensive because of wartime demand.

Table 3.10 indicates the extent to which merchant shippers were forced to respond to the higher risks of wartime sea-lanes. The prize vessels' large carrying capacity reflected the necessities of the agricultural staples of colonial commerce. Not surprisingly, the average prize was almost half again as large as the typical predator,

TABLE 3.10

Mean Tonnage, Crew Size, and Ordnance for Prizes Captured,
1739–1748

Prize Nationality	Tonnage		Size of Crew		Number of Carriage Guns		Number of Swivel Guns	
British	216	(18)	93	(21)	19	(46)	8	(9)
Spanish	244	(45)	96	(109)	15	(117)	12	(44)
French	255	(132)	119	(242)	19	(286)	7	(59)
Enemy of GB[a]	97	(11)	99	(6)	22	(10)	13	(2)
Grand Mean	241	(201)	111	(378)	19	(459)	9	(114)

Note: The figures in parentheses indicate the number of cases upon which the means are based. An analysis of variance revealed the differences in the means (except for crew size) were statistically significant at the .01 level.

[a]Includes prizes captured by British predators for which the nationality was unknown.

241 tons compared to 166 tons. (See Table 3.5 for comparisons.) The average for prize crews and ordnance, however, are quite striking. The merchantmen captured in the conflict carried complements and armament that virtually equaled their adversaries'. Clearly, defensive requirements greatly increased the costs of maritime commerce during the wars of 1739–1748.

IV

Chance and insecurity characterize maritime commerce in the 1740s. The number of British, Spanish, and French prizes indicate the extensive nature of privateering. The description of the shipping and ordnance suggests the substantial capital risked by the owners of both cruisers and merchant vessels, while thousands of mariners gambled with their lives. Privateering and naval prize actions hurt the efficiency of Atlantic commerce. Thousands of sailors, unnecessary for trade, sailed on heavily armed merchantmen and faced an armada of private warships bristling with men and guns, which had ceased to transport goods, turning instead to plundering others' cargoes.

Surprisingly, the prevailing view of economic historians is rather different. Increasing stability, not chance, and greater safety, not insecurity, characterize their portrait of eighteenth-century Atlantic commerce. Vessels engaging in transoceanic trade also enjoyed marked improvement in productivity. What accounted for this growing stability and increasing efficiency? Merchants were able to lower their costs by reducing crews and armaments and by employing vessels more efficiently designed for carrying cargoes. Douglass North stated the argument in an important article: "All improvements in manning efficiency during that period [1600–1770] came from a decline in crew requirements per constant average ship size. . . . It was the decline in piracy and privateering, permitting ships to reduce both manpower and armament, which contributed most to the fall in PSL [cost per day at sea of labor] prior to 1800."[73] James F. Shepherd and Gary M. Walton have taken North's argument even further: "The argument presented here is that crew reductions were made possible by the *elimination* of piracy and privateering [emphasis added]."[74] Merchants had lost numerous vessels to pirates and privateers during the seventeenth and early eighteenth centuries, but by the second or third decade of the 1700s, these predators had supposedly disappeared. As a result, Atlantic commerce became safer and more efficient.

There is little doubt that piracy declined and virtually disappeared in the early eighteenth century.[75] Certainly pirates caused few problems in the wars of 1739–1748. Reports of buccaneering activity appeared very rarely in the colonial press. In the spring of 1745 the *New-York Evening-Post* reported that "two St. Kitts Privateers are gone a Pyrating," but no further details were ever reported.[76] One year later two Antigua privateers captured the sloop *Pearl* which had been stolen by a Captain Wood for use as a pirate vessel. Although the *Pearl* was brought into Antigua, most of the pirates escaped.[77] When hostilities ended in 1748 only three stories concerning English piracy appeared in the colonial press. One involved an unsuccessful plot to take over the New York ship *Dragon*. Another reported that two boats from Montserrat intended "to go a pirating," though there is no evidence that they actually seized any commerce. The third account stated that the crew of the London privateer *Prince of Orange* was being sent home to stand trial "on a supposition of pyracy."[78] The only other cases of piracy reported in the colonies involved British Roman Catholics who were caught serving on Spanish and French privateers and were tried as pirates.[79]

Privateering, however, did not decline, and obviously was not "eliminated" in the 1740s, or for the rest of the eighteenth century. Given the widespread coverage of privateering in British and American newspapers, the countless references to private men-of-war in the correspondence of colonial merchants, and the numerous governmental rules and restrictions adopted to regulate privateers, it is difficult to see how Shepherd and Walton arrived at their erroneous conclusion. They emphasized the virtues of quantitative, empirical analysis and proclaimed that "no measures should ever be accepted on faith."[80] Curiously, this seems to have been the procedure adopted when they assessed the disappearance of privateering. North, Shepherd, and Walton essentially equated piracy with privateering—"the effects of privateering, consequently, were not much different from the effects of piracy"[81]—and concluded that both disappeared. Shepherd and Walton offered several quotations from the Board of Trade and contemporary West Indian residents to establish the problems of piracy at the turn of the century and of its eventual decline in the early eighteenth century. They concluded their discussion with a quotation from Shirley Hughson's 1894 study, which left the reader with the impression that the Carolina coast was safe and serene in

1741: "The pirates on the coast had been completely exterminated, and vessels came and went unarmed and unguarded without fear or interruption."[82] In fact, the Carolina coast was anything but safe during the 1740s. Numerous Spanish and French privateers operated there, often within plain sight of Charles Town Harbor. More than two hundred prize actions were fought on the Carolina coast between Cape Fear, North Carolina, and St. Simons Island, Georgia, during the wars of 1739–1748. Charles Town merchants Robert Pringle and Henry Laurens, as well as *South-Carolina Gazette* editor Peter Timothy, repeatedly criticized the Royal navy's inability to protect the colony's coastline.[83]

Professors North, Shepherd, and Walton provide statistical measurements to support their case for increasing shipping productivity—ton/man, ton/gun, and gun/man ratios. The ton/man ratios, derived by dividing a vessel's tonnage by its complement, were rising in the eighteenth century, thus indicating increasing efficiency. Similarly, the ton/gun ratios, derived by dividing a vessel's tonnage by the number of guns it mounted, were also rising. The same was true for gun/man ratios. All ratios suggest improving productivity for ocean shipping.

There are two problems with these data. First, all three periods cited by North (1715–1719, 1735–1739, and 1763–1764) and fourteen of the sixteen tables provided by Shepherd and Walton concern *peacetime* years. Surely an argument based on the demise of privateering must consider wartime, the only periods when private men-of-war were active. A fair test of their hypothesis was not attempted. Second, and more important, Great Britain and the American colonies were at war for twenty-four of the last forty-four years of the First British Empire (1739–1783). War was more common than peace. Far from declining, privateering expanded in the second half of the eighteenth century, and private warships were active in the early nineteenth century as well until the conclusion of the War of 1812. North, Shepherd, and Walton have demonstrated that crew sizes and ordnance declined in the 1700s, but clearly this did not result because privateering was eliminated. North suggested a more plausible cause for these reductions, which merits more consideration than the elimination of privateering: "an improvement in economic organization . . . and the development of markets and international trade."[84]

Table 3.11 suggests that ton/man, ton/gun, and gun/man ratios did not increase during wartime. Not surprisingly, these ratios for the predators are much lower than those presented by North,

TABLE 3.11
Ratios of Tons, Guns, and Men for All Predators and Prizes, 1739–1748

Ratio	T/M	T/G	G/M
Predators	3.20 (238)	15 (254)	.191 (410)
Prizes	7.38 (111)	22 (106)	.200 (335)
All Vessels	4.53 (349)	17 (360)	.195 (745)

Note: The numbers in parentheses indicate the number of cases upon which the ratios are based.

Shepherd, and Walton. Moreover, even the data for the prizes reveal inefficiencies. The ton/man ratios presented for predators and for all vessels in Table 3.11 are lower than North's data for 1735–1739 and 1763–1764. They are also lower than the corresponding ratios presented in fifty-four of the fifty-five categories included in Shepherd and Walton's work. The ratios for prizes do not display such marked differences, though they appear to have been less efficient than the Boston and Virginia vessels and about equal to the Barbados and Jamaica vessels described by Shepherd and Walton. Only New York shipping seems to have been less efficient than the prizes.

Piracy and privateering undermined the productivity of Atlantic commerce. Merchants faced higher costs and reduced efficiency because of the added increments of manpower and ordnance required for defense. Unlike piracy, privateering continued to plague the sea-lanes throughout the eighteenth century. It played a key role during the wars of 1739–1748 and continued to do so in subsequent imperial conflicts.

The purpose of warfare in the age of mercantilism was to expand (or protect) a nation's trade. Privateering made it possible to achieve this goal during the prosecution of the war itself. The desire for acquisition did not have to be postponed until the peace conferences commenced at the conclusion of hostilities. Imperial governments viewed prize actions as the way to augment national wealth and cripple the enemy's ability to wage war simultaneously. Thus the means became the ends. The lure of profits at the expense of an adversary's commerce appealed to the merchant communities in Europe as well as in the New World, and private property exerted an important influence in the maritime strategy of Britain, Spain, and France.

Chapter 4

THE COMPETITION FOR SEAMEN

O<small>N 5 JUNE 1741 THE NEWPORT SLOOP *REVENGE,* COMMANDED BY</small> Benjamin Norton, set sail on a privateering voyage against the Spanish. With only forty men aboard, the sloop first headed to Manhattan "to Gett more hands."[1] Recruiting proved difficult, however. On 8 June, Peter Vezian, Norton's quartermaster and author of the *Revenge*'s journal, noted that the sloop put in at Whitestone Point on the south side of the East River, "fired a Gun and beat the Drum to lett them know . . . we was" a privateer seeking recruits. "The Ferry boat Came off and told Us that we Cou'd not Gett hands for the Sloops fitted out by the Country [i.e., New York coast guard vessels] had Gott them all."[2] Then John Freebody, the *Revenge*'s principal owner, tried to enlist Lt. Gov. George Clark's assistance. "His Honour the Govr. . . . wou'd not Give him leave to beat up for Voluntiers." The city was "thined of hands by the 2 Country Sloops that were fitted out by the Council to Crueze after the Spanish privateers on the Coast." Lieutenant Governor Clark also informed Freebody that the duke of Newcastle had advised, "if Admiral Vernon or Genl. Wentworth should writte for more Recruits [for the Cartagena expedition] to Use his Endeavours to Gett them, so that he could not Give Encouragem't to any privateers to take their men away."[3]

The *Revenge,* nevertheless, remained in New York for another five weeks trying to fill its complement. Captain Norton also confronted desertion from the men he already had. Twelve men jumped ship after only two days in port. It is a "poor Encouragement to Gett hands when they leave Us so fast," Vezian confided to his journal. "After they were Gone I read the Articles to those on Board who Readily Signed So hope we shall Lead a peaceable Life. Remains out of the 41 hands that Came with Us from Rhode Island, 29 hands."[4]

The situation deteriorated when the *Revenge* was forced to compete with the New York privateer *Humming Bird*. Vezian recorded that on 3 July "We perceived that the three hands that had left Us on Board the *Humming Bird* privateer who had been Inticed by some of the Owners to leave Us by making of them drunk."[5] The two privateer crews nearly came to blows on 4 July when Norton led a boarding party to retrieve these men. After much shouting and threatening, they were returned. The *Humming Bird*'s captain gave up his New York recruiting efforts the next day and weighed anchor for Philadelphia.

The *Humming Bird* had barely cleared the East River when the *Revenge* suffered another setback. Some of the crew mistook a large ship entering the harbor for a Royal Navy vessel. Since the *Revenge* "had severall deserters from the Men a War they desired the Capt. . . . [to] Signal for Our pinnace that was then a shoare, That if she proved to be a Man of War they might Gett ashoar and Gett Clear from the Press." Fortunately, the ship was a merchantman, and "att night the Capt. Gave the people a pale of punch to Recover them of their fright."[6]

On 5 July the *Revenge* finally received some good news. The two coast guard vessels returned from chasing Spanish privateers, so their men were available for privateering. Nine days later the *Revenge,* fully manned with sixty-one officers and men, embarked "with the wind att WSW with a fresh Gale and by Gods Leave and Under his protection" for the West Indies on a "Cruize against the proud Dons the Spaniards." The captain "ordered the people a pale of punch to drink to a Good Voyage."[7]

This chapter examines the competition for seamen in American ports during the 1740s. The shortage of hands seriously hampered the sailing operations of the navy, coast guard, and merchant marine. Private men-of-war were not immune to these difficulties and also experienced problems obtaining full complements. Wartime conditions improved the financial rewards for mariners as increased demand for maritime labor caused seamen's wages to escalate dramatically. Merchants paid more than double the peacetime rates to entice sailors, while the privateers held out the allure of Spanish gold and Caribbean plunder. The navy and the coast guard also tried hard to procure additional hands. Instead of meeting competition with higher wages, however, the public men-of-war relied on a legally questionable policy of coercion, and press-gangs swept waterfront taverns and lodgings to ensnare "recruits." Despite the commanders' attempts to solicit, coax, cajole, seduce, and even kidnap seamen, the manpower shortage hurt all forms of maritime enterprise throughout the decade of hostilities, though mariners lucky enough to avoid the navy or capture by the enemy probably benefited from higher wartime wages.

The *Revenge*'s journal highlights the problems all captains faced during the wars of 1739–1748 when they tried to secure full crews. Scholars have been aware of the shortage of British seamen during the eighteenth-century colonial wars and have written about the navy's problems competing with the merchant marine and private men-of-war for available mariners. Historians have usually emphasized the privateers' attractiveness compared to the navy, and the seamen's preference for serving on private men-of-war. After surveying the navy's manpower problems in the West Indies, Richard Pares, for example, emphasized the struggle between the king's ships and the private men-of-war. "The competition of privateers for sailors was probably much severer than that of the merchant ships . . . Certainly the naval commanders in the West Indies were bitterer against them, and regarded them as a greater nuisance. In fact, they seem almost to have thought that the merchant ship owners were potential allies, or at least as great sufferers as themselves by the unscrupulous practices of the privateers."[8] Dora Mae Clark, Charles M. Andrews, and Richard B. Morris have all mentioned the stiff competition for seamen involving the navy, privateers, and the merchant service.[9]

More recent work has suggested that the supply of mariners was insufficient to man naval vessels and merchantmen. Ralph Davis has written that merchant shippers experienced numerous problems manning their vessels during wartime because they lost hundreds of men to the navy. "This view of the almost complete stripping of the merchant fleet of its seamen is, indeed, confirmed by the reading of day-to-day reports of the progress of impressment. . . . The shipowner therefore had great difficulty in getting seamen in wartime."[10] Approaching the manpower problem from the navy's point of view, Daniel A. Baugh has reached a similar conclusion: "In one very important respect the maritime resources of eighteenth-century Britain were not ample: there were not enough seamen to supply the wartime needs of both the navy and the merchant seamen."[11] Other scholars have written of the struggle to obtain men and have demonstrated that this competition was often violent and bloody.[12] Baugh has succinctly summarized the prevailing view of the results of this competition for manpower. "Because in wartime seamen were sought by merchants, privateers, and the navy, they naturally sold their services to the highest bidders, and the navy was not among them."[13] In the contest to attract mariners, most historians view the privateers as the obvious winners. The journal of the *Revenge* clearly reveals, however, that securing sufficient sailors was an arduous task for privateer captains as well. The *Revenge* spent thirty-six days in New York recruiting men and obtained only twenty additional hands. How long Freebody and Norton tried to sign on men in their home port of Newport remains unknown, but the *Humming Bird*'s skipper resigned himself to the impossibility of filling his complement at home and departed for Philadelphia.

I

Imperial conflict increased the demand for able seamen and caused a serious shortage of mariners in British colonial ports. The Royal Navy, colonial coast guard, and private men-of-war had seemingly limitless manpower needs as the ton/man ratios presented in the previous chapter suggest. The navy's requirements alone increased by more than 700 percent over the peacetime 1730s. Only about seven thousand to eight thousand officers and men comprised the Royal Navy's establishment during the prewar decade; at its peak strength in 1746–1747, more than sixty thousand men sailed in the king's service.[14]

This tremendous increase reduced the number of men available for other seagoing enterprises as numerous letters from Charles Town rice merchant Robert Pringle demonstrate. Pringle informed his brother Andrew in London that "Capt. Gregory [of the *Susannah,* bound from Charles Town to London] has been detain'd as he tells me purely for want of Hands, & is obliged to goe at Last Weak handed." Richard Partridge learned that his brig, *Richard,* was unable to depart for Europe because its complement remained unfilled. Francis Dalby, another London merchant, also received word that his ship, *Good Hope,* was finally ready to sail after having "been Detain'd some days for want of hands." Charles Town's shortage of mariners continued through the end of 1744. "Seamen are so very Scarce & Difficult to be Procurred here," Pringle wrote to Guernsey Island merchants Henry and John Brock in December.[15] Charles Town still lacked sailors in 1748 when Henry Laurens informed London businessman James Crokatt that "the *Amy* is now Loaded but wants Men, which I believe will detain her some days after the Bearer of this."[16]

The sailors' belief that they could earn more money elsewhere exacerbated these manpower shortages. Mariners sometimes adopted this view after they had signed on a trading vessel. As a result, desertion became a problem for the owners of trading vessels; this was common in Charles Town. Thus in 1743 the South Carolina legislature tried to prevent merchant sailors from jumping ship by enacting a tough, new statute. All white Carolinians were empowered under the new law to detain deserting mariners "or such as they suspect to be so." Those apprehended were confined in the city's workhouse until the masters of their vessels claimed them and paid the necessary charges. If the deserters' vessels had already sailed, the captives were available to other merchantmen. Not surprisingly, in the colony with the largest concentration of slave labor, this statute was similar to the provisions for runaway slaves and indicated scant concern for men unjustly detained. The law also contained fines for persons who assisted or harbored deserters and rewards for those who captured runaway mariners.[17]

Desertion, of course, was not limited to South Carolina. Moreover, masters and owners of commercial vessels were fairly certain of the deserters' intention. "RUN away from the Ship Westmoreland, John Dod Bonell, Commander, Richard Edwards, George Todder, John Pipe, Samuel Field, John Jackson, William Gessoys, and James Carroll, Mariners," stated an advertisement in the *Pennsylvania Gazette.* "The above Persons have all received advanced Wages, and absented themselves (as is supposed) to go out in the Privateers. Whoever takes up the above named Mariners and secures them in any Goal in this Province [Pennsylvania], shall have three Pounds for each, paid by WILLIAM PLUMSTEAD."[18] Apparently the men were not immediately apprehended because Plumstead ran the ad the following two weeks. Desertion became a common complaint during the wars of 1739–1748, and newspaper notices for absent seamen appeared throughout the colonies.[19]

Other commanders shared Plumstead's suspicions, and privateers became the favorite scapegoat for captains plagued by deserters, whether in the Royal Navy, the colonial coast guard, or the merchant marine.

Eighteenth-century British seamen wisely preferred to serve aboard merchantmen or private men-of-war rather than in the king's ships or colonial coast guard vessels. This added to the manpower shortages in the public men-of-war, where desertion was also a major problem. Tempted by higher wages in the merchant marine or by the prospects of privateering plunder, Royal Navy personnel often jumped ship in colonial ports. Gov. William Shirley informed the Massachusetts Assembly in 1742 of reports from Admiral Vernon concerning "Complaints made to him from the Commanders of His Majesty's Ships of War, that the Masters of Merchant Ships, and others in this Province, make a Practice of enticing away their Seamen."[20] Shirley wanted a law curbing this behavior but, receiving no cooperation from the legislature, he issued "A Proclamation to prevent the seducing & deserting of Mariners belonging to his Majesty's Ships of War."[21] The proclamation stated that "no Comr. of any Privateer or trading Ship shall entertain any Person till he hath by all reasonable Ways endeavoured to discover whether he hath deserted any Ship of War, nor whom he knows or is informed to be a Deserter on pain of twenty Pounds."[22] To enforce this proclamation, Shirley required all privateer and merchant captains to present a list of names, ages, and descriptions of all crew members to customs officials. A ten-pound (Mass.) fine would be levied for each man not listed. The customs office would then issue an attested crew list that Royal Navy officers could check each time they encountered a privateer or merchantman.[23]

Shirley's proclamation did not stop wartime desertion in Massachusetts. Adm. Peter Warren emphasized how desertion hindered even ordinary maintenance of naval vessels in Boston. "I sent the *Shirley* frigate last fall to clean at Boston, with directions to proceed and cruise to the southward with the *Wager*," Warren informed the Admiralty. "Her men leaving her, she was obliged to remain there all winter and did not arrive at Louisbourg till yesterday, 30 men short of complement. The captain used all possible diligence—so much [so] that he dared not set foot on shore for four months for fear of being prosecuted [by] the above Act [the Sixth of Anne, to be discussed below] or murdered by the mob for pressing."[24]

Warren's letter also outlines the navy's problems in trying to raise additional forces in New England. In early 1744 Shirley had asked the legislature for assistance in manning HMS *Bien Aimé,* then refitting in Boston before embarking for Cape Breton.[25] Twelve months later another manpower shortage threatened to weaken Massachusett's coastal defense. The Louisbourg expedition had captured a large French warship, but without sufficient sailors, the prize swung at anchor in Boston harbor. Shirley and Warren tried to attract mariners with the promise of a short enlistment. Warren "has given his Word of Honour," Shirley wrote, "that all voluntiers that will inlist to go aboard this Ship shall be put into Pay from the Time of their inlisting here, and be discharged upon his Return to Boston; and [I] shall in Consequence thereof forthwith issue my Proclamation for encouraging this Inlistment." Despite these efforts, Shirley knew there would be few volunteers, so he asked the legislature for help. "But as I fear we shall not be able to raise a sufficient Number of Men in that Way," he informed the lawmakers, "I must earnestly recommend it to you to assist me with your Resolutions for the impressing of Seamen for this Service."[26]

Desertion from the Royal Navy was certainly not limited to Massachusetts. Warren experienced similar difficulty when he careened HMS *Launceston* near New York City in 1744.[27] In fact, Warren informed the Admiralty that it would be difficult to prevent desertion almost anyplace in North America. "I beg I never clean or fill a ship on this continent without another to put my suspected men on board, for it is otherwise impossible to serve here with any honour."[28] Recently captured Louisbourg, far from any English-speaking communities, was "the only place in America that his Majesty's ships can clean at with any dispatch and prevent desertion, Warren asserted."[29] Newspaper ads also indicate that desertion was widespread, as naval officers placed notices for absent mariners in papers from New England to South Carolina. These ads often cited the enticement of higher wages in the merchant service. In 1740, for example, Capt. Vincent Pearse placed an ad in the *New-York Weekly Journal* in which he offered a reward of two pounds for the return of each deserter and ten pounds for information concerning the master of any merchantman enticing away sailors.[30] (See Figure 4.1.) Government officials even warned Royal Navy captains about the ease of desertion in American cities. Anthony Palmer, president of the Pennsylvania Council in 1748, confessed to Captain

WHereas the Seamen belonging to His Majesty's Ships station'd on the Continent of America, tempted by the high Wages given in the Merchants Service, have taken an unwarrantable Liberty of Deserting, by which means the Captains of His Majesty's Ships are put under a necessity of Impressing Seamen, to the Prejudice of the Trade for whose Protection they are design'd ; Therefore to prevent as much as possible such Desertion and Impressing for the future, I Capt. Peter Warren of his Majesty's Ship Launceston, now station'd at New-York, and compleatly mann'd, do hereby promise a Reward of Five Pounds New-York Money per Head, to any Person or Persons, who shall apprehend any Deserter or Deserters, belonging to the said Ship, and bring them to me, or put them into any County Jayl, giving me Notice thereof. As this is intended for the good of the Trade in general, and to keep his Majesty's Ship under my Command in a Condition to protect them, 'tis to be hop'd all Magistrates and Officers will use their Authority on this Occasion. Dated on board his Majesty's Ship Launceston, at New-York the 18th of October 1742.

Peter Warren.

WHEREAS by an Act of the Parliament of Great Britain, passed in the 6th Year of her late Majesty Queen ANNE, entitled, *an Act for the Encouragement of the Trade to America*, it is amongst other Things enacted, 'That every Commander of a Privateer or trading Ship in any part of America, shall, before he receive any Person to serve on board his Ship, by all reasonable Ways, endeavour to discover, whether such Person hath deserted any Ship of War; and if he shall entertain any such Person without such Endeavour, or which he knows or has been informed has deserted, such Commander shall forfeit for every such Offence Twenty Pounds, with Costs of Suit, to be recovered in any Court in her Majesty's Dominions. ' AND WHEREAS the following Persons, (to wit) George Reed, Samuel Watkins John M'Bride, John Eaton, William Gray, George Nickols, Peter Crown and William Clarke, did on the 22d Instant desert from his Majesty's Ship the Rye, at Boston: THESE are therefore to give Notice, that any Person who will apprehend all or any of the said Deserters, and deliver them to the Commander of any of his Majesty's Ships of War in this Harbour, or unto Mess. Nicklesen, Shubrick, and Comp. shall receive from the Person to whom delivered, the Sum of Twenty Pounds current Money for each Person to apprehended and delivered. AND, all Persons concerned, are hereby forewarned, to pay due Regard to the aforesaid Act of Parliament, of which the same will be carried strictly into Execution by CHARLES HARDY.

N.B. George Reed is aged 22 Years, 5 Feet 4 Inches high, of a brown Complexion, long Faced, flat Nose, and wears a Wig.

Samuel Watkins is aged 25 Years, fair Complexion, and 5 Feet 8 Inches high, has a Scar on the Left side of his Mouth, and short Hair, but sometimes a Wig.

John M'Bride is aged 44 Years, 5 Feet 5 Inches high, full Faced, hath long brown Hair.

John Eaton is aged 29 Years, 5 Feet 5 Inches high, of a brown Complexion, pitted with the Small-Pox, and wears a Wig.

William Gray is aged 22 Years, 5 Feet 7 Inches high, brown Complexion, thin Faced, and wears a Wig

George Nickols is aged 23 Years, 5 Feet 7 Inches high, brown Complexion, lusty, full Faced, and wears a Wig.

Peter Crown is aged 37 Years, and 5 Feet 9 Inches high, of a brown Complexion, long and thin Faced, and wears a Wig

William Clarke is aged 24 Years, and 5 Feet 6 Inches high, of a dark Complexion, hath a Scar on his Right Cheek, and wears a Wig.

Figure 4.1. Desertion was a chronic problem plaguing the Royal Navy throughout the wars of 1739–1748. Naval officers frequently advertised for deserters in the colonial press.

Captain Warren's ad appeared in the 4 November 1742 issue of the *Pennsylvania Gazette;* Captain Hardy's ran in the *South-Carolina Gazette* on 3 January 1743.

Masterson, commander of HMS *Hector,* that Philadelphia was too hospitable to the king's sailors. Replying to Masterson's request for a Delaware River pilot and for information concerning wharfage in Philadelphia, Palmer feared the *Hector*'s crew would probably jump ship en masse. "The danger mostly apprehended by the Council is, that you will not be able to keep your Sailors; this Port is on this account one of the worst in the World," Palmer admitted. "There is an abundance of ways to get out of Town, abundance of bad People to conceal & assist Runaways." Desertion had plagued the previous commander of the navy's

Pennsylvania station ship, Palmer continued. "Captn. Ballet experienc'd this & found it a hard matter to get Men."[31]

Manpower shortages also hampered colonial coast guard operations. The Massachusetts House of Representatives anticipated a lack of volunteers to serve on a newly purchased warship in July 1740, so it authorized the governor and council to press sufficient personnel to man the vessel.[32] Fearing an exodus of mariners during the buildup for the Louisbourg expedition, the Massachusetts assembly enacted legislation "to prevent seamen removing into distant parts to avoid their being impressed into His Majesty's service."[33] In 1746, Edward Tyng, commander of the colony's warship, *Massachusetts-Frigate,* petitioned Shirley "setting forth the great Difficulty he meets with in manning the said Ship."[34] Other provincial guard vessels also suffered. "The Commander of the *Boston-Packet* is inlisting Seamen for that Service," Shirley informed the legislators, "but it has been represented to me by the Committee of War, that it is not probable that many Men will inlist upon our Pay, when they can have much greater Wages in the Merchants Service." Shirley thought the situation called for "extraordinary Methods."[35]

Rhode Island's coast guard experienced similar difficulties. Because few men volunteered to serve on the colony's sloop, the legislature relied on impressment."[36] An inquiry concerning the capture of a French vessel off Point Judith, Rhode Island, in 1748, for instance, highlighted the problems of keeping the *Tartar,* the colony's sloop, fully manned. Captain Holmes had sailed without orders from the colony's chief executive, which prompted a legislative investigation. The inquiry's findings revealed the unpopular nature of Rhode Island's coast guard service. "It was resolved by the committee, that his going out without orders, or instructions from the Governor, or the Deputy Governor, was a great misdemeanor." The legislators condoned Holmes's motives, however. "It appeared to the committee, that it was without any bad design, and *principally to keep his men on board from deserting their service* [emphasis added]."[37]Holmes received only a reprimand.

It is ironic that Rhode Island experienced difficulties securing mariners and resorted to press warrants. Throughout the wars of 1739–1748, especially after France's entry, Newport was repeatedly accused of being a haven for sailors escaping Royal Navy press-gangs. William Shirley was Rhode Island's severest critic, especially during the Louisbourg expedition. Shirley wrote Rhode Island Governor Gideon Wanton twice in one week in June 1745 to secure mariners for a recently captured French warship, renamed HMS *Vigilant Prize*. The second letter berated Wanton's efforts and complained that Massachusetts's attempts to man the warship (a bounty for volunteers backed up by new press warrants) would be useless. "I find my endeavors will be to little purpose, whilst all mariners subject to be impressed here into His Majesty's Service, fly to Rhode Island to avoid it (as indeed has long been the practice) and are there sheltered and encouraged," Shirley fumed. "There are at this time many hundreds of foreign Seamen daily walking the streets of Newport, whilst scarce one is to be found in Boston." Shirley indicated that the king had authorized him to supply Warren with men and shipping. Wanton was bluntly told to put his colony in order and provide the needed sailors. "You will exert yourselves in the most effectual manner, for furnishing Mr. Warren with Seamen, which I am satisfied it is in the power of your Governmt to do, either by offering the same bounty to voluntiers as this governmt has done or by impressing." Shirley made it clear he was tired of Rhode Island's shielding seamen from impressment. "You will not permit your Colony to be an Asylum to all mariners coming into New England, for screening themselves from His Majesty's Service."[38] Josiah Willard, the Bay Colony's secretary, also attacked Rhode Island for harboring seamen and asked Warren to seek replacements in Newport instead of Boston.[39]

Six weeks after Shirley's scathing letter, Richard Partridge, Rhode Island's London agent, also warned Wanton of similar criticism levied by Warren and Christopher Kilby, Massachusetts's agent. Partridge hoped these attacks were groundless or else Rhode Island would earn the imperial government's animosity. He promised to demonstrate that Rhode Island had participated vigorously in the Cape Breton invasion, but was not optimistic. "I have had it several times thrown at me as if Rhode Island wou'd contribute very little if anything at all. If these things shou'd prove true it may make up hill work for me, both at Court and Parliament, but I hope otherwise."[40]

These attacks on Rhode Island's contributions to Cape Breton and the subsequent Canadian expedition prompted numerous letters to Partridge urging him to defend the colony. Rhode Island's defense was consistent: the colony had provided all the men it could spare. Rhode Island was a small colony, and most mariners already served on the province's numerous privateers. "The Colony was then exhausted of Men to an uncommon degree," Wanton explained to Partridge, "not twenty had ever return'd from the West India Expedition [the unsuccessful Cartagena incursion], We had lost many more in the Privateers and had then ten or twelve sail on a Cruise so that it was morally impossible to raise such a Number of Volunteers here at that Time as was desired."[41]

Wanton's defense was plausible. The colony had offered such large bounties to attract volunteers that Shirley and Warren complained it hurt recruiting in other colonies by undermining morale for men serving at lower wages.[42] Moreover, as has been shown, Rhode Island was not opposed to impressment. Much of what Wanton, Greene, and Partridge said was doubtless true. The Newport government had appropriated funds for the expeditions against New France and sought reimbursement from Westminster. Besides, Shirley's criticisms were not above suspicion. Blaming other colonies, especially Rhode Island, for the 1747 impressment riots that rocked Boston was to his advantage. In addition, the less Rhode Island received from the parliamentary grant covering the Cape Breton expenses, the more there would be for Massachusetts.[43]

Governor Shirley of Massachusetts also cast aspersions on the willingness of New York and Pennsylvania to supply men for the king's ships. In a long letter to the duke of Newcastle, Shirley explained that the Massachusetts General Court believed forcing men into the navy had driven hundreds of mariners into neighboring colonies to the detriment of Boston's trade while the commerce of Rhode Island, New York, and Pennsylvania expanded. In addition, riots had erupted in Boston, murders had taken place during a confrontation between seamen and press-gangs, and the colony's council had been intimidated from issuing additional press warrants. Shirley stopped short of telling Newcastle what to do. "I shall not presume to say what I think would be the proper Orders." He clearly believed, however, that Massachusetts press-gangs would encounter violence unless Whitehall applied impressment to the other northern colonies. "So long as Seamen shall continue to be impress'd here . . . no Regulations of those Impresses can effectually relieve this Province, unless some method is at the same time found to oblige the other Colonies, especially the neighbouring ones of Rhode Island; New York and Pennsylvania to furnish their proportion of Mariners for the King's Ships."[44] The conclusion emerging from these charges and countercharges is that navy and colonial coast guard vessels were often undermanned. Mariners sought the most attractive employment and whenever possible they obtained berths on merchantmen or private men-of-war rather than on warships in the royal or provincial service.

II

Private men-of-war frequently experienced problems obtaining full complements during the wars of 1739–1748. According to a Jamaican report in the early months of the conflict, "only two Privateers" had left the island "viz. a Sloop and a Brigantine; tho' several others would be fitted out if they could get Hands, who are so extream scarce."[45] Similarly, the owners of the New York privateer *Prince Charles,* commanded by Jacob Kierstede, failed to attract a full crew in Manhattan so they advertised for men in the *Pennsylvania Gazette.* Even with this expanded recruiting area, the *Prince Charles*'s owners ran the ad six weeks.[46] The owners of the Norfolk, Virginia, privateer, *Raleigh,* Walter Coode commander, likewise faced serious recruiting problems and resorted to soliciting sailors in the Quaker City. On 30 August 1744 the owners advertised they would receive men until 5 September when cruise would proceed "with all Expedition." Three months later, however, the *Raleigh* was still in Virginia, unable to sail until mid-December.[47] Then there was the case of the Newport privateer *Duke of Marlborough,* commanded by Benjamin Carr. Forced to recruit in New York because of Rhode Island's manpower shortages, Carr needed a cash advance from Manhattan merchant Gerard Beekman to cover the costs of this delay.[48]

In addition to recruiting problems, private men-of-war suffered from desertion. In early 1746 an ad in the *Pennsylvania Gazette* offered a reward of three pounds (Pa.) each for the return of seven men who had deserted from the Philadelphia privateer ship *Marlborough,* commanded by Christopher Clymer.[49]

Successful commanders, however, had little trouble securing men. Capt. Philip Dumaresque easily attracted a full complement when fitting out for a cruise in Boston.[50] Newport commander James Allen also experienced few recruiting problems in 1744, and, according to the *South-Carolina Gazette,* even had to turn men away: "The People were so far forward of sailing in so fine a Sloop, second to none but our Colony Sloop *Tartar,* and under so good a Commander, that he was forc'd to send ashore above 60 brave Fellows, who must wait a few Days longer for some other Privateers."[51] George Walker, a highly successful English privateer commander, attracted droves of sailors as he prepared for the first cruise of the Royal Family Privateers in 1746. Walker commanded four private men-of-war (each named after a member of the royal family) mounting more than one hundred carriage guns and manned by nearly one thousand men. Walker's earlier privateering success accounted for his ease of recruiting. "In one article, indeed, of our equipment, we had not the least difficulty, that of getting men: which is generally a cause of delay, and the most material business of preparing such expeditions," commented the anonymous chronicler of Walker's exploits. "For most of the officers and men of the *Boscawen* [Walker's previous command] continued close adherents to Mr. Walker; and the report of so great a private fleet to be fitted out, and the character and known success of the commander, had drawn together such numbers of seamen to offer themselves, that near as many were refused as would have manned a like number of ships; though at this time there was a great scarcity of hands, both in the government and merchant service."[52] Other successful recruiters included John Dennis of Newport; Samuel Bayard, Thomas Tucker, John Burgess, and Robert Troup of New York; and John Rouse of Boston."[53] Although these men rarely experienced recruiting problems, the author of Walker's adventures indicated that privateers as well as the navy and merchant service often suffered manpower shortages.

An examination of recruiting advertisements placed by privateer owners in the colonial press during the wars of 1739–1748 provides additional evidence that private men-of-war frequently encountered difficulties enlisting full complements. These ads appeared in newspapers in all major colonial ports throughout the 1740s. Even the fact of resorting to newspaper ads suggests recruiting problems. Normally, a privateer seeking mariners "beat up" for volunteers. That is, a privateersman literally beat a drum in an area of a port frequented by seamen to attract their attention. Prospective recruits would then learn of the impending voyage. The journal of the *Revenge* mentions that Captain Norton applied unsuccessfully to New York's lieutenant governor for permission "to beat about for hands." John Jones, owner of the Massachusetts privateer *Young Eagle,* complained to Bay Colony authorities that William Loud, a disgruntled mariner, interfered with recruiting procedures. "Notwithstanding your petitioner obtained Leave from the Government to beat up for Sailors to man the *Young Eagle* privateer John Rous Commander now bound on a privateering Voyage," Jones protested, "Yet the s^d Wm Loud in a riotous manner followed the Drum about the Town [Boston] cursing and abusing the Captain and Several times Colloured the Lieutenant." On 20 December 1741 Jones petitioned Governor Shirley to get rid of Loud by pressing him on one of the naval vessels anchored in Boston harbor. Loud had earlier served on the *Young Eagle*'s privateering cruise to the Wine Islands. He led an attempted mutiny, so Captain Dumaresque, then commander of the *Young Eagle,* had put Loud on a naval vessel in Gibraltar.[54]

If mariners wanted to serve on a privateer but did not see or hear a recruiting drummer, they could retire to a waterfront tavern where the articles for privateering voyages were commonly displayed. In New York, for instance, seamen might drop in at the Sign of the Pineapple, the Griffin, or the Jamaica Arms, all on the New Dock.[55] The Boatswain and Call in Front Street was the best Philadelphia pub for learning about privateering ventures. Mariners also frequented the Pewter Platter and the Crow and Thistle, also in Front Street, the Jolly Trooper in Arch Street, or Le Trembleur in Water Street. Newspaper ads directed sailors to these establishments for information concerning privateering cruises. Since tars normally patronized these taverns and therefore presumably knew of upcoming privateering voyages, resorting to newspaper ads suggests the difficulties of securing sufficient seamen.

These advertisements always stated the name of the vessel and commander and usually mentioned the number of carriage guns, swivels, and men that the private man-of-war would carry. A typical ad in the *Pennsylvania Gazette* began, "Now fitting out for a Cruising Voyage against his Majesty's Enemies, THE SHIP WILMINGTON, JOHN SIBBALD, Commander, Burthen about 300 Tons; to carry 24 Carriage and 24 Swivel Guns, with 150 Men."[56] The ads frequently mentioned the expected embarkation date; the *Wilmington* planned to sail in twenty days. The ads then directed interested seamen to contact the commander personally or go to one of the pubs to see (and sign) the articles for crew. These documents stipulated the terms of the voyage. Mariners considering the *Wilmington*'s cruise were instructed to "repair to the Commanders aforesaid, or to the Sign of the Boatswain-and-Call, near the Drawbridge, Philadelphia, where the Articles are to be seen, and sign'd by those that are willing to go the Cruize."[57] Occasionally, recruiting ads extolled the sailing qualities of the vessel or the commander's past successes. An ad for the schooner *George*, commanded by John Dougall, proudly proclaimed, "This Vessel has been compleatly repair'd, is well known to be a Prime Sailor, and has been very lucky, having taken a greater Value from the Spainiards, than any Privateer in his Majesty's Dominions."[58] An ad for the *Tartar* emphasized that it was a new vessel designed specifically for privateering; the owners of the *Pandour* made the same point.[59] These recruiting advertisements are shown in Figure 4.2.

Assessing the efficacy of these advertisements is difficult. Presumably, privateer owners would not have paid for them if they were unnecessary or ineffective. Recruiting ads appeared in all newspapers from Boston to Charles Town throughout King George's War. If they had not attracted men during the early years of the conflict, privateer owners probably would not have advertised in subsequent years. This would be especially true for ads recruiting men for different voyages made by the same vessel. If advertisements for the 1743 cruises of the *Wilmington* and the *George* had been ineffective, for example, why would their owners place similar notices the following year?

Recruiting advertisements that appeared in the *Pennsylvania Gazette* during the wars of 1739–1748 clearly demonstrate that privateers experienced problems obtaining full complements. (See Table 4.1.) Weeks and months passed by while a vessel sought enough hands. For two private men-of-war, the *Raleigh* (September to December 1744) and the *Marlborough* (November 1744 to February 1745), fully ninety days elapsed between the date of the first advertisement and the date of departure. To shorten the recruiting period before its second cruise in 1745, the *Marlborough* advertised for "able body'd Landsmen" as well as seamen. This may have worked because the recruiting period was trimmed to about five weeks. Even vessels that experienced little difficulty securing men (Adam Lister's 1745 cruise in the *Wilmington* and Alexander Katter's 1745 voyage in the *Warren*) failed to sail on their announced embarkation dates. In fact, of the fifteen advertisements stating a depature date, and for which the actual embarkation date is known, not one departed on schedule. Some were close. The *Wilmington* and the *Warren* missed by less

Philadelphia, April 17, 1745.
Now fitting out for a CRUIZING VOYAGE
against His Majefty's Enemies,

The S H I P
PANDOUR,
WILLIAM DOWELL
Commander ;
Burthen about 300
Tons ; to carry 24
Carriage Guns, moft-
ly 9 and 6 Pounders,
24 Swivels, and 30 Brafs Blunderbuffes, with
150 Men ; is a new Ship, built for a Priva-
teer, and every way completely fitted for that
Purpofe.

Now fitting out for a CRUIZING VOYAGE
against his Majefty's Enemies,

THE SNOW.
W A R R E N,
ALEXANDER KATTER
Commander;
Burthen about 220 Tons;
to carry 16 Carriage,
and 18 Swivel Guns,
with 130 Men.
A L S O, The old Scooner GEORGE,
JOHN DOUGALL, Commander,
To carry 12 Carriage, and 12 Swivel Guns,
and 100 Men.
This Veffel has been compleatly repair'd, is well
known to be a Prime Sailer, and has been
very lucky, having taken a greater Value
from the Spaniards, than any Privateer in his
Majefty's Dominions.
A L L G E N T L E M E N S A I L O R S,
and others, inclined to Enter on Board either
of the faid Privateers, (who are to go in Con-
fort) may Repair to the Commanders aforefaid,
or to the Sign of the *Boatfwain & Call* near
the Draw-Bridge *Philadelphia*, where the Articles are to be feen and figned, by thofe who
are willing to go the Cruife.
As they have their Guns, and every kind
of Ammunition ready, they will fail in 10 Days
at fartheft.

Philadelphia, May 18. 1744.
For a Cruize on a PRIVATEERING VOYAGE
against his Majefty's Enemies,

THE S H I P
TARTAR,
JOHN MACKEY,
Commander,
Burthen 300 Tons; 18
Carriage, and 20 Swivel
Guns, and 130 Men.
Fluth Fore and Aft, being a new Ship compleatly fitted
and equipped as a Ship of War for faid Voyage,
and will fail in Twenty Days.
A L L G E N T L E M E N S A I L O R S, and
Others, inclining to go on faid Cruize, may
repair to the Sign of the Crown and Thiftle, in
Front-Street, where the Officers attend; and the Arti-
cles are to be feen and figned.

Now fitting out for a CRUISING VOYAGE
against his Majefty's Enemies,

T H E S H I P
WILMINGTON,
JOHN SIBBALD,
Commander,
Burthen about 300 Tons ;
to carry 24 Carriage and
24 Swivel Guns, with
150 Men.
To fail in Twenty Days.
A L S O, The new Scooner G E O R G E,
WILLIAM DOWELL, Commander,
To carry 14 Carriage Guns, 14 Swivels, and 120 Men.
A L L G E N T L E M E N S A I L O R S,
and others, inclin'd to enter on board either of the
faid Privateers, may repair to the Commanders aforefaid,
or to the Sign of the *Boatfwain-and-Call*, near the
Drawbridge, *Philadelphia*, where the Articles are to
be feen, and fign'd by thofe that are willing to go the
Cruize.

Figure 4.2. Privateers often experienced difficulties securing full
complements and resorted to advertising for men in American newspapers.
These ads all appeared in the *Pennsylvania Gazette* (the *Wilmington,* on 17
May 1744; the *George,* on 8 November 1744; the *Tartar,* on 24 May 1744;
and the *Pandour,* on 18 April 1745).

than a week as did the *George* in June 1745. The *Pandour* and the
George, sailing in consort in 1746 under the command of William
Dowell and Robert Wood, did not leave, however, until seventy
days after their announced sailing date. Overall, the average delay
for these fifteen privateers was twenty-eight days. This is
undoubtedly a conservative figure and would have been larger if
such vessels as the *Raleigh,* the *Marlborough* (February 1745
cruise), or *Le Trembleur* (October 1746 cruise) had announced an
expected departure date.

TABLE 4.1

Privateering Recruiting Advertisements from the *Pennsylvania Gazette* during the Wars of 1739–1748

Vessel and Commander	Date of First Ad	Date of Last Ad	Announced Departure (Days)	Actual Departure	Amount of Delay (Days)
Dursley Galley, William Neate[a]	9 July 41	23 July 41	—	—	—
Victory, Adam Lesler	16 July 41	23 July 41	10	—	—
George, John Sibbald	16 July 41	23 July 41	10	—	—
Surprize, Joseph Redmond[b]	21 Oct. 42	25 Nov. 42	—	—	—
Wilmington, John Sibbald	28 April 43	9 June 43	None	16 June 43	—
George, William Dowell	28 April 43	9 June 43	None	16 June 42	—
Wilmington, John Sibbald	17 May 44	7 June 44	20	28 June 44	22
George, William Dowell	17 May 44	7 June 44	20	28 June 44	22

TABLE 4.1 CONT.

Vessel and Commander	Date of First Ad	Date of Last Ad	Announced Departure (Days)	Actual Departure	Amount of Delay (Days)
Tartar, John Mackey	24 March 44	7 June 44	20	5 July 44	22
Le Trembleur, John Seares	14 June 44	21 June 44	8	30 June 44	8
Raleigh[c], Walter Coode	30 Aug. 44	6 Sept. 44	"all Expedition"[d]	7 Dec. 44	—
Warren, Alexander Katter	8 Nov. 44	22 Nov. 44	10	6 Dec. 44	18
George, John Dougal	8 Nov. 44	22 Nov. 44	10	6 Dec. 44	18
Cruizer, William Clymer	15 Nov. 44	22 Nov. 44	8	6 Dec. 44	13
Marlborough, Christopher Clymer	15 Nov. 44	12 Feb. 45	None	19 Feb. 45	—
Prince Charles[e], Jacobus Kierstede	14 Dec. 45	8 Jan. 45	14	21 Jan. 45	24
Wilmington, Adam Lister	5 March 45	5 March 45	10	19 March 45	4

TABLE 4.1 CONT.

Vesssel and Commander	Date of First Ad	Date of Last Ad	Announced Departure (Days)	Actual Departure	Amount of Delay (Days)
Pandour, William Dowell	18 April 45	30 May 45	"all Expedition"	30 May 45	—
George, Robert Wood	18 April 45	30 May 45	"all Expedition"	30 May 45	—
Warren, Alexander Katter	13 June 45	27 June 45	10	27 June 45	4
George, John Dougal	13 June 45	27 June 45	10	27 June 45	4
Dreadnought, John Cunningham	22 Aug. 45	10 Oct. 45	"all Expedition"		—
Marlborough, Christopher Clymer	31 Oct. 45	28 Nov. 45	21	6 Dec. 45	15
Pandour, William Dowell	17 Dec. 45	25 Feb. 46	14	11 March 46	70
George, Robert Wood	17 Dec. 45	25 Feb. 46	14	11 March 46	70
Warren, Alexander Katter	27 March 46	10 April 46	21	—	—

TABLE 4.1 CONT.

Vessel and Commander	Date of First Ad	Date of Last Ad	Announced Departure (Days)	Actual Departure	Amount of Delay (Days)
Le Trembleur, Obadiah Bowne	28 Aug. 46	16 Oct. 46	"all Expedition"	30 Oct. 46	—
Le Trembleur, Obadiah Bowne	23 July 47	13 Aug. 47	"all Expedition	—	—
Pandour, William Dowell	8 Oct. 47	12 Nov. 47	"all Expedition"	19 Nov. 47	—
Le Trembleur, Abraham Matthews	9 June 48	23 June 48	14	30 June 48	7

[a]The *Dursley Galley* was actually a letter of marque vessel hired by the Royal Navy to carry provisions from Philadelphia to Jamaica. These recruiting ads stated that hands would receive wages "and one half of all prizes . . . as privateers g e n e r a l l y divide . . . ."

[b]The *Surprize* was probably a letter of marque ship.

[c]The *Raleigh*'s home port was Norfolk, Virginia.

[d]The *Raleigh*'s recruiting ad did not indicate a specific date of departure. Instead, the owners stated the vessel would sail as soon as possible, i.e., "with all Expedition will proceed on such a Cruise . . . ." As can be seen, other privateer owners announced their embarkation dates in this manner.

[e]The *Prince Charles*'s home port was New York City.

The *Marlborough*'s recruiting ad provides a clue to understanding the competition for seamen. The navy, privateers, merchant service, and colonial coast guard wanted experienced mariners, not merely untrained recruits, to fill their complements. During the age of sail, vessels required hands possessing much expertise and experience. Going aloft to trim sails required competence during the day in calm seas; in the dark, in heavy weather, or under enemy fire, handling the sails was far more demanding. Seamen's skills were not learned overnight. The historian Ralph Davis has suggested that all the operations of a sailing vessel required a year or two to learn. For this reason the Newfoundland and Iceland fisheries and the Newcastle coal trade were held in high esteem in Britain during the seventeenth and eighteenth centuries as nurseries for seamen.[60] During the 1740s, however, competition for trained mariners, who were always in short supply, led captains of vessels such as the *Marlborough* to accept landsmen in their crews.

III

Seamen clearly benefited from the short supply and strong demand for maritime labor as mariners' wages increased markedly. The tense conditions in Europe caused by Anglo-Spanish rivalry during the 1730s led to a partial mobilization of Britain's fleet, boosting merchant seamen's monthly wages to approximately thirty-five to forty shillings sterling in 1733–1735. As tensions eased, wages fell to more normal peacetime levels of twenty-three to twenty-five shillings, where they remained until hostilities commenced.[61] Mariners' wages rose dramatically in the fall of 1739. The *Boston Evening-Post* reported that seamen in Jamaica "may have 20 Guineas, besides many other Advantages, for the Run Home [i.e., England]."[62] In Britain, sailors demanded fifty shillings, a month from merchant shippers in 1740; from 1745 to 1748 monthly wages averaged fifty-five shillings.[63] The upward spiral in seamen's wages during the War of Jenkins' Ear provoked statutory wage controls. For the twelve-month period beginning 25 March 1741, seamen's wages were limited to thirty-five shillings per month. This act, however, was unsuccessful and was not renewed.[64] Merchant marine wages averaged about 50 percent above peacetime levels during the 1740s.[65]

North American wages also reflected the high wartime demand for sailors. Robert Pringle wrote Henry and John Brock concerning their ship, *Anne Galley,* then taking on a cargo of rice and deerskins in Charles Town Harbor. "It happens well that Provisions are Cheap here. & that your Sailors are on Easie & Low wages & stay by the Ship. There being now Fifteen & Twenty Guineas given to Sailors for the Run to Europe."[66] The seamen on William Pepperrell's Massachusetts merchantman *Charming Molly* received sixteen pounds (Mass.) per month in 1747, four times higher than the wages Pepperrell paid during the 1730s.[67] Manhattan merchants also faced higher wartime wage bills. Gerard Beekman paid Timothy Anborn and Allen Mackintosh, both hands on Beekman's sloop *Dolphin,* seventy-five shillings (N.Y.) per month (about forty-two shillings sterling) during the winter of 1748. Richard Price, another "Mariner" on the *Dolphin,* received £5 15s. (N.Y.) per month (about sixty-four shillings sterling).[68]

Merchant seamen normally received their wages at the end of their voyages, although advances might be paid when a sailor signed on board, or in a port of call during the voyage. A parliamentary statute prohibited captains from advancing sailors more than half of their wages, to discourage them from jumping ship after receiving their pay.[69] Desertion increased during wartime whenever the scarcity of seamen in a port of call boosted the prevailing wages to higher than normal levels. Merchants therefore normally advanced sums to sailors to keep them from deserting, another indication of the conflict's beneficial effect on maritime labor.

The low wages in the Royal Navy and the colonial coast guard, especially when compared with the merchant marine's inflated wartime level of pay, help explain why so many men deserted from the empire's warships. The navy's pay scale remained static for nearly 150 years. In 1653 parliamentary authorities set naval wages for able seamen at twenty-four shillings per month and for ordinary seamen at nineteen shillings per month. These rates did not change until British tars violently challenged the navy and the government during the great mutinies at Spithead and the Nore in 1797.[70] Out of his meager wages the British seaman had to pay six pence to the sailors' hospital at Greenwich, six pence to the Chatham Chest (a fund for injured sailors' medical expenses), four pence to his ship's chaplain, and another two pence to his vessel's surgeon. In addition, since the navy refused to provide uniforms, further deductions were required to purchase apparel from the ships' pursers.[71]

During peacetime, monthly wage rates in the navy and the merchant marine were roughly equal. Once hostilities erupted, however, a large differential appeared. In addition to this wage gap, the navy was also incredibly slow in paying its men. As in the merchant service, naval seamen received their wages at the end of cruises. At least, that is how the mariners were supposed to be paid. "Keep the pay, keep the man" was the navy's cynical wage policy during the eighteenth century. If a seaman' s wages were withheld for a considerable time, say a year or two, a relatively large amount of back pay accumulated. Naval authorities believed these accumulations deterred desertion. As a result, Royal Navy tars were not paid for years on end. During the Nore mutiny of 1797, there were ships in the fleet that had not been paid off for eight, ten, twelve, and in one case, fifteen years.[72] The British sailor's abhorrence of such treatment is not difficult to understand.[73]

Service aboard American public men-of-war was no more popular than on the king's ships because colonial coast guard wages also held little attraction for provincial sailors. Table 4.2 presents the monthly wage rates for seamen in the Massachusetts and Rhode Island coast guards for years in which rates are extant. The Pennsylvania Council's estimate for sailors' wages for a proposed cruise to patrol the Delaware capes in 1748 is also included. These figures indicate that guarding the British North American coast was hardly a lucrative undertaking. Only the proposed wages for the Pennsylvania guard vessel equaled the merchant marine's prevailing wage rate. Massachusetts's pay never approached the wages mariners could earn on merchantmen. The low pay, coupled with inflation, drove Massachusetts wages below even the Royal Navy's in 1747. Rhode Island sailors fared better than their northern neighbors, but they still lagged far behind the merchant service.

Not surprisingly, the coast guard attracted few volunteers. In January 1746, Capt. Thomas Sanders, commander of the provincial sloop, *Massachusetts,* petitioned the Bay Colony for higher wages. Apparently, Massachusetts paid its sloop's mariners even lower wages than sailors on other provincial vessels. Governor Shirley supported this petition, informing the legislature that Sanders "was not able to support himself and Family nor to get able-bodied Seamen to navigate the Province Sloop, under the scanty Allowance you have made for them, so much lower than that of the other Commanders and Seamen in the Pay of the Province."[74] Sanders's

TABLE 4.2
Monthly Wage Rates in the Colonial Coast Guard during the Wars of
1739–1748

Year	Massachusetts		Rhode Island		Pennsylvania	
1740	£ 6	(22s. 10d.)				
1741	£ 8[a]	(22s. 2d.)				
1742	£ 8	(29s. 1d.)				
1743	£ 8	(29s.)				
1744	£ 8	(27s. 1d.)	£ 8	(27s. 1d.)		
1745	£ 8	(24s. 9d.)	£ 8	(24s. 9d.)		
1746	£ 8	(24s. 10d.)	£ 8[b]	(24s. 10d.)		
1747	£ 8	(17s. 3d.)	£14	(30s. 3d.)		
1748	£12.10	(27s. 4d.)	£14	(30s. 8d.)	£5	(57s. 5d.)

Sources: Worthington Chauncey Ford *et al.*, eds., *Journals of the House of Representatives of Massachusetts* (Boston, 1919–1971), XIX, 122–123; XX, 202; XXI, 208–209; XXII, 155–156, 216; XXIII, 393–394; XXIV, 12, 68, 96, 349; Ellis Ames *et al.*, eds., *The Acts and Resolves, Public and Private, of the Province of the Massachusetts Bay . . .* (Boston, 1869–1922), XIII, 94, 106, 118, 225, 367, 535; John R. Bartlett, ed., *Records of the Colony of Rhode Island and Providence Plantations in New England* (1859; reprint ed., New York, 1968), IV, 568, 575; V, 16, 90–92, 101, 167–168, 216, 246; George E. Reed, ed., *Pennsylvania Archives, Fourth Series: Papers of the Governors* (Harrisburg, Pa., 1900), II, 67–68.

Note: The figures in parentheses are the sterling values of the colonial currencies. John J. McCusker, *Money and Exchange in Europe and America, 1600–1775: A Handbook* (Chapel Hill, N.C., 1978), 316, provided the exchange rates.

[a]The Massachusetts legislature set these wages at £2 new tenor. For comparison, Table 4.2 expresses all Massachusetts wages in old tenor. (£1 new tenor was approximately equal to £4 old tenor.) See McCusker, *Money and Exchange,* 133.

[b]Rhode Island also paid each volunteer a bounty of 40s. (R.I.).

plea was successful, and the assembly raised the wages for the *Massachusetts*'s officers and men.[75]

Prompted, perhaps, by this success, Capt. Edward Tyng,

commander of the provincial warship *Massachusetts Frigate,* also requested more money. Tyng's application emphasized "the great Difficulty he meets with in manning the said Ship by Reason of the lowness of the Wages allowed by the Government." Shirley again supported the increase "for it seems impracticable for Capt. Tyng to make up his Complement without it." After defeating two proposals, the legislature finally granted an increase of forty shillings.[76]

Massachusetts faced more recruiting difficulties in 1746. The assembly authorized Shirley to fit out the *Boston Packet* for guard duty, but he doubted if a full complement could be secured because of the colony's low wages. "The Commander of the *Boston-Packet* is inlisting Seamen for that Service; but it has been represented to me by the Committee of War, that it is not probable that many Men will inlist upon our Pay, when they can have much greater Wages in the Merchants Service."[77]

Massachusetts legislators were more tightfisted the following spring and flatly refused another petition for higher wages from Captain Tyng. Wages remained at 1746 levels, and if few men enlisted, the government would rely on coercion: "If a sufficient Number of Seamen do not appear to inlist, the Captain-General [Governor Shirley] be desired to cause an Impress for that Service."[78]

In addition to monthly wages, sailors in the navy and the coast guard also received prize money from vessels their warships captured. How much prize money augmented a seaman's income is hard to determine. Sailors in the coast guard probably benefited little because their vessels captured few prizes (less than 2 percent of the prizes included in the data file). The navy is another matter, as the king's ships captured hundreds of vessels in American waters. The historian Peter Kemp has estimated that prize money doubled the income of the navy's lower deck seamen: "If one might guess at an all-round average, prize money brought in to the sailor approximately as much again as his naval pay each year."[79] Unfortunately, Kemp provides no evidence to support his "guess." If he were correct, the navy's pay would have approximated wages in the merchant marine. There is simply too much evidence to contradict this dubious assumption, however.

Although the navy captured hundreds of valuable enemy vessels, lower-deck seamen received a very small proportion of the prize money. By statute, all naval prizes were divided according to royal guidelines, which gave the lion's share of the money to captains, commodores, and admirals.[80] When a naval vessel captured a prize, the captain received three-eighths of the capture's value if the prize had been taken by one man-of-war. If more than one warship engaged the prize, all the commanders shared the three-eighths. If the captain sailed under the command of an admiral or a commodore, the captain surrendered one-eighth to his superior. Of the remaining five-eighths, one belonged to the lieutenants (including captains of marines and land forces aboard, if any). Another one-eighth went to the junior officers and the boatswain, gunner, purser, carpenter, master's mate, surgeons, and chaplain. The midshipmen and more important petty officers (boatswain's mate, gunner's mate, carpenter's mate, master-at-arms, yeomen, coxwains, and the sergeants and corporals of the marines) received one-eighth. Only the remaining two-eighths belonged to the lesser petty officers, soldiers, and lower deck sailors who constituted the overwhelming majority of the ship's company.[81] The Massachusetts coast guard followed the navy's distribution scheme for prize money.[82] As the historian Julian Gwyn has observed, "In wartime a captain in an active service theatre of operations had to be very unlucky not to share in a few prizes. . . . For an admiral actively engaged at sea the making of a modest fortune was almost a certainty from the war of 1739–48 onwards."[83]

Peter Warren, commander of naval forces during the Louisbourg expedition, earned a fortune in prize money during King George's War. William Shirley estimated that Warren netted "near Seventy thousand Pound[s] Sterling" from the Louisbourg assault alone.[84] Throughout the conflict, Warren earned at least £127,405 sterling in prize money.[85] The able seaman was hardly as fortunate. The British victory over the French fleet in the Bay of Biscay in October 1747 illustrates the disparities in the navy's distribution of prize money. Lower-deck seamen who participated in this decisive victory received about £60 sterling, while Admirals George Anson and Warren, commanders of the British squadron, split £48,358.[86] In 1747 alone, Anson pocketed nearly £100,000 while Warren received £48,099.[87] Charles Town merchant Robert Pringle disapproved of the large sums naval officers received in prize money. When Thomas Frankland, commander of HMS *Rose,* escorted the French prize *Conception,* worth nearly £100,000 sterling, into Charles Town, Pringle complained that "the Captains of the kings Ships having Certainly too large a Share of Prizes especially when they happen to be of so great Value. The Prize Money ought to be Limitted & some proper fund appointed to appropriate Same."[88] The *Conception* was the most valuable prize brought into South Carolina during the war. As an investor in privateers, Pringle may have resented the navy's competition with private enterprise in the taking of prizes.

Besides awarding most prize money to the gentlemen of the quarterdeck, the navy undermined the value of lower-deck shares by its tardiness in distributing prize money. Essentially, the navy observed the same cynical policy for prize money that it employed in paying wages. Seamen received prize shares long after the captures had been sold and the proceeds divided. This was another attempt to prevent desertion.[89] A succinct example of this practice is provided in the *Boston News-Letter*'s report concerning the ship *Grand Juste,* taken by HMS *Success,* and condemned in the Massachusetts vice-admiralty court. Naval tars paraded in Boston streets "with Cockades in their Hats" anticipating their prize shares when their voyage ended. "We may be pretty well assur'd," the *News-Letter* concluded, "there will be few or no Deserters, to occasion an Impress of Men for the Success while each Man belonging to her has a hopeful Prospect of receiving a good round Sum for this Share."[90]

Unlike the merchant fleet, the coast guard, and the navy, private men-of-war did not secure full complements by paying high wages or relying on press-gangs. Instead, privateers attracted sailors with the prospect of windfall gains earned by capturing enemy vessels. British prize law allowed privateer owners and crews to divide their prizes as they chose.[91] To induce mariners to join privateering voyages, the owners of private warships usually offered liberal prize shares, which provided for two-thirds of the proceeds for the officers and men and one-third for the owners.[92] The rewards for privateersmen on successful predators could be substantial. In 1744, for example, each mariner sailing with Captains Hall and Lamprier, two colonial privateers cruising in consort, received a prize share of three hundred pounds after capturing a rich Spanish register ship in the Windward Passage.[93] Each man on the New York privateer *Dolphin,* commanded by Richard Langdon, earned 110 pieces of eight (about eighteen pounds sterling) from capturing a single sloop during their 1745 cruise.[94] The crew of Capt. Thomas Grenall's brig *Batchelors,* also from Manhattan, pocketed prize shares of more than forty pounds from another successful 1745 voyage.[95] Determining the average value of privateering prize money is obviously difficult. Some private men-of-war captured numerous prizes, and their crews received substantial gains. Other mariners sailing on unsuccessful warships earned no prize money at all. On the whole, if a typical colonial privateer sloop captured a prize of average value, the privateersmen could expect to share prize money worth more than twice the highest average monthly wages paid to sailors in the merchant fleet and nearly.six times the monthly wages paid in the Royal Navy.[96]

IV

The colonial coast guard and the Royal Navy could not compete with merchant shippers and privateers to attract colonial seamen so imperial authorities relied on impressment. The colonies' low wages precluded price competition. New England assemblies occasionally raised their wage rates, but the increases were few and far between. Parliament callously refused to augment Royal Navy wages until forced to do so when the fleet mutinied in 1797. Because governments could coerce sailors to man their warships, the coast guard and the navy refused to compete. Impressment, however, was extremely unpopular and caused numerous problems for British and American officials.

Although impressment secured manpower, it hurt Anglo-American commerce, the empire's *raison d'être,* in several ways. First, and most obvious, the navy's extensive manpower requirements limited the availability of sailors for merchantmen, forcing up wage rates for the remaining mariners. Privateers worsened this situation. Some colonial merchants blamed private men-of-war for the shortage of seamen, but most businessmen criticized the navy. After all, since privateers could not press men, the merchant marine could at least compete with private men-of-war for manpower. They could not compete with press-gangs.

Fear of impressment was another factor that hurt imperial commerce. Eighteenth-century British tars were terrified of serving on the king's warships, and rightfully so. Mariners clearly had few, if any, economic incentives to join the navy since the low wages and slow payment were common knowledge. The risks of battle were another disincentive. Combat was not the only threat to a sailor's physical well-being, however. Naval discipline was rigorous and relied heavily on corporal punishment. Floggings with the cat-o'-nine-tails, beatings from the boatswain's rattan, running the gauntlet, being locked in irons, and capital punishment for a myriad of offenses were part of the daily routine in the king's service.[97] Shore leave was nearly nonexistent because the navy thought it would increase desertion. As a result, British sailors received few respites from the navy's rigors. Given the Royal Navy's disincentives for lower-deck seamen, it is much harder to account for a mariner's voluntary enlistment (some did join willingly) than to explain why so many seamen strenuously avoided naval service.

Impressment exacerbated mariners' fears of the navy because it made practically every sailor a potential victim. Although some avenues of commerce received protection from impressment, virtually all merchant seamen, officers excluded, were vulnerable to press-gangs. As nurseries for seamen, the British fisheries were largely sheltered from impressment. The colliers, Thames watermen, and transports supplying the armed forces were also frequently spared from the gangs. Political connections or heroism in the face of the enemy sometimes earned protections from impressment. Massachusetts Governor Belcher sought exemptions for an associate in 1740. "I ask your friendship," Belcher wrote Captain Warren, "in this difficult Juncture, that His [Massachusetts merchant Major Sewall] men may not be taken from him, & his Voyage thereby ruin'd—your kind offices in this matter I should take as an Article of your particular Respect to me."[98] The Admiralty released sailors pressed from the merchantman *Prince of Orange* and issued one-month protections "as an Encouragement to them for their gallant Defence of the Ship." The *Prince of Orange* had earlier refused to surrender to a powerful Spanish privateer during a voyage from St. Kitts to London.[99]

Most sailors were little sheltered from impressment because the navy observed only one basic rule when coercing sailors. Supposedly, only men from inbound vessels were liable to impressment; outward bound merchantmen were theoretically off limits.[100] Commerce dictated this concession because outward-bound vessels denuded of mariners might be incapable of completing their voyages, and trade would suffer. Manpower losses from nearly completed voyages, however, were not as serious for the owners of merchantmen. The impact on mariners returning home after a transatlantic (or even longer) voyage, only to be impressed for naval service, could certainly be devastating. Not surprisingly, the navy did not always follow this rule. Captain

Townsend of HMS *Tartar* pressed numerous hands from the *Emma Susannah* as it departed Charles Town for Boston in 1740.[101] Because seamen continually faced impressment, shipowners were forced to offer higher wages to induce mariners to risk the press-gangs. In this way, impressment added to the wartime inflation of wages in the merchant marine.[102]

The mere presence of naval warships increased seamen's wages. Mariners afraid of impressment avoided ports frequented by the Royal Navy. Thus station ships hurt colonial commerce. Robert Pringle, who bitterly criticized the navy throughout King George's War, attacked the service's negative impact on trade before the war even began. "I am to acquaint you that the Merchant Shipping here suffer very much by the King's Ships that are from time to time Station'd here, who Instead of Encourageing & being a Help & protection to our Navigation are a Nuisance & very much Distress same in a great many Respects."[103] Pringle emphasized that press-gangs drove mariners to other ports. Once hostilities commenced and sailors became scarce, Pringle blasted the navy. "Merchant Ships are Greatly Oppress'd here by the King's Ships Impressing their Hands, which make Sailors Wages Run very high."[104]

Boston also faced manpower shortages because of the navy's presence. When two naval vessels left Boston in 1739 for new stations on the Carolina coast (undoubtedly to Robert Pringle's chagrin!), Bay colony mariners breathed a sigh of relief: "Early Yesterday Morning His Majesty's Ships *Tartar* and *Squirrel* sail'd from Nantasket for South Carolina to the great Joy of our Sailors, many of whom had retired to the Country, and others hid themselves in Town, to prevent their being impress'd to serve on board those Ships."[105] In 1745 the Boston Town Meeting complained to the provincial legislature about the navy's adverse effect on commerce. The Bostonians lamented:

> That they labour under insupportable Grievances by Means of the late repeated Warrants to impress Seamen for his Majesty's Ships . . . by which Means the Number of Seamen impressed, and those who have fled to the neighbouring Governments for Protection from Impresses, added to those who went in the Sea Service to Cape-Breton, amount to more than three Thousand, whereby the neighbouring Governments have not only had a sufficient Number of Seamen to navigate their Trade with, but also so large a Surpliss of Men as to enable them to Man within the Province of New-York and Colony of Rhode-Island thirty Sail of Privateers.

The town meeting concluded by emphasizing the disastrous impact impressment had on commerce. "The once cherished now depressed, once flourishing now sinking Town of Boston, have been so far from being able to Man any Privateers, that she has wanted Men to Man the Merchant Vessels, to the inexpressible Loss and Damage of her Merchants."[106] Clearly, Boston's civic leaders believed the king's ships hurt the city's economy.

British warships continued to press men in American ports throughout the wars of 1739–1748 and during the subsequent French and Indian War. Benjamin Franklin complained about impressment in 1759 in phrases reminiscent of Robert Pringle or the Boston Town Meeting. "New York and Boston have so often found the Inconvenience of . . . Station Ships that they are very indifferent about having them: The Pressing of their Men and thereby disappointing Voyages, often hurting their Trade more than the Enemy hurts it."[107] Paradoxically, the station ships that supposedly aided colonial trade by safeguarding it from enemy predators hurt commerce by worsening the manpower shortage. The *Boston Evening-Post* reported an incident that graphically summarizes American fears of impressment:

> Watertown, August 20. Yesterday (being Lord's Day) a very odd Adventure happened here, which had it been on any other Day would have been comical enough; 'tis this: We, as well as many other Country Towns, had for some Days been under strange Apprehensions of the *Press Gang* coming among us, and it unhappily fell out, that Yesterday Two Boston Gentlemen spent the Sabbath with us, one of which had a laced Jacket and Hat, and the other a red Face and a red Coat, which with us are very shrewd Signs of their being Military Men. In the Forenoon, it being hot, the Gentlemen were only seen at their Lodgings, or among the shady Trees, which however gave the Alarm; in the Afternoon they came to Meeting, sat down in a Pew, and behaved very civily; but in the Time of Service, one of them (being hot) look'd out of the Window, only for this Benefit of the Air, which however was thought to be done on purpose, that he might give the Signal to the rest of the Gang, who were supposed to be somewhere at Hand. This put our Men out of all Patience, and first, two who were in the Pew with the Gentlemen, got out, who were soon follow'd by many others; some in as private and sly a Manner as possible, and others jump'd out of the Windows; so that in short, we lost Twenty of our Congregation, some of whom (I am told) ran into the Woods for their better Security until the Danger was over: However, they are all now

returnedd [sic], and the Town restored to its former Tranquility. 'Tis remarkable that the Gentlemen were much surprized to observe such a Disturbance in the Meeting, and utterly ignorant that themselves were the Cause of it.[108]

Despite the navy's widespread use of press-gangs in America, the legality of impressment was questionable, especially the pressing of privateersmen and American seamen. The confusion resulted from the Prize Act of 1708, "an act for the encouragement of the trade to America," commonly referred to as the Sixth of Anne or the American Act. This statute explicitly exempted all Americans and British mariners serving on privateers or merchantmen trading to America from impressment into the Royal Navy:

> That no mariner or other person who shall serve on board, or be retained to serve on board any privateer, or trading ship or vessel, that shall be imployed in any part of America, nor any mariner, or other person, being on shoar in any part thereof, shall be liable to be impressed or taken away, or shall be impressed or taken away, by any officer or officers belonging to any of her Majesty's ships of war, impowered by the lord high admiral, or any other person whatsoever.[109]

The statute was precise. How, then, could American and British seamen sailing on private men-of-war or in the colonial trade be legally impressed?

The answer lies in a series of questionable opinions issued by the Crown's legal officers. Essentially, the government's attorneys argued that the Sixth of Anne expired in 1713 when Queen Anne's War ended. Sir Edward Northey, England's attorney general, stated in 1716, "I am of opinion the whole American Act was intended, and appears to have been intended only for the war."[110] Northey's rationale is obscure because nothing in the act provided for expiration at the conflict's conclusion. In addition, British and American admiralty courts supply incontrovertible evidence that this law was in force in 1739.

The Privy Council authorized colonial governors to issue letters of marque in 1739. Privateers were required to send prizes to Britain or the colonies for admiralty proceedings. When this action occurred, the Sixth of Anne was the only statute regulating prize adjudication. All prizes tried in 1739 and the first three months of 1740 were proceeded against under the American Act because only the 1708 law prescribed the admiralty courts' procedural steps. If the Sixth of Anne had expired in 1713, there would have been no judicial process for prize cases.[111]

Americans were well aware that the Sixth of Anne protected colonists and privateersmen from impressment. In his proclamation encouraging privateers, Massachusetts Governor Belcher promised all the privateersmen exemptions from impressment: "All their Mariners and Soldiers duly inlisted shall be freed from all Impresses for any other Service whatsoever."[112] New York and Charles Town newspapers reprinted Belcher's proclamation.[113] South Carolina Lieutenant Governor William Bull's proclamation also guaranteed immunity from impressment for all privateersmen.[114] Two weeks after Belcher's pronouncement, the *Boston Evening-Post* devoted its front page to excerpts from the Sixth of Anne, including the act's ninth section, which contained the protection from impressment.[115]

Apparently England's Privy Council, the High Court of Admiralty, the colonial vice-admiralty courts, and the chief executives of Massachusetts and South Carolina, not to mention thousands of colonial and British seamen, believed the Sixth of Anne was in force in 1739 when the first letters of marque were issued and the first prizes were tried. Members of Parliament also thought the act was operative during the war's early months. In November 1739 when the House of Commons considered stricter regulations for private men-of-war, legislators examined the American Act to see if they could improve it.[116] Both houses of Parliament worked on legislation throughout the winter of 1739–1740, and a new bill became law on 19 March 1740.[117]

The Prize Act of 1740 replaced the 1708 statute. Virtually every clause in both laws addressed the adjudication of prizes taken by the Royal Navy and private vessels with letters of marque. Many sections were virtually verbatim. There were some important changes, however. Americans and Britons serving on privateers or in the colonial trade no longer enjoyed immunity from impressment. Parliament had finally ended the controversy over the American Act, or so it seemed. Yet confusion existed because Westminster did not specifically repeal the Sixth of Anne, and Whitehall still instructed royal governors to enforce the 1708 act. William Shirley's 1741 instructions, for example, required enforcement of the Sixth of Anne.[118] Given the contradictions and ambiguities in London concerning the American Act, confusion in the colonies is understandable.

The Royal Navy believed impressment in America was legal, so naval commanders pressed privateersmen and merchant seamen in the colonial trade after the 1740 bill became law. The Philadelphia privateer *Victory,* commanded by John Sibbald, nearly paid a high price for a press-gang's actions. Sibbald lost all but a handful of his crew in Jamaica in 1741. During its passage home, the undermanned *Victory* narrowly escaped capture by two Spanish privateers.[119] The navy also pressed men from John Bannister's Newport privateer *Victory* in Jamaica in 1741.[120] Numerous letters of Robert Pringle document impressment from vessels in the colonial trade.

Although the 1740 Prize Act failed to protect these mariners, merchants like Bannister and Pringle asserted that their seamen were exempt from impressment. Bannister informed a London correspondent of an impending trip to England "in order to recover the £20 Ster[1]. for each man the Admiral pressed out [of] Powers [commander of the *Victory*] at Jamaica (when a Private man of War) Agreeable to Act of Parliament[.]"[121] Bannister referred, of course, to the Sixth of Anne, which provided that naval officers would forfeit twenty pounds plus legal costs for each man illegally pressed from privateers or merchantmen trading to America. The irrepressible Pringle even convinced a Royal Navy captain that the American Act protected merchant seamen from impressment. In 1742 Pringle secured the release of several men pressed from the *Richard*, then loading in Charles Town harbor. Pringle related this success at the navy's expense to his brother, Andrew. It seems that Captain Hallin had been "detain'd for Want of Hands, as all the other Vessells are, having had Some of his people impress'd by the Commander of the Kings Ships with whom [I] have had Some Dispute about the Same." Pringle continued, "However [I] have oblig'd them to Return Capt. Hallin's & believe [I] am the first in the Place that has oblig'd them to doe So, having made them Sensible that I was Determin'd to Sue them according to the Act of Parliament in the Case made & provided."[122] After Captain Forrest, commander of HMS *Wager,* pressed two men from the sloop *Philadelphia,* John Stinson, the sloop's master, filed a damage suit in a Boston court under the Sixth of Anne.[123] Admiral Warren, discussing impressment's unpopularity in Manhattan with New York Governor George Clinton, blamed the situation on the American Act. "The spirit against pressing continues as violent as ever in your government," Warren asserted. "Indeed it will do so in all the colonies till some measures are taken upon it by the British

Parliament, either by repealing the clause of 6 Anne [c. 37], which forbids pressing in America or by some other means. You see they prosecute upon the Act without any regard to the attorney's and solicitor general's opinions that the force of the Act expired with [that] war."[124] Obviously, some naval officers and royal governors, not to mention most merchants and seamen, believed the Sixth of Anne was not dead.

Imperial authorities were aware of this confusion. In the summer of 1743 Thomas Corbett, secretary to the Admiralty, informed the colonial governors that the American Act had expired in 1713.[125] In October 1743 Whitehall officials reiterated the navy's right to press Americans and Britons engaged in privateering and the colonial trade. Yet three years later Admiral Warren complained to Corbett that "the Act of 6: Anne which forbids pressing in the colonies continues in force, which all the law courts abroad construe it to do. . . . It occasions continual prosecutions against sea officers who cannot avoid pressing."[126] This impasse concerning impressment in America continued throughout the 1740s.

Although the imperial government upheld the right to force men into the king's service, it directed Royal Navy officers to exercise discretion when coercing colonial sailors. "In the Press Warrants which we give the Captains of His Majesty's Ships in America, they are strictly required not to distress either the Merchant Ships, or the Privateers," the Lords of the Admiralty asserted.[127] Essentially, London's position affirmed that mariners could be pressed but that press-gangs should always use restraint and moderation.

It seems unlikely that Captain Sibbald of the *Victory* thought the navy exercised much discretion while stripping nearly all the hands from his vessel. Similarly, Capt. John Griffiths of the Rhode Island privateer *Caesar* probably thought a press-gang failed to take "great Care no Indiscreet or Unreasonable Use" of its press warrant when taking thirty-five men from his vessel in 1744.[128] Certainly, South Carolinians thought the king's service less than discreet when a press-gang murdered a Charles Town seaman and then fled to avoid prosecution.[129] Bostonians were similarly outraged when navy "recruiters" killed two Massachusetts mariners who each possessed protections from the press issued by Peter Warren.[130] The Boston Town Meeting petitioned the provincial legislature for relief from impressment, especially from press-gangs that behaved like "lawless Rabble."[131] Boston's great anti-impressment riots of 17–

20 November 1747 clearly revealed the impossibility of coercing men into the navy without violence and distress.

V

The controversies over the Sixth of Anne and impressment in general illustrate the severe manpower shortage that gripped the British Empire during the eighteenth century. When the Admiralty resorted to impressment, problems arose from the American Act because the navy could not coerce American mariners or the thousands of native British tars sailing in the colonial trade or on private men-of-war. The Sixth of Anne had earlier prevented the navy from maintaining its complement in Boston before the 1711 Walker expedition against Canada. The American Act created even more headaches for naval officials in the 1740s.

Although the Sixth of Anne hampered the Royal Navy, Parliament did not repeal the law. Impressment was so completely hated in Britain and the colonies that Westminster probably thought it politically unwise to rescind the statute. Instead, Parliament merely omitted the section granting protection from impressment in the prize law of 1740. To placate colonial opposition, Whitehall ordered the navy to exercise care and discretion when kidnapping men from privateers or merchantmen in the American trade. Parliament did not explicitly repeal the American Act until 1775, thus ending the debate concerning its supposed expiration in 1713. Presumably, this action would have been unnecessary if the Crown's legal officers had been correct.[132]

Obviously, mariners found the navy's discretion grossly inadequate. It is, of course, highly unlikely that any press-gang could have acted moderately. Given the navy's notorious reputation, no press-gang could employ restraint and still obtain any men. Colonial opposition to impressment was not restrained, especially in Boston where the press was often hot. In 1741 Governor Shirley even had to persuade the Massachusetts General Court that ordering Castle William's battery to fire on HMS *Astrae,* whose commander had pressed several Bay Colony mariners, was not in the best interest of Massachusetts's war effort.[133] In 1747 when press-gangs swept through Boston harbor pressing indiscriminately, a mob exceeding three hundred persons resisted with cutlasses and clubs. The rioters seized several press-gang members, threatened Governor Shirley's residence after he protected naval personnel, assaulted and locked a deputy sheriff in the stocks, threw stones and brickbats at the

Massachusetts capitol, and burned a barge on the Boston Commons which they incorrectly thought belonged to the navy. Before the riots ended, Adm. Charles Knowles threatened to bombard the town.[134] Despite the violent confrontations impressment often caused, the naval historian N.A.M. Rodger has suggested that press-gangs were pleasant assignments: "There was a holiday element in being sent pressing either by sea or by land."[135] However accurate this assessment may be for Great Britain, it certainly fails to describe the press in America.

The navy was not alone in its desperate attempts to obtain men. The colonial coast guard also resorted to impressment. Ironically, many colonial officials who protested loudly against naval impressment authorized press-gangs of their own. The Massachusetts House of Representatives and the Rhode Island Assembly did not shrink from coercing seamen into the colonial service.

Letters of merchants such as Robert Pringle, correspondence of naval officers like Peter Warren, and numerous American newspaper reports testify to the inadequate supply of maritime labor. As a result, seamen's wages continually increased. The navy's manpower requirements created a vicious circle of a shortage of mariners, higher wages, press-gangs, an exodus of sailors to safer ports, an even shorter supply of men, higher wages, more press-gangs, and so on. The privateers' demand for sailors added even more pressure on the supply of men.

Throughout the conflict, private men-of-war were criticized for draining seamen from the navy and the merchant marine. Historians have echoed these charges and asserted that droves of mariners deserted from the navy, fled from the press, and jumped ship from merchantmen to sign on privateers. Even private men-of-war faced manpower shortages, however, and were forced to advertise for crews or sail from port to port seeking men. Privateers were not great magnets that easily attracted full complements.

During the wars of 1739–1748 British and American seamen had four major avenues of employment. Paradoxically, wartime improved mariners' working conditions. For a large variety of reasons, they shunned the navy and the colonial coast guard whenever possible. The merchant service and privateers were more attractive. Yet these employers frequently experienced a shortage of sailors. There were simply too few seamen available for wartime duty.

Chapter 5

THEATERS OF OPERATIONS: BRITISH COLONIAL PRIVATEERS

In the summer of 1744 Dr. Alexander Hamilton, the Maryland physician, traveled the Atlantic coast from Annapolis to Maine and back. During his overland trek, Hamilton observed the varying customs and habits of the residents of Britain's northern colonies and filled his travelogue, the well-known *Itinerarium,* with interesting anecdotes concerning colonial politics, the quality of roadside taverns, impressions of northern cities, and the foibles of New York's Dutch inhabitants. Because he toured the East Coast during the height of the wars of 1739–1748, Hamilton's account is especially useful in assessing the impact of imperial warfare on colonial society. The Scottish-born physician repeatedly focused his attention on the progress of the maritime conflict involving Britain, Spain, and France. More particularly, Hamilton discovered a widespread and very active interest in privateering.

The Anglo-Spanish war and the prospect of French entry into the conflict as Britain's enemy was the topic of conversation at the outset of Hamilton's trip. "After supper," Hamilton recorded at Tradway's tavern on his second night away from home, "the conversation turned upon politicks, news, and the dreaded French war."[1] Several days later near Darby, Pennsylvania, the same topic nearly caused a young Quaker and a privateer boatswain to come to blows.[2] Dinner conversation in Philadelphia echoed the discussions of the Maryland countryside: "The [dinner] company divided into committees in conversation; the prevailing topick was politicks and conjectures of a French war."[3] Uncertainty concerning French foreign policy ended during Hamilton's stay in Philadelphia when declarations of the Anglo-French war reached the Quaker City on 10 June. During the official announcement of hostilities, over four thousand people, more than one-fourth of Philadelphia's population, gathered in the streets to hear the governor's proclamations.[4] A large parade was led "by about 30 flags and ensigns taken from privateer vessels and others in the harbour which were carried by a parcell of roaring sailors."[5]

After leaving Philadelphia Hamilton was besieged for information during his journey to New York. "The country people whom I met asked in generall whether war had been proclaimed against France."[6] At Raretan Ferry near Perth Amboy, New Jersey, Hamilton encountered two other travelers. "First of all (as is naturall) we enquired concerning news." Again, the war dominated conversation. Hamilton learned that an English sloop had narrowly escaped capture by a French privateer that "had the impudence to pursue her into the hook at the entrance to [New] York Bay."[7] This interest in privateers and prize actions became a major theme throughout Hamilton's subsequent observations concerning the hostilities.

Hamilton spent nearly a month in New York, sailing up the Hudson to Albany and Schenectady, passing ten days in Manhattan, and traveling across Long Island. During this visit he frequently noted the results of the prize war. "We met two sloops from [New] York," Hamilton recorded during his cruise up the Hudson, "by whom we had news of a French privateer taken by Captain Ting [Edward Tyng], master of the Boston gally." Back in Manhattan, Hamilton recorded other British successes. "I dined at Todd's [a Manhattan tavern] and went in the afternoon to see the French prizes in the harbour. Both of them were large ships. . . . Warren [Royal Navy Captain Peter Warren], who took the St. Francis, has gained a great character. His praise is in everybody's mouth, and he has made a fine estate of the business." News from the prize war could also be disappointing, however. "We heard news of a coasting vessel belonging to N. England taken by a French privateer in her passage betwixt Boston and Rhode Island. . . . We had news this day [9 July] of an English vessel loaden with ammunition and bound for New England being taken on the coast."[8]

After leaving New York, Hamilton proceeded to New London, Connecticut, where he witnessed a near panic caused by fears of

French privateers. "The inhabitants were alarmed this night att a sloop that appeared to be rowing up into the harbour, they having heard a little before a firing of guns out in the Sound and seen one vessell, as they thought, give chase to another. There was strange clamour and crowd in the street, chiefly of women." Hamilton recorded that this mysterious sloop did not strike its colors when fired upon by the Connecticut coast guard sloop, which happened to be in the harbor. After a second shot "which whistled thro' her rigging, she struck and made answer that it was one Captain Trueman from Antegua. Then the people's fears were over, for they imagined it was old Morpang, the French rover, who in former times used to plunder these parts when he wanted provision."[9]

Hamilton noticed an even greater interest in privateering as he left Connecticut and entered Rhode Island. In Newport Hamilton recorded the attractiveness of the female population as well as the reputation of the city's private men-of-war. "This place is famous for privateering." He also saw what the profits of privateering could provide when he and Dr. William Moffat visited Godfrey Malbone's palatial country seat in nearby Portsmouth. "I went with the Doctor att 10 a'clock to see a house about half a mile out of town, built lately by one Captain Malbone, a substantial trader there. It is the largest and most magnificent dwelling I have seen in America."[10]

Hamilton's interest in prizes and privateers continued in Boston. There he strolled along the waterfront observing captured French merchantmen and surveyed "a ship upon the stocks that was intended for a privateer." Hamilton also frequented the city's public houses where he discussed privateering over a few drinks. "I spent the evening with Mr. Parker [a Boston merchant] where I drank good port wine and heard news of six prizes carried into New York by the company of privateers there."[11]

On his way home to Annapolis Hamilton returned to Newport. Once again he commented on the leading role privateering played in the city's economy. "In time of war this place is noted for privateering, which business they carry on with great vigour and alacrity. The island has fitted out now 13 or 14 privateers and is dayly equipping more. While I stayed in this place they sent in severall valuable prizes."[12] Newport's enthusiasm for privateering spilled over from its countinghouses to the city's salons. When Hamilton accompanied an acquaintance to a meeting of Newport's Philosophical Club, he "was surprized to find no matters of philosophy were brought upon the carpet. They talked of privateering and the building of vessels."[13]

On his way to New York Hamilton decided upon a change of scenery and rode along the Connecticut coast instead of crossing Long Island Sound and retracing his earlier route. The landscape was different, but the news was the same. In Milford he learned about Philadelphia privateers who had captured several enemy merchantmen. At Turtle Bay (an inlet in New York's East River) a fellow traveler gave Hamilton "a whole pacquet of news about prizes and privateering, which is now the whole subject of discourse."[14] Hamilton was tired of such reports by the time he reached Manhattan, where he accepted a dinner invitation from Stephen Bayard, New York's mayor. Many of the city's political luminaries were present including James DeLancey, the colony's chief justice, and Daniel Horsmanden, the city recorder. Hamilton, however, found the dinner conversation boring: "The table chat ran upon privateering and such discourse as has now become so common that it is tiresome and flat."[15] Hamilton left early and went to the Hungarian Club where discussion again concentrated on "the taking of some tobacco ships near the capes of Virginia, which furnished matter for conversation all night."[16]

Hamilton's portrait of the colonies during wartime suggests that many Americans—merchants, farmers, tavern keepers, artisans, government officials, mariners—displayed an awareness and concern for King George's War in general, but it was the scramble for prizes at sea that commanded their greatest attention. Throughout his travels, whether in the large port cities of Boston and Philadelphia, the privateering centers of Newport and New York, the country towns of Connecticut, or just along the road in public houses, Hamilton observed widespread interest in the exploits of private men-of-war.

Numerous sources corroborate Hamilton's observations of 1744. Thus every colonial governor encouraged the fitting out of privateers; assemblies loaned arms and ammunition to privateer owners; and merchants in every leading port invested in seafaring predators, while mariners by the thousands enlisted to serve on board. Finally, newspapers throughout the colonies from Boston to Barbados published hundreds of accounts of captures involving American privateers. The evidence, in short, clearly reveals that privateering was extensive whether measured by the ports that participated, the number of private men-of-war that embarked on cruises, or the merchants, captains, and seamen who sought prizes. It also indicates the impressive scope of the privateers' operations as they pursued enemy merchantmen from Newfoundland's Grand Banks to the Caribbean year after year throughout the decade. Privateering was also impressive when compared with the efforts of the Royal Navy in American waters and the various expeditions against Spanish and French colonial possessions. To understand the nature and impact of imperial warfare in America then, an examination of privateering is essential.

I

All the leading ports in British North America and the British West Indies fitted out private men-of-war. Each port's activity can be assessed in different ways. One might, for instance, count the privateers that sailed from each city, but this would miss repeated cruises by individual private men-of-war. Alternatively, one might count the prizes captured by a city's privateers, but this would not necessarily indicate the commitment of a city's resources to privateering, since a few skillful or lucky commanders from one port might seize several prizes while another's larger fleet sailed home empty-handed.

The method adopted here for measuring each port's participation is to determine the number of privateers at sea in each year of the hostilities. This takes into consideration multiple voyages by the same captain. If, for example, Capt. John Lush of New York embarked on one or more cruises in 1740, he would be counted as one "yearly privateer." If Lush sailed in 1741, 1742, and 1743, three yearly privateers are recorded. The calculation is conservative. Some yearly privateers undertook more than one cruise per year, but the nature of the data prevents a more precise measure. Ideally, the time at sea for each private man-of-war should be determined, but though colonial newspapers reported hundreds of captures, they seldom stated the length of time cruisers had been on the hunt. Fortunately, this problem is not serious. Privateering voyages appear to have been lengthy: the average duration of ninety-four cruises conducted by Newport, New York, and Philadelphia privateers was nearly seven months.[17] It would have been difficult for a captain to make more than one or two voyages a year.

By identifying the types of vessels fitted out as private men-of-war, one can estimate the crew complements and the value of shipping employed in privateering.[18] The numbers of yearly

TABLE 5.1

Yearly Privateers and Privateering Berths from British Colonial Ports,
1739–1748

Port	Yearly Privateers		Privateering Berths[a]	
	N	%	N	%
Boston	29	6.2	2,591	7.1
Newport	117	25.1	9,309	25.6
New York	105	22.6	10,328	28.4
Philadelphia	47	10.1	4,646	12.8
Charles Town	36	7.7	2,553	7.0
West Indies[b]	112	24.0	5,372[c]	14.7
Other[d]	20	4.3	1,605	4.4
Totals	466	100.0	36,404	100.0

[a]Several procedures were employed to estimate yearly privateering berths. For cases listing crew size there was no need to estimate. When data on crew size were missing, estimates were based on the type of vessel—ship, snow, brig, etc.—using the mean crew size for all British colonial privateers of that type. (See chapter 3.) When data were missing for crew size and vessel type, no estimate was made.

[b]Includes Bermuda.

[c]This estimate suffers rather dramatically from missing data.

[d]Includes Cape Fear, N.C.; Norfolk, Va.; Frederica, Ga.; Portsmouth, N.H.; and New Jersey.

privateers and yearly privateering berths for the leading British colonial seaports are presented in Table 5.1.[19] The types of vessels and their value for each port are indicated in Table 5.2. These tabulations demonstrate that the colonies risked many men and substantial capital in the maritime war.

These data also indicate a strong correlation between urban development and participation in the prize war. Privateering ventures required entrepreneurial ability, shipping, and manpower. The largest seaports—Boston, Newport, New York, Philadelphia, and Charles Town—possessed more of the requisites than did smaller communities such as Providence, Perth Amboy, or Norfolk.

Organization of a privateering cruise required experienced merchants unafraid of taking risks and in command of sufficient

TABLE 5.2

Types and Value (£ Sterling) of Yearly Privateers, 1739–1748

Port	Schooners	Sloops	Brigs	Snows	Ships	Other[a]	Missing	Value
Boston	1 (233)	9 (2,646)	12 (8,668)	3 (2,394)	0	0	4	£13,941
Newport	4 (932)	68 (22,896)	14 (10,616)	12 (10,153)	8 (13,597)	0	11	£58,194
New York City	0	39 (14,579)	43 (34,605)	7 (6,961)	13 (20,197)	1	2	£76,342
Philadelphia	9 (2,377)	6 (1,765)	6 (4,942)	9 (9,898)	12 (18,850)	1	4	£37,832
Charles Town	8 (2,837)	9 (3,045)	4 (3,388)	3 (1,982)	5 (7,516)	5	3	£18,775
West Indies[b]	10 (3,071)	31 (11,324)	13 (9,248)	6 (5,967)	1 (2,519)	6	45	£32,129
Other[c]	3 (735)	7 (2,639)	4 (3,051)	3 (2,345)	1 (1,261)	0	2	£10,031
Totals	35 (10,185)	169 (58,894)	96 (74,518)	43 (39,700)	40 (63,940)	13	70	£247,237

Note: Estimated values are based on the Philadelphia construction costs from 1735 to 1754 presented in John J. McCusker, "Sources of Capital Investment in the Philadelphia Shipping Industry," *Journal of Economic History*, XXXII (1972), 146–157. The estimates consider the difference between measured tons and tons burden and also assume that private men-of-war were vessels converted to privateers, not new-built craft.

[a]Includes galleys, boats, and pettyaugers. Lack of data precludes calculations of values.
[b]Includes Bermuda.
[c]Includes Cape Fear, N.C.; Norfolk, Va.; Frederica, Ga.; Portsmouth, N.H.; and New Jersey.

capital to acquire strong sailing vessels, substantial ordnance, and enough provisions for a long voyage. They needed skilled captains with established reputations to attract large crews. Once a privateer captured an enemy merchantman, the owners' business skills were especially important because profits did not materialize until the prize was condemned in a vice-admiralty court and the vessel and cargo were sold to advantage. Business correspondents, warehouse facilities, and market information were all necessary for success. Privateering was obviously not a business for amateurs. The overwhelming majority of privateer investors listed their profession as "merchant" when they applied for a letter of marque. Of eighty-nine bonds for Rhode Island letters of marque, for example, only two (2 percent) failed to list merchants among the investors.[20] Many leading businessmen in the large seaports owned shares in private men-of-war, including John Bannister, Godfrey Malbone, and John Brown of Newport; Thomas Hancock of Boston; the Livingstons, Beekmans, and Van Hornes of New York; and Robert Pringle of Charles Town. To minimize risks, few cruisers were owned by a single investor.[21]

In addition to entrepreneurial ability, shipping and manpower were also available in the larger ports. Some vessels were constructed specifically for privateering; Alexander Hamilton observed one on the stocks in Boston, for example. The owners of the Philadelphia privateers *Pandour* advertised that their vessel was a "new ship, built for a Privateer."[22] Most private men-of-war, however, were converted merchantmen. Thus communities with large merchant fleets could rapidly dispatch private men-of-war when hostilities erupted in 1739 and when France became involved in 1744. In addition, the principal ports more easily supplied the enormous numbers of men needed for privateering crews. These vessels were manned almost to the gunwales since crews of fifty to seventy were normal even on schooners and sloops. Such requirements placed severe pressures on the maritime labor market because merchantmen also sailed with large crews during wartime to protect themselves from enemy predators and because colonial governments competed for mariners to man the vessels that patrolled their coasts. In addition, the Royal Navy vessels assigned to the North American station "recruited" colonial sailors by impressment. Although crews were often difficult to secure, bigger cities offered the amplest supply of men. Not all of the men sailing on privateers were experienced mariners; some were landsmen seeking adventure, gain, or escape from rural boredom. The largest ports probably attracted more of these recruits than the smaller outports.

Dr. Hamilton correctly portrayed Newport as a center of privateering. (See Figure 5.1.) The Rhode Island capital led the British colonies in the number of yearly privateers and ranked second in privateering berths. Newport's participation in the prize war began early. Soon after learning of the Privy Council's authorization of letters of marque and reprisal against Spain, Rhode Islanders commenced cruising operations.[23] Before the end of 1739 seven privateers sailed out of Naragansett Bay, establishing Newport as Britain's most important colonial privateering port, a position it retained throughout the Anglo-Spanish war. After the hostilities expanded in 1744, the *New-York Weekly Post-Boy* commented on the increased interest in privateering. "Several stout Privateers are fitting out at Boston, and two at New-London, but none can come up to the brisk and brave Rhode-Islanders."[24] Newport continued to play a prominent role in the prize war, but surrendered its position as the leading privateering port during the conflict with France. (See Table 5.3.)

New York City vied with its northern neighbor as the center of privateering. (See Figure 5.2.) Although few New York privateers cruised during the War of Jenkins' Ear, Manhattan merchants succumbed to a privateering fever between 1744 and 1748. In each of these years New York ranked either first (1746–1748) or second (1744–1745) among British colonial ports in the number of vessels and men raiding Spanish and French commerce.

Figure 5.1. A view of Newport, Rhode Island, from a painting done c. 1740. Newport was the fifth largest city in America during the 1740s. Alexander Hamilton, the peripatetic Maryland physician, commented on Newport's preeminence in the prize war: "This place is famous for privateering."

TABLE 5.3

Yearly Ranking of British Colonial Participation in Privateering by Port, 1739–1748

Year/Rank	1	2	3	4	5	6	7	Totals
1739	NEWPORT	B.W.I.[a]	NEW YORK	BOSTON	OTHER[b]	NO OTHER PVTRS.	NO OTHER PVTRS.	16 PVTRS.
	7 Pvtrs.	3 Pvtrs.	2 Pvtrs.	2 Pvtrs.	2 Pvtrs.			1031 Berths
	507 Berths	72 Berths[*]	144 Berths	120 Berths[*]	188 Berths			3 Missing
1740	NEWPORT	B.W.I.	NEW YORK	BOSTON	CHAS. TOWN	PHILA.	NO OTHER PVTRS.	33 PVTRS.
	12 Pvtrs.	10 Pvtrs.	5 Pvtrs.	3 Pvtrs.	2 Pvtrs.	1 Pvtr.		1962 Berths
	947 Berths[*]	309 Berths[*]	323 Berths	229 Berths[*]	82 Berths	72 Berths		7 Missing
1741	NEWPORT	B.W.I.	BOSTON	OTHER	PHILA.	NEW YORK	CHAS. TOWN	29 PVTRS.
	9 Pvtrs.	5 Pvtrs.	4 Pvtrs.	4 Pvtrs.	4 Pvtrs.	2 Pvtrs.	1 Pvtr.	1645 Berths
	530 Berths[*]	144 Berths[*]	301 Berths[*]	216 Berths[*]	210 Berths	144 Berths	100 Berths	8 Missing
1742	NEWPORT	B.W.I.	PHILA.	BOSTON	OTHER	NO OTHER PVTRS.	NO OTHER PVTRS.	20 PVTRS.
	10 Pvtrs.	5 Pvtrs.	2 Pvtrs.	2 Pvtrs.	1 Pvtr.			1255 Berths
	815 Berths	164 Berths[*]	129 Berths	72 Berths[*]	75 Berths			3 Missing
1743	NEWPORT	B.W.I.	PHILA.	CHAS. TOWN	NEW YORK	BOSTON	NO OTHER PVTRS.	25 PVTRS.
	7 Pvtrs.	7 Pvtrs.	4 Pvtrs.	4 Pvtrs.	2 Pvtrs.	1 Pvtr.		2009 Berths
	526 Berths	525 Berths	349 Berths	337 Berths	200 Berths	72 Berths		1 Missing
1744	NEWPORT	NEW YORK	B.W.I.	PHILA.	BOSTON	CHAS. TOWN	OTHER	70 PVTRS.
	19 Pvtrs.	15 Pvtrs.	13 Pvtrs.	9 Pvtrs.	9 Pvtrs.	3 Pvtrs.	2 Pvtrs.	5992 Berths
	1507 Berths	1619 Berths	524 Berths[*]	960 Berths	921 Berths	311 Berths	150 Berths	10 Missing[c]

TABLE 5.3 CONT.

Year/Rank	1	2	3	4	5	6	7	Totals
1745	B.W.I.	NEW YORK	NEWPORT	PHILA.	CHAS. TOWN	BOSTON	OTHER	102 PVTRS.
	35 Pvtrs.	22 Pvtrs.	18 Pvtrs.	11 Pvtrs.	7 Pvtrs.	6 Pvtrs.	3 Pvtrs.	8928 Berths
	1915 Berths*	2318 Berths	1792 Berths	1401 Berths	477 Berths	651 Berths	374 Berths	16 Missing
1746	NEW YORK	NEWPORT	B.W.I.	PHILA.	CHAS. TOWN	OTHER	BOSTON	59 PVTRS.
	19 Pvtrs.	12 Pvtrs.	9 Pvtrs.	8 Pvtrs.	8 Pvtrs.	2 Pvtrs.	1 Pvtr.	4986 Berths
	1907 Berths	997 Berths	495 Berths	786 Berths	572 Berths	120 Berths	109 Berths	4 Missing
1747	NEW YORK	B.W.I.	NEWPORT	CHAS. TOWN	PHILA.	OTHER	NO OTHER	57 PVTRS.
	20 Pvtrs.	14 Pvtrs.	11 Pvtrs.	5 Pvtrs.	4 Pvtrs.	3 Pvtrs.	PVTRS.	4452 Berths
	1814 Berths	583 Berths	994 Berths	351 Berths	500 Berths	210 Berths		6 Missing
1748	NEW YORK	B.W.I.	NEWPORT	CHAS. TOWN	PHILA.	OTHER	BOSTON	55 PVTRS.
	18 Pvtrs.	12 Pvtrs.	11 Pvtrs.	6 Pvtrs.	4 Pvtrs.	3 Pvtrs.	1 Pvtr.	4144 Berths
	1859 Berths	694 Berths*	641 Berths*	323 Berths	239 Berths	272 Berths	116 Berths	12 Missing

Note: The rankings are based on the number of yearly privateers.
[a]Includes Bermuda privateers.
[b]Includes privateers from Cape Fear, N.C.; Norfolk, Va.; Frederica, Ga.; Portsmouth, N.H.; and New Jersey.
[c]Missing indicates the number of privateers for which the type of vessel was unknown.
*The estimate for the number of berths is too low because of missing data for vessel type and crew size for 20% of the yearly privateers.

Figure 5.2. A view of New York and Fort George, c. 1735. New York was the third largest city in British North America and was the leading center of colonial privateering during the 1740s.

Several factors account for the ascendancy of Newport and New York in privateering. Both ports possessed large numbers of vessels and mariners, and their merchants may have been motivated to participate in the speculative business of privateering because of their secondary position in the regular channels of commerce. Each port operated in the shadow of a larger neighbor. Boston dominated the overseas trade of New England, while Philadelphia was the premier port of the Middle Atlantic colonies.[25] Newport and New York merchants may thus have had more to gain from privateering. Both cities also drew on a tradition of successful prize activity. Rhode Island Governor John Wanton had been heavily involved in privateering during Queen Anne's War, and William Wanton, a younger kinsman, was an early investor in 1739.[26] The Wantons' economic and political position provided an excellent example of what success in privateering could mean. Richard Partridge, Rhode Island's London agent, recalled "the Wars of the late Queen," when "the Privateers from the Colony of Rhode Island did more Execution ag^st the Privateers of the Enemy that infested their Coasts than all the Ships of War of the Massachusetts or indeed of all the Colonys in those parts put together."[27] Manhattan merchants had also invested in privateering in the wars of King William and Queen Anne. Several of the same families—the Van Hornes, Philipses, and Provoosts—sent out private men-of-war in the 1740s.[28]

Although Boston, Philadelphia, and Charles Town ranked among the largest American cities, New York and Newport were far more active in privateering. A few Massachusetts and Pennsylvania businessmen who bought shares in private men-of-war apparently accepted Newport merchant John Bannister's assessment of privateering investments: "In case of a French Warr I don't think theres any business near so profitable as a proper Vessell or two well fitted out a Privateering."[29] Most prosperous merchants in Boston and Philadelphia, however, saw things differently, being less inclined to take the risks associated with privateering than their fellows in Newport and New York. Religion was also a factor in Philadelphia, where many leading businessmen were Quakers. The Pembertons, the Whartons, John Reynell, Isaac Norris II, John Smith, and John Bringhurst, among others, were members of Philadelphia's Quaker establishment. Reynell believed that the peace testimony precluded Quakers from even purchasing prize goods captured by American privateers, let alone investing in private men-of-war. He chastized Elias Bland, his former apprentice, for being more concerned with the bottom line than with religious scruples when Bland sent a consignment of prize goods to Philadelphia:

> The Shaggs I Suppose are Prize Goods, & I was in hopes thou was so much a Fr^d. as to have born a faithfuller Testimony against that Iniquitous Trade of Privateering, than to so farr Encouraged it, as to Purchase Part of their Stollen Goods: I think we as a People ought not to have any thing to do with them, & I desire for the future thou will keep they self clear of it for I believe it is agreeable to the mind of God that wee Should. There has been a great [deal] brought in & sold here & Some things very low, that a good Profit might [have] been made on them, but the Substantiall Part of Fr^ds. were of Opinion we ought not to have any thing to do with them & I think they were right for how inconsistant it is for us, to Declare against the Trade as Unlawfull, Yet asoon as they bring in any Prizes go & Purchase The Goods.[30]

The Quakers' decision to shun privateering ventures reduced Philadelphia's role in the prize war. (See Figure 5.3.)

As the conflict dragged on and expanded to include France, Bostonians devoted increased resources to the war effort, but not to privateering. Military contracts with the imperial government for supplying British forces in Newfoundland, Annapolis Royal, and Louisbourg engaged the attention of leading merchants. Thomas

Figure 5.3. A view of Philadelphia from the east, c. 1735. Although Philadelphia was the second largest port in colonial America and boasted a bustling harbor, the Quaker city played a peripheral role in privateering because of the religious scruples of many Quaker merchants.

Hancock, for example, owned shares in the Boston privateers *Speedwell* and *Young Eagle* during the War of Jenkins' Ear. After 1745 he preferred the more profitable and safer supply contracts, which became his "absorbing interest." Other leading Boston merchants profited from such lucrative contracts.[31] Boston's expanding role in the war against France claimed much of the city's resources. The 1745 Louisbourg campaign required more than three thousand men.[32] The expedition and the use of frequent press-gangs to man the Royal Navy and Massachusetts coast guard drove hundreds of seamen out of Boston. This exodus hindered Boston's commercial activity, and the city's trade decayed as the conflict lengthened.[33] It also prevented businessmen from turning to privateering and increased the number of Boston merchants who clearly envied the cruising fleets of Newport and New York.[34] (See Figure 5.4.)

Charles Town's role in privateering was limited by the lack of shipping. Although the city was the South's busiest port, most commercial vessels entering the harbor were not locally owned. (See Figure 5.5.) In his 1740 report to the Board of Trade, Robert Dinwiddie, surveyor general of customs for the southern department, stated that South Carolinians owned only twenty-five vessels.[35] The correspondence of Charles Town merchant Robert Pringle reveals that local businessmen often experienced difficulty securing shipping during the 1740s to export rice, the colony's chief staple. Before the declaration of war in 1739, Pringle was apprehensive concerning the wartime supply of shipping. "We have the greatest Crop of Rice this Year by much that has ever yet been produc'd in the Province & if the Apprehensions of a War Continue, We are afraid of not having Shipping enough to Carry it of[f]."[36] Pringle echoed these fears throughout the fall and winter of 1739–1740. In a letter to Thomas Burrill, his Hull, England, correspondent, Pringle indicated that his fears had been confirmed. "We have not had so many Shipping here this Season as usual occasion'd by the War."[37] The squeeze on shipping did not ease during the Anglo-Spanish war; France's entry into the conflict exacerbated the problem.[38] South Carolina Governor James Glen reported that the shipping picture was little improved by the end of the war in 1749. "We have few or no ships of our Own. We depend in great measure upon those sent from Britain, or on such as are built in New England for British merchants, and which generally take in this country in their way to England to get Freight."[39] Examination of available shipping registers confirms this view. Only 30 vessels averaging 32 tons were registered in South Carolina between 1735 and 1739. Although registration increased to 134 by 1749, the overwhelming majority of these craft were small sloops and schooners under 22 tons, too small for privateering.[40] Between 1734 and 1749 only 15 vessels larger than 50 tons were registered in South Carolina.[41] As a result, Carolina merchants were unable to devote much tonnage to privateering. In 1744, when Pringle headed a local syndicate investing in a privateering venture, he sent Capt. Mark Anderson to London to obtain suitable vessels.[42]

Charles Town also faced a shortage of mariners. Slaves composed nearly half of the city's population. Although blacks served on colonial vessels, it is doubtful that privateer owners recruited them for crews, since they may have felt it unwise to arm slaves. Such caution must have been especially prevalent after the Stono Rebellion of 1739. The Negro Act, passed after the slave insurrection to calm white fears and quell black resistance, increased surveillance of blacks' activities and probably precluded much recruiting of black privateersmen.[43] Charles Town's white population failed to provide a sufficient number of sailors. On numerous occasions, Pringle informed his business correspondents that their vessels' scheduled departures had been delayed "for want of Hands."[44] Henry Laurens, the future Charles Town slave merchant, also complained about the city's shortage of mariners.[45] This scarcity of shipping and manpower prevented Charles Town from playing a larger role in privateering.

Figure 5.4. A view of Boston from the southeast, 1743. Boston was the largest city in British North America. Its commitment to military contracts and the 1745 Louisburg expedition, however, limited investments in privateering voyages.

Figure 5.5. A view of Charles Town, before 1739. Charles Town was the largest city in the Southern colonies and boasted an impressive transatlantic commerce. The shortage of locally owned shipping and lack of mariners limited its involvement in privateering ventures.

If Dr. Hamilton had expanded his journey to include the many ports that dotted the British West Indies, he would undoubtedly have penned numerous references to the many privateers and prizes that passed through these Caribbean harbors. The island colonies accounted for nearly one out of every four British colonial yearly privateers. In the War of Jenkins' Ear, the number of West Indian privateers ranked second only to Rhode Island's. When the conflict escalated in 1744, so did the islands' participation in privateering. In 1745, the prize war's most active year, the West Indies led the British colonies in the number of vessels seeking enemy merchantmen.

At first glance, the role of the British West Indies appears surprisingly large. Like Charles Town, the islands depended on shipping from other ports, and black slaves formed the majority of the population.[46] Nevertheless, the islands possessed a key advantage for privateering ventures: they were ideally located for preying on the richest trade routes of the Spanish and French Empires. The Caribbean was the principal theater of operations for American privateers. The attraction of merchantmen carrying the lucrative agricultural staples of the West Indies and the lure of the fabled treasure ships of New Spain made the area a magnet for cruisers from all belligerent nations. In addition to location, the island colonies, like Newport and New York, had a long and successful history of privateering as well as a body of seamen and ships' officers thoroughly experienced in this kind of venture.[47] For these several reasons, the British West Indian colonies were among the leaders in sending out private men-of-war.

As Hamilton's *Itinerarium* reveals, enthusiasm for privateering was widespread, and colonists from New England to Barbados joined in the war at sea. They also boasted of their accomplishments: " 'Tis computed that there are and will be before Winter 113 Sail of Privateers at Sea, from the *British American* Colonies; most of them stout Vessels and abundantly well mann'd. A Naval Force, equal (some say) to that of the Crown of *Great-Britain* in the time of Queen Elizabeth."[48] It is impossible to miss the sense of pride that equated America's privateers with the famous navy of Drake and Hawkins.

II

Privateering ebbed and flowed with fluctuations of Spanish and French commerce, and can therefore be divided into two periods,

1739–1743 and 1744–1748. During the first phase only Spanish commerce was vulnerable to capture. Because the French stayed aloof from the fighting, their merchantmen could not be taken as prizes. At the same time, French warships were unable to seize British vessels. With the maritime war limited to Britain and Spain, the first phase of the conflict was less active than the second. The numbers of yearly privateers and privateering berths indicate the smaller scale. Every colonial port from Boston to the British West Indies dispatched fewer vessels in the first half of the hostilities than in the second, as reflected in Table 5.3.

Americans responded enthusiastically to George II's proclamation in 1739 authorizing privateering against Spain. In addition to seeking financial gains, colonists wanted to retaliate for Spanish "depredations" against British shipping.[49] Newport residents exploded with "universal Joy" when they heard the king's proclamation; similar reactions occurred in other ports.[50] Sixteen colonial privateers entered the war in the last four months of 1739, and thirty-three cruised in 1740, the peak year in the war against Spain. This boom created a demand for naval stores and ordnance that exceeded American supplies. "We have as yet fitted out but three Privateers," wrote Newport merchant John Bannister in the fall of 1739. "Occasion'd [by] the want of Warlike Stores which are not to be got but have great Reason to think those 3 will make it richly worthwhile."[51] A year later at the height of the War of Jenkins' Ear, Bannister still experienced difficulties obtaining privateering supplies. "I wrote you Pressing about the Guns you s^d youd Keepe and without which [I] cant send our Sloope Victory to Sea therefore begg. you wont fail. shipping the Guns by first Convayance. . . . We have our Water and provisions on board and shall sail next week if the disapointment of the guns dont prevent[.]"[52]

American expectations of success against Spain bore fruit early in the conflict. In January 1740, for instance, Bannister informed some business associates of the exploits of the privateer sloop *Virgin Queen*, commanded by Charles Hall. The *Virgin Queen* had "attack'd the Town of Porto Plate [Puerto Plata] on Hispaniola and took it[,] also the fort with 6 Cannon[.] they plunder'd the Town and afterwards Burnt it[. They] took a Prise in the Harbour [and] Carr^d. her to New Providence where the Effects was Condemn'd[.]" Bannister, who owned one-third of Hall's sloop, related news of other successes. "[They] went out on a Second Cruise and in a few days took three prises Vallued at thirty thousand pounds and was fitting out for a third Cruise[.]" Captain Hall had already remitted nearly ten thousand pounds to Bannister and his partners, and an additional two thousand pounds was waiting in New Providence in the Bahamas. Bannister hoped for even more profits: "[I] expect daily to hear of his further good Success."[53] News of Hall's good fortune spread beyond Newport. The *Boston News-Letter* commented, "He had met with such extraordinary Success that he designs to spend the Summer in those seas: He is now double mann'd. . . . Capt. Hall's Owners design to have his Statue cut out of a Block of Marble to stand upon a handsome Pedestal with each Foot upon a Spaniard's Neck."[54]

Bannister's other privateers shared Captain Hall's good fortune. "The Revenge[,] Capt Allen[,] belonging to Capt. [John] Brown and myself has cleared us £120,000 Curr^cy [approximately £22,587 sterling] in 6 prises in the Bay of Mexico," Bannister noted in 1740.[55] Capt. Joseph Power in the sloop *Victory* attacked the Spanish colonial town of Aroonoque "in which was a Considerable Plunder and in the Harbour also took two Rich Prises[,] one of [th]em has been Eighteen months on the Co[a]st [of New Spain and] had on Board a Great Quantity of Cash and Laden with Cocoa."[56] Power's success impressed the *Pennsylvania Gazette*: "Upon the whole we reckon he's made the greatest Voyage of any Privateer this War."[57]

Other American privateers enjoyed success in 1740 at Spain's expense. Newport merchant Godfrey Malbone received a letter of congratulations from Massachusetts Governor Jonathan Belcher after Malbone's privateer *Charming Betty* captured the ship *Oratava*.[58] Capt. James Collingwood, the *Charming Betty*'s commander, added to Malbone's profits by escorting another prize valued at two thousand pounds into Charles Town.[59] Capt. Richard Langdon in the New York privateer *Stephen & Elizabeth*, sailing in consort with Captain Hall in the *Virgin Queen*, brought another Spanish merchantman into the Carolina capital. Robert Pringle approved of the French claret that was part of the prize's cargo and sent a gift of three dozen bottles to his brother in London.[60]

Buoyed by his early triumphs, Bannister planned to increase his privateering investments in 1741. Another of his privateers, Capt. Elisha Berry in the *Revenge,* had recently taken a prize into St. Kitts. Bannister expressed confidence that "this with our former Success has put us upon fitting out another large Sloope 117 tons which expect will Sail some time in April and are now upon Setting up another large vessel for Same employ; Provided there be a french war we shall have near 30 Sail out of this Port Privateering."[61] There was no French war in 1741, 1742, or 1743, however, and Bannister's plans to send out the large sloop did not materialize. That vessel was still in Newport the following August. "Our Sloope the New Revenge 116 Tons[,] Capt Allen[,] We have in Such Readiness that upon advice of a french warr [we] can send her to sea in 48 hours[.]"[62] Spanish commerce alone could not support increasing numbers of British colonial privateers; consequently fewer private men-of-war sailed in 1741 and 1742 than in 1740. The Royal Navy's buildup for the Cartagena expedition also contributed to the decline of privateering. Public and private warships competed for Spanish commerce, and large concentrations of the king's ships diminished the prospects of colonial privateers.[63] Certainly Adm. Edward Vernon, commander of the naval forces in the Cartagena expedition, ordered his captains "to take, sink, burn or destroy" all Spanish vessels they encountered.[64]

When France finally entered the war privateering investments increased dramatically, and the American press exuberantly described preparations to launch more predators in the colonies and in the mother country.[65] Pringle's privateering investments are a case in point. Early in 1744 Pringle informed his brother that he was considering a privateering venture that combined Charles Town and London merchants. "Each Person to be £50 Ster. Concern'd & if it can be brought to Bear, I mean if there can be gott Fifty or Sixty Subscribers, it will be undertaken."[66] He was unsure, however, if the scheme could attract sufficient capital. The picture altered after France joined the conflict, and by July Pringle was confident of securing investors. "As we now have a War with France [I] doubt not of Getting Subscribers enough, & perhaps some Gentlemen in London may have desir'd to be Concern'd with us."[67] Similar activity by many other colonial investors made 1744 and 1745 the busiest years of the maritime war. Nearly 40 percent of the yearly privateers and 41 percent of the privateering berths were recorded in this period.

Supplies of munitions in American ports fell short of demand just as they had in the 1740 privateering boom. "[I] wish thou may be so lucky as to send a Parcel of Powder per the Mary, & that she may Arrive soon. what came per Cap[t] Seymour has been sold by the

Quantity at £18 per bb [barrell]," John Reynell wrote from Philadelphia in 1744. "Expect it will be Plenty enough next Year, but the Number of Privateers fitted and fitting out here, makes the Demand for Powder much greater than usual."[68] Reynell was still trying to import more gunpowder the next summer.[69] Apparently, supplying the tools of war did not violate his Quaker convictions.

Spanish and French commerce had its limits, and American privateers experienced diminishing returns by 1746. That same year the convoy system devised by the comte de Maurepas, French minister of marine, reduced American captures by allowing two large convoys to elude the Royal Navy and colonial privateers.[70] This signaled the end of the privateering boom, and in 1746 owners began to seek buyers for their vessels. On 26 June the *Pennsylvania Gazette* announced the sale of the privateer ship *Marlborough*. This was not simply a transfer of ownership; the advertisement stated that the *Marlborough* would be sold "as a Merchant Ship." Its ordnance would be sold separately.[71] It is unlikely that the *Marlborough*'s owners would have held two sales if interest in privateering had been high. Other Philadelphia privateer owners began to sell vessels and munitions. On 27 July 1747, "All the armament, & c. belonging to the Privateer brigantine George" went on the auction block on Inglis's wharf.[72] The carriage guns, small arms, powder, and a variety of sails belonging to the private men-of-war *Wilmington* and *George* were sold at Allen's wharf.[73] The privateer ship *Pandour* and all its "warlike stores" were advertised for sale on 13 August 1747, while a vendue sale was scheduled for 26 November 1747 as the owners of the privateer snow *Warren* decided to liquidate their investment in the maritime conflict.[74]

Merchants in other colonial ports cut back their privateering investments after the peak years of 1744–1745. Two Virginia cruisers were auctioned in 1746.[75] A year later Newport entrepreneur Samuel Vernon commented on privateering's decline. "[I] am glad you are so well pleased with his [Vernon's brother William's] Sale of your Guns," Vernon wrote to Thomas and Adrian Hope, "but [I] do assure you no Person would be able to dispose of such Parcel for half that Money, the Business of Privateering not being in so great Esteem with us now."[76] Privateering activity in European sea-lanes also waned in the war's closing years. The anonymous author of the exploits of George Walker, the Bristol, England, privateer commander, discussed a 1748 cruise off the

Portuguese coast. "Though in this last part of our cruise we met not with the success we had been accustomed to hope for, yet we had no cause to lament our particular ill-luck in competition with the better fortune of others; for of several king's ships and letters of marque which we chased and came up with, not one as we could learn had within this time met any prize."[77] By the summer of 1748 privateering activity had declined nearly 50 percent from the peak year of 1745.

III

British colonial privateers sailed Atlantic waters from Newfoundland to the Spanish Main, but they concentrated where the pickings were richest, taking by far the greatest number of prizes in the Caribbean. (See Table 5.4.)[78] West Indian goods were worth considerably more than North American products. The rich staples of the Indies—sugar, molasses, cocoa, coffee, indigo, logwood—fetched better prices than fish and furs. Spanish treasure ships, though elusive, were also alluring. In addition, the North American continental possessions of Spain and France generated less trade than their West Indian colonies. Traffic between France, Quebec, and Cape Breton or between Cadiz and Florida was insufficient to attract many privateers. Moreover, the commerce of Mexico, Louisiana, Central America, South America, and Asia passed through the Caribbean.[79] For these reasons, the West Indian theater of operations accounted for 682 prize actions, nearly nine times as many as in more northerly waters.

It is difficult to be precise about British colonial privateers' Caribbean cruising lanes. The colonial press generally reported that a prize had been taken in the West Indies and nothing more. Newspaper readers learned, for instance, that Charles Davidson, commander of the Newport privateer *St. Anne,* captured the *Amiable Teresa* in the Caribbean and that the Philadelphians Alexander Katter in the *Warren* and John Dougall in the "old Schooner" *George* seized the *Lewis Joseph, St. Anne,* and another French merchantman in the West Indies.[80] Of the 682 Caribbean prize cases, 192 (28 percent) listed only "West Indies" as the place of action. For an additional 220 Caribbean cases (32 percent) the place of action can be inferred from the point of embarkation and/or destination of the prize or the port to which the prize was taken. Capt. Thomas Greenall, commander of the New York brig *Batchelor,* for example, forced an enemy ship aground on

TABLE 5.4

British Colonial Privateers' Theaters of Operations, 1739–1748

Year	Caribbean Prize Actions		North American Prize Actions	
	N	%	N	%
1739	3	0.4	0	0.0
1740	45	6.6	2	2.5
1741	19	2.8	3	3.7
1742	35	5.1	4	5.0
1743	33	4.8	0	0.0
1744	88	12.9	48	60.0
1745	145	21.3	4	5.0
1746	106	15.6	5	6.3
1747	118	17.3	6	7.5
1748	90	13.2	8	10.0
Totals	682	100.0	80	100.0

Combined Theaters	N	%
Caribbean	682	89.5
North American	80	10.5
Totals	762	100.0

Hispaniola and also escorted two merchantmen into Jamaica in 1745. Greenall probably took these prizes in the Caribbean, though the news reports did not indicate the place of action.[81] Captain Harwood, another privateer commander, captured a French sloop in 1745. Though the place of action is unknown, the prize's destination (Curaçao), its point of embarkation (Guadeloupe), its cargo (sugar), and the colony to which it was taken (St. Kitts), all suggest that Harwood took his prize in the West Indies.[82]

Since 270 of the Caribbean prize actions fought by American privateers (40 percent) indicated a specific West Indian location, it is possible to examine the colonists' major Caribbean cruising areas. (See Table 5.5.) The sea-lanes around Cuba and Hispaniola, where most of Spain's colonial commerce aggregated, were the most popular. Fleets from Veracruz on the Gulf of Mexico and from Portobello and Cartagena on the coast of New Granada rendezvoused at Havana to take advantage of favorable winds and

TABLE 5.5

Caribbean Cruising Areas of British Colonial Privateers, 1739–1748

Cruising Area	N	%
Mexico[a]	7	2.6
Cuba[b]	71	26.3
Hispaniola[c]	54	20.0
Caicos Islands	11	4.1
Puerto Rico and the Virgin Islands	16	5.9
Martinique, Guadeloupe, and the Windward Islands	44	16.3
Coast of New Granada[d]	34	12.6
Other[e]	33	12.2
Totals	270	100.0

[a]Includes general references to Mexico as well as cases referring specifically to Veracruz and Campeche.

[b]Includes the Old Bahama Channel off Cuba's northeast coast.

[c]Includes the Windward Passage.

[d]Includes the northern coast of what is now Colombia and Venezuela; Panama east of the Canal Zone; and the islands of Salt Tortuga, Curaçao, Aruba, and La Orchilla.

[e]Includes Caribbean locations from the Bahamas in the northwest to Surinam in the southeast. None of these areas was referred to in more than five cases. Nine cases from Bermuda are also included.

currents in the Florida Straits and the Old Bahama Channel. At Havana, they also enjoyed the protection of greater numbers and the presence of Spanish men-of-war.[83] French vessels also sailed in this area, going to or from the sugar colony of Saint-Domingue on Hispaniola. Many British colonial privateers operated in the shipping lanes north of Cuba, the Windward Passage between Cuba and Hispaniola, and the Mona Passage off Hispaniola's east coast. Moreover, this area was the closest to British North American ports. The second major cruising area lay six hundred miles east of Hispaniola. Martinique and Guadeloupe were France's most important sugar colonies, and their commerce attracted American privateers that lay to windward and picked up merchantmen sailing to or from the French possessions. Along the Spanish Main, the southernmost theater of British privateering operations in the Caribbean, private men-of-war preyed on vessels en route to

Cartagena and Portobello or raided the coastal commerce from Panama to Cayenne.

Compared to the Caribbean, the war in northern waters was a modest affair, though marked by a flurry of activity in 1744. (See Table 5.4.) Many northern prize actions were defensive, as homeward-bound privateers escorting Caribbean prizes fought off Spanish cruisers along the coast. In 1742, for example, Boston Captain John Rouse, commanding the *Young Eagle,* and two St. Kitts privateers—Robert Flower in the *Bonetta* and William Wilkinson in the *Mary*—were taking prizes to New England. Off Florida they encountered a Spanish fleet and were forced to defend themselves. Rouse and his consorts not only saved their prizes but also captured three Spanish privateers.[84] After 1744 French commerce in the Cape Breton area and fishing vessels on the Newfoundland banks became fair game for British privateers. Of the forty-eight actions occurring in 1744, thirty-nine took place near Louisbourg or Newfoundland. Captain Rouse played the most active role in these Anglo-French encounters. The *Boston News-Letter* reported in August that Rouse had captured eight French vessels and carried them into Newfoundland. In September Rouse commanded four private men-of-war in a raid on a French settlement on the "back side of Newfoundland," resulting in a total victory. In addition to plundering the town, the New Englanders captured five French letter of marque ships riding at anchor in the harbor and more goods (chiefly fish, oil, and munitions) than they could load on their vessels.[85] After the surrender of Louisbourg in 1745, prize actions in the north were limited mainly to efforts to save Spanish and French prizes seized in the Caribbean or to recapture British vessels taken by enemy privateers. (See Table 5.6.)

IV

Finally, the extensive nature of privateering during the wars of 1739–1748 can be gauged by comparing the actions of American private men-of-war with those of the Royal Navy in American waters and by examining the manpower employed in privateering with the number of British colonists who participated in the conflict's other military operations.

The Royal Navy devoted considerable resources to the maritime war in America. Operating off the North American coast and from the navy's Caribbean stations in Jamaica and Antigua, the king's ships mounted major offenses against Cartagena and Louisbourg and

TABLE 5.6

North American Cruising Areas of British Colonial Privateers, 1739–1748

Cruising Area	N	%
Newfoundland Banks	32	40.0
Cape Breton[a]	11	13.8
New England—New York Coast[b]	6	7.5
Carolina Coast[c]	17	21.2
Florida	9	11.2
Other[d]	5	6.2
Totals	80	100.0

[a]Includes Canso and Cape Sable.

[b]Includes Cape Cod, Martha's Vineyard Sound, and Sandy Hook, N.J.

[c]Includes all prize actions from Cape Fear, N.C., to St. Simons Island, Ga.

[d]Includes Delaware capes, the Virginia capes, and two general references to "the Coast of North America."

also participated extensively in the prize war, attempting to protect British and American vessels from enemy predators and cruising the sea-lanes in search of Spanish and French merchantmen. On the whole, the navy enjoyed only mixed success. Admiral Vernon failed to capture Cartagena, but naval forces commanded by Commodore Warren combined with William Pepperrell's New England militia to seize the "Gibraltar of the New World."[86] The navy's record in the prize war was also mixed. Although Royal Navy vessels fought hundreds of prize actions in American waters and contributed to British sea power by intercepting Spanish and French commerce, the king's ships could not prevent enemy warships from seriously disrupting British colonial trade, as chapter 6 will demonstrate.

The Royal Navy fought hundreds of prize actions in American waters. Although naval vessels interfered with enemy commerce, colonial privateers dealt Spanish and French shipping a more serious blow. (See Table 5.7.) The navy's prize actions paralleled the privateers' activities very closely. The Anglo-Spanish war was much smaller than the conflict's second phase beginning in 1744. Fewer than one-fourth of the navy's prize actions occurred before France declared war. Naval vessels also pursued enemy merchantmen in the same shipping lanes as the privateers, and the Caribbean accounted for more than three-fourths of naval prize

TABLE 5.7
Royal Navy's American Theaters of Operations, 1739–1748

Year	Caribbean Prize Actions		North American Prize Actions	
	N	%	N	%
1739	4	1.5	1	1.3
1740	14	5.3	2	2.6
1741	22	8.4	1	1.3
1742	11	4.2	3	3.9
1743	18	6.9	3	3.9
1744	69	26.3	13	16.9
1745	50	19.1	17	22.1
1746	15	5.7	9	11.7
1747	30	11.5	5	6.5
1748	29	11.1	23	29.9
Totals	262	100.0	77	100.0

Combined Theaters	N	%
Caribbean	262	77.3
North American	77	22.7
Totals	339	100.0

actions. The major difference between Table 5.4, which presents the British colonial privateers' theaters of operations, and Table 5.7 is the scale: American private men-of-war fought more than twice as many prize actions in North American waters and in the Caribbean as the Royal Navy.[87]

Privateering was also extensive when compared to the number of Americans who saw action in the conflict's other military operations. British colonists were involved in three major campaigns against the Spanish and French. In 1741, Americans participated in the ill-fated Cartagena expedition. In 1745 militia forces from the northern colonies, especially New England, joined with the navy and colonial coast guard to capture Louisbourg. A year later, American troops mobilized for an assault on Quebec. These were the largest military operations in which provincial forces participated. Each of the first two expeditions included three thousand to four thousand Americans, while nearly eight thousand recruits enlisted for the invasion of Canada.[88] More Americans served on privateers than in these campaigns. (See Table 5.1.) Berths on colonial private men-of-war exceeded thirty-six thousand, well over double the manpower devoted to the Cartagena, Louisbourg, and Quebec expeditions combined. Although it is likely some mariners sailed on more than one privateering voyage, the evidence still strongly suggests that more colonists fought against King George's enemies in America's private navy than in the king's own forces.[89]

V

The widespread coverage of private men-of-war in the American press, the attention predators and prizes received in travelers' accounts like Hamilton's *Itinerarium,* and the numerous references to the maritime conflict in the correspondence of colonial merchants and officials demonstrate the importance of privateering for British North America. Moreover, American colonists devoted considerable resources in pursuit of enemy prizes. Merchants in the leading seaports fitted out scores of vessels carrying thousands of men to capture Spanish and French merchantmen. Privateering boomed in the early years of the War of Jenkins' Ear. After chafing for years because of their inability to get even with Spanish *guarda-costas,* Americans jumped at the chance for revenge. When French commerce was thrown open to British warships in 1744, privateering increased dramatically.

Newport and New York were the leading privateering ports. Operating in the shadows of larger seaports, Rhode Island and Manhattan merchants had more incentive than their Boston and Philadelphia counterparts to invest in the prize war. In addition, Massachusetts's primary role in the Louisbourg and Quebec expeditions diminished Boston's participation in privateering by siphoning off thousands of men for the campaigns and by driving away hundreds of seamen who sought to avoid navy press-gangs. Important Quaker merchants also limited Philadelphia's role in the prize war by shunning investments in private men-of-war because of religious convictions. Manpower and shipping limitations prevented Charles Town from playing more than a peripheral role.

British colonial privateering provides insights concerning Spanish and French colonial commerce. Despite the bitter rivalry between the northern English colonies and the French communities on Cape Breton and in the St. Lawrence Valley, the North American theater of operations received little attention from American warships. Quebec might have threatened the New England and New York frontiers and might have checked British westward expansion, but New France's maritime commerce offered limited rewards, so few British privateers cruised in northern waters. This was also true of Spanish Florida. Because the richest prizes sailed in the Caribbean, the overwhelming majority of American privateers cruised in the West Indies throughout the decade of hostilities.

British colonial privateering was also extensive when measured by its wide geographic theaters of operations. French and Spanish merchantmen sailing from Newfoundland to the tropics risked capture by private men-of-war. Vessels hauling fish and furs from Quebec and Cape Breton, sugar and spice from Cuba and Cap François, or bale goods and bordeaux from Spain and France struck their colors to American privateers. The specter of capture always loomed over the horizon.

Important as it was, British colonial privateering was only one aspect of this maritime conflict. King George's enemies also dispatched hundreds of private men-of-war to prey on British North American shipping. An examination of Spanish and French privateers is required before the impact of privateering on colonial America in the 1740s can be assessed.

Chapter 6

THEATERS OF OPERATIONS: SPANISH AND FRENCH PRIVATEERS

T HE CAROLINA COAST WAS FREE OF SPANISH PRIVATEERS IN November 1739, or so Royal Navy Captain Peter Warren informed the Admiralty. "I do not hear as yet that there has been any Spanish privateers out, nor of any of our trade being taken."[1] Warren was writing shortly after the War of Jenkins' Ear had been declared, during a period of anxious anticipation as merchants in North American and Caribbean ports rushed to fit out private men-of-war to prey on the trade of the British and Spanish Empires. Six months later Carolina commerce was still secure when Charles Town merchant Robert Pringle recorded the capture of a Spanish privateer. "A Few Days ago a Spanish Privateer of 16 Guns and 87 Men, was brought in here by his Majesty's ship the *Shoreham,* Capt. Boschawen, taken off the Havana and is the only Privateer that has yet appear'd from that place."[2] This was the first Spanish privateer seen in the Carolina capital. Unfortunately for Pringle and other American merchants from St. John's, Newfoundland, to Bridgetown, Barbados, hundreds of other privateers from Havana, St. Augustine, Cap François, and Martinique subsequently cruised in American waters. As the war continued, enemy predators appeared with alarming frequency, and their influence on American shipping became increasingly devastating.

British North Americans were keenly aware of the enemy's damaging actions. The same newspapers that lavished attention on British colonial privateering successes also published hundreds of accounts of British vessels that became enemy prizes. Spanish and French privateers prowling in the Caribbean and off the Carolina coast, the Virginia capes, the Delaware capes, and the northern coast made maritime commerce a risky business. Enemy cruisers captured vessels and cargoes worth hundreds of thousands of pounds sterling. These predators also broadened American interest in the prize war. Residents of Boston and Charles Town, who owned few private men-of-war, probably paid as much attention to the privateers' exploits as the citizens of the privateering centers of Newport and New York. Despite the efforts of the Royal Navy, the provincial coast guard, and British colonial privateers, Spanish and French privateering voyages continued profitably until the Treaty of Aix-la-Chapelle ended the hostilities.

The success of enemy privateers demonstrates the importance of privateering during the eighteenth century. Private men-of-war disrupted the commerce of the most important ports in British America while they augmented the wealth of Spanish and French colonies by sending their prizes home to Florida, Cuba, Saint-Domingue, and Martinique. The privateers increased Spanish and French sea power, but because they were privately owned, manned, and equipped, they did not drain the treasuries of Spain, France, or their colonies. The disruption of British colonial commerce during the wars of 1739–1748 provides graphic evidence of the value of this marriage of patriotism and the pursuit of profit.

I

Enemy privateering operations were extensive as Spanish and French private men-of-war pursued British merchantmen relentlessly in American waters for nearly a decade. Although enemy vessels cruised throughout the hostilities, Spanish and French privateering activity closely paralleled the pattern of their British counterparts and can be divided into two periods, 1739–1743 and 1744–1748. France remained neutral during the first phase of the conflict, so only Spanish cruisers assaulted British commerce. With French warships out of the struggle, the first period was therefore less active than the second. The War of Jenkins' Ear ushered in a boom in Spanish privateering in 1740, the first full year of the conflict. Merchants in St. Augustine, Havana, and other colonial ports were eager to send out warships to capture British merchantmen. After two years of expansion, Spanish prize actions declined in 1742–1743, a pattern that closely mirrored

British cruising activity. Greater protection for British shipping offered by Royal navy convoys may explain this downturn in Spanish privateering. The French declaration of war against Britain in 1744 sparked a new phase in the maritime conflict as French warships entered the fray. This increase in enemy activity continued throughout the rest of the war. Only the end of hostilities curbed Spanish and French private men-of-war as Britain's Atlantic commerce provided an abundance of prizes for enemy predators.

Spanish and French privateers attacked British merchantmen throughout the hostilities, as the yearly pattern of enemy prize actions presented in Table 6.1 indicates. Unlike Table 5.1, which measured yearly privateers, Table 6.1 is based on cases of private men-of-war engaging British vessels. The data concerning Spanish and French privateers supplied by the North American press were too sparse to construct a table similar to Table 5.1. American newspapers, however, were extremely sensitive to captures of British craft by Spanish and French warships. As a result, the yearly operations of enemy cruisers can be examined using prize actions.

TABLE 6.1

Yearly Prize Actions in America, 1739–1748

Year	Spanish and French Privateers		British Colonial Privateers	
	N	%	N	%
1739	0	0.0	2	0.3
1740	25	3.4	47	6.2
1741	72	9.8	22	2.9
1742	32	4.3	39	5.1
1743	20	2.7	32	4.2
1744	69	9.4	136	17.8
1745	139	18.9	147	19.3
1746	113	15.4	109	14.3
1747	144	19.6	124	16.3
1748[a]	122	16.6	101	13.3
Totals	736	100.0	762	100.0

[a]Includes one prize action from 1749.

For comparison, Table 6.1 also includes actions involving British colonial privateers.

British North Americans were fully aware of the upswing in Spanish privateering in 1740. This was especially true for South Carolinians since only newly created and sparsely settled Georgia separated the Palmetto Colony from Spanish Florida. St. Augustine, less than 250 miles from Charles Town, had dispatched numerous *guarda-costas* in the prewar years. After 1739 the Florida port became a center of Spanish privateering, ranking second to Havana as the capital of Spanish private men-of-war. More Carolina vessels struck their colors to St. Augustine privateers, and the Florida port received more Carolina prizes than any other enemy port. Don Manuel de Montiano, St. Augustine's governor, invested in privateering ventures, and one of his captains, Don Juan de Leon Fandino, commanded the *guarda-costa* that captured Capt. Robert Jenkins in 1731. Fandino had cut off Jenkins's ear, thus providing the most interesting name of the several intercolonial wars.[3]

Charles Town residents clearly appreciated St. Augustine's threat to South Carolina commerce. Early in 1740 the Carolina legislature agreed to support Gen. James Oglethorpe in an expedition against the Florida capital. Robert Pringle thought this venture "is like to Come to nothing, this Province not being in a condition to give any tolerable assistance."[4] Pringle was right. After a clumsy operation in conjunction with Royal Navy vessels commanded by Capt. Vincent Pearce, the attack fizzled.[5] Pringle hoped, however, that a new British initiative would capture the Florida privateering port. "All the Kings Ships before St. Augustine have left the place without Effecting any thing and are gone to their Respective Stations," he wrote to his brother. "And all the Troops are also withdrawn from thence after an Inglorious Expedition and haveing been before the place Two Months. The Miscarriage of said Expedition is Laid at General Oglethorpes Door and that our want of Success is entirely Oweing to his unaccountable Bad Conduct and Ill Management." Pringle expected, however, "that my Lord Cathcart and Admiral Vernon will have instructions to take St. Augustine, Otherwise I am Affraid it will Still Remain in the possessions of the Spaniards which will prove of the Utmost Ill Consequences and worse than ever before to So. Carolina."[6]

Lord Cathcart and Admiral Vernon did not capture St. Augustine, and Spanish privateers continued to operate off the Carolina coast.

The sloop *Sally,* bound to Charles Town from Madeira laden with one hundred pipes of wine, was taken during the summer of 1740 by a St. Augustine privateer.[7] A small Spanish cruiser chased a Carolina coastal vessel in October, while another enemy privateer menaced the coast. In March 1741 the *Anchona* was captured after leaving Charles Town.[8] In the fall of 1741 a Spanish privateer captured the *Polly, Hawke,* and *Squirrel.* The three prizes, which were carrying more than twenty-one hundred barrels of Carolina rice to markets in Lisbon and Cowes, England, were sent to St. Augustine. The Spaniards also took the *Martha* and the *Caesar* and equipped them to assist in the privateering cruise.[9]

The perils of the Carolina coast became common knowledge throughout British America. Newport merchant John Bannister informed an associate that "most of our Carolina Vessells Loaded with Naval Stores have been taken by the Spanish privateers there having been no less than five sale [sail] on the [Carolina] Coast at once."[10] The *Pennsylvania Gazette* published an article concerning St. Augustine privateers based upon the account of John Lucas, an English prisoner who escaped from the Florida capital. According to this report, at least thirty-six British vessels had been escorted into St. Augustine. Some of them (like the *Martha* and the *Caesar*) had been subsequently refitted as Spanish privateers and cruised between South Carolina and the Virginia capes. The article closed with a comment concerning South Carolina's dismal defenses: "Lucas further informs us, that the Spaniards say, *The English at Carolina are certainly asleep, otherwise they'd not let us take their Vessels even on the Bar of Charlestown* [emphasis in original]."[11]

The Chesapeake sea-lanes were also hard hit by Spanish privateers in the early years of the War of Jenkins' Ear. In the spring of 1741 five enemy cruisers menaced the Virginia capes, and one of them, the Havana privateer *St. John,* captured five merchantmen off the Old Dominion's shores. The *St. John*'s success finally forced its skipper, Captain Lewis, to cut short his voyage. After dispatching crews to sail its prizes, the *St. John* was too undermanned to seize additional vessels.[12] There was no respite for Virginians following Lewis's departure as Capt. Don Francisco Larango soon captured the *Patuxent* and *Argyle* at the entrance to Chesapeake Bay.[13] Reports of other Spanish privateers cruising just outside Capes Charles and Henry prompted the Virginia House of Burgesses to fit out two warships to patrol the coast.[14] Just south of Cape Henry in

Albemarle Sound, Spanish private men-of-war operated so close to Edenton, North Carolina, that the colony's governor put the militia on alert in case the enemy landed forces to plunder nearby plantations.[15]

Spanish assaults on Chesapeake commerce continued in 1742, led by the notorious Capt. Don Juan de Leon Fandino. After a successful prize action off Charles Town, Fandino headed north to Virginia. Between 14 March and 30 April, the Spanish privateersmen captured six British merchantmen before turning south with their prizes.[16] Unfortunately for Captain Fandino, he was unable to enjoy the profits of his conquests. Capt. Thomas Frankland, commander of HMS *Rose,* captured Fandino in the Old Bahama Channel en route to Havana. Frankland also recaptured three of Fandino's prizes, which he escorted, along with the Spanish captain and his crew, to Charles Town.

Much to the relief of British North America, Captain Fandino was sent to Britain.[17] He had been a notorious adversary. Pringle asserted, "[He] has made great Depredations on our Shipping for upwards of these twenty years past, being the most Noted of all the Spanish Guarda Costa's."[18] Less polite were the comments in the *Pennsylvania Gazette*: "Don Juan, etc. Captain of the Privateer, has done more Mischief to the English Trade, before and since the War, than any four Privateers the Spanish have. He is the same insolent Villain that cut of[f] Capt. Jenkins's Ears, and sent them to our King: People less polite and humane than the English, might now think of returning that barbarous Compliment."[19]

The northern British colonies were spared the privateering raids that plagued the Carolina coast and the Virginia capes. France remained aloof from the War of Jenkins' Ear so Cape Breton and Quebec vessels did not cruise in the North Atlantic until 1744. A few Spanish warships, however, menaced the northern coasts. Zebulon Witham of Gloucester, Massachusetts, informed the Bay Colony Council that he had been captured by a Spanish privateer in November 1741 off the Virginia capes. "While he was Prisoner wth the Spaniards he understood that the s^d. Privateer Ship intended for the Coast of New Eng^d. and the Sloop was to cruize on the Coast of Virginia and Pennsylvania."[20] Upon receiving this information, Governor Shirley wanted to dispatch Capt. Edward Tyng in the provincial snow. A shortage of mariners led Shirley instead to turn to the legislature for a bounty to encourage private men-of-war to pursue the enemy privateer. The Massachusetts General Court complied with Shirley's request and authorized a bounty of ten pounds (Mass.) for every man on board an enemy privateer or naval vessel at the beginning of an engagement. This bounty applied to all Massachusetts privateers and letter of marque ships engaging the Spanish between Newfoundland and South Carolina.[21]

In May 1741 the New York Assembly appropriated four hundred pounds (N.Y.) to fit out two sloops to engage two Spanish privateers recently spotted off the colony's coast. (These were probably the two "Country Sloops" mentioned in the journal of the privateer *Revenge*.)[22] Rhode Island dispatched its colony sloop, the *Tartar,* to seize two Spanish private men-of-war—possibly the same warships that prompted New York's actions.[23] A month later Pennsylvania Lieutenant Governor George Thomas informed the legislature about four Spanish privateers that had recently captured five prizes. In addition, two other enemy cruisers had chased vessels bound to Philadelphia, and one of them, belonging to Philadelphia merchants, had been driven ashore near Egg Harbor, New Jersey, less than thirty-five miles from Cape May and the entrance to Delaware Bay. Thomas urged the assembly to dispatch a coastal patrol vessel and tried to embarrass the legislators by emphasizing their inactivity in juxtaposition to the actions of their northern neighbors. "I recommend it to your Consideration whether it will not be very disreputable to this Province as well as disadvantageious to the Trade of it, to remain inactive. When Boston, Rhode Island, & New York, are fitting out Vessels of fforce to secure their navigation by attacking the Enemy." The Quaker-dominated legislature, however, would not be embarrassed.[24]

After France entered the conflict, enemy privateering in North American waters and in the Caribbean increased markedly. Spanish and French prize actions in 1744 rose by 245 percent over the previous year. (See Table 6.1.) Spanish and French prize actions in 1747, their busiest year of the war, registered an increase of 620 percent over 1743. British colonists had been apprehensive concerning the prospects of a French war; the dramatic escalation of the prize war indicates their fears were justified.[25] Pennsylvania Lieutenant Governor Thomas warned that French opposition marked a new and more dangerous phase of the conflict. "We have not now the Slothful Spaniard only to deal with. The French are an active, enterprizing Enemy, and however quiet we are at present, or however secure we may now think ourselves, it is not to be doubted but they are Meditating a Blow to be struck where they think it may be done with the least Danger and most advantage to themselves.''[26] Thomas was fearful that this blow would be struck against Pennsylvania—and with good reason.

II

Spanish and French privateers attacked British commerce off North America at its weakest points: along the Carolina coast and the capes of Virginia and Delaware. The British islands in the Caribbean attracted enemy warships as well. These had been the favored targets in the War of Jenkins' Ear, and they continued to draw the largest numbers of Spanish and French private men-of-war after France joined the conflict. Table 6.2 presents the theaters of operations for Spanish and French privateers and reveals that enemy privateers divided their attention rather evenly between North America and the Caribbean. Of the 736 prize actions included in

TABLE 6.2
Spanish and French Privateers' Theaters of Operations, 1740–1749

Year	Caribbean Prize Actions		North American Prize Actions	
	N	%	N	%
1740	14	3.6	11	3.2
1741	19	4.9	53	15.2
1742	18	4.7	14	4.0
1743	13	3.4	7	2.0
1744	30	7.8	39	11.2
1745	84	21.7	55	15.8
1746	93	24.0	20	5.7
1747	75	19.4	69	19.8
1748	40	10.3	81	23.2
1749	1	0.3	0	0.0
Totals	387	100.0	349	100.0

Combined Theaters	N	%
Caribbean	387	52.6
North American	349	47.4
Totals	736	100.0

the table, nearly one-half took place off the North American coast while the remaining actions occurred in the Caribbean.

The distribution of prize actions reflects the trade patterns in the British Empire. The North American colonies accounted for hundreds of thousands of pounds sterling in imports and exports every year, and so did Britain's Caribbean sugar islands. Robert Dinwiddie, surveyor general of customs for the southern district, wrote to the Board of Trade on 29 April 1740 concerning the volume of colonial commerce. "I have been at a great deal of Trouble and Expence to inform Myself of the Trade of his Majesty's American Empire, and the annuall amount of the National Produce of each Colony or Plantation," Dinwiddie informed the board. "I give You the following Thoughts, Observations and Calculations, which is partly from my own knowledge and the best informations I possibly could get."[27]

Dinwiddie's figures indicate that the North American and West Indian colonies provided an enormous amount of commerce for the enemy to attack. Exports from the continent (including Newfoundland but excluding Hudson's Bay) amounted to £2,290,000 annually, about three-fifths of the total from Britain's New World possessions. The West Indies (including Bermuda) annually shipped goods valued at £1,455,000, about two-fifths of the total of American exports.[28] English customs records corroborate Dinwiddie's view of the substantial trade generated in both the British West Indies and the mainland colonies, though Caribbean commerce exceeded North America's in official values. From Christmas 1738 to Christmas 1739, the last year before the War of Jenkins' Ear and closest to Dinwiddie's 1740 report, West Indian exports to Great Britain totaled £1,569,102, compared to £801,035 from the North American colonies.[29] Thus the West Indies accounted for two-thirds of Britain's colonial imports. These figures understate the mainland colonies' commerce, however, because they concern only goods bound for the mother country. Most exports from New England, New York, Pennsylvania, and New Jersey were destined for ports outside Great Britain.[30] Because of this extensive traffic, Spanish and French privateers divided their attention between both theaters of operations. The French loss of Cape Breton in June 1745 probably explains the Caribbean's primacy after 1745. Before that defeat, the North American theater was the busier of the two. Deprived of a base north of Florida, enemy privateers must have found it easier to attack British commerce in the Caribbean where the Spanish and French islands supplied good harbors and adequate shipping and manpower.

Although the majority of Spanish and French American prize actions were fought in the Caribbean, pinpointing their prime areas of attack is impossible because newspaper accounts frequently mentioned only that the action had occurred in the "West Indies." More often, the place of action had to be inferred from the point of embarkation and/or destination of the prize or the port to which the prize was taken. About three-fifths of the 387 Spanish and French Caribbean prize actions suffered from indefinite data concerning the place of action. Table 6.3, which is based on 150 enemy prize actions that indicated a specific West Indian location, suggests where Spanish and French privateers sought their prizes.

In the eastern Caribbean, Martinique was the hub of enemy privateering. Operating from Fort Royal and St. Pierre, French private men-of-war captured numerous merchantmen bound to and from the British Leeward and Windward islands. The "swarm" of enemy privateers sailing from Martinique was widely remarked upon in the American press: " 'Tis said there are 15 Privateers out of Martineco, and 8 out of Guadaloup;" "the French Privateers are so numerous and strong among the Islands, that it is dangerous for our Vessels to stir out;" "enemy predators were so numerous that even our Vessels of Force run's a great Hazard of being taken."[31] Antigua, the most valuable colony in the British Leewards,

TABLE 6.3

Caribbean Cruising Areas of Spanish and French Privateers, 1740–1748

Cruising Area	N	%
Bermuda	12	8.0
Bahamas	11	7.3
Jamaica and Windward Passage	23	15.3
Gulf of Honduras	15	10.0
Curaçao and South American Coast	14	9.3
Windward Islands	16	10.7
Leeward Islands	46	30.7
Other[a]	13	8.7
Totals	150	100.0

[a]Includes Cuba, Hispaniola, and Puerto Rico.

exporting annually goods worth £240,000, was especially hard hit by Martinique privateers who captured a "considerable Number of Vessels," including twelve or thirteen Boston merchantmen and two more from Rhode Island.[32]

Antigua's situation deteriorated in 1746. Capt. Joseph Osgood, master of the Boston merchantman *Endeavour,* reported from the island that "there are no less than thirty-two Privateers out of Martineco, which makes it a wonder if any Vessel escapes, and there are but few that do."[33] By the summer of 1746 markets in Martinique and Guadeloupe were "glutted with Provisions, etc. while our own Islands are in great Distress for want." Reports from the Leewards suggested that five out of six British vessels struck their colors to French warships.[34] A returning British prisoner stated that Martinique predators "brought in 4 or 5 Prizes of a Day; that they had at least 30 or 40 English Prizes in the Harbour, when he came away."[35] Many planters, merchants, and agents in the Leeward Islands and Barbados criticized the Royal Navy for inadequate protection and petitioned the Admiralty for more men-of-war to cruise off their colonies.[36] The Royal Navy did cruise against French shipping in the Leewards, and naval frigates captured French vessels from Martinique. As one report suggested, however, although the navy was active, the task was too large: "Our Ships are Cruising all round the island [Martinique], still 20 Sale [sail] of Frenchmen are safe arrived."[37]

Things were so bad in Antigua and Barbados in 1746 that the islands took more direct action. Antigua's government purchased and fitted out a French privateer sloop that Capt. Samuel Bayard in the New York private man-of-war *Hester* had recently captured. This move paid off as four days later the sloop seized a French privateer.[38] American newspapers reported that Barbados adopted a similar course of action. "We hear from Barbados that the Trade of that Place being still much interrupted by the French Privateers, they were obliged to agree with Captain Fielding, of the Leostaff Privateer of Bristol, England, to cruize off the Island for twelve Days, for which it is said he was to have Five Hundred Pounds."[39] Fielding responded by capturing three French private men-of-war on the eighth day of his cruise. This action proved only a temporary deterrent, however, and after several British merchantmen had been seized within the very sight of Bridgetown, the colony hired Captain Grantham, a Bermuda privateer commander, to patrol the coast. Grantham subsequently engaged a French privateer for four hours but was unable to capture it.[40] The islands' problems continued the next year as more than fifty privateers operated from Martinique in the fall of 1747.[41]

Farther west, Jamaica attracted large numbers of Spanish and French privateers. According to Dinwiddie, Jamaica possessed the most valuable commerce in the British West Indies, accounting for annual exports of half a million pounds sterling.[42] Sugar ships left Jamaica by sailing through the Yucatan Channel west of Cuba to the Straits of Florida or through the Windward Passage between Cuba and Hispaniola. These routes teemed with enemy cruisers as Havana, the leading Spanish privateering port, and Cap François on Hispaniola, another privateering center, were well-placed to intercept this extensive traffic.[43] In the summer of 1745 eighteen French privateers cruised the island's shipping lanes disrupting trade.[44] Merchantmen bound to the northern colonies were forced to wait at Point Morant before attempting to sail through the Jamaica Channel and Windward Passage because Spanish and French private men-of-war were simply too numerous to elude.[45] A Jamaican dispatch in late 1745 estimated losses at £130,000 for vessels taken off the island's coast.[46] Early in 1746 Spanish galleys avoided Royal Navy cruisers and seized British merchantmen.[47] In February 1746 an English fleet bound from Jamaica to Portobello worth £150,000 sterling was intercepted, as were four vessels bound from England and Ireland and five more sailing to Jamaica from Boston.[48] About the same time Captain Snell, the skipper of a Boston merchantman, wrote home that "the French Privateers are as thick as Bees about Jamaica, and that he dare not venture out with his Ship."[49] In July 1747 enemy privateers seized nineteen merchantmen bound from Jamaica to the North American colonies and escorted them into various Hispaniola ports.[50]

Despite all of the prizes, Jamaicans were fortunate to possess a Royal Navy station on their island. Although the navy was often criticized for inactivity, the king's ships frequently patrolled the coasts and captured or destroyed large numbers of enemy privateers. Reports such as the following often appeared in the colonial press: "Admiral Davers keeps the Men of War under his Command constantly out upon a Cruize, which gives great Satisfaction to the Islanders [Jamaicans], and all such as trade to those Parts."[51] There were simply too many Spanish and French privateers for the navy to prevent British losses.[52]

TABLE 6.4

North American Cruising Areas of Spanish and French Privateers,
1740–1748

Cruising Area	N	%
Northern Colonies[a]	30	8.6
Delaware Capes[b]	54	15.5
Virginia Capes[c]	86	24.6
Carolina Coast[d]	149	42.7
Other[e]	30	8.6
Totals	349	100.0

[a]Includes all North American prize actions north of the Delaware capes, including Newfoundland and the Grand Banks.

[b]Includes Delaware Bay and Delaware River.

[c]Includes North Carolina prize actions between Cape Lookout and Albemarle Sound.

[d]Includes all prize actions from Cape Lookout, N.C., to St. Simons Island, Ga.

[e]Includes prize actions off Florida and general references to "the coast of North America."

Enemy activity in North American shipping lanes is easier to locate than in the Caribbean. Of the 349 Spanish and French prize actions fought in the northern theater of operations, only 22 (6 percent) suffered from uncertainty concerning the place of action.[53] Table 6.4 presents the major Spanish and French cruising areas on the North American coast.

The extensive rice and naval-stores commerce of Carolina suffered most from Spanish and French privateers. Carolina's rich commerce, weak coastal defenses, and proximity to Spanish ports account for this region's popularity among enemy private men-of-war. Despite the Royal Navy's Carolina station, this southern theater of North America was open to enemy attack. The chronic shipping shortage in Charles Town and the thinly settled province of Georgia prevented extensive cruising by British privateers in the area. In addition, the many capes and islands off the North Carolina coast provided sheltered rendezvous points for Spanish and French warships. Enemy commanders sent prizes to Ocracoke Island near Cape Hatteras and Cape Lookout for safekeeping until they were ready to sail home. Privateers also took on water and slaughtered beef in the Outer Banks.[54]

Enemy privateers also found the Virginia capes especially attractive. The extensive trade of Virginia and Maryland passed between Cape Charles and Cape Henry at the entrance to Chesapeake Bay. The capes funnelled all British merchantmen entering or leaving the bay through a narrow twelve-mile channel. Yet this passage was much too wide for a fort on either cape to command. Spanish and French privateers concentrated off the capes and captured incoming vessels carrying hardware, wine, textiles, and other European goods, and outgoing merchantmen laden with tobacco and wheat.

The Delaware capes were another popular cruising ground. Between Cape May, New Jersey, and Cape Henlopen, Delaware, lay the entrance to Delaware Bay. The maritime commerce of Philadelphia, the second largest city in British North America, passed through this narrow twelve-and-a-half-mile channel. These capes, like those of Virginia, funnelled British merchantmen through the slender passage and greatly eased cruising operations for enemy privateers. Pennsylvania vessels laden with bread, flour, other foodstuffs, and lumber for casks, bound for Europe or the West Indies, became easy targets. Philadelphia-bound merchantmen with European and Caribbean cargoes ran this gauntlet as well.

Spanish and French privateers often took prizes in all three areas during a single cruise. Embarking from ports in the West Indies or St. Augustine, enemy cruisers intercepted merchantmen off Georgia and the Carolinas before raiding British shipping off the Virginia and Delaware capes. South Carolina's commerce faced double jeopardy when the Spanish and French privateers sailed home. The latter years of the conflict witnessed a series of devastating privateering cruises during which the enemy began taking prizes off the Carolina coast before continuing to the northern cruising grounds.

Despite the success of the dramatic, sweeping forays up the North American coast, many enemy privateers restricted their operations to the coast of Carolina. In the spring of 1745 Don Julian Joseph de la Vega sailed from St. Augustine in consort with a French and a Spanish sloop. Cruising in sight of Charles Town harbor, they forced seven merchantmen to haul down their colors.[55] Throughout the summer of 1745 the *South-Carolina*

Gazette published numerous accounts of enemy privateers attacking British commerce on the colony's undefended coast. In June five Havana privateers were sailing off the colony's shore. There was even an unconfirmed report that Captain de la Vega had returned. A September report revealed the weakness of British opposition: "Last Tuesday Afternoon a Spanish Privateer Schooner had the Impudence to chase in two Vessels quite over this Bar."[56]

Although the pace of the prize war slackened in 1746, the *South-Carolina Gazette*'s columns still carried the depressing news of enemy captures. One report indicated that the dreaded de la Vega in a large brigantine, accompanied by three other privateers, had left Havana for the Carolina shipping lanes. This unsettling news "had so alarm'd the coasting Commanders here, that for 10 Days past, every Time a Brigt hath been seen by them . . . they have made the best of their Way into Port, reporting they had been chas'd by Don Julian off Cape Romain."[57] Farther north, Capt. Don Pedro Arracoche of Havana conducted a successful privateering cruise near Cape Fear. Arracoche seized the *Elizabeth* and the *Brunswick,* both bound to Cape Fear from New York City. Before heading back to the Caribbean Arracoche captured the *St. George* and the *Increase.*[49] Carolinians must have enjoyed some satisfaction when George Gyles, commander of the Bristol, England, privateer *Prince Charles,* escorted *La Packavet Real,* commanded by Don Pedro de Avillo, into Charles Town in December. De Avillo was Arracoche's consort. In any case, *La Packavet Real* had taken four prizes on the coast before Captain Gyles captured it just outside Havana harbor.[59]

Enemy successes at South Carolina's expense increased in 1747. Capt. Stephen Bernard (or Berrerd), commander of a Havana privateer sloop, captured the *Industry,* the *John,* the *Mary,* and three other merchantmen off the Carolina coast before heading north to menace Philadelphia's sea-lanes. In the Delaware River Bernard seized the ship *Mary* and manned his prize to cruise against British shipping. On his return to Havana, he took the ship *Patience* off Cape Fear as it was heading for London carrying rice and naval stores from Charles Town. (Unfortunately for Bernard, both the *Patience* and the *Mary* were subsequently recaptured by the *Isabella* and the *Walker,* two American privateers sailing in consort from Charles Town and Frederica, Georgia.)[60] St. Jago Gaultier, captain of a small Spanish privateer mounting only six carriage guns, captured the schooner *Dorchester* and a sloop off

Edisto Island, South Carolina, and escorted them into St. Augustine.[61] To prevent further losses Charles Town businessmen hired the sloop *Endeavour,* commanded by Capt. Charles Walker, to patrol the coast. Unfortunately, Walker failed to capture any enemy warships, and Spanish and French privateering continued.[62]

South Carolina merchants suffered from Spanish and French privateers until peace was finally proclaimed in 1748. Charles Town merchant Henry Laurens chronicled British losses in letters to his business associates during the final years of the war. "Our Coast has for some Weeks past been grosly insulted by two or three Piccaroon Privateers," he wrote in June 1747, "[they] Sent their Boat and took a Pettiagua Loaded with Rice, *within the Bar* [emphasis added]."[63] Spanish activity continued brisk in August when Charles Town residents hired the *Endeavour* to pursue enemy privateers after learning that HMS *Aldborough,* the province's station ship, had been damaged in a storm. The city's merchants had earlier attempted to hire a vessel to patrol the coasts but were unable to agree on financial terms.[64] Writing to London merchant Alexander Watson, Laurens prefaced a list of six recently captured vessels with the melancholy statement: "We have been very unlucky in our Shipping on this Coast, a great Number of them being taken by Spanish and french Privateers."[65]

Laurens discussed the bleak commercial outlook resulting from the enemy's constant attacks on shipping in North America and Europe. "I am very sorry to observe your Ships from Boston having Suffer'd so greatly by the enemy, but 'tis no more than common nowadays to trade from all parts of America & especially this Province," he informed a Massachusetts merchant. "Our Ships are taken on one Side or the other constantly. Such as escape Privateers on this side fall in with them in the Channel so that very few arrive safe. We have Lately had eight or ten Sail of Loaden Vessels taken on this Coast besides small Pettiaguas etc. drove on Shoar and plunder'd."[66]

The first eight months of 1748 differed little from the previous three years. The *South-Carolina Gazette* continued to inform the war-weary merchant community of the latest enemy successes. There were a few rays of light, however. The legislature fit out two sloops, the *Pearl* and *Nonpareil,* that captured several enemy cruisers and convoyed vessels past enemy privateers.[67] The *Isabella,* a Charles Town private man-of-war, seized the richly laden French ship *St. Jacques* and sent it into Charles Town.[68]

There were also accounts of the peace negotiations underway at Aix-la-Chapelle.[69] Much of the news remained bad, however, as Spanish privateers took prizes in plain sight of Charles Town harbor, and enemy privateersmen sacked the town of Brunswick, North Carolina.[70] Even the long-awaited peace treaty failed to halt enemy captures as St. Augustine and Havana privateers claimed to have no confirmation of the cessation of hostilities.[71]

Spanish privateers also plagued Virginia shipping in 1744–1748. Don Francisco Larango returned to Virginia waters in 1744 and took three prizes off the capes. Sailing with a Captain Figaroa, the privateers next captured the *Mary and Susannah,* bound to Virginia from Bermuda, and two sloops sailing for North Carolina. On their way home, Larango and Figaroa intercepted the *Lydia* of Philadelphia on the Carolina coast.[72] Enemy activity increased in 1745. Capt. Edmund Freman, master of a Cape Cod whaling vessel, told the *Pennsylvania Gazette* of a successful Spanish privateer snow operating off the Virginia capes. The Spaniards captured Freman's whaler and three other vessels before releasing him and eighty-two other prisoners near Cape Henlopen. Freman stated that during his captivity the Spaniards continually sought their consort, a powerful ship mounting thirty-six guns.[73] This predator was busy capturing three tobacco ships sailing from Maryland to Scotland.[74] At least two other Spanish private men-of-war disrupted British shipping east of the Chesapeake Bay. A Spanish snow and sloop sailing in consort took four prizes including a Nantucket sloop commanded by Captain Swain, who was among forty-three prisoners released before the Spaniards sailed home.[75] Three other English vessels had better luck. Capt. Edward Dixon, master of the *Howard,* successfully defended his vessel when attacked by a Spanish warship on the tobacco coast and then safely escorted the *Mayflower* of Whitehaven and the *Loving* of Biddeford on the homeward voyage to England.[76]

Conditions improved in 1746 and 1747, but Chesapeake commerce was hit hard in 1748. The Spanish privateer *Confirmation* seized three vessels off the capes in April and also engaged the *York* but was unable to capture it.[77] Another Spanish warship took three prizes inside the capes within sight of Norfolk.[78] Two enemy privateers seized the *Triton,* but fortunately for Captain Askew, his crew, and his owners, HMS *Otter* and *Hector* subsequently recaptured the vessel, though the privateers escaped.[79] French Captain Deveaux in the *Royale* made a profitable visit to the Chesapeake in 1748, capturing the *Mercury Galley, Speedwell,* and another merchantman.[80] Even the Peace of Aix-la-Chapelle failed to halt privateering off the Virginia capes as Capt. Jean Lartique in the privateer *Le Royal* from Petite Goave, Saint-Domingue, captured the snow *True Briton* off Cape Charles on 18 June, nearly three weeks after the legal deadline for French captures. The Newport privateer *Defiance,* commanded by Capt. John Sweet, recaptured the *True Briton* and escorted it to Rhode Island, thus saving the owners from a total loss.[81] Capt. Juan Ferdinando of St. Augustine seized the *Endeavour* in October 1748. This incident occurred some three months after the 29 July deadline for Spanish privateering, but Ferdinando claimed ignorance of the hostilities' conclusion.[82]

Carolina and Chesapeake commerce suffered chronic losses from Spanish and French private men-of-war during 1744–1748, yet the most dramatic enemy privateering attacks took place farther north off the Delaware capes. This area had experienced few disruptions in 1744–1746. Capt. John Joseph Le Gross of Louisbourg captured at least four prizes east of Delaware Bay in 1744. Benjamin Franklin mentioned these captures in an unsuccessful attempt to appropriate funds for coastal defense during a heated debate in the Pennsylvania Assembly in February 1745.[83] Beginning with a major raid in 1747, however, Spanish and French privateers rocked Philadelphia's maritime commerce. Captain Lahaye, commander of the Cap François sloop *Marshal Vaudroy,* mounting fourteen carriage guns and carrying 150 men, began the raids by seizing his first two prizes off the Carolina coast. Then on 28 August he captured a Philadelphia sloop homeward bound from New Providence Island off the Delaware Capes. The *Ranger* became the fourth prize of his voyage. On 1 September the *Marshal Vaudroy* took the *London* and *George and Mary,* two tobacco ships bound from the Chesapeake to Hull, England. The next day Lahaye intercepted another vessel named the *London,* and he seized the sloop *Charity* from Philadelphia bound for Antigua on 7 September. The Philadelphia ship *Boston* became the ninth prize on 10 September as it entered the Delaware capes homeward bound from Jamaica. Lahaye next turned his sights on the *Cumberland* as it headed for Philadelphia, but after a nine-hour chase, the British vessel escaped. Weakened from dispatching so many prize crews to man his captures, Lahaye turned south for the voyage home to Saint-Dominque. The *Marshal Vaudroy* completed this successful cruise by raiding the town of Beaufort, just west of Cape Lookout on the North Carolina coast.[84]

These captures quickly raised alarms concerning the Delaware Bay's weak defenses. Anthony Palmer, president of the Pennsylvania Council and acting chief executive, warned the assembly that the colony's military weaknesses must be corrected as soon as possible. After recounting the *Marshal Vaudroy*'s numerous prize actions, Palmer informed the legislators that a party of Spanish and French raiders had sailed up the Delaware River to Newcastle (a scant twenty-five miles from Philadelphia) and plundered two plantations, abused the owners, carried off slaves and other property, and capped off their incursion by capturing a "valuable ship" bound to Philadelphia from Antigua. Palmer was afraid Philadelphia's porous coastal defenses would permit more privateers to return in the spring of 1748. The Spanish and French might even attack the capital unless the assembly acted.[85] The legislature refused to budge, however.

Concerned citizens led by Benjamin Franklin intervened in the debate over Pennsylvania's defenses. Late in 1747 Franklin attacked the Quaker legislators and merchants who refused to beef up the colony's military in a pamphlet titled, *Plain Truth; or, Serious Considerations on the Present State of the City of Philadelphia and Province of Pennsylvania. By a Tradesman of Philadelphia.* Franklin spearheaded the formation of a volunteer militia and helped set up a lottery to raise three thousand pounds for erecting batteries to defend the city, all at private cost.[86] The legislature's "irresponsibility" infuriated council president Palmer, who informed the British commander at Louisbourg: "We have the Misfortune to have an Assembly consisting chiefly of Quakers." Philadelphia needed cannon, and Palmer had written to Cape Breton hoping to borrow some.[87] He sent similar requests to the governors of New York and Massachusetts.[88]

Palmer also asked the Royal Navy for help. He reiterated the legislature's inactivity and his fears concerning enemy privateers to Adm. Charles Knowles, commander of the navy's Jamaica station:

> We need not tell you, who are so well acquainted with the Condition of the Colonies, that the Majority of the Assembly consisting of Quakers, their Principles wou'd never suffer them to put this Province into a posture of Defence, nor to fit out Vessels for the protection of their Trade; encourag'd by this, the Coast was last year

invested with swarms of French & Spanish Privateers, numbers of our Vessels were taken within our own Capes, & the Enemy seeing no resistance seiz'd our Pilots & fell a plundering the Plantations Situate on the Bayside. This Success more than answering their expectation, we are told by Prisoners who have been lately carried into the Enemie's Ports, that great preparations are making & mighty Schemes concerted for our Ruin.

Palmer impressed upon Knowles the devastating impact for the navy and the West Indies in general if Philadelphia fell or if its commerce were destroyed. "This [the loss of Philadelphia's trade] is an Event of so much Importance to His Majesty, as His Majestie's Fleet in the West Indies are to be supplied with a great part of their provisions from hence, & His Majestie's Subjects there cannot get many of the necessaries of Life but from the Continent."[89] Palmer's anxieties about enemy private men-of-war had been fed, as he indicated to Knowles, by the reports of increased Spanish and French preparations related by returning British prisoners-of-war. Edward Seymour, lieutenant of the New York privateer *Dragon* and recently released from Havana, asserted that twenty-five Spanish privateers were fitting out to cruise off the Delaware capes in the spring of 1748.[90]

The *Pennsylvania Gazette* kept Philadelphia abreast of the attempts to bolster coastal defenses. Doubtless many Philadelphians welcomed the arrival of HMS *Otter* to protect Pennsylvania's commerce and the loan of some cannon from New York.[91] Philadelphia merchant John Swift informed his uncle in London that the city's volunteer militia numbered eight hundred armed men, including Swift. He had earlier asked his London relative to send him a weapon because he felt "bound in Reason, Duty and Honour to have one of some kind or other, and my Fowling piece has no Bayonet to it." Swift also reported that the battery was under construction and another lottery to raise six thousand pounds for Philadelphia's fortifications was underway. In addition, twelve cannons had arrived from New York. "With these," Swift concluded, "we shall be able to make some assistance in case of an attack."[92]

The Pennsylvania Council tightened security in the Delaware River and Bay by issuing new regulations for pilot boat captains. Beginning 10 April 1748 all pilots were strictly enjoined from boarding any inward-bound vessel "until the Commander thereof, or some of the Mariners or People, have first come on Shore, to the End it may the more certainly be known whether such Vessel belongs to *British* Subjects." The regulations were in effect for the height of Pennsylvania's shipping season, 10 April to 25 September, and would last until the war ended.[93] With these few precautions, Philadelphians anxiously awaited the dreaded arrival of the enemy's privateers. The wait was a short one.

The *Marshal Vaudroy* began its 1748 privateering voyage with three captures off the North Carolina coast in April.[94] The sloop then turned north and seized three merchantmen off the Delaware capes. To avoid guarding numerous prisoners, the Frenchmen put their captives ashore after stripping them "of everything they had that was valuable."[95] Captain Berneau, another Cap François privateer commander, joined the *Marshal Vaudroy* in the hunt for British prizes and captured two sloops lying at anchor in Cape May harbor.[96] Berneau had already seized six merchantmen at the entrance to Delaware Bay. The *Marshal Vaudroy* took two more prizes before turning south for the return voyage to Saint-Domingue. The Cap François privateer completed its successful cruise by capturing the *Three Brothers* off False Cape, Virginia.[97]

The French privateers' successes prompted council president Palmer to urge the assembly for funds to fit out a vessel to pursue the enemy. "It is from your House only that the Merchants and Traders expect Protection," he asserted, "and if that be now refused, or proper Measures neglected to disperse the enemy, our Port must continue blocked up, our inward bound Vessels inevitably lost, and a total Stagnation of Trade must follow, which will certainly bring Poverty and Ruin upon many of our Inhabitants."[98] The legislature peevishly replied that since Palmer was well-aware of their views on this matter, it would serve no useful purpose to repeat them. If a vessel were sent out, the enemy would probably sail away only to return when the coast was clear. The legislators further contended that the cost of maintaining a guard vessel on constant alert was "too heavy" and even superfluous since Palmer had already indicated that the navy was dispatching a vessel to guard the coasts.[99]

The situation on the Delaware capes deteriorated. In May, HMS *Otter,* the new station ship, suffered serious damage in an engagement with the enemy while en route to Philadelphia and was unable to patrol Delaware Bay. In addition, other privateers had joined the *Marshal Vaudroy* and Captain Berneau. The

Pennsylvania Council received a dispatch from Salem, New Jersey, stating that a Spanish privateer was now lying in the Delaware River about ten miles from Newcastle. The communiqué contained a rather unflattering description of the enemy commander: "The Spanish Capt. is of a savage, barbarous disposition, & declared frequently that he wou'd rob, plunder, & burn whatever he cou'd."[100]

Capt. Vincent de Lopez, commander of the Havana private man-of-war *St. Michael,* proved to be a man of his word. Acting in consort with Captain Ramong, commander of the Havana privateer *La Fortune,* de Lopez robbed, plundered, and burned throughout May. The two privateers captured eleven merchantmen in and around Delaware Bay. On one occasion, de Lopez attempted to seize a ship from Jamaica while it was anchored at Newcastle. The combined firing of the shore batteries and the vessel's carriage guns stopped the privateers from scoring yet another success.[101] During the last week of May, de Lopez landed some of his men at Elsingborough, New Jersey, but the Salem County militia was on the alert and forced the raiders back on the *St. Michael.*[102] On his return to Havana, de Lopez tarried in Chesapeake Bay and captured five more prizes before leaving the North American coast.[103]

Enemy privateers seriously interrupted Philadelphia's maritime commerce and plunged the province into a series of political recriminations. The *Pennsylvania Gazette* stated that the port had been effectively closed down by the enemy's warships: "All foreign trade is now at a stand, and the port as much shut up, as if the river was frozen."[104] This was not an exaggeration, as the customhouse notices, printed weekly in the *Gazette,* indicated that no vessels had entered in or out of the city.[105] John Swift reported, "There has been so many Vessels taken of late, that I begin almost to despair, that any will get safe. To save myself the trouble of writing you News, I shall send you with this one of Franklin's Papers, by which you will see what a Glorious Condition Quakerism is like to bring this Province to."[106] In New York City Gerard Beekman received word of Philadelphia's closing. "Yesterday Came Express to our Govournor from Philadelphia that Just before their fleet was to Sail outward bound under Convoy of the wolf man of war, a Vessell arrived from Boston who had bin taken at Cor [?] within the Capes by don Pedro who Lay there with a 36 gun Ship and 7 other privateers so that their harbour is intirly blockt up and Like to be this Summer."[107]

Beekman asked Peleg Thurston to warn John Channing and the Newport merchant community of these developments "least their Interist May fall in his [i.e., the Spanish privateer's] hands."[109] Fortunately, the port was not closed very long. On 9 June the *Pennsylvania Gazette* reported, "The Enemies Privateers have left our River at Present." On 4 July, Beekman wrote that he hoped the sloop *Caster* had already arrived in Philadelphia and that she would soon be ready to sail again.[109]

The assembly's failure to support measures to lift the privateers' siege of the Delaware capes produced another round of vitriolic messages between the two houses of the legislature. On 9 June the council issued yet another demand for the lower house to fit out a vessel for commercial protection. The legislators again cited the presence of HMS *Otter,* ignoring that vessel's inability to pursue privateers. The council was not satisfied with these arguments and charged the Quaker-dominated assembly with being derelict in its duty to protect the colony.[110] Enemy privateering success continued, and not until news of the Peace of Aix-la-Chapelle reached Philadelphia in mid-August was the threat of further losses to Spanish and French privateers finally over.[111]

III

Privateer commanders cruised in the busiest shipping lanes and also planned their voyages to coincide with the height of the shipping season. This was true for all privateers, whether they were Spanish or French or British, whether they operated in the West Indies or off the coast of North America. An examination of the seasons in which the privateers operated illuminates the patterns of shipping for the British, Spanish, and French Empires in the mideighteenth century.

Colonial exports were, of course, overwhelmingly agricultural. Flour and wheat from the Middle Atlantic provinces, tobacco from the Chesapeake, rice and naval stores from Carolina, and sugar, molasses, coffee, indigo, and cocoa from the Caribbean composed the cargoes in vessels bound from the Americas. As a result, the annual cycle of crop cultivation largely determined the seasons of merchant shipping. In addition, climatic conditions—the heavy weather in the North Atlantic from November to early spring and the hurricane season in the West Indies from July to mid-October— also influenced the patterns of oceanic commerce.

The impact of ocean weather and the growing seasons of

American staple crops clearly affected the seasonal patterns of Spanish and French prize actions in the North American theaters of operations during the wars of 1739–1748. (See Table 6.5.) The North Atlantic's severe winter storms and gales hindered privateering operations for Spanish and French warships. Prize actions declined in the fall and did not pick up again until the cold weather abated. The end of March ushered in the privateering season as well as the beginning of spring. April, the busiest spring month, witnessed an increase of nearly 40 percent over the previous four months' activity. The pace of privateering accelerated in the summer, and June was the busiest month of the year. Altogether spring and summer accounted for two-thirds of all enemy North American prize actions. Privateering began to taper off as the fall progressed. As winter approached, privateering in North America nearly ceased. Only the Carolina coast witnessed much activity.

Rice governed the pattern of South Carolina's commerce. Armies of black slaves planted the crop in the spring, cultivation continued throughout the summer, and the threshed grain was packed for shipment in the fall.[112] Because Carolina streams and creeks could not accommodate oceangoing vessels, the rice was sent to Charles Town for shipment to European markets. Robert Pringle outlined this yearly pattern to Richard Thompson whose vessel, the *Friend,* had arrived in Charles Town in July.

> It is with much Concern that I have to acquaint you that you have sent said Vessell in the worst of times by coming here at this Season of the Year which is a great deal too late & we have generally little or no Trade in the hot Season of June, July, & August & there is now no good Rice of the Crop left fit to Ship to Europe to be purchas'd & Pitch & Tar are very Scarce as there is none hardly comes to Town in this Season. . . . We never expect any Vessells to come to load here after the month of May & what Shipping happen to come at this Season generally go up our River & Lye there for the Crop till October or November. No Ship ought to arrive here later than April or Earlier for the Crop than the month of September or October."[113]

Although Thompson was unaware of the proper times to arrive in Charles Town, Spanish and French privateers were not. They plagued Carolina merchants in the fall and spring. Pringle bitterly criticized the Royal Navy for inactivity in the fall and spring.[114] As noted earlier, Captain de la Vega and his two consorts arrived off

TABLE 6.5

Privateering Seasonal Pattern: Prize Actions in North American Waters,
1739–1748

Season	Northern Colonies[a]	Delaware Capes[b]	Virginia Capes[c]	Carolina Coast[d]
Spring				
March	0	0	1	7
April	0	0	17	31
May	5	5	18	7
Seasonal Subtotal		93 actions, 29.0%		
Summer				
June	3	18	18	9
July	5	8	15	7
August	3	5	8	24
Seasonal Subtotal		123 actions, 38.3%		
Fall				
September	5	10	1	21
October	1	4	3	11
November	2	6	4	10
Seasonal Subtotal		78 actions, 24.3%		
Winter				
December	1	0	0	5
January	2	0	0	11
February	1	0	1	6
Seasonal Subtotal		27 Actions, 8.4%		
Yearly Total		321 actions, 100.0%		

Note: Because British colonial privateers fought only eighty prize actions on the North American coast and since many of those were defensive in nature, only Spanish and French actions are included in this table.

[a]Includes all North American prize actions north of the Delaware capes, including Newfoundland and the Grand Banks.

[b]Includes Delaware Bay and Delaware River.

[c]Includes North Carolina prize actions between Cape Lookout and Albemarle Sound.

[d]Includes all prize actions from Cape Lookout, N.C., to St. Simons Island, Ga.

the Carolina coast in April to begin their privateering operations. Henry Laurens wrote his most dismal accounts of enemy activities in November at the end of the busy fall season. More than 40 percent of the prize actions on the Carolina coast occurred in April, September, and October.

Prize actions off the Virginia capes ebbed and flowed according to the seasonal nature of tobacco cultivation. The colonists planted seeds in the early spring and transplanted the tobacco in June. Six weeks later it was cut and placed in barns for curing before being packed into hogsheads for shipment to market. The first packaged tobacco appeared in October, and the bulk of the crop was dockside during the next two or three months. As a result, seventeenth-century English tobacco ships sailed for Virginia and Maryland in autumn, and because of deteriorating weather conditions and loading delays in the Chesapeake, the ships seldom returned to Europe until spring. The Chesapeake fleet's sailing times changed in the early eighteenth century. Vessels from Britain arrived in the early spring after the winter gales and cleared for home during the summer. Changes in tobacco marketing arrangements facilitated this alteration in the shipping season. Resident factors and storekeepers reduced loading delays, thus substantially lowering the large labor and victual costs of wintering in Virginia and Maryland.[115]

Spanish and French privateers timed their voyages for the spring and early summer, and April, May, June, and July accounted for nearly four-fifths of the prize actions on the tobacco coast. Enemy predators learned this seasonal pattern long before the 1740s, and the tobacco trade had been hard hit during the Anglo-Dutch and Anglo-French wars of the seventeenth century.[116] To prevent further losses, the British Privy Council adopted a plan of annual convoys in 1707. Vessels arrived from England in October and departed from the Chesapeake in May. Although convoys reduced losses in the latter years of Queen Anne's War, they were unsuccessful in the wars of 1739–1748.[117] Captains Fandino, Larango, de Lopez, and other Spanish commanders took prizes off the capes with seeming impunity. French privateers led by Captains Lahaye and Deveaux enjoyed similar success. The Royal Navy still provided convoys. Capt. Thomas Gregory, for example, advertised on 16 March 1747 that "His Majesty's ship Folkstone, under my command, will sail for England about the 12th of June: All masters of merchantmen, who incline to take benefit of the convoy, are desired to be ready with their ships in Hampton Road by that time."[118] Station ships also cruised inside the bay and off the capes to capture enemy warships. The king's ships, however, were unable to stop losses of British merchantmen to Spanish and French privateers.

North of the Chesapeake the prize war was largely confined to the spring and summer. The severity of the North Atlantic in winter was an important factor in determining this season. From the beginning of the conflict, British naval officers expected little activity in northern waters during the winter. Captain Warren informed the Admiralty of his plans to abandon the New England coast during cold weather. "[Capt. Townshend] brought me orders to make reprisals on the Spaniards, and I shall be at sea in ten days with a clean ship and 140 men. And as it is impossible to employ this ship on this coast during the winter, I propose to cruise to the southward, which I hope their lordships will approve of."[119]

Northern colonial officials also cut back provincial coast guard operations during the winter. At the end of October 1740, the Rhode Island legislature voted to haul up the colony's guard vessel and remove all her stores and rigging because there was little point in patrolling the coast by that date.[120] After Zebulon Witham reported that a Spanish privateer was cruising off the Virginia capes in November 1741 and that it might head toward New England, Governor Shirley wanted to dispatch a provincial vessel to guard the coast. The Massachusetts General Court, however, thought winter cruising operations were impracticable; besides, the sailors had already been discharged for the cold weather months. The legislators thought the vessel "ought to be completely furnished & ready by the Middle of February" at the earliest. This schedule did not change. In January 1745 the House of Representatives received Shirley's request to have the province vessel ready to cruise by the end of February.[121] When the house provided for an additional guard vessel in June 1744, it stipulated that its cruise should end in mid-October.[122] Shirley wrote Rhode Island Governor William Greene in September 1744 to inform him that three Cape Breton privateers were cruising off the New England coast.[123] Like Shirley, Greene was alarmed by these French warships and asked the legislature to extend the cruise of the colony sloop until 31 October. The legislature, however, refused the governor's request.[124] Robert Pringle also believed that privateering activity in northern waters would cease by late fall. Writing to Massachusetts merchant John Erving, Pringle arranged for his wife's return to

Charles Town from a Boston visit. "By the 1st of November it is to be hop'd there will be no risque in Coming by sea from your parts, as by that Time of year the Coasts will be pretty Clear of Spanish Privateers."[125]

The payment of wages for New England coast guard crews also indicates that colonial governments considered winter operations unnecessary. In the warm weather months the governments kept full complements (if they could be raised) on the payroll. After the middle of October, however, only the captain, a few officers, and a handful of lower-deck seamen received wages to look after the colony vessels while they were in port for the winter.[126]

Pennsylvania's problems with enemy privateers were also largely confined to warm weather months. Captain Larango, the well-known Spanish privateer commander who attacked Pennsylvania commerce in 1744 and 1745, arrived off the Delaware capes during the summer.[127] Well-aware of the dangers to commerce that warm weather would bring, John Reynell informed an English correspondent in March 1745, "I look upon it that the Danger of Shipping is nothing neigh so great now, as it will be some time hence, when we may Reasonably Expect there will be Privateers on the Coast."[128] In the great raid of 1747, Captain Lahaye's *Marshal Vaudroy* took its first prize in Philadelphia sea-lanes on 28 August and turned south before the middle of September. In the political recriminations following Lahaye's cruise, Pennsylvania Council President Palmer repeatedly voiced his fears for the following spring and summer. When the council tightened the security by regulating Delaware Bay pilots, the new rules were in effect from 10 April to 25 September, the height of the shipping season. The French and Spanish privateers who closed the port of Philadelphia in 1748 began their operations on the Carolina coast in April (perfect timing, according to Pringle) and reached the Delaware capes in May.

The annual cycle of privateering in the tropics differed greatly from the North American theater of operations. The hurricane season, lasting from July to mid-October, influenced Caribbean commerce. Shipowners wanted their vessels out of West Indian waters during this dangerous season. London insurers even doubled the premiums on ships that remained in the Caribbean after 31 July. Sugar production also affected the West Indian shipping season. The first sugar canes were ready for cutting in January, and the harvest continued until about July. Milling, boiling, and processing were required before the sugar could be packed for shipment to Europe. Ships arrived steadily in the islands from November until July, when the bad weather began.[129]

The seasonal pattern of Caribbean prize actions shown in Table 6.6 reveals the merchants' respect for hurricanes and the growing cycle of sugar cane. Privateering was brisk in the winter and early spring as vessels arrived to load the new crop. Prize actions declined during the hurricane season. August and September were the slowest months with privateering activity falling 120 to 140 percent compared to the peak months of March and February. Prize actions picked up again in late fall and steadily increased with the approach of the new season.

The timing of British and Franco-Spanish Caribbean prize actions also suggests a different pattern for the belligerents' West Indian commerce. Privateering activity declined for all nations during the hurricane season, indicating a decline of merchantmen in the West Indies. British activity resumed in November, the posthurricane season accounting for more prize actions than the season preceding the storms. Spanish and French privateering, however, declined even more from November to February than it had during the hurricane season. November to January were the slowest months of the year for enemy activity in the Caribbean.

The major shifts in British privateering activity responded to the influx of Spanish and French merchantmen into the Caribbean. The overwhelming majority of these vessels came from Europe because the French and Spanish North American colonies, unlike their British counterparts, contributed little tonnage to West Indian shipping. This also accounts for the much higher number of British prize actions in Table 6.6. Numerous Spanish and French warships were busy annoying British sea-lanes farther north. Because Spanish and French merchantmen embarked from Europe and were unhampered by North Atlantic storms, they arrived in the Caribbean throughout the winter. This probably explains why American privateers were so busy from November to March.

The different pattern of Spanish and French West Indian privateering results from the dual nature of Britain's Caribbean commerce. Numerous vessels from the British Isles arrived in the West Indies, and, like the Spanish and French sugar ships, they sailed for the islands during the late fall and winter months. In contrast to the Spanish and French West Indian trade, however, North American merchantmen also played a key role in Caribbean

TABLE 6.6
Privateering Seasonal Pattern: The Caribbean Sea, 1739–1748

Season	British Prize Actions		Enemy Prize Actions	
	N	%	N	%
Prehurricane Season				
March	69		56	
April	40		55	
May	46		54	
June	41		23	
Seasonal Subtotal	196	28.7	188	48.6
Hurricane Season				
July	55		35	
August	28		24	
September	33		23	
October	47		39	
Seasonal Subtotal	163	23.9	121	31.3
Posthurricane Season				
November	69		19	
December	62		18	
January	96		13	
February	96		28	
Seasonal Subtotal	323	47.4	78	20.2
Total	682		387	

Combined British, Spanish, and French Prize Actions	N	%
Prehurricane	384	35.9
Hurricane	284	26.9
Posthurricane	401	37.5
Total	1,069	100.0

commerce. Hundreds of vessels from New England, New York, and Philadelphia exchanged goods in the West Indies. Because North Atlantic weather conditions limited winter sailings, American merchantmen arrived in the tropics later than European vessels, thus accounting for the variation in enemy West Indian operations.

IV

The numerous Spanish and French privateering successes revealed the vulnerability of British colonial commerce and elicited considerable criticism concerning the Royal Navy's inability to protect American trade. Merchants throughout the British Empire castigated the navy for failing to prevent British shipping from falling into the enemies' hands. Because the Admiralty was fully aware of the merchant community's influence on the government in London, protecting maritime commerce received a high priority.[130] Certainly the correspondence of naval commanders in the Caribbean and North America reveals a marked concern for guarding merchantmen sailing in American waters. Admiral Vernon, commander of naval forces in the Caribbean from 1739–1742, issued numerous orders to his subordinates for protecting West Indian vessels. In October 1739, for example, Vernon ordered Captain Harcourt, commander of HM Sloop *Drake*, "to continue cruising on the North side of this island [Jamaica] for the protection of Port Antonio and the coasting trade of this island by giving them convoy round to the North East end whenever they shall apply to you for it." Vernon continued, "You will employ yourself in cruising off the port of St. Iago on Cuba for intercepting of anything going out or coming into that port, as it is from the privateers from that port to be apprehended the danger of our coasting trade will be most exposed."[131] Vernon issued similar orders throughout his West Indian tour of duty, and his successors followed suit. On the North American station, officers also received orders for safeguarding British merchantmen.[132] Great Britain's formidable naval power, however, could not stop the seizure of hundreds of vessels.

Not surprisingly, those areas hardest hit by enemy privateers complained about the navy's inability to protect trade. South Carolinians were especially bitter. Pringle was infuriated by what he considered the naval commanders' inexcusable inaction. After a Spanish privateer had chased a small vessel near Charles Town in October 1740, Pringle fumed because the navy did nothing. "The two Kings Ships Station'd here are both Lying up and have been so ever since the middle of July last. It is a pity that they were not expos'd in the publick Prints."[133] Pringle also informed his brother that several vessels bound for Europe were "obliged to go without the Kings Ship the *Phonix,* Capt. Fanshaw, altho' he Lay ready in our Road, Yet he would not Stir to See the Ships off the Coast."

Moreover, South Carolina's government had been forced to dispatch its own warships to pursue a Spanish privateer because the navy refused to leave port.[134] In 1741 the Carolina Assembly offered rewards for privateers to safeguard the coast because the navy could not stop enemy cruisers. After Capt. John Rous of the sloop *Speedwell* returned with a captured Spanish privateer, the *South-Carolina Gazette* commented on Captain Fanshaw's efforts. "The same Day likewise return'd Capt. Fanshaw, in his Majesty's Ship the Phenix,—With his usual Success, he having been out some Weeks past and luckily met with no Enemy.—WE now begin to hope that Capt. Rous's Vigilence and Courage will spoil the Spaniards future Gleanings, they have made but too good a Harvest already."[135] Captain Fanshaw's lack of zeal may have caused him some trouble with the Admiralty. The *Pennsylvania Gazette* subsequently reported he had been court-martialed and docked six months' pay, though the specific charges were not mentioned.[136] Occasionally, the navy's blundering cost its men prize money. Pringle noted in 1742, "General Oglethorpe has had the good fortune to make a Prize of the Pay goeing to St. Augustine[. Its] Value is said about £16,000 Sterling, and we have at present four Kings Ships in the Harbour who if they had been on their Duty might Certainly have mett with said Prize."[137]

Pringle criticized the navy throughout the War of Jenkins' Ear. When HMS *Rye* replaced HMS *Phoenix* early in 1742, Pringle commented, "We have had no King's ships on a Cruize for these Ten months past, so badly is this Coast taken care of."[138] The *Rye*'s arrival did not improve this situation, however. "Notwithstanding all the King's Ships Station'd on this Coast, we have just Receiv'd a List of Six Ships Lately taken whereof the *St. Andrew,* William Greig, from this [port] with Rice for Cowes [England] is one and Carry'd to Havana. The Commanders of the King's Ships here doe not doe their duty. One of them Capt. Hardy who Arrived from England about four Months agoe and has not been out of Port Since so that our Trade is very precarious."[139] Northern colonists also learned of Hardy's inactivity when the *New-York Weekly Journal* published an attack concerning his lack of initiative.[140]

Pringle singled out Hardy for a bitter attack concerning his role in the Spanish invasion of Georgia in 1742. "If it had not been thro' the bad Conduct and Cowardice of Capt. Hardy of the King's Ships here, we had Destroy'd all their Shipping before they could have got away." Pringle hoped that Hardy "will be Broke" when London authorities received an accurate account of the action.[141] Pringle was not alone in criticizing Hardy's conduct in this action. Eliza Lucas, a member of the Carolina planter class and notable indigo experimenter, informed her father that Hardy's performance had "greatly disgusted the Gov. and Council as well as the rest of the Inhabitance."[142] South Carolina Lieutenant Governor William Bull excoriated the navy in general and Captain Hardy in particular in a letter to George II. "Many of the Commanders of such Ships as have been Stationed here for some Years past declaring themselves Accountable to no Authority here for any of their proceedings or behaviour; have layed up in harbour as they pleased instead of Cruizing for the Protection of the Trade whilst at the same time this Province have upon several Emergencies been Obliged for that reason to fit out Vessels to do, what was their duty to have done." Bull turned his attention to Captain Hardy. "And in particular the present Commanding Officer of Your Majestys Ships upon the Station who from the time of his arrival here, the beginning of January last never put to Sea again until he went in relief of Your Majesty's Troops at St. Simons in July."[143] Bull added that Hardy refused to pursue the enemy's forces as the council had suggested, which resulted in the Spaniards' safe retreat to Florida. Despite these attacks, Hardy was not "broke," and he remained on the Carolina station until the end of 1743.[144]

West Indian merchants also criticized the navy's attempts to safeguard the empire's Caribbean commerce. In May 1740 Barbados and the Leeward Islands complained about the navy's protection and petitioned Westminster for additional naval vessels.[145] North American newspapers reported that Spanish privateers successfully interrupted Jamaican commerce.[146] The navy was criticized for inactivity. "We have nothing remarkable stirring here," commented a Jamaican correspondent in November 1743. "The Fleet is safe moor'd at Port Royal, except a few cruising Ships, and the Admiral passing his Time in profound Tranquility with a Brace of Mistresses in the Country, and he is at present despised by every Body here."[147]

Even when praising active and successful naval commanders, the colonial press criticized most of the king's officers. The *Virginia Gazette* congratulated Warren, then a captain, for his successes against Spanish privateers, but Warren's fellow officers suffered by comparison. "If some of the Commanders of the King's Ships would take Example from the brave Captain Warren, who by his

Courage and Vigilence has taken 5 or 6 Spanish Prizes within these few Months, our Coast would be more secure, our Trade protected, as it ought to be, and they would better deserve his Majesty's Pay, than they have done some Time past; by lying close in a State of Indolence, instead of Activity."[148] Warren prompted a similar response when he arrived in Antigua in late 1743 as commodore of the Leeward Island station. "At his Arrival he ordered all the Men of War out of English Harbour, to their great Surprize, who would rather tarry and eat roast Beef and Pudding on Shore, than to fight at Sea for Sallet and Soop; but the Crabs begin to crawl out of the Mangroves, tho' with great Reluctance."[149]

The navy was under fire as well for its failure to protect European sea-lanes during the War of Jenkins' Ear. In London, Richard Partridge, Rhode Island's colonial agent, wrote that English merchants "complain heavily of their losses by the Spaniards which indeed has been very great . . . and now are applying to Parlmt for redress."[150] Although additional men-of-war were stationed in the Channel and the Bay of Biscay, British merchantmen still faced capture. Spanish privateers "are as thick and as little disturbed in the Channel and on the Coast of England as ever," the *Pennsylvania Gazette* reported in August 1742.[151]

France's entry into the conflict exacerbated the navy's problems. The increased number of enemy prize actions presented in Tables 6.1 and 6.2 demonstrates the king's ships' inability to curb Spanish and French private men-of-war. Not surprisingly, North American and West Indian colonists continued their barrage of criticism of the navy. After publishing a report that three Spanish privateers captured a vessel within sight of Charles Town, the *South-Carolina Gazette* commented that the king's officers had not pursued the enemy because of concern about the hurricane season. The *Gazette* then snidely suggested the navy had arbitrarily lengthened the storm season to excuse their inactivity.[152]

South Carolina Governor Glen indicated his dissatisfaction with the navy in 1746. Writing to Admiral Warren, Glen emphasized the importance of active naval patrols on the vulnerable Carolina coast. "You are perfectly acquainted with every circumstance relating to this province. It is needless for me to enter into particular details of it, further than to say that the security of our trade and the safety of the colony is in great measure dependent upon the protection of His Majesty's ships of war stationed here." Despite this disclaimer, Glen proceeded to lecture Warren on the importance of active naval officers. "Nothing but ships of force cruising upon the coast can deter privateers from watching for our trade, and even landing on our coast. They have done [so] (alas, with impunity) within these last few days, and carried off the people that were the guard of one of our lookouts." Glen wanted more warships on the Carolina station. To get them he emphasized the value of South Carolina's trade with Great Britain, and closed with an unsubtle reference to the Admiralty. "For these reasons (as all this is well known to the lords of the Admiralty) I make no doubt that they will have given orders for other ships to attend on the service of this province. Until such assistance arrives, I thought it my duty to represent to you the present situation of this frontier colony, having neither ship nor sloop. Therefore I desire you will send us such assistance as you can spare."[153] Apparently Warren was unable to satisfy the Carolinians because complaints about the navy and reports of enemy privateers infesting the coast continued until the hostilities ended.[154]

West Indian merchants and legislators also bombarded imperial authorities with criticisms of inadequate protection after France joined the conflict. Peter Warren defended himself and Capt. Charles Knowles against complaints from Barbados merchants in 1745. "For my own part, I have done all in my power to protect them and all the colonies and islands where I have been during my stay at these places. If it had not too much appearance of vanity, I could send their lordships public testimonies of satisfaction I have given in general here, and to that island [Barbados] in particular from which the complaint has arisen."[155] Warren survived this criticism, doubtless because of his excellent record against Spanish and French cruisers. Other commanders were not so fortunate. In 1746 enemy warships successfully raided Antigua's commerce. Philadelphia merchant John Reynell commented on these losses to his London friend, Daniel Flexney, and laid the blame squarely on Commodore Lee, commander of the Leeward Island station. "It cannot be denied but that there has abundance of Vessels been taken off of the Island of Antigua very much owing to the Neglect of Commodore Lee who has taken hardly any care to protect the Trade of that Island by keeping Cruisers out but has laid in the Harbour with the King's Ships, and suffered the Merchants Vessells to be taken almost under his Nose which is a most cruel Affair."[156] Antigua businessmen concurred with Reynell's analysis and called for Lee's removal. The island's legislators bitterly complained to

London, and their political clout compelled the Admiralty to relieve Lee of command at the end of 1746.[157]

Although the Admiralty received complaints throughout the war, it would be incorrect to view the navy as having been totally inactive. Occasionally, the colonists applauded the efforts of the king's ships. Lord Banff, commander of HMS *Hastings,* the Virginia station ship, was even the subject of a poem.

> SCOTIA boasts thy Birth, thy Actions, Fame;
> BANFF, is thy Title: Now a glorious Name!
> Ensigns of Honour shall around thy Breast
> Thy Trophies crown the British Souls carest.
> Hence sure of GEORGE'S aid and Neptune's Smiles,
> Iberian Pride shall dread our Western Isles.[158]

The *South-Carolina Gazette,* usually one of the navy's strongest critics, also praised naval commanders on occasion. In September 1744 when Capt. William Newnham, commander of HM Snow *Spy,* departed the Carolina station for England, the *Gazette* applauded his service. "During Capt. Newnham's Stay here, he has given uncommon Satisfaction; as have also all the other Commanders of his Majesty's Ships *at present* on this Station [emphasis in original]."[159] Again in 1747 the navy received a compliment (albeit a left-handed one) instead of criticism from the *Gazette* when the paper declared the old proverb "that to send a British Man of War after a French Privateer, was but sending a Cow after a Hare" was no longer true.[160]

With hundreds of Spanish and French privateers chasing British merchantmen in the West Indies, North America, and Europe, the Royal Navy faced an arduous, indeed an impossible, task. The frequent criticism of the navy's efforts from throughout the empire, though exaggerated at times, demonstrates that Europe's most powerful navy could not protect wartime commerce adequately. There were simply too many enemy predators. Royal Navy officers realized these insurmountable difficulties. Peter Warren, an active and successful commander, stated the problem succinctly. "Were the whole British fleet employed here [American waters] for their protection only they could not secure them from falling into the hands of the enemy."[161]

V

Chapters 5 and 6 have demonstrated that the lure of privateering off the North American coast and in the Caribbean characterized the wars of 1739–1748. The bulk of the conflict's maritime activity did not consist of great arrays of men-of-war engaging each other or of ships of the line shelling stout citadels to conquer enemy cities. The scramble to capture prizes, not territorial conquest, was the top priority. The alleged Spanish depredations during the 1730s had caused hostilities to erupt in 1739, and the attempt to capture merchantmen or to elude warships was the primary activity in American waters until the Peace of Aix-la-Chapelle ended the struggle.

The Spanish, French, and British colonies expended much effort during the maritime prize war. Merchants in Havana, St. Augustine, Cap François, and Martinique, and their counterparts in Newport, New York, Jamaica, and New Providence, sent out hundreds of privateers to seize enemy merchantmen. Thousands of mariners, attracted by the prospect of plunder, sailed on these warships. Interest in the prize war, however, was clearly not limited to its participants. Because of enemy activity, Philadelphians and Bostonians, Connecticut Yankees and the Carolina gentry, Chesapeake tobacco growers and West Indian sugar planters, displayed a keen awareness of maritime engagements. Merchants like Henry Laurens and John Reynell, who chose not to invest in privateers, were just as interested in and informed of prize actions as businessmen, like John Bannister and Robert Pringle, who did. Although the Laurenses and the Reynells might not gain windfall profits from successful prize actions, they could certainly suffer substantial losses from enemy victories.

The wide geographic theaters of operations reinforced the prize war's impact on the belligerents' New World empires. Merchantmen sailing in virtually every area of the Atlantic from Newfoundland to the equator risked capture by an enemy cruiser. The agricultural staple trades of the Carolinas, the Chesapeake, and especially the Caribbean sustained losses at the hands of private and public men-of-war. The predators were well-aware of the major avenues of commerce and timed their voyages to coincide with the height of the shipping season in each theater of operations. Their ability to disrupt trade was graphically demonstrated off the Delaware capes in 1747 and 1748 when French and Spanish privateers brought the commercial traffic of Philadelphia to a halt.

The interruption of trade caused by privateers demonstrates the inability of nation-states in the mideighteenth century to protect commerce. Superior to her French and Spanish counterparts, Britannia may have ruled the waves, but the king's ships could not prevent the loss of hundreds of vessels and hundreds of thousands of pounds sterling in cargoes to enemy privateers. Historians, concentrating on the navy and the growing power of the eighteenth-century state, have painted a picture of increasing safety and stability in transoceanic commerce.[162] Yet during the wars of 1739–1748, the most powerful European navy could not check the enemy's privateers. Spanish and French prize actions increased in the conflict's latter years, and only peace halted their progress. At the same time, the Spanish and French navies were unable to stop British colonial private men-of-war.

Privateering was one of the most important facets of imperial warfare for eighteenth-century American ports. Newspapers in Boston, New York, Philadelphia, and Charles Town devoted more coverage to prize actions than to other New World military events. The siege of Louisbourg, of course, attracted tremendous attention, but it was largely limited to the summer of 1745. Alexander Hamilton, the peripatetic Maryland physician, could well have been describing the content of the colonial press and not a fellow traveler's conversation when he wrote "a younge gentleman . . . gave me a whole paquet of news about prizes and privateers, which is now the whole subject of discourse."[163]

Chapter 7

THE IMPACT OF PRIVATEERING ON COMMERCE

Hundreds of warships plying the North Atlantic and intercepting merchantmen seriously crippled the colonial commerce of Britain and her enemies. Chapters 5 and 6 have revealed that virtually all the belligerents' transatlantic trade faced capture. Privateers preyed on vessels carrying fish, flour, and other produce from northern North America. Ships laden with tobacco from the Chesapeake and rice from the Carolinas became lucrative prizes. The Caribbean's rich sugar commerce attracted even more captors than the other cruising theaters. Captains sufficiently skillful or lucky to elude capture in American waters ran another gauntlet of predators as they approached Europe. Merchants suffered from privateering even when their vessels successfully completed voyages because warships caused enormous increases in the costs of doing business. This chapter analyzes the economic impact of privateering during the wars of 1739–1748.

Although private men-of-war infested Atlantic sea-lanes throughout the hostilities, assessing their financial impact is difficult. First, there are two major levels of analysis, the national (aggregate) viewpoint and the vantage point of the individual privateer. On the national level, what effect did British colonial privateering have on Spanish and French commerce and how did British Atlantic trade fare against the enemy's private men-of-war? On a more personal level, how successful (or unsuccessful) was an individual privateer? Did the owners and crew of, for example, the

Revenge of Newport or the *Greyhound* of New York, earn or lose money from their prize actions? Was privateering profitable for the individuals who risked their lives and capital? A second major economic issue related to privateering concerns the indirect expense that private men-of-war imposed on the Atlantic merchant community. The number of vessels captured represents the most dramatic evidence of the privateers' destructive impact, but was this the sole measure of their effect on commerce? How did privateering affect freight rates, insurance premiums, and seamen's wages? Although the answers to these questions are enigmatic and elusive, it can be shown that privateering exerted an enormous influence on Atlantic commerce during the 1740s.

I

American privateers seriously disrupted the commerce of Britain's enemies. The number of captures is the clearest evidence of their impact. More than 800 vessels surrendered to colonial private men-of-war. (See Table 7.1.) Although assessing the value of these prize vessels and cargoes is difficult, an informed estimate can be offered. The data file contains information concerning the

TABLE 7.1
Nationality of Prizes Captured by British Colonial Privateers, 1739–1748

Nationality	N	%
French	308	37.2
Spanish	226	27.3
Enemy of Great Britain[a]	195	23.5
British[b]	65	7.8
Neutral[c]	34	4.1
Pirates	1	.1
Totals	829	100.0

Note: The number of prizes should be viewed as an understatement. The press probably did not report every capture. Moreover, some newspaper accounts were too vague to be included in the data file.

[a]Includes prizes of unknown nationality. The colonial press usually referred to these as "enemy prize" or simply "prize."

[b]Comprises British vessels recaptured en route to enemy ports.

[c]Includes Dutch, Danish, Portuguese, and (before 1744) French vessels.

value of some of these prizes. Using these data, it is possible to determine an average value for the prizes. Multiplying this average prize value by the total of 829 yields an estimate of the value of enemy shipping seized by colonial private men-of-war. The data file includes values expressed in pounds or pieces of eight for 109 prizes captured by British colonial privateers. After these values were converted from colonial currencies and Spanish coinage into their sterling equivalents, they totaled £968,972.[1] Values for an additional 44 captures were based on appraisals of the worth of the cargoes and prize vessels.

Of the 829 successful prize actions involving British colonial privateers, 532 (64 percent) contained data concerning the prize's cargo. Unfortunately, much of this information was rather vague. The cargoes of 38 prizes, for example, were described as being "rich," while 10 others were characterized as "of no great value." An additional 65 enemy vessels were privateers, so it is difficult to determine if they carried cargoes. Specific commodities found in the prizes' holds were listed in 229 cases. The *Medusa of Nants,* captured by Capt. John Sibbald in the Philadelphia ship *Wilmington,* for example, carried "Sugars, Indigo, and some Pieces of Eight."[2] The New York privateer *Elizabeth,* commanded by Thomas Barnes, took the ship *Le Bon* in 1744 as it transported salt, flour, and cordage to Cape Breton from La Rochelle.[3] "A very valuable Cargo of Dry Goods" became the property of William Duthy, captain of the Charles Town privateer *Mercury,* after he seized the French sloop *Usrow Angelica.*[4] John Albine in the *Catherine* dispatched a French sloop to New York "laden with Sugar and Rum."[5] Captain Strawbridge in the Newport privateer *Prince Frederick* captured a French snow in 1748, "her Cargoe consisting of Sugar, Cocoa and Coffee, reckon'd to be a pretty good Prize."[6]

These cases listing specific commodities suggest the broad outlines of the French and Spanish goods intercepted by British colonial privateers. Not surprisingly, given the most popular cruising theaters of American private men-of-war, West Indian products accounted for the largest proportion of cargoes. Sugar, indigo, cocoa, molasses, rum, and coffee comprised the goods in about half of these prize cargoes. Vessels carrying European products, especially "dry goods," "bale goods" (which included textiles, hardware, and other manufactured goods), and wine, accounted for about one-third of the prize ladings. The remaining cases contained cargoes of provisions (including beef, fish, and livestock), money, naval stores, timber, hides, and other semiprocessed goods.

Although these cases indicate the contents of prize cargoes, they could not be used to estimate the values for those cargoes because they did not provide quantity breakdowns. Without some idea of the number of hogsheads of sugar and rum or barrels of flour and beef or hundredweights of cocoa and indigo, calculating even rough estimates for the value of the prize cargoes would be impossible. Fortunately, other cases in the data file contained more detailed information concerning prize cargoes.

Seventy-two prizes provided quantity breakdowns for all or some of their cargoes. Captains Morris and Ingorsol, cruising in consort in 1745, captured a French snow carrying "200 Hogsheads of Sugar, &c."[7] *Le Barrie,* a French prize taken by the New York privateer *Triton,* was transporting twenty tons of wine and fifteen tons of flour as well as some soap, candles, and dry goods to Cap François when it was forced to strike its colors.[8] Capt. Thomas Greenall in the privateer *Hester* took a French ship laden with 750 hogsheads of sugar on 5 December 1745.[9] The *St. Anne,* a French ship sent to New York by Capt. Martin Bicker, commander of the privateer *Phoenix,* was conveying 200 hogsheads of sugar and "some Coffee, Cotton and Ginger" from Guadeloupe to France in 1748.[10] Using eighteenth-century price data it was possible to estimate the value of the cargoes in forty-four of these cases.[11] These estimates are conservative because only those products with quantity data were included in the appraisals. In the examples just cited, the soap, candles, and dry goods were excluded from the estimate of *Le Barrie*'s cargo. The value for the *St. Anne*'s prize goods was based only on the 200 hogsheads of sugar; the coffee, cotton, and ginger were ignored. Since the prize vessel itself was a valuable piece of property, an appraisal of the ship was added to each of these estimates.[12]

Despite the problems encountered in preparing these estimates, the results proved to be rather close to the average value of the 109 prizes that contained recorded values. The average for the 109 prizes was £8,890 sterling; the mean for the 44 estimates was £9,691. Using these estimates, the 829 prizes taken by American privateers were worth about £7,561,000 sterling. This substantial amount was roughly equivalent to 30 percent of the total trade (exports plus imports) of France and its American colonies during 1739–1748.[13]

King George's War seriously disrupted French colonial trade. Commerce between France and the West Indies fell by nearly 50 percent from 1743 to 1745.[14] The activities of French fishermen on the Grand Banks also declined. Granville, a leading French port in the Newfoundland fishery, dispatched an average of seventy-six fishing vessels per year during 1730–1744 but an average of only five vessels per year from 1745 to 1748.[15] Trade between New France and the French West Indies also suffered. Exports from the islands to Quebec dropped 39 percent from 1743 to 1744. In 1745, Quebec's Caribbean imports were 72 percent below prewar levels. Exports from New France to the Antilles followed a similar pattern, falling by nearly 60 percent from 1743 to 1744. Despite a modest recovery in 1745, the value of Canadian shipments to the Caribbean still registered a decline of 43 percent compared to 1743.[16]

Spain's colonial commerce also suffered as British sea power caused Spanish merchants to suspend regular trade with America.[17] The major fleets that supplied the Spanish colonies with goods and returned with treasure did not sail in the 1740s. No *flotas* (the trading fleets that operated between Cadiz and Veracruz) or *galeones* (the fleets sailing between Cadiz and Cartagena and Portobello) embarked during the conflict. Instead, the Crown authorized individual merchantmen carrying registered cargoes (hence their designation as "register ships") to engage in the colonial trade. Though less predictable than regularly scheduled *flotas* and *galeones,* the register ships failed to elude British predators. Nearly 60 percent of these vessels were captured, and Spanish exports to America declined. Imports from the Spanish West Indies fell as well. Cuban tobacco remittances to Spain fell markedly from prewar levels. The situation deteriorated as the conflict dragged on, and remittances for 1745–1749 fell 17 percent compared to 1740–1744. Spanish tobacco consumption declined noticeably and did not reach pre-1740 levels until 1762. Cuban sugar exports also slowed to a trickle. Trade within the Spanish Caribbean dropped as well. The total value (imports plus exports) of Havana's nonpeninsular commerce dipped 54 percent between 1735 and 1740. Although trade had recovered somewhat by 1745, Havana's Caribbean imports and exports were only two-thirds of their 1735 values.[18] Despite these setbacks, much treasure from Mexico ultimately arrived in Spain. On three occasions treasure fleets eluded British naval vessels and privateers.[19]

TABLE 7.2

Home Ports of British Colonial Privateers that Captured Prizes,
1739–1748

Port	N	%
Boston	60	7.2
Newport	194	23.4
New York City	230	27.7
Philadelphia	64	7.7
Charles Town	29	3.5
West Indies[a]	152	18.3
Other[b]	14	1.7
Consorts from Different Ports	70	8.4
Unknown	16	1.9
Totals	829	100.0

[a]Includes Bermuda.

[b]Includes Cape Fear, N.C.; Norfolk, Va.; Frederica, Ga.; Portsmouth, N.H.; and New Jersey.

The home ports of successful American privateers are presented in Table 7.2. New York, Newport, and the West Indian ports captured the great majority of the prizes, and the data also suggest that New York's private men-of-war were the most successful on a per-privateer basis. They furnished 23 percent of the yearly privateers (see Table 5.1) yet seized 28 percent of the prizes. Only Boston, with a much smaller number of both privateers and prizes, matched this record.[20] The New Yorkers' success may have resulted in part from the use of larger, more heavily manned vessels than were employed by their Newport and West Indian counterparts; Manhattan merchants fitted out more brigs and fewer sloops.[21]

British colonial privateers, of course, were not the only predators raiding Atlantic sea-lanes. Unfortunately for American merchants, Spanish and French private men-of-war were also active in the prize war, and they dealt a damaging blow to British colonial trade. The data file lists 635 cases of British and American vessels captured in the Caribbean and off the coast of North America. Not surprisingly, these losses are reflected in British import and export statistics. An analysis of these records for 1740–1748 reveals that Britain's total trade (imports plus exports) with its American colonies fluctuated with the ebb and

TABLE 7.3

Britain's Trade with the American Colonies in Pounds Sterling
(Official Prices), 1740–1748

Year	Imports from Britain	Exports to Britain	Trade Trade[a]
1740	£1,258,653	£2,217,919	£3,476,572
1741	1,438,678	2,449,919	3,888,597
1742	1,483,300	2,022,115	3,505,415
1743	1,438,827	2,439,292	3,878,119
1744	1,033,381	1,947,778	2,981,609
1745	940,072	1,731,158	2,671,230
1746	1,456,719	1,841,497	3,298,216
1747	1,351,106	1,745,122	3,096,228
1748	1,498,077	2,533,082	4,031,159

Sources: Charles Whitworth, *State of the Trade of Great Britain in Its Imports and Exports, Progressively from the Year 1697* (London, 1776), 44–52. Whitworth's statistics have been augmented using Jacob M. Price, "New Time Series for Scotland's and Britain's Trade with the Thirteen Colonies and States, 1740–1791," *William and Mary Quarterly,* 3d Ser., XXXII (1975), 322–325.

Note: The colonies included in this table are the mainland provinces from Georgia to Massachusetts, Newfoundland, Antigua, Barbados, Jamaica, Montserat, Nevis, and St. Kitts. The table begins with 1740, the first year included in Price's "New Time Series."

[a]Total trade is the sum of imports and exports.

flow of the prize war.[22] (See Table 7.3) The limited nature of the War of Jenkins' Ear did not seriously interrupt Britain's imperial commerce. France's entry into the conflict signaled a sharp escalation of the prize war and produced a marked decline in the volume of Britain's colonial trade. Exports from the British West Indies to the mother country fell by 18 percent in 1744; British imports from North America declined by 25 percent. Colonial imports also suffered. Caribbean purchases of British goods dropped by £162,681 sterling (down 37 percent) while North American consumption decreased by £201,511 (down 23 percent). Britain's total trade with the colonies dipped even more in 1745, the prize war's busiest year. British colonial commerce revived in the later stages of the conflict, but it did not return to prewar levels until after the Peace of Aix-la-Chapelle.

The total value of prizes captured by enemy warships did not represent the total cost of the prize war. Although each belligerent lost hundreds of thousands of pounds sterling in cargoes and vessels, these losses were partially offset (at the national level) by captures made by their own privateers. As the historian Ralph Davis has argued, "It is far from certain, however, that captures, numerous as they were, inflicted as much damage on the shipowning community as other, less dramatic, features of war."[23] These other features included huge increases in freight rates, marine insurance premiums, and seamen's wages, which substantially escalated wartime business costs.

Merchants feared that the uncertainty of the sea-lanes caused by enemy warships would decrease the volume of shipping engaged in maritime trade. Fewer vessels meant higher freight rates. Charles Town's merchants were especially concerned about inadequate shipping because of the port's small merchant fleet and proximity to enemy privateers. Rice merchant Robert Pringle worried continually about the lack of shipping needed to transport Carolina rice to European markets. "We have the greatest Crop of Rice this Year by much that has ever yet been produc'd in the Province," Pringle wrote to a Hull, England, correspondent, "& if the Apprehensions of a War Continue, We are afraid of not having Shipping enough to Carry it off[f]."[24] This dearth of shipping caused higher freight rates. "Freight will Govern according to the News we may receive wether we may expect Peace or Warr, Affairs at home seeming as yet to be Still Doubtful."[25] In addition to higher freight rates, Pringle feared inadequate shipping would lower the price of Carolina rice and increase the costs of imported goods. "If the Shipping doe not arrive it [the Carolina rice crop] will be very low in Price this Season & as the Continued apprehensions of a Warr makes navigation Precarious, the Produce of the Islands, Vizt. Rum, Sugar, & Molasses will be Scarce here & high in Price."[26]

The rates for transporting Charles Town rice to London listed in Pringle's letterbook confirm his prewar fears. The cost of shipping the colony's staple to its European markets nearly doubled during the wars of 1739–1748. In December 1739 Charles Town residents learned about the Spanish war. Pringle wrote his brother in London that he was "apprehensive that we shall want Shipping to Carry off

our Crop of Rice & believe Freight for London will be at £3.10/
[sterling] per Ton."[27] Six months later freight had risen by more than
20 percent. "We have not had so many Shipping here this Season as
usual occasion'd by the War," Pringle explained to Thomas Burrill,
"so that Freight is very high being at £4.5/per ton for London."[28]
Freight continued to climb upward in 1742 and 1743. In late 1743
the constant rumors concerning French entry into the war made the
picture even bleaker. "Freight is not Likely to be less this Season as
we have this Year a very Large Crop of Rice," Pringle declared.
"Shipping will be Scarce & Freight high As long as the Warr
Continues and more especially if a French Warr should happen
which seems to be very Likely."[29]

After France joined the conflict, Pringle's letters became even
gloomier. He wrote Boston merchant John Erving, "As we
apprehend a Scarcity of Shipping here next Crop by reason of the
War with France & Spain, it is Thought Freight will be high tho at
[the] Sametime Our Produce being of but Small Value [we] wont
afford it."[30] In January 1745 Pringle despaired that bills of
exchange could not be obtained in Charles Town, the price of rice
continued to fall, and freight rates soared to £6 sterling per ton.[31]
Freight rates continued to rise until the hostilities ended. Charles
Town merchant Henry Laurens noted it cost £6.10.0 sterling to ship
a ton of rice to London in the spring of 1748, an increase of 86
percent over 1739 levels.[32]

The increasing freight rates caused by the prize war were not
limited to Carolina's rice trade. The Chesapeake's extensive
tobacco commerce also experienced sharp increases in shipping
costs. Before the war erupted, freight charges for Maryland tobacco
fluctuated very little. In the peacetime period, 1714–1738, the
average cost of shipping tobacco to London was just under £7
sterling per ton.[33] This price stability ended in the first shipping
season during the War of Jenkins' Ear. Freight charges in 1740
jumped to £9–10 per ton, an increase of more than 35 percent over
the peacetime rate. (See Table 7.4.) Freight averaged about 30
percent higher than pre-1740 levels throughout the Anglo-Spanish
war. When the hostilities escalated in 1744, the cost of shipping
tobacco rose again. The highest freight rates occurred in 1747 and
1748, when French and Spanish privateers were most active in
North American waters.[34] The costs of transporting Maryland's
staple to market during King George's War were more than 60
percent higher than prewar levels.

TABLE 7.4
Tobacco Freight Rates, Maryland to London 1739–1749

Year	Rate Per Ton (£ Sterling)	Increase Over Prewar Level (%)
1739	7	—
1740	9–10*	35.7
1741	9	28.6
1742	9	28.6
1743	9	28.6
1744	9–12*	50.0
1745	12–13*	78.6
1746	13–14*	92.9
1747	16	128.6
1748	8–16*	71.4
1749	7	—

Source: James F. Shepherd and Gary M. Walton, *Shipping, Maritime Trade, and the Economic Development of Colonial North America* (Cambridge, 1972), 191–192.

*The midpoint of the range of freight rates (i.e., 9.5 for 1740, 10.5 for 1744, etc.) was used to calculate the percentage increase in transportation costs.

The maritime prize war also increased the cost of transporting West Indian sugar. The proximity of British, French, and Spanish Caribbean colonies attracted numerous warships, and the West Indies comprised the busiest New World theater of operations for the belligerents' private men-of-war. This resulted in soaring sugar freight rates. The normal peacetime cost of shipping a hundredweight of sugar from Barbados to London was 3s. 6d. sterling. This increased by a shilling (29 percent) in response to the declaration of war against Spain. At the height of King George's War, freight reached 7s. 6d.–8s., more than double the peacetime rate.[35] Vessels engaged in the West Indian-North American trade also experienced hefty increases in transportation costs. Normal peacetime freights between Philadelphia and the West Indies averaged about 5s. a hundredweight. The prize war pushed this up to 7s. 6d.–9s., an increase of 50–80 percent.[36]

Philadelphia merchants worried about higher business costs

because of the prize war. "Thou must Endeavour now to buy very Cheap because I expect Fr[t]. and insurance will be higher than usual," John Reynell advised a London correspondent in early 1740.[37] Spanish privateering successes and wartime mobilization caused a shortage of shipping and thus higher freight rates in the Quaker City, America's second largest port. Reynell described these changing business conditions as he informed another associate why he had been unable to secure a vessel to transport some lumber. "[I have] waited to See whether [I] could give thee any Expectation of Loading a Vessel with Staves &c and have now to advise thee that [I] believe it will not be in my Power to do it." Freight rates soared, and many shipowners were reluctant to send out their vessels, especially if the cargo was only a prosaic lading of timber. Reynell continued, "The Fr.[t] thou mentionest is Large, and formerly we could get 'em carryed for much less. but as 3 or 4 of our Vessells have been lately taken by the Spaniards and 8 or 10 taken up to Carry off Soldiers, and a great many to Carry Provisions for the Men of War &c it has made Vessells Scarce and Fr.[t] high so that hardly any Body cares to let out their Vessells to Carry only Lumber."[38]

French entry into the war only made matters worse. Reynell wrote in July 1744, "Since my last Warr has been Declared here against the French King, which we are afraid will very much Effect our Trade. I believe it will Occasion English goods to rise with us, for it will be more difficult to get 'em. Insurance will be high, and fewer Vessells will be coming and perhaps some of them will be taken."[39] That fall business slumped noticeably, prompting Reynell to comment, "Trading is Exceeding dead here[;] hardly anything goes forward but Privateering."[40] For a principled Quaker, the business outlook was bleak indeed. Numerous other references in Reynell's letters indicate wartime freight rates remained high.

As Reynell's letters suggest, higher premiums for marine insurance accompanied rising transportation costs. Privateers increased the risks of maritime commerce. As a result, more merchants sought insurance for their vessels and cargoes. The greater wartime risk and the increased demand for policies escalated marine insurance rates. An examination of premium income and payments for losses of the London Assurance Company, one of the two joint-stock marine insurance houses in England, illustrates the unsettling impact the prize war had on maritime commerce.[41]

Immediately preceding the War of Jenkins' Ear, the company's premium income averaged just under ten thousand pounds sterling per annum. With the advent of hostilities, revenue soared. In 1741 premium income reached thirty thousand pounds. Receipts more than doubled when France entered the war, and London Assurance took in nearly eighty thousand pounds in premiums in 1744–1745. After a brief downturn in 1746, premium income topped one hundred thousand pounds toward the end of King George's War. The fluctuations in the company's premium revenue closely followed the events of the prize war.

The London Assurance Company's payments for losses also approximated the conflict's contours. Payments in 1740 were approximately twelve thousand pounds. They rose to eighteen thousand pounds in 1741 as the Spanish prize war increased losses. Outlays declined, as the prize war did, until France declared war on Britain. Payments for losses in 1744–1745 jumped to nearly fifty thousand pounds. Before the war ended, London Assurance's payments to policyholders approached eighty thousand pounds a year.

The company's premium income increased because more merchants purchased insurance and because insurance rates rose. These rates responded to the risks of capture by enemy predators. Premiums for vessels sailing in the English Channel or the West Indies, both favorite privateer cruising grounds, were higher than those for voyages to and from safer locations. Rates between London and Genoa in 1739–1740 reflect this pattern. In June 1739 insurance for a voyage between these ports cost 21s. percent. In July, the premium rose to three pounds. By August, the rate reached five guineas, and from October 1739 to March 1740, it hit eight guineas percent (that is eight guineas per one hundred guineas value). Policyholders could save two guineas from the August rate and three guineas from the October–March rate if their vessels sailed in a convoy, which clearly reveals the influence of the risks of capture on insurance rates.[42]

The business activities of William Braund, a prominent English insurance underwriter, reveal that premiums charged by private underwriters paralleled London Assurance's increases. In 1741 Braund had the misfortune of losing thirty-five risks. He suffered twenty-two losses in November alone, the result of Spanish privateering successes. The consequence of these disasters was a tremendous increase in insurance premiums, especially for vessels sailing in dangerous waters. When Braund insured a ship bound from St. Kitts to London the next winter, he charged the high premium of 40 percent of the value of the ship and its cargo.[43]

The proximity of enemy colonies and the lucrative sugar trade made the Caribbean a risky area for merchant shipping. As a result, insurance costs for voyages between London and the sugar islands were high. The standard peacetime rate for a passage from Barbados to London was 2½ to 5 percent of the value of the vessel and its cargo, depending on the season. Insurance for Jamaican voyages fluctuated between 5 and 8 percent. These rates increased when the War of Jenkins' Ear began. Jamaicans paid 12 percent while Barbados residents remitted 7 percent. This differential reflected the risks of enemy warships. Located in the center of the most dangerous privateering waters, Jamaican commerce was more vulnerable than the trade of Barbados. When France declared war in 1744, insurance rates for Barbados climbed to 25 guineas because the island was near Martinique, a center of French privateering.[44]

North American colonists trading with the West Indies also faced higher wartime insurance premiums. The average peacetime rate from the mainland to a British sugar colony was around 4 percent. This figure soared during the wars of 1739–1748. Premiums for voyages from Salem, Massachusetts, to Barbados rose to 18–23 percent during 1747–1748; voyages from Salem to Jamaica reached 23–25 percent in the same years.[45]

Philadelphia merchants complained about the inflated cost of marine insurance during the wars of 1739–1748. John Reynell grumbled that premiums for a voyage from Pennsylvania to Bristol, England, jumped nearly 78 percent during the War of Jenkins' Ear.[46] After France joined the conflict, Reynell thought insurance might be prohibitively expensive. "I am very uneasy about the Goods I have already writ for," he informed London merchant Elias Bland in June 1744, "on Acco‌ᵗ. of the rumour we have of Insurance being got up very high, so high that if it be true, we shall never be able to get the Money for them again that they Cost." Hearing that premiums might reach 20 percent, Reynell instructed Bland to ship the goods on several different ships without insurance and simply hoped for the best.[47] Although Philadelphia premiums did not reach the rumored 20 percent, they were high, as Reynell indicated to London merchant Thomas Taylor. "Thou orders me to Insure the full Value [on a cargo of Philadelphia goods bound to Jamaica], which can't be Done here, without giving what I judge to high a Premᵐ. 15 per Cent at least."[48] Insurance remained high in the spring of 1747. Philadelphia merchant Samuel Powel asked David Barclay, his London correspondent, to insure goods shipped on the *Boneta Packet,* bound from Philadelphia to Jamaica, but only if the premium did not exceed 14 percent.[49] Premiums in London and Philadelphia were so high that shippers explored the possibilities of insuring their goods in Holland.[50]

British merchants were not alone in facing dramatic increases in insurance rates. Spanish and French businessmen also faced spiraling marine insurance premiums. Normal French peacetime rates of 3 or 4 percent in 1742 jumped to 6 percent in 1743.[51] One month after the 1744 declaration of war, the owners of the *Trois Marie* had to pay 16 percent for insurance on a passage to Canada from Rouen. By the end of May underwriters in Rouen charged between 26 and 36 percent for a transatlantic voyage.[52] At the height of the prize war insurance rates varied from 35 percent in Cadiz to 40 percent in most French cities.[53] The *Pennsylvania Gazette* cheerfully informed its readers of these added costs to French merchants. "We are assured, that Premiums on Insurance on the *French* Ships from St. Domingo for France, are risen from 25 to 45 Guineas per Cent. a certain sign how fearful the Trading French are of their Property, when the British Men of War keep the Seas."[54]

The records of Robert Dugard's Société du Canada, an important Rouen mercantile house, demonstrate the influence of escalating insurance rates and the catastrophic impact of losing vessels. Dugard's company traded with New France, Louisbourg, and the French West Indies. During the peacetime years from 1729 (the company's founding year) to 1742, the company's assets rose from 22,001 to 620,182 *livres.* The war brought disaster, however. Insurance premiums jumped tenfold between 1742–1743 and 1744–1745. Such increases made it difficult to turn a profit even from a successfully completed voyage. In 1744 Dugard's ship *Union* sailed safely from Rouen to Martinique but still recorded a loss of 31,363 *livres* because of the high cost (28 percent) of insurance.[55] Some of Dugard's other vessels were less fortunate; British predators captured one-third of the company's ships.[56] Dale Miquelon, the historian of the Société du Canada, has summarized the conflict's effect on Dugard's enterprise: "The war with the English had destroyed a magnificent commercial undertaking just at the moment when it had ceased to require the reinvestment of every *écu* it earned and was expected to begin paying handsome annual dividends. No one had the heart to rebuild it."[57]

Ironically, British merchants probably paid higher insurance premiums because of British privateering successes since French shipowners obtained insurance in England from the two joint-stock companies and the private underwriters.[58] Many Englishmen opposed this seemingly unpatriotic commerce because it cushioned the financial damage the enemy suffered from successful British prize actions. If Parliament prevented French merchants from obtaining insurance in Britain, the enemy's colonial trade would suffer a serious blow. The lack of British insurance, the *Pennsylvania Gazette* observed, "cannot fail of being extreamly fatal to the French Commerce, more especially that which they carry on to the West-Indies."[59] Besides easing financial losses from prize actions, insuring French vessels increased costs for British businessmen. The *Pennsylvania Gazette* expressed a widespread desire when it hoped British privateering victories would cease to make this business profitable for English insurers.[60] Newport merchant John Bannister worried that French losses would drain the assets from English insurance companies and threaten their solvency. He urged William Handley, a London business associate, to collect insurance for the loss of the *Lee Frigate* as soon as possible. "Pray Loose no Time in Recovering this Insurance as in all probability our Ships of War will destroy the French Navigation in the West Indies which of Course will Very much hurt many of your underwriters."[61] Eventually, English insurance of French commerce became sufficiently unpopular to prompt parliamentary legislation prohibiting the practice in 1748. This action lapsed with the Peace of Aix-la-Chapelle, however, and British firms insured French shipping during wartime until Parliament ended this business for good in 1793.[62]

The dramatic escalation in merchant seamen's wages was another business cost that soared during the wars of 1739–1748. Like the increases in freight and insurance rates, the maritime prize war helped cause the higher wage bills. The shortage of mariners prevented full complements on merchantmen as well as the king's ships, privateers, and colonial coast guard vessels. This excess demand for seamen raised monthly wages in the merchant marine from the normal peacetime level of twenty-three to twenty-five shillings to fifty to fifty-five shillings during the height of the conflict.[63] Longer delays in port while shipowners tried to secure full complements further increased business expenses.

Thus the prize war cost British, Spanish, and French commerce much more than the value of ships and cargoes captured by enemy cruisers. Although the majority of merchantmen completed their voyages safely during the hostilities, they were still affected by privateering. Freight rates rose dramatically. More merchants purchased insurance at inflated prices. Seamen's wages more than doubled. The severe manpower shortage forced vessels to ride at anchor while owners and agents frantically sought mariners. Waiting for convoys added to the turnaround time spent in port and caused prices to plummet when numerous vessels arrived simultaneously. The prize war caused all of these added expenses.

II

Although hundreds of British, Spanish, and French merchantmen struck their colors to private men-of-war, privateering was not an easy or safe way to earn a living. On the contrary, it was a difficult and often dangerous business. Privateers had to seek out prospective prizes, overtake them, ascertain if they were liable for seizure, subdue them, and then successfully dispatch them to a friendly port for condemnation. Each step in this process included problems and hazards. For many British colonial private men-of-war, the obstacles proved insurmountable. The total number of captures was large, but many individual privateers were unsuccessful.

Capturing an enemy merchantman was an arduous undertaking. After sighting a vessel, the privateer's first task was to determine the prospective prize's nationality. This was often difficult. Because the threat of capture always loomed over the horizon, shipowners frequently instructed their captains to avoid speaking with other vessels and steer clear of all other craft at sea. As a result, merchantmen fled at the first sight of a sail. Privateers, therefore, had to overhaul a sighted vessel to see if it belonged to the enemy and was liable for capture.

The journal of the Newport privateer sloop *Revenge* reveals the difficulties of overtaking merchantmen. "Saw a top Sail Vessell and a Sloop," reads the entry for 19 July 1741. "Bore down upon her but it Coming Calm could not Speak with her."[64] Poor weather conditions hindered the *Revenge* again on 29 July. "Saw a Sloop. Gave Chase but the Weather being Calm was forced to Gett out Our Oars. Fired our Bow Chase to bring her too, but we tacking about and the people in Confusion, Night Coming on, it being very Foggy, Coud not Speak to her."[65] On the morning of 3 August the *Revenge* chased a schooner. The pursuit persisted throughout the following afternoon, but with little success. "Att 5 PM. Gave her a Gun in hopes to bring her too, to know who she was, but she did not mind it neither hoisted any Colours. she bore down upon Us, then takt and bore away. We fired 10 Shott but all did not Signify for she hug'd her Wind and it Growing dark and having a Good pair of heels we lost Sight of her."[66]

Even overhauling a vessel and forcing it to come under a privateer's bow did not guarantee a successful prize action. Frequently private men-of-war discovered that a prospective prize belonged to a fellow countryman. "Saw a Sail under Our Lee Bow about a League Dist.," reads the *Revenge*'s journal for 15 July 1741. "All hands was Called upon Deck and Gott Ready to Receive her had she been an Enemy. We fired one of our Bow Chases and brot. him too. she was a Sloop from Nantucket."[67] This was only one of many similar disappointments during the *Revenge*'s cruise. Other predators shared this experience. The Philadelphia privateer *Marlborough*, commanded by Capt. Christopher Clymer, seemingly chased the entire British merchant fleet in 1745. The privateersmen returned home from a cruise during which they had stopped seventy vessels only to discover they were all British! "Tho' he [Clymer] has made an industrious Cruise," commented the *Pennsylvania Gazette*, "it has not proved a successful One."[68] Capt. George Walker, "commodore" of the Bristol, England, Royal Family Privateers, encountered similar bad luck in 1748.[69]

Some vessels stopped by American private men-of-war belonged to citizens of neutral countries and could not be legally captured. British colonial privateers were well aware of this fact. To obtain letters of marque, commanders were required to sign a sworn statement testifying that they would obey instructions issued by George II which clearly prohibited seizing neutral vessels. Moreover, privateer owners and commanders had to post a bond of fifteen hundred to three thousand pounds sterling (depending on the size of the crew) to insure compliance with the king's directives.[70]

Most American privateer commanders obeyed these instructions. In 1740 Capt. John Lush in a New York privateer, for example, stopped a merchantman which, proving to be a French neutral, he subsequently released.[71] On 17 September 1741 the Newport privateer sloop *Revenge* suffered a similar misfortune. Two days later the *Revenge* chased another vessel and pursued it throughout the night and all the next day. The *Revenge* finally overhauled its quarry only to discover that it had been chasing another French vessel. On 20 September the *Revenge* encountered yet another French craft.[72] So much time and effort expended on neutral vessels must have been discouraging.

Unfortunately for neutral merchants (and British diplomats), not all British colonial privateers scrupulously observed neutral rights. Neutral vessels, especially Dutch merchantmen, were captured throughout the conflict. British privateers usually justified their actions by claiming their quarry had been trading with the enemy which compromised the prize's neutrality.[73] Colonial admiralty judges often agreed with the privateers. On 9 January 1740 Massachusetts Vice-Admiralty Judge Robert Auchmuty condemned the *Amsterdam Post,* despite the fact the vessel was Dutch.[74] Samuel Pemberton, a Rhode Island admiralty judge, condemned three Dutch vessels in the fall of 1742 for trading with the Spanish.[75] Subsequent Rhode Island admiralty judges also condemned neutral vessels (usually Dutch) captured by American privateers.[76] Judges in other British colonies rendered decisions that adversely affected neutral merchantmen.[77]

Not surprisingly, British privateers irritated Dutch officials. In 1742 Curaçao merchants and mariners took direct action against three American private men-of-war. After learning that two privateers from St. Kitts and one from Rhode Island were careening at Aruba, the Dutch colonists dispatched a fourteen-gun ship with 140 men and captured the Englishmen. The Dutch then incarcerated the captains, whipped the crews, and sold the privateer vessels. "The Reason they assigned for this conduct was, that the said Privateers had some Time before taken a Dutch Ship, and so thought fit to make Reprisals,'' commented the *Pennsylvania Gazette.*[78]

The Dutch government also complained frequently through diplomatic channels about the illegal activities of British privateers. After numerous incidents, King George II ordered all privateer captains to sign a statement indicating they had read and would comply with a 1674 treaty of amity and friendship concluded between England and Holland.[79] This new requirement failed to solve the problem, and complaints continued throughout the war. In 1746 Dutch diplomats in London protested the actions of English privateers. Amsterdam authorities issued a not terribly subtle hint of reprisals unless London curbed the private men-of-war.[80] Capt. James Mann informed New York City officials that he had been detained by authorities in Curaçao for five days after the New York privateer *Dolphin*, commanded by Capt. Michael Beesley, had seized three Dutch sloops. Mann reported that "the People of Coracoa are very uneasy about this Affair."[81] The obviously illegal capture and subsequent condemnation of the Dutch ship *Vrow Dorthea* in Charles Town in 1748 embarrassed Henry Laurens. "The Condemnation or rather Seizure & Condemnation of that Ship is look'd upon here as a piece of Grand injustice not expected from Carolina."[82]

Although Dutch authorities protested illegal seizures, neutral prizes constituted a small proportion of the American privateers' successes. Only sixty-two captures involving neutral vessels (fifty-three of them Dutch) appear in the data file. British colonial privateers seized only thirty-four of these vessels. Although the number of neutral captures is probably understated, neutral vessels did not comprise a large percentage of colonial privateers' prizes.

Once a private man-of-war was fortunate enough to sight a vessel, overtake it, and determine that it was, indeed, an enemy merchantman, the privateer then had to force the prospective prize to strike its colors. This was often difficult. As chapter 3 has indicated, many merchantmen carried carriage guns and ample crews to man them. Prizes often tried to repel attacks. In the summer of 1742 a Newport privateer commanded by Capt. John Rouse suffered fifty men killed in action while taking a Spanish ship.[83] A St. Kitts private man-of-war commanded by Captain Harriot lost eighteen men plus many wounded when it engaged a French vessel near the Caicos Islands in 1744.[84] Capt. William Dowell of the Philadelphia privateer schooner *George* fought for four hours with a French ship carrying twenty-four guns in the fall of 1744 and sustained casualties of eight men killed and fifteen wounded. Dowell was then forced to sail to Bermuda to repair the schooner's rigging. Despite these losses and the French vessel's escape, the captain and crew were "far from being discouraged, [and] design another Three-Months Cruize before they return home."[85] Seventy-three cases in the data file record fatalities for British colonial privateersmen in prize actions. The average number killed was five. Casualties included officers as well as lower-deck seamen. The following privateer commanders were killed in action during the wars of 1739–1748: David Donahew of Boston, Captain Cunningham of Jamaica, John Hopkins of Providence, and John

Albine, John Johnson, Edward Menzies, and Thomas Tucker, all of New York.

Spanish and French privateers also encountered stiff resistance during prize actions. A Spanish man-of-war sustained fourteen men killed during a two-hour engagement with the *Martha*, Captain Browse master.[86] Captain Fiske and his crew killed twenty Spaniards and wounded nine others during a five-hour struggle in the Gulf of Honduras in 1744. After suffering many casualties, Fiske's Boston sloop struck its colors and was escorted into Campeche, Mexico.[87] A French privateer of ten guns and seventy-five men attacked the ship *Wrightson and Isabella* of Sunderland, England, off the coast of Holland in 1745. In the ensuing five-hour battle, the privateer attempted to board the merchantman three times. Finally, the Frenchman sheered off to sail away. One last shot from the English vessel, however, blew up the privateer, resulting in the loss of its entire crew. When the *Wrightson and Isabella* arrived in England, the Lords Commissioners of the Admiralty recommended that the king award Capt. Richard Hornby a gold chain and medal worth one hundred pounds sterling and issue a bounty of five pounds for each crewman "to encourage others, under like Circumstance, to exert themselves in the Defence of their Ships."[88] In a 1748 engagement with the Barbados sloop *Hawk*, seventeen hands from the Spanish privateer *Grand Diable* lost their lives.[89] The data file includes fifty-one cases with information for enemy privateersmen killed in prize actions; the average number of fatalities was seven. The duration of prize actions provides another clue to the difficulties predators frequently faced when forcing merchantmen to surrender. For the 122 cases in the data file containing information about the length of an engagement, the average prize action lasted nearly five hours.

In addition to attacking enemy vessels, privateers occasionally raided enemy settlements. These assaults were the prize war's deadliest operations. The bloodiest engagement involving privateers occurred on 4 September 1748 when two Havana private men-of-war attacked Brunswick, North Carolina. During the engagement eighty Spaniards were killed and thirty-seven were captured. Shore batteries sank one of the invaders' vessels, but the other escaped with a merchantman carrying naval stores and most of the town's valuables.[90] British privateers also sustained heavy casualties while assaulting enemy towns. A raid on a Spanish West Indian island in 1741 killed more British colonial privateersmen than any other action in the conflict. Capt. Charles Davidson, commander of the Newport sloop *St. Andrew,* lost fifty-three of his eighty-man crew in this unsuccessful attack.[91] Captain Wallis of the Boston privateer *Vernon* lost fifty men in 1740 during a disastrous raid in the Canary Islands.[92]

Even after an enemy vessel had hauled down its colors, it was still too early for a privateer's crew to contemplate profits. Until an admiralty judge condemned the prize, the privateers earned no financial rewards. After capturing an enemy vessel the privateer commander had to decide whether to send or escort the prize to a friendly port for admiralty proceedings. This was an important decision. If the prize was merely dispatched under the direction of several members of the crew, the captain risked losing the prize if the prisoners overpowered the prize crew. Sailors on the New York brigantine *Catharine* won their freedom by overpowering the Spanish prize crew attempting to sail the brig to San Sebastian, Spain.[93] Samuel Coon, first mate on the Charles Town schooner *Charles,* led a successful uprising against a prize crew two days after Captain Berneau's French privateer had captured the schooner.[94] On the other hand, if the privateer commander accompanied his prize to a friendly port instead of employing a prize crew, valuable cruising time would be lost. It was a difficult choice.

Privateers also risked encountering a stronger enemy warship (or several warships) even if they escorted prizes to a British port. In 1740 Captain Bennet in a Jamaican privateer chanced upon two Spanish private sloops-of-war after they had taken a Jamaican merchantman. Bennet recaptured the prize as well as the two sloops.[95] In June 1745 three Dunkirk privateers, the *Real,* the *Princess de Penthievre,* and an unidentified consort, enjoyed great success in the North Sea, capturing the ship *Mary,* bound for Charles Town from Newcastle-upon-Tyne; the ships *Cambridge* and *Baltimore,* from Virginia for London; the ship *Sea Horse,* bound from Maryland for London; a Scottish ship laden with corn; and two German vessels sailing for Bristol from Bremen. Instead of dispatching their prizes under the direction of prize crews, the French cruisers accompanied them home. On 5 July off Oostende (Belgium), however, two twenty-gun frigates, HMS *Bridgewater,* commanded by Lord George Graham, and HMS *Sheerness,* commanded by Captain Gordon, attacked the Frenchmen and their prizes. In the ensuing four-hour battle, the king's ships recaptured all the prizes except the Scottish ship, and took the *Real* and the *Princess de Penthievre* as well.[96] HMS *Advice* recaptured the ship *Beulah,* James Child master, after it had been taken by a Bayonne privateer.[97] On 10 July 1748 the New York private man-of-war *Royal Catharine,* commanded by John Bill, deprived the Spanish privateer *Grand Diable* of a valuable prize by retaking the New York brigantine *Concord.*[98]

Spanish and French privateers were not alone in losing prizes to enemy warships. Capt. John Colt, commander of a St. Kitts private man-of-war, seized two Spanish vessels off Cuba in 1740 and accompanied them to Jamaica. En route, a Spanish man-of-war chased Colt's vessel. Since the privateersmen could not escape and keep their prizes, they decided to stand and fight. The two prizes remained in British custody, but Colt and his crew were captured and brought into Santiago de Cuba.[99] In 1744 the Rhode Island private man-of-war *Young Godfrey,* sailing in consort with the *Koulikan* privateer of Jamaica, captured a Spanish ship. While the three proceeded to Cartagena to ransom the prize, two heavily armed French privateers intercepted them. During the prize action, the French retook the Spaniard and sunk the *Young Godfrey.* The *Koulikan* was lucky to escape. Katherine Malbone, wife of Newport merchant Godfrey Malbone, the *Young Godfrey*'s owner, thought the Jamaicans were more than lucky. In a letter to her son Godfrey, Jr., for whom the *Young Godfrey* was named, Mrs. Malbone cast aspersions on the Jamaicans' courage and claimed the *Koulikan* had actually "run away" from the fight.[100]

The famous French privateer commander Morepang captured Captain Gatman's Boston privateer and Gatman's prize off Cape Breton in 1744.[101] Another French privateer recaptured the prize ship seized by Capt. Robert Troup, commander of the New York privateer brig *Hester,* in 1747. This prize did not remain in French hands long, as it was subsequently taken by a British colonial privateer and escorted into Rhode Island.[102] The *Pennsylvania Gazette* reported what was probably the most extreme example of warships encountering enemy cruisers after taking a prize:

> We have received Advice, that the King William Privateer of this Port [Bristol, England], is sail'd into Cork, without her last Prize . . . which had been taken and retaken no less than six Times, viz. first by the Benson Privateer; then by a St. Maloe's Privateer; again by the Prince Charles Privateer; then by another French Privateer; and

fifthly, by the King William in his Way thither, who seeing two large Ships of 30 Guns each, about ten Leagues of[f] Cape Clear [Ireland], was oblig'd to leave the Prize, and make the best of their Way off.[103]

There are 106 cases in the data file in which one predator engaged another after a prize had been taken. In the 25 cases involving British colonial privateers, American cruisers successfully defended their captures about half the time while enemy warships recaptured the prize(s) or even subdued the privateer in the remaining half. The enemy's record was worse, losing prizes in most of the 75 cases involving a British warship. Clearly, private men-of-war could not rest easily after a successful prize action until their capture was moored in a friendly harbor.

The difficulties of sighting enemy merchantmen, overhauling them at sea, subduing them in battle, and finally escorting them to a British port proved to be so great that a sizable proportion of British colonial privateers failed to take a single prize. The distribution of prize actions involving American privateers is summarized in Table 7.5. Nearly one-fourth of colonial private men-of-war did not capture any Spanish or French vessels. In addition, nearly three-eighths failed to seize more than one enemy merchantman. Nearly half participated in fewer than five successful prize actions. Only forty-three British colonial privateers took more than four enemy vessels.

To facilitate taking Spanish and French prizes, many British colonial privateers embarked on voyages in groups of two or more. The practice of sailing in consort complicates the analysis of successful prize actions. More than a third of the merchantmen captured by American privateers were taken in actions involving consorts. Thus, Table 7.5 indicates the number of privateers participating in successful captures of enemy vessels, not the number of different prizes taken by American private men-of-war. John Dennis of Newport, for example, was one of the most successful colonial privateer commanders in the 1740s. As captain of the *Defiance* and later as skipper of the *Prince Frederick,* Dennis participated in sixteen successful prize actions, eleven when sailing by himself and five while sailing in consort. Samuel Bayard, commander of the New York privateer *Hester,* captured five prizes when sailing alone and fourteen when sailing in consort. New York captains Thomas Seymour of the *Clinton* and *Dragon* and Richard Jefferies of the *Greyhound* and *Polly* participated in eighteen and

TABLE 7.5
Participation of British Colonial Privateers in Successful Prize Actions,
1739–1748

Number of Successful Prize Actions	Number of Privateers	%
0	73	23.6
1	42	13.6
2–4	151	48.9
5–9	28	9.1
10 or more	15	4.8
Totals	309	100.0

twenty-two successful prize actions, respectively. Sixteen of Seymour's prizes and eighteen of Jefferies's were taken when sailing in consort.

Cruising in consort increased the firepower of privateers, but it diminished the share of a prize each private man-of-war received. A consort agreement signed by the owners of the Newport sloops *Revenge* and *Success* on 10 November 1744, for example, stated that the proceeds of any prizes were to be divided equally.[104] Thus the two ships sailing together would have to seize merchantmen at least twice as valuable as either could have taken alone for the agreement to be advantageous. Since many prizes were taken in consort, the proceeds to the owners and crews of the *Hester* or the *Greyhound* or the *Clinton* were not as substantial as the numbers of their successful prize actions might suggest. Easing the difficulties of privateering lessened its rewards.

Capturing merchantmen and dispatching them to friendly ports for admiralty proceedings was so difficult that some privateers did not bother to send their prizes to port. Instead, the captors released the prize vessel and crew after the captives promised to pay a ransom. To ensure compliance, the privateersmen held a prize crew officer hostage. Capt. John Griffith, commander of a Newport privateer, for example, released a rich Spanish register ship in 1743 after the Spaniards agreed to pay a large sum of money. "The Owners of he[r] will clear, it is said, Ten Thousand Pound[s] at least," the *New-York Weekly Journal* reported.[105] Another Rhode Island cruiser, the *Prince Frederick,* commanded by Capt. William

Hopkins, took seven prizes in 1743; five were ransomed; and Hopkins escorted the others to Newport.[106] Enemy predators also ransomed prizes. Capt. Jacques Brasson, commander of the French private man-of-war *Chamflour,* captured an Irish ship bound for South Carolina in 1745. Instead of proceeding to a French port with his prize, Brasson ransomed the ship and took the prize's first mate hostage. Unfortunately for the privateers, HMS *Augusta,* commanded by Capt. John Hamilton, captured the *Chamflour,* ending the ransom agreement: "The Owners are discharged now from the Obligation, Capt. Hamilton having sent in the Mate of the Cork Ship with the Bond, to be given up by the Owners."[107]

American merchants instructed colonial captains to try to ransom their vessels when captured by enemy privateers. John Reynell ordered Edward Dowers, master of the ship *Bolton,* bound in the summer of 1746 from Philadelphia to Antigua and thence to England, "In case of being taken, Endeavour to ransom if thou cans't for Twelve Hundred Pounds Sterling (if Sugar Loaden, may'st advance as much more as thou thinks Reasonable) and Draw for the Same on [James] Birkett and [Nathaniel] Booth of Antigua, on Elias Bland of London, or on us here the Bills shall be honourably paid and the Hostage fully Satisfied for his time, Expences etc."[108] Manhattan merchant Gerard Beekman gave Capt. William Collins, master of the sloop *Dolphin,* similar instructions: "As you[r] Vessell is Loaded only with Lumber and is very old Can be of Lettle worth to an Enimy. in Case you Should be taken Which God forbid you may Give them fifty Pounds Sterling as a ransom for her again for She will not be worth that to them."[109]

It is difficult to determine how often prizes were ransomed during the hostilities. Apparently, it was quite common in Europe. The French government printed forms in French and English with special headings for each French admiralty jurisdiction to facilitate ransoming, thus suggesting that ransoms occurred frequently.[110] Early in 1744 English officials issued instructions to limit the number of prizes ransomed by British public and private men-of-war. "No Commander of any Man of War or Privateer shall ransom any Ship taken as Prize, when such Ship may conveniently be brought into some Port of his Majesty's Dominions." If a prize were ransomed, written reasons and preparatory examinations similar to those employed in vice-admiralty cases were required to be sent to admiralty officials. Commanders of privateers and letter of marque ships who contravened these instructions risked the forfeiture of their commissions as well as legal proceedings against the bonds for their letters of marque.[111] Despite these indications that ransoming occurred frequently in European waters, the data file includes only thirty cases of prizes ransomed in North American and Caribbean shipping lanes. The proximity of numerous privateering bases in England and France probably accounts for the greater reliance on ransoming in Europe compared to the New World.

III

The maritime prize war exerted a marked impact on Atlantic commerce. In the aggregate, privateers captured hundreds of vessels worth thousands of pounds sterling. The financial success of the individual privateer, however, is much less certain. It is difficult to determine whether privateering was profitable for the men who owned and fitted out British colonial private men-of-war. Nor is it easy to ascertain if the crews who "dream[ed] of nothing but mad Bulls, Spaniards and bagg[s] of Gold"[112] obtained the chimera of rich plunder.

Identifying privateer owners is a major obstacle that obscures the question of the financial success of individual private men-of-war. Because so many records required by British prize statutes (bonds for letters of marque, journals of privateering voyages, etc.) no longer survive, the owners of most privateers are impossible to discover. The most valuable sources of privateering during the wars of 1739–1748, the colonial press and vice-admiralty court records, rarely provide the names of privateer owners.

Even when the names of owners are known, problems still exist. Since privateering was such a speculative investment, few vessels were owned by one individual. To minimize losses, warships were frequently owned by several men, though it is usually impossible to determine each owner's share in a given privateer. John Gidley and Sueton Grant owned the Newport privateer *St. Andrew* in 1740, but the records do not indicate if they were equal partners.[113] In 1744 Solomon Townsend, Jonathan Tillinghast, Samuel Freebody, and John Channing owned the privateer sloop *Queen of Hungary,* but again it is impossible to determine if they owned equal shares.[114] These difficulties of owner identification are familiar to students of seventeenth- and eighteenth-century British shipping because the problem applies generally to merchant vessels as well as privateers.[115]

The dearth of business records is another problem in analyzing the financial success of privateering. Although the bonds for Rhode Island letters of marque indicate that John Brown was a substantial investor in private men-of-war, his mercantile papers are missing so it is nearly impossible to determine if Brown's privateers were profitable. The same is true for John Bannister and William and Samuel Vernon. They invested in Newport private men-of-war, but their few surviving papers lack a clear statement concerning profit and loss. Robert Pringle invested in several privateers in England and South Carolina, but his letterbook is silent about gains (or losses) resulting from those investments.

The persistence of investors provides a clue to the financial rewards of privateering. Potential financiers of privateers probably would not undertake such projects unless they expected the outcome to be as lucrative as alternative ventures. Thus, if the men who invested in private men-of-war in 1740 or 1741 continued to own privateers throughout the conflict, or if an individual invested in 1744 and did so for the next several years, it seems reasonable to assume these investors earned returns on their capital.

The names of seventy-three different investors in Rhode Island privateers are included in eighty-nine bonds for letters of marque. An examination of these individuals' persistence of investment reveals mixed results, as Table 7.6 indicates. For most investors, privateering was probably only a passing interest and perhaps only minimally rewarding. The number of moderately persistent investors suggests that Rhode Island businessmen realized some earnings from privateering. Eight individuals invested in three different years while an equal number invested in four separate years. This equaled the duration of the Anglo-French war. (The other seven invested in two different years.) The remaining five investors risked their capital in both phases of the maritime conflict. Such persistence suggests that privateering was, indeed, profitable.

The Rhode Island letters of marque provide another clue for assessing the profitability of privateering. A strong commitment to privateering (measured by the number of privateers in which an individual invested in a single year) suggests these investments were lucrative. Prudent men would probably not invest in several private men-of-war if they were losing money. Table 7.7 reveals that a measure of investors' commitment to privateers, like their persistence, yields inconclusive results concerning the financial rewards of privateering. A large majority of investors owned shares

TABLE 7.6

Persistence of Investment in Rhode Island Privateers during the Wars of
1739–1748

Category of Investors	Number of Investors	%
Low Persistence	45	61.6
(Invested in 1 year only)		
Moderate Persistence	23	31.5
(Invested in 2–4 different years)		
High Persistence	5	6.9
(Invested in 5–8 different years)		
Totals	73	100.0

Source: Bonds for Rhode Island Letters of Marque, Rhode Island Notary Public Records, IV–V, Rhode Island State Archives, Providence.

in only one privateer in a given year. Only twenty-two colonists thought privateering sufficiently profitable to invest in more than one private man-of-war in a given year. Fewer than 3 percent invested in more than three in a year.

On the basis of these two indicators, it seems safe to conclude that most of the seventy-three investors in Rhode Island privateers did not realize substantial returns on their investments. At the other end of the spectrum, men like Brown and Bannister, who invested in eight different years of the conflict, or Grant and Malbone, who owned shares in four and five privateers in a single year, would not have continually sunk money into losing ventures.

The measures for persistence and commitment reveal the existence of a small, elite group of Newport privateer investors. A close correlation existed among the colonists who displayed a high persistence in and a strong commitment to privateering investments. Seven of the eight investors who ranked in the strong commitment categories in Table 7.7 also risked their capital in more than one year of the hostilities. In addition, the average number of years in which these seven invested was 5.3. (Had it not been for a freak accident, this figure would probably have been even larger. On 17 September 1744, Grant, Gidley, and Nathaniel Coddington, leading citizens of Newport and investors in private men-of-war, were surveying the stores of their privateer *Prince*

TABLE 7.7

Strength of Investors' Commitment in Rhode Island Privateers during the
Wars of 1739–1748

Category of Commitment	Number of Investors	%
Weakest Commitment	51	69.8
(Annual investment in one pvtr.)		
Weak Commitment	14	19.2
(Annual investment in two pvtrs.)		
Strong Commitment	6	8.2
(Annual investment in three pvtrs.)		
Strongest Commitment	2	2.8
(Annual investment in four or five pvtrs.)		
Totals	73	100.0

Source: Bonds for Rhode Island Letters of Marque, Rhode Island Notary Public Records, IV–V, Rhode Island State Archives, Providence.

Frederick when a pistol fired accidently, causing the gunpowder in their warehouse to explode. All three owners and an employee died from injuries sustained in the blast.[116]) Besides investing heavily in privateering, these men were also among New England's leading merchants.[117] It is doubtful that such knowledgeable businessmen would have invested in several privateers each year throughout the conflict unless these investments were profitable. (See Table 7.8.)

Despite these suggestions of financial rewards, the profitability of Rhode Island privateering is still uncertain. It is likely that Godfrey Malbone, a leading member of Newport's mercantile community, lost money investing in privateering. In a letter to Godfrey, Jr., Katherine Malbone revealed the results of her husband's privateering investments. "Your father has had such bad luck it is thought by most people he has lost forty thousand pound [Rhode Island currency, about £6,200 sterling] but he will not give over for he is now fitting out two Ships [the *Prince of Wales* and *Duke of Cumberland*] which i hope will be as lucky as the rest has been unlucky."[118] Malbone also discussed his losses in a letter to his son. "I have had very ill Success Since the war commencd I have Lost nigh fifty Thousand pounds our currency [about £7,755 sterling]— however I am now maiking a Vigorous Attempt."[119]

TABLE 7.8
Newport's Leading Privateering Investors during the Wars of 1739–1748

Name of Investor	Number of Years Invested	Largest Number of Pvtrs. in One Year
John Bannister	8	3
John Brown	8	3
Peleg Brown	4	3
Nathaniel Coddington	2	3
Sueton Grant	4	4
Godfrey Malbone	7	5
William Mumford	4	3
Mean	5.3	3.4

Source: Bonds for Rhode Island Letters of Marque, Rhode Island Notary Public Records, IV–V, Rhode Island State Archives, Providence.

Unfortunately for the Malbone family, the *Prince of Wales* and *Duke of Cumberland* captured no rich prizes. Instead, their voyage ended in financial calamity. Godfrey, Jr., received these bleak tidings in a letter from Judge Edward Scott, his uncle:

> It is with very great Regret & a deep Concern that I send you the following advise, In Decr past your father fitted out from hence on a Cruise against His Majesty's Enemies two fine new Ships, of which he was sole Owner, excepting a Quarter Part of one of them . . . the Night after they sailed there was a most violent Snow Storm, & it is much feared that they both of them founder'd neither of them having been since heard of, so that every body here as well as your Father himself give over the said Ships as lost, his Interest in them was very considerable not less as he has informed me than Forty Thousand Pounds [approximately £6,200 sterling].

These losses had a direct impact on Godfrey, Jr., who was then studying law at Lincoln's Inn in London. "It would be, I doubt not," Scott's letter continued:

> more agreeable to your Inclination to tarry longer, but as your Father's great Losses since the Commencement of the present War with France, amounting in the whole to above Sixty Thousand Pounds [more than £9,300 sterling], incapacitate him to support so

great an Expence as must unavoidably attend your prosecuting your
Studies at the Inns of Court in London, You ought & must submit to
return home without Delay.[120]

Apparently, these setbacks convinced Malbone to stop investing in
privateers. He is not listed as an owner in the bonds for Rhode
Island letters of marque after 1746.

John Bannister enjoyed greater success in his privateering
investments. (See Figure 7.1.) He owned shares in the Newport
privateers *Virgin Queen, Revenge,* and *Victory* during the early
years of the War of Jenkins' Ear. All seemed to be doing well since
Bannister's correspondence mentions numerous Spanish prizes
taken by his cruisers.[121] Bannister thought wartime conditions were
favorable, and privateering was one of the most attractive
investment opportunities. He wrote in 1740, "This Year shipping
has done mighty well on Acct. of the high Freights, and if the
Rupture Continues freight will still hold up but in case of a French
Warr I don't think theres any business near so profitable as a proper
Vessell or two well fitted out a Privateering."[122]

Bannister's enthusiasm for privateers waned, however, because of
problems with one of his captains. Charles Hall, commander of the
Virgin Queen, was unreliable in remitting the proceeds of his
captures. Although the *Virgin Queen* successfully seized Spanish
prizes, its Newport owners did not count the profits. Finally,
Bannister replaced Hall with Capt. John Cane.[123] This was difficult
to accomplish since the *Virgin Queen* was in Jamaica. Bannister
notified Daniel Vanburg, his Jamaican correspondent, to assist
Cane. Bannister also asked Vanburg to initiate legal action against
Hall to recover the value of prizes the sloop had taken.[124] Bannister
never collected the overdue remittances, however. In a heated
letter to the West Indian merchant, in which he indicated his
dissatisfaction with Vanburg's attempts to recover funds from Hall,
Bannister revealed that he had sold his interest in the *Virgin
Queen*.[125]

This incident suggests that even the owners of successful
privateers encountered difficulty in receiving satisfactory returns
on their investments. It also illustrates the problems privateer
owners faced when their captains did not escort prizes into their
home ports. Other privateer owners lost money because their
captains failed to remit funds. In June 1745 the New York privateer
Polly, commanded by Capt. William Morgan, was sunk in Delaware

Figure 7.1. John Bannister was an important Newport merchant and a leading investor in private men-of-war.

Bay while returning from a successful cruise. The *Polly*'s loss was not accidental; Captain Morgan attempted to abscond with a chest of money belonging to the *Polly*'s owners, or at least that is what they claimed. When Morgan was subsequently jailed in Norfolk, Virginia, he denied any wrongdoing. Instead, he and several members of his crew swore before a local magistrate that the *Polly*'s lieutenant had made off with the prize money. Either way, the privateer's owners lost income.[126] Morgan may have been telling the truth because the *Polly*'s owners did not prosecute him. Five months later Morgan embarked on another voyage as the lieutenant of the Norfolk privateer *Raleigh*. Morgan's new owners probably regretted their decision to hire him since proceeds from two prizes taken by the *Raleigh* never made it to Virginia. Morgan and two fellow officers were accused of gambling away the prize money in St. Kitts. They denied the charges and offered a reward to discover the identity of the "ill-designing People" who had "slanderously and maliciously" reported they had lost their owners' money.[127] Whether or not Morgan and his associates had been slandered, the *Raleigh*'s owners still lost money on a successful cruise.

Robert Pringle also lost money because of his involvement with a *successful* privateer. (See Figures 7.2 and 7.3.) Although Pringle owned no shares in the London private man-of-war *Revenge,* commanded by Capt. James Wimble, he advanced the captain seventy-five pounds sterling for refitting when the vessel was in Charles Town in 1742. Naturally, Pringle expected a return on his money, either from the *Revenge*'s London owners or from prizes that Wimble would take in American waters. Eventually, the South Carolinian had to write off the advance as a loss. The merchants Wimble identified as the privateer's owners refused to honor Wimble's bills of exchange. Even though the *Revenge* enjoyed a successful cruise, Wimble never remitted any funds to the Charles Town merchant. Pringle did not give up easily. His association with the *Revenge* elicited twenty-one different letters between 6 December 1742 and 24 April 1745. During this period Pringle wrote his business correspondents in London, New Providence Island, Boston, St. Kitts, Jamaica, and Newport, in addition to Wimble, in an effort to recoup his cash advance. These attempts suffered a serious setback when Wimble died in 1744. Pringle's last letter concerning Wimble indicated his acceptance of the bad debt. "I observe You have been so Good as to enquire into Capt. Wimbles affairs, but am afraid there will be nothing obtain'd," he wrote to Kingston, Jamaica, merchant James Henderson.

Pringle experienced another misfortune from privateering in 1747: he was captured by the Spanish while sailing to England. "This day [11 August 1747] the Ship James, in which I was Passenger, was taken by a Spanish Privateer Sloop, Capt: Diego Lanchez, Com^r: . . . the Spaniards took everything from us excepting what was then on our Backs."[129] Pringle, his fellow passengers, and the ship's crew were taken to St. Augustine, Florida, where he remained until 26 October. During his captivity the Charles Town merchant kept a journal, noting his expenses for

Figure 7.2. Robert Pringle was an influential Charles Town rice merchant and privateering investor. His letterbook is a valuable source for Charles Town's commercial activities during the 1730s and 1740s.

purchasing presents for his captors and provisions for himself and recording several British vessels that had run aground on the Florida coast during severe weather. While Pringle remained a prisoner, other British captives escaped and headed to Georgia. "Last night [14 September], Say 10 A Clock, Five English Sailors Ran away with a Canoe to goe to Frederica."[130] About six weeks later Pringle also left St. Augustine for Frederica aboard the flag-of-truce schooner

Figure 7.3. Robert Pringle's handsome house in Charleston, South Carolina, is evidence of Pringle's business abilities.

Speedwell. Finally, on 22 November Pringle succeeded in returning to his Charles Town home.

Because difficulties could arise when privateers sent prizes to distant ports, owners usually directed their captains to send all prizes home whenever possible. The instructions, issued to all commanders of Rhode Island private men-of-war, required that "all such Ships and Vessels with their Lading and Merchandizes whatsoever which You shall happen to seize or take You are to bring into Your Commission Port If you can."[131] Sending prizes home allowed the owners to supervise directly the disposition of the prize and cargo after condemnation in a vice-admiralty court. This supervision could save much time and money. Delays caused by writing instructions to correspondents in faraway cities, commissions charged by those correspondents for their services, and the need to sell cargoes in unfamiliar and often glutted markets diminished the value of prize cargoes and vessels.

Privateer owners enjoyed only partial success in having prizes sent home. Of the 443 prizes listed in the data file that were captured by British colonial privateers and for which the port to which the prize was taken is indicated, only 241 (54 percent) were sent to the privateers' home ports. Obviously, private men-of-war could not always comply with their owners' desires, especially if a prize had been taken in the West Indies or the Wine Islands and the privateer's home port was Newport or Boston. This is another circumstance obscuring the profitability of privateering.

The financial rewards earned by privateering investors are clearly difficult to determine. The owners' business correspondence is sparse, and their persistence and commitment to privateering investments are not always reliable indicators. Definitive figures concerning the profitability of privateering may never be established. It is possible, however, to suggest a general framework to assess the financial rewards of private men-of-war. The average value for prizes captured by British colonial privateers, mentioned at the beginning of this chapter, is the departure point. The mean value for the 109 prizes with recorded values for their cargoes was £8,890 sterling; the average of the 44 estimates was £9,691. These figures overstate the average value that each privateer received from the prizes because they do not consider the practice of sailing in consort. The 109 prizes were taken by 157 privateers; 71 private men-of-war captured the 44 prizes with estimated values. The mean values of these prizes thus became £6,172 sterling (109 cases) and £6,005 (44 cases). The average value for all 153 prizes, a sample of nearly one-fifth (19 percent) of the 829 prizes captured by British colonial privateers, was £6,120 sterling.

The average prize value can be viewed as the "gross revenue" of privateering. Some deductions are necessary to determine the owners' net receipts. First, the costs of vice-admiralty proceedings reduced the £6,120. The various fees charged by the judge, register, and marshal of the court plus the numerous expenditures for unlading the cargo and conducting the vendue sales probably ate up about 15 percent of the prize's value. Next, the owners divided the remaining £5,202 (average value less condemnation costs) with the crew. British prize law allowed privateer owners and crews to divide their prizes as they chose.[132] Evidence concerning the division of prizes is sparse, but existing agreements indicate the owners usually received one-third of a condemned prize while the ship's company pocketed the rest. The articles of agreement concluded between the owners and company of the Newport privateer sloop *Revenge* on 3 September 1743 called for such a division.[133] The owners and crew of the Newport private sloop-of-war *Success* had a similar arrangement in 1744.[134] A recruiting advertisement for the New York privateer *Prince Charles,* commanded by Jacobus Kierstede, announced that "the Men are to draw two Thirds of all Prizes, without any Deduction for Arms, Ammunition and Provision."[135] In 1746 the owners and crews of the privateer brigantines *Prince Frederick* of Newport and *Dolphin* of New York divided their prizes in the same fashion.[136] Thus the owner's share of the average prize was £1,734 sterling (one-third of £5,202).

Out of their third, the owners had to pay the costs of the cruise— the provisions consumed by the crew and the charges for the vessel and ordnance. Privateer owners escaped one major expense encountered by owners of merchantmen: there was no wage bill.

Provisions on a typical privateer during the 1740s normally consisted of one pound of meat, one pound of bread, a quarter of a quart of beans, peas, or corn, and one half-pint of rum per man per day.[137] Thus on an average cruise of seven months, each privateersman consumed approximately one barrel of meat, nearly two hundredweights of bread, almost seven bushels of beans, peas, or corn, and washed it all down with about fourteen gallons of rum. Using the same eighteenth-century price data employed to estimate the values of prize cargoes, the costs of provisioning a private man-of-war during King George's War can be approximated. Because these costs were subject to fluctuating commodity prices and were directly related to the size of the vessel and crew, it is impossible to present one figure as "the average cost of provisioning a privateer." Victual estimates for a ship with an average complement of 131 men, for example, varied from a low of £370 sterling to a high of £560. The same is true for other vessel types. Since sloops comprised the largest number of American private men-of-war, it would be most efficacious to use the average cost of provisioning one of these single-masted vessels in estimating the owners' costs. The first major expense debited to the owners' account was £257 sterling, the average cost of victualing the 72-man crew of a sloop for seven months.[138]

Estimating the charges for the privateering vessel and ordnance is more difficult than calculating the cost of provisions because less evidence exists concerning these expenses. If the investors did not already own a vessel and purchased a new one, the costs would be substantial. During this period new sloops in Philadelphia cost between £3.10.0 and £5.6.0 sterling per measured ton. At an average of 130.5 tons (87 tons burden), a new sloop would cost between £457 and £692.[139] If the investors fitted out one of their own vessels, the expense would then depend upon the opportunity costs of employing that vessel in other enterprises. Such costs are impossible to determine since so much depended upon the war's impact on an individual's business.

An estimate prepared for the Pennsylvania Council provides a glimpse of the costs of a vessel and ordnance for a cruising expedition. In 1748 the council considered dispatching a warship to protect Pennsylvania commerce from Spanish and French privateers. The legislators estimated it would cost about £300 Pennsylvania currency (about £172 sterling) per month to hire a vessel and equip it with sufficient ordnance or about £1.9.0 sterling per man per month.[140] Using this figure to estimate the costs of a privateer vessel, this translates into about £10 per man for the duration of the normal seven-month cruise. Thus the typical American private sloop-of-war with its average complement would cost its owners around £720 sterling for the vessel and ordnance.[141]

According to these estimates, the major expenses for dispatching a privateer sloop manned by seventy-two men for a seven-month cruise were in the neighborhood of £1,000 sterling. Evidence from the correspondence of two privateer owners supports the accuracy of this estimate. John Bannister discussed his privateering investments with a business associate in 1739. "Had I had orders from You to have Invested your Effects In such Mannar as I should have thot most Advantageous, I should have Interested you in the Sloope Virgin Queen a Small Privateer which was fitted out [by] three of us[.] the whole out fitt [cost] no more than £2400 this Currency."[142] The sterling cost of outfitting the *Virgin Queen* was about £480. This was a very small privateer, however. Its complement was only thirty-six men. Employing the same method to calculate the costs of the "average privateer sloop," but substituting thirty-six for the crew size, the estimated cost of fitting out the *Virgin Queen* would be £465 sterling, a close approximation (97 percent) of the actual costs. In 1744 Robert Pringle participated in a scheme to raise £3,000 sterling for a privateering cruise involving two vessels. Pringle and his associates fitted out large vessels, probably a snow and a ship, not sloops. This accounts for the higher expense.[143] The estimated costs of equipping a snow and a ship as privateers in 1744 were £3,289 sterling, a figure within 10 percent of the actual outlay.

On the basis of the average value of prizes taken by American privateers and the estimates of costs incurred in fitting out a colonial private man-of-war, it is possible to speculate about the profitability of British colonial privateering during the wars of 1739–1748. If an average private sloop-of-war captured a prize of average value, the sloop's owners would receive a return on their seven-month investment of about 78 percent. This translates into an annual rate of return of better than 130 percent.[144] Obviously, privateering could be very rewarding. Substantial profits could be earned if a privateer made one cruise and captured a single prize of only average value. Many predators intercepted more than one prize per cruise, and many captures were worth more than £6,120. The profitability for these privateers must have been large indeed. James G. Lydon, the historian of New York privateering during the 1740s, believes that Manhattan privateering investors realized windfall returns. "The average profit received by the known shareholders . . . approximated 140 percent."[145] On the other hand, nearly one-fourth of the British colonial privateers listed in the data file failed to capture even one enemy merchantman. The owners of these privateers, like Godfrey Malbone, probably lost their capital.

The financial rewards earned by the crew members of private men-of war can also be estimated. These mariners divided two-thirds of the value of prizes after the costs of admiralty justice had been deducted. Therefore, out of £6,120 for the average prize, the ship's company divided about £3,468. Assuming a seven-month cruise and a complement of seventy-two men, each prize share was worth about £48, or 137s. per month. Wages in the merchant marine rose from their normal peacetime rates of 23–25s. per month to 55*s*. a month in 1745–1748. The Royal Navy's wages remained notoriously low throughout the conflict as able-bodied seamen received only 24*s*. per month. Thus, the rewards from privateering more than doubled the highest average monthly wages paid to merchant seamen and were nearly six times the Royal Navy's monthly wage rate.[146] Lower-deck mariners as well as privateer owners could reap substantial rewards from prize actions.

IV

This chapter has obviously assumed that economic motivation predominated in decisions to join privateering ventures whether as investor, captain, or crew member. A brief consideration of noneconomic motivation is in order, however, before concluding this discussion. Although the prospect of windfall gains was clearly important, the owners of private men-of-war and their sailors were not mere "economic men." Part of their desire to fit out warships and attack enemy vessels stemmed from patriotic fervor. The "universal Joy" in Newport that greeted the 1739 proclamation authorizing letters of marque and the "Spirit of Privateering" that prevailed in New York in 1744 owed much of their intensity to British nationalism and a desire to retaliate for "depredations" against British shipping.[147]

British privateers demonstrated their patriotism throughout the war by risking their lives and their vessels in a decidedly uneconomic activity—attacking enemy privateers. True, British private men-of-war engaging enemy privateers were eligible for bounty money of £5 sterling for every man on board the enemy warship at the beginning of the action according to provisions in the Prize Acts of 1740 and 1744. The procedures for obtaining the bounty were cumbersome, however, and payments were slow and difficult to collect.[148] Besides, with the average complement of 149 men on French privateers, British predators stood to gain only £745 for their trouble. Merchantmen were clearly more attractive and safer targets. For these reasons the historian Richard Pares has argued that British privateers seldom engaged enemy private men-of-war: "Nor was it likely that the privateers, whatever their size, would do their country much service in the way of attacking the enemy's privateers and ships of war. After all, it was not their business to do so." Pares conceded that occasionally privateers engaged Spanish and French predators, but these actions were probably mistakes: "The commanders cannot often have gone out of their way to seek them, or entered into them with their eyes open."[149] Despite this lack of financial incentive, British colonial privateers engaged in 128 prize actions with their French and Spanish counterparts and captured sixty-eight enemy privateers and sank fourteen others. These engagements followed the general contours of the prize war; most encounters occurred after 1744 in the Caribbean.

The details of these prize actions clearly reveal the nationalistic sentiments of the privateersmen and their owners. Newport privateer investor John Bannister seemed eager for his predator, the *New Revenge,* to encounter a Spanish privateer during a 1741 cruise. "I hope [the *New Revenge*] may be of Some Service not Doubting She'l make her way Good with any of the Spanish Vessells and shall be glad were it her fortune to meete with the Best Privateers of em all."[150] Successful privateer captains earned the gratitude of local merchants for engaging Spanish and French private men-of-war. Philadelphians learned in 1746 that the residents of Bridgetown, Barbados, applauded Capt. Peter Marshall, commander of the Newport privateer *Prince Frederick,* for attacking two French privateers that had harassed the island's shipping.[151] New York Captain John Burgess received much praise and a gift of silver plate after he seized the French privateer *Mars* off Sandy Hook, New Jersey, and escorted it into New York.[152] Newport Captain John Dennis's popularity soared in St. Kitts because he captured so many French private men-of-war in 1746 and 1747.[153] Another report concerning Captain Dennis provides additional evidence that colonial privateer commanders were not solely motivated by the bottom line:

> Tuesday last arrived here [Philadelphia] Captain Hazelton, mentioned in one of our former Papers to have been taken by a French Privateer, and carried into Martineco. During his Stay there, which was two Months, there were above Twenty Vessels sent in by their Privateers: And in which Time Captain Dennis, of Rhode-Island, had been cruizing off and on in Sight of the Town, and sent a Message to the Governor, by a Vessel from St. Eustatia, desiring him to send out two of his best Privateers to him, and he would shew him some Sport. Upon which, a Snow and Sloop was fitted out in an extraordinary Manner, and sent out; the Snow mounted sixteen Carriage Guns, and had about 240 Men on board, besides a Number of Gentlemens Sons, who went out Voluntiers, to share in the Honour of bringing Dennis in.

As it turned out, the French failed to engage Dennis but encountered instead the Bristol, England, privateer *Leostaff,* commanded by Captain Fielding, who captured the snow and inflicted heavy damage on the sloop.[154] The incident reveals that Dennis and his French adversaries fought for something more than profit, while Fielding was not averse to attacking heavily manned and armed enemy warships. Privateering involved a marriage of patriotism and the pursuit of profit.

A definitive pronouncement concerning the profitability of American privateers during the wars of 1739–1748 remains elusive. Yet privateering clearly offered the prospect of windfall profits to the owners of successful private men-of-war. Moreover, it was unnecessary for a privateer to seize a Spanish galleon loaded to the gunwales with gold and silver or to capture scores of vessels laden with sugar, molasses, cocoa, and other staples to make substantial gains. The capture of a single prize of average value was enough to yield an annual profit of more than 130 percent on the capital invested. The potential profitability of privateering was considerable, and many investors in this wartime enterprise probably realized financial gains.

This prospect of profit was important in mobilizing support for imperial warfare within the British colonial mercantile community. Success in the prize war also explains why ports like New York benefited from colonial conflict, while others like Boston, which dispatched few privateers, did not. In any event, privateering did not disappear from the Atlantic during the eighteenth century. Merchants and mariners continued to believe, as they had in earlier times, that they could make their fortunes from the decks of private men-of-war.

AFTERWORD

PRIVATEERING AND COLONIAL AMERICA

P RIVATEERING PLAYED AN IMPORTANT ROLE THROUGHOUT THE HISTORY of colonial America. From the expansion of Elizabethan England in the late sixteenth century through the War for Independence, Americans dispatched thousands of private men-of-war to cruise against enemy shipping. Privateering did not decline in the eighteenth century and was certainly not eliminated. In addition, the disruption of an adversary's maritime commerce continued to dominate American naval thinking until the end of the nineteenth century. Privateers sailed the Atlantic during the War of 1812, and the destruction of commerce occupied a central position in European and American naval policy until private warships were abolished by treaty in 1857—and even then the United States refused to ratify the international agreement. Privateering and prize actions dominated America's maritime outlook until Alfred Thayer Mahan took up his persuasive pen in the 1890s and advocated a new naval policy based on the destruction of an enemy's fleet, not his commerce.

The inability of nation-states to support the staggering expenditures necessary for large, powerful navies gave rise to privateering. National treasuries could not bear the cost of fleets capable of safeguarding Atlantic shipping lanes. The governments of Great Britain and the other European colonial powers (and subsequently the United States government as well) tried to augment their sea power by encouraging the private sector to equip

222

and man private men-of-war. Attracted by the possibilities of windfall profits, merchants in London, Bristol, Dunkirk, Bayonne, Cadiz, and San Sebastian in Europe, and Newport, New York, the British West Indies, Havana, St. Augustine, Martinique, and Cap François in America sent out thousands of vessels during the conflicts of the seventeenth and eighteenth centuries. Naval prize money motivated officers and men in the service of European monarchs and provides additional testimony to the enormous influence of prize actions.

Privateering was a popular and important maritime enterprise in mideighteenth-century America. Imperial officials at Whitehall and Westminster devoted increasing attention to the privateers' expanding operations. British authorities had begun to regulate private men-of-war during Queen Anne's War in 1708, and the Prize Acts of 1740 and 1744, as well as the various instructions to privateersmen, were additional efforts to control colonial warships. The adjudication of prizes in American vice-admiralty courts suggests that London enjoyed only partial success, however. In their zeal to issue condemnations, admiralty judges circumvented the provisions of the law. Privateering brought money into American ports, and colonial admiralty courts were only too eager to share in the profits.

The large number of American ships and men that sought prizes also documents the popularity of privateering. More than three hundred individual private men-of-war were equipped and manned in the British colonies from 1739–1748. The private warships were substantial craft, as large sloops and brigantines averaging between eighty and one hundred tons burden were the most popular privateer vessels. These vessels carried large crews and considerable armaments representing substantial investments in labor and capital. Although the long-term trend in eighteenth-century Atlantic shipping pointed to less heavily armed and manned merchantmen, the era's numerous conflicts arrested this tendency.

The maritime prize war of 1739–1748 highlighted the British Empire's one glaring deficiency as a naval power: an inadequate supply of trained mariners to man the naval and merchant fleets. The recruiting of sailors for private men-of-war exacerbated this shortage. Indeed, contemporary naval officials and merchants blamed the privateers for the lack of tars, and historians have frequently echoed these charges. Private men-of-war, however, also faced great difficulties filling their complements. This competition to attract seamen doubled the level of mariners' wages, sharply escalating the costs of doing business in wartime. Ironically, wartime conditions benefited sailors as merchants were forced to pay more to tempt available seamen to risk naval press-gangs. Eighteenth-century sailing vessels required skilled personnel. Because governments were incapable or unwilling to devise an effective method to increase the supply of trained sailors, there were always manpower shortages during wartime.

American privateering was extensive as all major colonial ports participated in the prize war. Newport and New York fitted out the most private men-of-war, followed by the British West Indian ports. Privateering probably attracted merchants who did not dominate the more normal channels of commerce. Because of its highly speculative nature, many businessmen probably eschewed privateering's high risks when they could earn profits in more stable avenues of trade.

British colonial privateers concentrated on the Caribbean, site of the most important shipping lanes in the Spanish and French Empires. The overwhelming majority of prize actions involving American predators occurred in the West Indies. Privateersmen dreamed of capturing the fabulously wealthy Spanish treasure ships that sailed through the Old Bahama Channel bound for Cadiz. This treasure proved elusive, however, and private men-of-war settled for more prosaic cargoes of sugar, cocoa, coffee, indigo, and other West Indian products. Colonial cruisers also intercepted vessels laden with European goods that had been dispatched to the islands in exchange for tropical produce. The Caribbean was the primary theater of operations because Spanish and French North American commerce was insufficient to support continued deployment of British private men-of-war.

Spanish and French privateers also exerted a strong influence on colonial America during the hostilities. Enemy cruisers harassed British shipping, especially after France entered the conflict in 1744. The activities of Spanish, French, and British privateers demonstrated clearly that Europe's most powerful navies could not provide adequate protection for Atlantic trade. French and Spanish predators divided their efforts between the North American coast and the West Indies. America's tobacco, rice, and sugar commerce suffered as a result. In addition, Spanish and French private men-of-war halted Philadelphia's commerce in 1748, revealing that even major colonial cities were vulnerable to attack.

The prize war had serious adverse effects on the belligerents' maritime commerce. The colonial trade of Britain, Spain, and France declined sharply during the 1740s. Losses to enemy privateers totaled in the millions of pounds sterling. This was only part of the prize war's price tag, however. The scramble for prizes increased business costs dramatically, as freight rates, insurance premiums, and seamen's wages soared.

Privateers were successful at the aggregate or national level, but the fortunes of individual private men-of-war are more difficult to determine. A large minority of colonial cruisers failed to capture a single enemy merchantman, while many American privateers seized only one prize. The owners of these vessels probably lost money on their investments. Windfall profits were possible, however. If a privateer sloop captured a prize of only average value, its owners stood to earn profits exceeding 100 percent while its crew could pocket prize money surpassing wages in the king's service or the merchant marine. Moreover, both investors and privateersmen simultaneously demonstrated laudable patriotic spirit.

Privateering was synonymous with imperial warfare during the mercantilist world of the seventeenth and eighteenth centuries. Merchants had invested heavily in private men-of-war before King George's War, and privateering played the leading role in America's war effort during the 1740s. The French and Indian War, the American Revolution, and the Napoleonic Wars (including the War of 1812) all witnessed increasing numbers of private warships. The increasing security of Atlantic commerce depicted by some scholars often proved illusory during the chronic warfare of the last half of the eighteenth century and the first fifteen years of the nineteenth. As long as nations needed to mobilize private capital to augment sea power, and naval fleets could not control wartime shipping lanes, privateering dominated American maritime conflict and exerted a major influence on colonial commerce.

APPENDIX:

THE PRIVATEER DATA FILE

The major evidential base for this study is a computer data file containing 3,973 instances of prize actions constructed primarily from news reports published in the colonial press. Vice-admiralty court records and other government documents have also been utilized. A prize action is defined as an encounter between a predator (privateer, naval vessel, colonial coast guard vessel, etc.) and an enemy craft. An action succeeded when the latter was captured, whether by armed struggle or by surrender at the approach of the warship. Each prize action constitutes a case in the data file; each report that a privateer was embarking on a cruise also constitutes a case. Each case in the file contains a series of variables pertaining to prize actions. These variables provide information about the most important aspects of privateering.[1]

The first step in the construction of the data file was a thorough examination of the *Pennsylvania Gazette,* the best American newspaper for research on the period, 1739–1749. Several factors dictated the *Gazette*'s selection. First, Benjamin Franklin was one of America's best newspaper editors, and he devoted considerable attention to imperial hostilities, especially the maritime conflict. Second, Philadelphia's central location on the Atlantic seaboard facilitated reporting the news from the more northern and southern colonies. Third, virtually all issues of the *Gazette* during the wars of 1739–1748 have survived.[2]

226

The second step in creating the data file was to supplement the *Pennsylvania Gazette*'s coverage of the prize war with articles from newspapers from the other major American seaports. The *Boston News-Letter* provided the best coverage of the war in New England, so it was examined in preference to Boston's other papers. The *South-Carolina Gazette* was Charles Town's only newspaper in the 1740s; fortunately it was also one of the best in the colonies. Four newspapers were required to cover New York because none of Manhattan's papers boasted a continuous run throughout the war. Williamsburg's *Virginia Gazette* provided information about the war's impact in the Chesapeake, but the large number of missing issues limited its usefulness.

The data file was completed by entering cases from other privateering sources. The vice-admiralty court records for the mainland colonies were the most important additional sources. Bonds for Rhode Island letters of marque also contained valuable information, albeit for a small number of cases. These bonds, which were similar to a security deposit filed with the colony's vice-admiralty court to ensure compliance with British prize law, provided the names of privateer owners, captains, vessels, and shipping details. The Rhode Island Admiralty Lists also indicated the names of owners, captains, vessels, and the duration of privateering cruises. Finally, some miscellaneous papers in the Massachusetts Archives provided a few additional cases.

Table A.1 reveals that the colonial press provided the overwhelming majority of cases in the data file, and the *Pennsylvania Gazette* accounted for more than half of the cases. This preponderance resulted from the research design. As mentioned, all cases from the *Gazette* were entered into the data file first. Cases from the other newspapers were included only if the prize actions they reported were not mentioned in Franklin's paper or if they contained more information than the *Gazette*'s accounts. Duplicate reports, were, of course, rigidly excluded from the data file. Cases from the other sources were then entered if the prize actions they documented had been missed by the press or if they provided more complete information. Again, duplicate cases were deleted from the file.

The following is a list and brief description of the variables included in each case in the data file.

SOURCE:
Indicates the data source for each case.
DATE:
Indicates the date of the data source in which the case appeared. This is normally the date of a colonial newspaper. Cases from sources other than the colonial press received the date from the letter of marque, vice-admiralty decree, or other appropriate source.

TABLE A.1
Sources for the Privateer Data File

Source	N	%
Boston News-Letter	568	14.3
New-York Evening-Post	267	6.3
New-York Gazette	13	.3
New-York Weekly Journal	148	3.7
New-York Weekly Post-Boy	174	4.4
Pennsylvania Gazette	2,153	54.2
Virginia Gazette	27	.7
South-Carolina Gazette	502	12.6
Colonial Vice-Admiralty Court Records[a]	73	1.9
Mass. Archives[b]	14	.4
R.I. Admiralty Lists[c]	21	.5
R.I. Bonds for Letters of Marque[d]	13	.3
Totals	3,973	100.0

[a]Massachusetts Vice-Admiralty Court Records, V, Suffolk County Courthouse, Boston; Rhode Island Vice-Admiralty Court Records, Rhode Island Admiralty Papers, I–VIII, Rhode Island State Archives, Providence; Minutes of the Vice-Admiralty Court of the Province of New York, I–II, (photostats), Library of Congress; Pennsylvania Vice-Admiralty Court Records, Boxes 1 and 2, (photostats), Lib. Cong.; South Carolina Minutes of the Vice-Admiralty Courts at Charles Town, Boxes 4 and 5, (photostats), Lib. Cong.

[b]Massachusetts Archives, LXIV, Maritime, 1740–1753, Massachusetts State House, Boston.

[c]Maritime Papers: Colonial Wars, 1723–1760, 82–124, R.I. State Archs.

[d]Bonds for Rhode Island Letters of Marque, Rhode Island Notary Public Records, IV–V, R.I. State Archs.

CATEGORY:

Indicates the predator's nationality and status—privateer, naval vessel, letter of marque ship, etc.

PRIZENAT:

Indicates the prize vessel's nationality.

Name Variables: CAPTAIN, SHIP, PRIZE, PRIZECAPT

These variables indicate the names of the predator commander and vessel (CAPTAIN and SHIP) and the names of the prize vessel and master (PRIZE and PRIZECAPT).

HOMEPORT, PRIZEHOME:

Indicate the home port of the predator (HOMEPORT) and the prize (PRIZEHOME).

TYPE, PRIZETYPE:

Indicate the type of vessel (ship, sloop, schooner, etc.) in which the predator (TYPE) and prize (PRIZETYPE) sailed.

TONS, PRIZETONS:

Indicate the tons burden of the predator (TONS) and prize (PRIZETONS) vessels.

MEN, PRIZEMEN:

Indicate the number of men serving on board the predator (MEN) and prize (PRIZEMEN) vessels.

GUNS, SWIVELS, PRIZEGUNS, PRIZESWIVELS:

Indicate the number of carriage guns and swivel guns carried on board the predator (GUNS and SWIVELS) and prize (PRIZEGUNS and PRIZESWIVELS) vessels.

DESTINATION, EMBARKATION:

Indicate, respectively, the prize vessel's destination and port of embarkation.

PORTAKEN:

Indicates the port to which the prize was dispatched or escorted after a successful prize action.

ACTIONPLACE:

Indicates the geographical place where the prize action occurred.

ACTIONHOURS:

Indicates the prize action's duration in hours.

Casualty Variables: CAPKILL, CAPWOUND, CAPPRIS, PRIZEKILL, PRIZEWOUND, PRIZEPRIS:

Indicate the number of men who were killed, wounded, or captured during a prize action on board the predator (CAPKILL, CAPWOUND, and CAPRIS) and prize (PRIZEKILL, PRIZEWOUND, and PRIZEPRIS) vessels.

Variables, VALUEPD, CURRENCY, VALUE8:

Indicate the value of the prize vessel. VALUEPD indicates the data source expressed the value in pounds; CURRENCY indicates if VALUEPD refers to pounds sterling or the currency of a British colony. VALUE8 indicates that the data source expressed the value in Spanish pieces of eight.

PRCARGO:
Provides information concerning the prize's cargo.

PVTRSAIL, PRIZESAIL:
Indicate the sailing arrangements of the predator (PVTRSAIL) and prize (PRIZESAIL) vessels during the prize action.

Although the privateer data file is the most complete source on the maritime prize war of 1739–1748, it has limitations. Because the file was constructed from British North American sources, it is more complete for British colonial privateers than it is for Spanish and French predators. The file has more valid observations for the names of American privateer commanders and vessels, for example, than for their enemy counterparts. Missing data is more of a problem for Spanish and French prize actions. The same is true for actions involving the Royal Navy. The file is also more reliable for North American prize actions than for engagements occurring in European sea-lanes, where few American private men-of-war ventured. Despite these caveats, the data file presents a reliable picture of the prize war because colonial newspapers were very much concerned about British vessels captured by the enemy. Although the data for a Spanish or French privateer may be incomplete, American editors devoted great attention to their actions. British vessels taken by the enemy were important news items.

Notes

NOTES TO THE INTRODUCTION

1. Alexander O. Exquemelin's *De Americaeneche Zee Roover* (Amsterdam, 1678), translated into English as John Esquemeling, *Bucaniers of America* (London, 1684) is the most famous account of seventeenth-century buccaneering. It ran through five English editions by 1699 and was also translated into French, Spanish, and German. Using the pen name Charles Johnson, Daniel Defoe contributed an important collection to the literature on piracy, *A General History of the Pyrates*, ed. Manuel Schonhorn (Columbia, S.C., 1972; orig. publ. in 2 vols., London, 1724, 1728).

2. Marcus Rediker, " 'Under the Banner of King Death': The Social World of Anglo-American Pirates, 1716 to 1726," *William and Mary Quarterly*, 3d Ser., XXXVIII (1981), 203–227, and *Between the Devil and the Deep Blue Sea: Merchant Seamen, Pirates, and the Anglo-American World, 1700–1750* (Cambridge, 1987); Robert C. Ritchie, *Captain Kidd and the War against the Pirates* (Cambridge, Mass., 1986); B.R. Burg, *Sodomy and the Perception of Evil: English Sea Rovers in the Seventeenth-Century Caribbean* (New York, 1983).

3. James F. Shepherd and Gary M. Walton, *Shipping, Maritime Trade, and the Economic Development of Colonial North America* (Cambridge, 1972), 80–90; Douglass C. North, "Sources of Productivity Change in Ocean Shipping, 1600–1850," *Journal of Political Economy*, LXXVI (1968), 953–970.

4. Michael Roberts, "The Military Revolution, 1560–1660," in Michael Roberts, *Essays in Swedish History* (Minneapolis, 1967), 195–225. See also Geoffrey Parker, *The Military Revolution: Military Innovation and the Rise of the West, 1500–1800* (Cambridge, 1988).

5. Steven Saunders Webb, *The Governors-General: The English Army and the Definition of the Empire, 1569–1681* (Chapel Hill, N.C., 1979), stresses the

importance of military rather than commercial considerations for England's overseas expansion. However true this may have been for the seventeenth century (and certainly Webb's thesis has been forcefully attacked), it is of doubtful validity for the eighteenth century, especially the 1740s.

NOTES TO CHAPTER 1

1. J. Franklin Jameson, ed., *Privateering and Piracy in the Colonial Period: Illustrative Documents* (New York, 1923).

2. James G. Lydon, *Pirates, Privateers, and Profits* (Upper Saddle River, N.J., 1970).

3. Pauline Maier, "Isaac Sears and the Business of Revolution," in Pauline Maier, *The Old Revolutionaries: Political Lives in the Age of Samuel Adams* (New York, 1980), 59–60.

4. Seventeenth-century privateers may have been marginal men, but their Elizabethan predecessors included some of England's wealthiest and most respected merchants and mariners. See Kenneth R. Andrews, *Elizabethan Privateering: English Privateering during the Spanish War, 1585–1603* (Cambridge, 1964).

5. Robert C. Ritchie, *Captain Kidd and the War against the Pirates* (Cambridge, Mass., 1986); Hugh F. Rankin, *The Golden Age of Piracy* (New York, 1969), 152–158; I.K. Steele, *Politics of Colonial Policy: The Board of Trade in Colonial Administration, 1696–1720* (New York, 1968), chap. 3.

6. Richard Pares, *War and Trade in the West Indies, 1739–1763* (Oxford, 1936), chaps. 1–2; Jean O. McLachlan, *Trade and Peace with Old Spain: A Study of the Influence of Commerce on Anglo-Spanish Diplomacy in the First Half of the Eighteenth Century* (Cambridge, 1940), chap. 4; Geoffrey J. Walker, *Spanish Politics and Imperial Trade, 1700–1789* (Bloomington, Ind., 1979), 205–209; Ernest G. Hildner, Jr., "The Rôle of the South Sea Company in the Diplomacy Leading to the War of Jenkins' Ear, 1729–1739," *Hispanic American Historical Review,* XVIII (1938), 322–341.

7. Walker, *Spanish Politics,* 68–74; McLachlan, *Trade and Peace,* 46–47, 78–79.

8. John Charles Martin Ogelsby, "War at Sea in the West Indies, 1739–1748" (Ph.D. diss., University of Washington, 1963), 5; Pares, *War and Trade,* 22–23; John Robert McNeill, *Atlantic Empires of France and Spain: Louisbourg and Havana, 1700–1763* (Chapel Hill, N.C., 1985), 89–91.

9. *Boston News-Letter,* 5 and 26 Mar. 1730.

10. See, for example, *ibid.,* 16 Apr. 1730; *Pennsylvania Gazette* (Philadelphia), 16 Mar., 10 July, 26 Oct. 1733, 31 Oct. 1734, 3 Jan., 14 Mar., 15 June, 10 Aug. 1738.

11. *Bos. News-Letter,* 5 Mar. 1730.

12. *Pa. Gaz.,* 7 Oct. 1731; *Bos. News-Letter,* 14 Oct. 1731.

13. *Boston Evening-Post,* 25 July 1737.

14. McLachlan, *Trade and Peace,* 78–121; Pares, *War and Trade,* 28. Colonists

could follow the progress of these negotiations in the press. See *Boston Gazette,* 11 June and 23 July 1739; *Pa. Gaz.,* 9, 26 Apr., and 3 May 1739.

15. *Pa. Gaz.,* 26 Apr. 1739.

16. Daniel A. Baugh, *British Naval Administration in the Age of Walpole* (Princeton, N.J., 1965), 22; Richard Pares, *Colonial Blockade and Neutral Rights, 1739–1763* (Oxford, 1938), 6–7, 17; Pares, *War and Trade,* 46–47.

17. W.L. Grant and J. Munro, eds., *Acts of the Privy Council of England: Colonial Series, 1613–1783* (1908–1912; reprint, Nendeln, Liechtenstein, 1966), III, 636.

18. *Bos. Gazette,* 20 Aug. 1739; *New-York Weekly Journal,* 27 Aug. 1739.

19. *Bos. Eve.-Post,* 27 Aug. 1739.

20. *Ibid.*

21. Massachusetts Archives, LXXXII, Minutes of the Council, 1733–1753, 326–363, Massachusetts State House, Boston.

22. *N.-Y. Wkly. Journ.,* 20, 27 Aug., and 24 Sept. 1739; Lydon, *Pirates, Privateers, and Profits,* 87.

23. *Pa. Gaz.,* 23 Aug. 1739; *Virginia Gazette* (Williamsburg), 31 Aug. 1739; *South-Carolina Gazette* (Charles Town), 15 Sept. 1739.

24. Carl Bridenbaugh, *Cities in Revolt: Urban Life in America, 1743–1776,* rev. ed. (New York, 1971), 63–64. For an eloquent statement of Quaker principles concerning privateering, see John Reynell to Elias Bland, 11 Feb. 1745, John Reynell Letterbook, 24 May 1744–4 Oct. 1745, Historical Society of Pennsylvania, Philadelphia.

25. Bannister to Hugh Vans, 19 Aug. 1741, John Bannister Copy Book, 1730–1742, 188, Newport Historical Society, Newport, R.I.

26. *Pa. Gaz.,* 30 Aug. 1744.

27. *New-York Weekly Post-Boy,* 17 Sept. 1744.

28. *New-York Gazette,* 29 Oct. 1744. Jacob M. Price, "Economic Function and the Growth of American Port Towns in the Eighteenth Century," *Perspectives in American History,* VIII (1974), 176.

29. *Pa. Gaz.,* 5 Mar. 1745.

30. *Ibid.,* 5 Jan. 1745.

31. *Ibid.,* 27 Sept. 1745.

32. *Ibid.,* 3 Mar. 1746.

33. *Ibid.,* 24 July 1746.

34. *Bos. News-Letter,* 27 Jan. 1747.

35. *N.-Y. Wkly. Post-Boy,* 13 June 1748.

36. *Pa. Gaz.,* 6 June 1745. Tucker commanded the New York privateer *Mary Anne.*

37. 13 Geo. II, 1740, c. 4, in Danby Pickering, ed., *The Statutes at Large . . .* (Cambridge, 1762–1807), XVII, 360–370. Chapter 2 discusses British prize law.

38. Newcastle to the Governor and Company of Rhode Island, 18 Apr. 1740, in

Gertrude Selwyn Kimball, ed., *The Correspondence of the Colonial Governors of Rhode Island, 1723-1775* (1902-1903; reprint, Freeport, N.Y., 1969), I, 149-150. This act also benefited Royal Navy officers enormously because it greatly increased their share of prize money. See Julian Gwyn, *The Enterprising Admiral: The Personal Fortune of Admiral Sir Peter Warren* (Montreal, 1974), 318.

39. *Pa. Gaz.,* 14 June 1744.

40. John R. Bartlett, ed., *Records of the Colony of Rhode Island and Providence Plantations in New England* (1859; reprint, New York, 1968), IV, 560-561.

41. *Captain Peter Warren v. Ship Le St. Francois Xavier* (1744), Minutes of the Vice-Admiralty Court of the Province of New York, I, 162, (photostats), Library of Congress.

42. Clinton to the Board of Trade, 9 Oct. 1744, in Edward B. O'Callaghan, ed., *Documents, Relative to the Colonial History of the State of New York* (Albany, 1853-1887), IV, 262.

43. Ellis Ames, Abner C. Goodell *et al.,* eds., *The Acts and Resolves, Public and Private, of the Province of the Massachusetts Bay . . .* (Boston, 1869-1922), III, 218.

44. *Pa. Gaz.,* 27 Oct. 1743.

45. McNeill, *Atlantic Empires,* 91.

46. *Pa. Gaz.,* 22 Mar. 1748.

47. For a useful discussion of this scholarly argument see C.H. Wilson, "Trade, Society and the State," in *The Economy of Expanding Europe in the Sixteenth and Seventeenth Centuries,* vol. IV of *The Cambridge Economic History of Europe,* ed. E.E. Rich and C.H. Wilson (Cambridge, 1967), 495, hereafter cited as "Trade, Society, State"; and Immanuel Wallerstein, *The Modern World-System II: Mercantilism and the Consolidation of the European World-Economy, 1600-1750* (New York, 1980), 37-38.

48. Eli F. Heckscher, *Mercantilism* (London, 1935), 2 vols.; Jacob Viner, "Power Versus Plenty as Objectives of Foreign Policy in the 17th and 18th Centuries," *World Politics,* I (1948). See also Charles Wilson, " 'Mercantilism': Some Vicissitudes of an Idea," *Economic History Review,* 2d Ser., X (1957), and Walter E. Minchinton, ed., *Mercantilism: System or Expediency* (Lexington, Mass., 1969).

49. W.A. Speck, "The International and Imperial Context," in Jack P. Greene and J.R. Pole, eds., *Colonial British America: Essays in the New History of the Early Modern Era* (Baltimore, 1984), 395.

50. D.C. Coleman, "Mercantilism Revisited," *Historical Journal,* XXIII (1980), 791.

51. For useful discussions concerning mercantilism and the balance of trade see Wilson, "Trade, Society, State," 496-503; John J. McCusker and Russell R. Menard, *The Economy of British America, 1607-1789* (Chapel Hill, N.C., 1985), 35-38; Michael Kammen, *Empire and Interest: The American Colonies and the Politics of Mercantilism* (Philadelphia, 1970), 4-8.

52. Jan De Vries, *The Economy of Europe in an Age of Crisis, 1600-1750* (Cambridge, 1976), 239-240; Kristof Glamann, "The Changing Patterns of Trade," in Rich and Wilson, eds., *Cambridge Economic History of Europe,* IV, 210-211;

Rudolph C. Blitz, "Mercantilist Policies and the Pattern of World Trade, 1500–1750," *Journal of Economic History*, XXVII (1967), 39.

53. Wilson, "Trade, Society, State," 514.

54. Kristof Glamann, "European Trade 1500–1750," trans. Geoffrey French, in *The Sixteenth and Seventeenth Centuries*, vol. II of *The Fontana Economic History of Europe*, ed. Carlo M. Cipolla (London, 1974), 428.

55. Walter L. Dorn, *Competition for Empire, 1740–1763* (New York, 1940), 8–9; Speck, "The International and Imperial Context," in Greene and Pole, eds., *Colonial British America*, 385.

56. McCusker and Menard, *Economy of British America*, 37–38; Wilson, "Trade, Society, State," 495–521; Dorn, *Competition for Empire*, 7–12; Betty Behrens, "Government and Society," in *The Economic Organization of Early Modern Europe*, vol. V of *The Cambridge Economic History of Europe*, ed. E.E. Rich and C.H. Wilson (Cambridge, 1977), 573–574, hereafter cited as "Government and Society."

57. De Vries, *Economy of Europe*, 242.

58. Wilson, "Trade, Society, State," 569; Behrens, "Government and Society," 522–523.

59. Quoted in Christopher Hill, *The Century of Revolution, 1603–1714* (London, 1974 ed.), 185.

60. The term is Wallerstein's; see *Modern World-System II*, chap. 2.

61. De Vries, *Economy of Europe*, 122–123, 253; Wallerstein, *Modern World-System II*, 114, 246–284; Dorn, *Competition for Empire*, 8; Wilson, "Trade, Society, State," 536–537.

62. Dorn, *Competition for Empire*, 126.

63. Michael Roberts, "The Military Revolution, 1560–1660," in Michael Roberts, *Essays in Swedish History* (Minneapolis, 1967), 195–225; Geoffrey Parker, *The Military Revolution: Military Innovation and the Rise of the West, 1500–1800* (Cambridge, 1988).

64. De Vries, *Economy of Europe*, 203–207; Samuel E. Finer, "State- and Nation-Building in Europe: The Role of the Military," in Charles Tilly, ed., *The Formation of National States in Western Europe* (Princeton, N.J., 1975), 84–163; David G. Chandler *et al.*, "Armies and Navies," in *The Rise of Great Britain and Russia, 1688–1715/25*, vol. VI of *The New Cambridge Modern History*, ed. J.S. Bromley (Cambridge, 1970), 741–833, hereafter cited as "Armies and Navies."

65. Michael Duffy, "The Foundations of British Naval Power," in Michael Duffy, ed., *The Military Revolution and the State, 1500–1800* (Exeter, Eng., 1980), 51–56, 82; De Vries, *Economy of Europe*, 205; Chandler *et al.*, "Armies and Navies," 792.

66. Behrens, "Government and Society," 567.

67. Michael Duffy, "Introduction: The Military Revolution and the State, 1500–1800," in Duffy, ed., *Military Revolution*, 1; see also Behrens, "Government and Society," 555–567, and Finer, "State- and Nation-Building," in Tilly, ed., *Formation of National States*.

68. David J. Starkey, "The Economic and Military Significance of British Privateering, 1702–83," *Journal of Transport History*, 3d Ser., IX (1988), 50–51.

69. Baugh, *British Naval Administration*, 112–113; Gwyn, *The Enterprising Admiral.*

70. Stephen Saunders Webb emphasizes the importance of military conquest as the primary basis of the English Empire in *The Governors General: The English Army and the Definition of the Empire, 1569–1681* (Chapel Hill, N.C., 1979). For perceptive criticism of Webb's argument see Richard R. Johnson, "The Imperial Webb: The Thesis of Garrison Government in Early America Considered," *William and Mary Quarterly*, 3d Ser., XLIII (1986), 408–430, and Ian Steele, "Governors or Generals?: A Note on Martial Law and the Revolution of 1689 in English America," *WMQ*, 3d Ser., XLVI (1989), 304–314.

71. Baugh, *British Naval Administration*, 22; see also Sir Herbert Richmond, *The Navy in the War of 1739–48* (Cambridge, 1920), I, xx–xxi, 30–35; and Dorn, *Competition for Empire*, 106–108.

72. See especially Alfred Thayer Mahan, *The Influence of Sea Power upon History, 1660–1783* (New York, 1890).

73. See, for example, Richmond, *The Navy in the War of 1739–48;* Julian S. Corbett, *England in the Seven Years' War: A Study of Combined Strategy* (London, 1907), 2 vols.; and Gerald S. Graham, *Empire of the North Atlantic: The Maritime Struggle for North America* (Toronto, 1950). For a recent, overly glowing view of life in the king's ships and a scathing assessment of privateering, see N.A.M. Rodger, *The Wooden World: An Anatomy of the Georgian Navy* (Annapolis, Md., 1986), 128–129, 160, 185–186. An exception to the trend among naval historians to criticize (or largely ignore) privateering is Geoffrey Symcox's *The Crisis of French Sea Power, 1688–1697: From the Guerre d'Escadre to the Guerre de Course* (The Hague, 1974).

74. Andrews, *Elizabethan Privateering.*

75. Michael Craton, "The Role of the Caribbean Vice Admiralty Courts in British Imperialism," *Caribbean Studies*, XI (1971), 5–20; Dorothy S. Towle, ed., *Records of the Vice-Admiralty Court of Rhode Island, 1716–1752* (Washington, D.C., 1936), 100.

76. Hiller B. Zobel, *The Boston Massacre* (New York, 1970), 33.

77. Although the High Court of Admiralty Papers in the Public Record Office comprise a veritable treasure trove of records for English privateering, they offer meager rewards for historians of American private men-of-war before the American Revolution. For valuable and perceptive studies employing H.C.A. sources, often using sophisticated quantitative analysis, see Andrews, *Elizabethan Privateering;* W.R. Meyer, "English Privateering in the War of 1688 to 1697," *Mariner's Mirror*, LXVII (1981), 259–272, and "The Channel Island Privateers, 1793–1815," in A.G. Jamieson, ed., *A People of the Sea: The Maritime History of the Channel Islands* (London, 1986), 173–194; Walter E. Minchinton and David J. Starkey, "Characteristics of Privateers Operating from the British Isles Against America, 1777–1783," in Timothy J. Runyan, ed., *Ships, Seafaring and Society: Essays in Maritime History* (Detroit, 1987), 251–274; and Starkey, "Significance of British Privateering," *Jrn. Transport Hist.*, 3d Ser., IX (1988), 50–59. The large collection

of prize papers, H.C.A. 32, contains records pertaining to privateers from Great Britain, not the colonies; see List & Index Society, *High Court of Admiralty: Index to Prize Papers, 1739–1748* (London, 1973). Because American privateers had their prizes condemned in colonial courts, only appeal cases were forwarded to London. Appeals were rare. Of the 215 extant prize cases in the records of the mainland vice-admiralty courts, only 13 (6%) were definitely appealed.

78. Jameson, ed., *Privateering and Piracy*, 381–429.

79. H.S. Vaughan, ed., *Voyages and Cruises of Commodore Walker* (London, 1928), xiv.

80. For the *Greyhound*'s capture, see *New-York Evening-Post*, 5 and 19 Jan. 1747; *Pa. Gaz.*, 27 Jan. 1747; the *Queen of Hungary*'s action was reported the *Pa. Gaz.*, 9 May 1745. Boston's Old North Church contains a plaque commemorating Capt. Gruchy's exploits and his gift of four beautifully carved wooden statues. The plaque reads: "In memory of Thomas James Gruchy Junior warden of the Church and Merchant adventurer from Jersey who in parlous times as Captain of the Privateer Queen of Hungary took from a French ship in the year 1746 the four figures of cherubim now in front of the organ[.]" See Figure 1.6.

81. For commentary concerning the circulation of news in the colonial press see Ian K. Steele, *The English Atlantic, 1675–1740: An Exploration of Communication and Community* (New York, 1986), chap. 8, 132–167, and Warren Bertram Johnson, "The Content of American Colonial Newspapers Relative to International Affairs, 1704–1763" (Ph.D. diss., University of Washington, 1962), 135–136, 452.

82. Please see the Appendix for a discussion of the methodology employed to examine the press and other privateering sources.

NOTES TO CHAPTER 2

1. W.L. Grant and J. Munro, eds., *Acts of the Privy Council of England: Colonial Series, 1613–1783* (1908–1912; reprint, Nendeln, Liechtenstein, 1966), III, 636.

2. George II to the Governor and Company of Rhode Island, 15 June 1739. (Newcastle signed this letter.) Gertrude Selwyn Kimball, ed., *The Correspondence of the Colonial Governors of Rhode Island, 1723–1775* (1902–1903; reprint, Freeport, N.Y., 1969), I, 106–108.

3. *Ibid.*, 108.

4. See, for example, the bond for a letter of marque signed by Capt. James Allen, John Brown, and Peleg Brown in Rhode Island Notary Public Records, IV, 416–419, Rhode Island State Archives, Providence.

5. *Boston Evening-Post*, 26 Nov. 1739.

6. Richard Pares, *Colonial Blockade and Neutral Rights, 1739–1763* (Oxford, 1938), 45; James G. Lydon, *Pirates, Privateers, and Profits* (Upper Saddle River, N.J., 1970), 86–87, 89, 95. On Morris's role in New York's factional politics, see Patricia U. Bonomi, *A Factious People: Politics and Society in Colonial New York* (New York, 1971), chap. 4.

7. Grant and Munro, eds., *Acts of the Privy Council*, III, 636.

8. A copy of these instructions is printed in J. Franklin Jameson, ed., *Privateering and Piracy in the Colonial Period: Illustrative Documents* (New York, 1923), 347–354.

9. Pares, *Colonial Blockade,* 46, 65.

10. Helen J. Crump, *Colonial Admiralty Jurisdiction in the Seventeenth Century* (London, 1931), 120.

11. 6 Anne, 1708, c. 37, in Danby Pickering, ed., *The Statutes at Large . . .* (Cambridge, 1762–1807), XI, 433–443.

12. *Ibid.,* 434–435.

13. *Ibid.,* 435–436.

14. *Ibid.,* 437.

15. *Ibid.,* 438.

16. *Ibid.,* 438–443.

17. 13 Geo. II, 1740, c. 4, *ibid.,* XVII, 360–370. Lydon states that this new act "expressly exempted privateersmen from impressment," but the act contained no such provision; see Lydon, *Pirates, Privateers, and Profits,* 86. Chapter 4 discusses impressment.

18. 13 Geo. II, 1740, c. 4, in Pickering, ed., *The Statutes at Large,* XVII, 368.

19. *Ibid.,* 364.

20. *Ibid.,* 369.

21. *Ibid.,* 366–367.

22. 17 Geo. II, 1744, c. 34, *ibid.,* XVIII, 252–263.

23. *Ibid.,* 254–255.

24. *Ibid.,* 263.

25. For the expansion of American privateering after 1739 compared with earlier conflicts, see Lydon, *Pirates, Privateers, and Profits;* Sydney V. James, *Colonial Rhode Island: A History* (New York, 1975), 117–118, 132; Carl Bridenbaugh, *Cities in Revolt: Urban Life in America, 1743–1776,* rev. ed. (New York, 1971), 61–69. For the escalation of American privateering during the American Revolution and the War of 1812, see William M. Fowler, Jr., *Rebels under Sail: The American Navy during the American Revolution* (New York, 1976), 22–24, 244–247; and Jerome R. Garitee, *The Republic's Private Navy: The American Privateering Business as Practiced by Baltimore during the War of 1812* (Middletown, Conn., 1977).

26. Crump, *Colonial Admiralty Jurisdiction,* 128; Carl Ubbelohde, *The Vice-Admiralty Courts and the American Revolution* (Chapel Hill, N.C., 1960), 18–22; Richard B. Morris, *Government and Labor in Early America* (1946; reprint, New York, 1965), 232.

27. Michael Craton, "The Role of the Caribbean Vice Admiralty Courts in British Imperialism," *Caribbean Studies,* XI (1971), 5–20.

28. Charles M. Andrews "Introduction," to Dorothy S. Towle, ed., *Records of the Vice-Admiralty Court of Rhode Island, 1716–1752* (Washington, D.C., 1936), 19.

29. Partridge to Governor Richard Ward, 21 Feb. 1743, in Kimball, ed., *R.I. Gov. Correspondence,* I, 224–225.

30. John R. Bartlett, ed., *Records of the Colony of Rhode Island and Providence Plantations in New England* (1859; reprint, New York, 1968), V, 60.

31. Strahan to Corbett, 1 Feb. 1744, in Kimball, ed., *R.I. Gov. Correspondence,* I, 243–245.

32. For the assembly's reactions see Bartlett, ed., *Records of Colonial R.I.,* VI, 107. See Kimball, ed., *R.I. Gov. Correspondence,* II, 273–276, 291–292, for Partridge's activities. Evidence of Andrews's privateering investments are in Rhode Island Notary Public Records, V, 322.

33. Pares, *Colonial Blockade,* 131.

34. For Gidley's privateering investments see the bonds for letters of marque in Rhode Island Notary Public Records, IV, 419, 468, 479.

35. Greene to the duke of Newcastle, 15 Mar. 1744, in Bartlett, ed., *Records of Colonial R.I.,* V, 79–80.

36. Burton A. Konkle, *The Life of Andrew Hamilton, 1676–1741: "The Day-Star of the American Revolution"* (1941; reprint, Freeport, N.Y., 1972), 5–9, 16, 66–106.

37. *Dictionary of American Biography,* s.v. "Auchmuty, Robert"; John A. Schutz, *William Shirley: King's Governor of Massachusetts* (Chapel Hill, N.C., 1961), 11–12.

38. M. Eugene Sirmans, *Colonial South Carolina: A Political History, 1663–1763* (Chapel Hill, N.C., 1966), 181, 247, 278–279.

39. Bonomi, *A Factious People,* 71, 304–307, 314.

40. Konkle, *Andrew Hamilton,* 47–60; Sirmans, *Colonial South Carolina,* 247, 278–283.

41. For a detailed breakdown of vice-admiralty court decisions for each colony and each judge, see Carl Eliot Swanson, "Predators and Prizes: Privateering in the British Colonies during the War of 1739–1748" (Ph.D. thesis, University of Western Ontario, 1979), 45–48.

42. Hiller B. Zobel, *The Boston Massacre* (New York, 1970), 33.

43. *Griffith* v. *Snow Lady de la Rosara* (1744), *Bennetland* v. *Schooner Magdalene* (1744), *Cranston* v. *Spanish Sloop* (1744), Rhode Island Vice-Admiralty Court Records, Rhode Island Admiralty Papers, II, 88–90, 104–110, 111–115, R.I. State Archs.

44. *Jefferies et al.* v. *Sloop Grand Diable* (1746), *Burgess et al.* v. *Brig Le Mar/Dispatch* (1748), Minutes of the Vice-Admiralty Court of the Province of New York, I, 214–222, II, 88–97 (photostats), Library of Congress.

45. Reynell to Henry Sherburne, Jr., 15 May 1746, John Reynell Letterbook, 5 Oct. 1745–29 May 1747, Historical Society of Pennsylvania, Philadelphia.

46. Reynell to Sherburne, 7 July 1746, *ibid.* From libel to final decree, this case lasted eleven weeks.

47. Craton, "Role of the Caribbean Vice Admiralty Courts," *Carib. Stud.,* XI (1971), 11.

48. *Boston Gazette,* 2 June 1740.

49. *Baudry* v. *Davidson* (1742), Massachusetts Vice-Admiralty Court Records, V, 94–97, Suffolk County Courthouse, Boston. John J. McCusker, *Money and Exchange in Europe and America, 1600–1775: A Handbook* (Chapel Hill, N.C., 1978), 316, provided the sterling exchange rates for all conversions in this chapter.

50. Bannister to Hugh Vans, 8 Jan. 1742, John Bannister Copy Book, 1730–1742, 238, Newport Historical Society, Newport, R.I.

51. *Bowne* v. *Ship Victory* (1745), *Bowne* v. *Ship Apollo* (1745), Pennsylvania Vice-Admiralty Court Records, Box 1, 290–293 (photostats), Lib. Cong.

52. Pringle to Bennett, 16 Sept. 1742, in Walter B. Edgar, ed., *The Letterbook of Robert Pringle* (Columbia, S.C., 1972), I, 414.

53. Pringle to Bennett, 5 July 1742, *ibid.,* 385.

54. *Hadden et al.* v. *Sloop Dolphin* (1747), *Troupe et al.* v. *Sloop Flore de la Mere and Prize Goods* (1748), *Wainman et al.* v. *Snow Thomas and Mary* (1748), *Bill et al.* v. *Snow Concord* (1748), *Menzies et al.* v. *Brig Charming Mary* (1748), and *Troupe et al.* v. *Brig Ave Maria et al.* (1748), New York Vice-Admiralty Court Minutes, II, 48–51, 77–85, 85–87, 99–115, 115–119, 120–132.

55. *Sweet* v. *Sloop Young Johannes* (1747), R.I. Vice-Admiralty Court Records, V, 119–128.

56. *Sweet* v. *Snow True Briton* (1748), *ibid.,* VI, 107–118, VII, 33.

57. *Griffith* v. *Snow Caulker* (1743), *ibid.,* I, 91–102.

NOTES TO CHAPTER 3

1. Douglass C. North, "Sources of Productivity Change in Ocean Shipping, 1600–1850," *Journal of Political Economy,* LXXVI (1968), 953–970, and James F. Shepherd and Gary M. Walton, *Shipping, Maritime Trade, and the Economic Development of Colonial North America* (Cambridge, 1972).

2. Daniel A. Baugh, *British Naval Administration in the Age of Walpole* (Princeton, N.J., 1965), 112.

3. Julian Gwyn, *The Enterprising Admiral: The Personal Fortune of Admiral Sir Peter Warren* (Montreal, 1974).

4. The Spanish colonies also maintained coast guard vessels—the *guarda-costas.* Once hostilities erupted, however, the American press only differentiated between Spanish privateers and the Spanish navy; *guarda-costas* were not mentioned. It was impracticable, therefore, to include *guarda-costas* in this discussion of colony vessels. Moreover, since many *guarda-costas* were actually privately owned vessels sailing with government permission to take prizes, they were indistinguishable from privateers. See Jean O. McLachlan, *Trade and Peace with Old Spain: A Study of the Influence of Commerce on Anglo-Spanish Diplomacy in the First Half of the Eighteenth Century* (Cambridge, 1940), 78–121; Richard Pares, *War and Trade in the West Indies, 1739–1763* (Oxford, 1936), 22–28, 52, 126; John Robert

McNeill, *Atlantic Empires of France and Spain: Louisbourg and Havana, 1700–1763* (Chapel Hill, N.C., 1985), 89–91.

5. Massachusetts Archives, LXIV, Maritime, 1740–1753, 70, 89–90, Massachusetts State House, Boston.

6. Worthington Chauncey Ford *et al.* eds., *Journals of the House of Representatives of Massachusetts* (Boston, 1919–1971), XIX, 123.

7. Law to Wanton, 3 Mar. 1746, in Gertrude Selwyn Kimball, ed., *The Correspondence of the Colonial Governors of Rhode Island, 1723–1775* (1902–1903; reprint, Freeport, N.Y., 1969), I, 408. For other letters concerning joint cruises of these sloops, see 261–262 and 267–269.

8. *New-York Evening-Post,* 10 Aug. 1747.

9. *Pennsylvania Gazette* (Philadelphia), 2 Dec. 1746 and 30 Apr. 1747.

10. George E. Reed, ed., *Pennsylvania Archives, Fourth Series: Papers of the Governors* (Harrisburg, Pa., 1900), I, 686–744, 852–860.

11. Samuel Powel to Gabriel Manigault, 27 May and 4 June 1747; Powel to Robert Wheatle, 30 May 1747, Samuel Powel Letterbook, III, 70, 82, Historical Society of Pennsylvania, Philadelphia. John Swift to John White, 30 May and 13 July 1747, John Swift Letter Book, 1747–1751, Hist. Soc. of Pa. *Pa. Gaz.,* 14 May and 15 Dec. 1747, and 2 and 16 June 1748.

12. Mass. Archs., LXIV, 60–62.

13. *Ibid.,* 63–65.

14. Bannister to Hugh Vans, 8 Jan. 1742, John Bannister Copy Book, Newport Historical Society, Newport, R.I., hereafter cited as Bannister Copy Book.

15. *Pa. Gaz.,* 3 Dec. 1747.

16. *Ibid.,* 15 Sept. 1748. Other stories concerning the *Bethel*'s capture appeared in the *Gazette*'s issues for 1 and 29 Sept. and 6 Oct. 1748.

17. *Ibid.,* 1 Sept. 1748. The exchange rate used for conversion to sterling is contained in John J. McCusker, *Money and Exchange in Europe and America, 1600–1775: A Handbook* (Chapel Hill, N.C., 1978), 310.

18. *Pa. Gaz.,* 1 Dec. 1748.

19. For the importance of trading and buccaneering in the earlier period see Kenneth R. Andrews, *Elizabethan Privateering: English Privateering during the Spanish War, 1585–1603* (Cambridge, 1964) and Richard S. Dunn, *Sugar and Slaves: The Rise of the Planter Class in the English West Indies, 1624–1713* (Chapel Hill, N.C., 1972).

20. The total of 2,598 is the number of cases in the data file involving British captors. Since many privateers and naval vessels participated in more than one prize action, it does not mean there were 2,598 *different* British predators.

21. Joseph A. Goldenberg, *Shipbuilding in Colonial America* (Charlottesville, Va., 1976), 77.

22. Howard I. Chapelle, *History of American Sailing Ships* (London, 1936), 11, and *The Search for Speed under Sail, 1700–1855* (New York, 1967), 10; Goldenberg, *Shipbuilding in Colonial America,* 78; Arthur P. Middleton, *Tobacco*

Coast: A Maritime History of Chesapeake Bay in the Colonial Era (Newport News, Va., 1953), 217.

23. Privateer owners frequently advertised in the newspapers for crews and stressed aspects of their ventures likely to produce a rewarding voyage—their captain's reputation, past successes, lucrative profit-sharing arrangements, and the vessel's seaworthiness. Significantly, these advertisements rarely stated that the craft was a "new ship, built for a Privateer." See the recruiting ad for the Philadelphia ship, *Pandour, Pa. Gaz.,* 18 Apr. 1745.

24. Chapelle, *Search for Speed,* 26–27.

25. Middleton, *Tobacco Coast,* 217, 252, 255; Goldenberg, *Shipbuilding in Colonial America,* 77. The tonnage figures presented here and throughout this analysis are tons burden, or deadweight tonnage.

26. Chapelle, *Search for Speed,* 26–27.

27. Goldenberg, *Shipbuilding in Colonial America,* 78; Middleton, *Tobacco Coast,* 217.

28. Chapelle, *Search for Speed,* 11; Goldenberg, *Shipbuilding in Colonial America,* 78.

29. Middleton, *Tobacco Coast,* 217; Chapelle, *History of American Sailing Ships,* 41; Goldenberg, *Shipbuilding in Colonial America,* 78.

30. Goldenberg, *Shipbuilding in Colonial America,* 79. See chapter 5 for a discussion of the colonial ports' roles in privateering.

31. Chapelle, *Search for Speed,* 27.

32. John Bannister to Capt. Joseph Harrison, 7 Dec. 1739, Bannister Copy Book, 41–42; *Boston Gazette,* 17 Dec. 1739; *Pa. Gaz.,* 3 and 29 Jan. 1740. Bannister owned the *Virgin Queen.*

33. *Pa. Gaz.,* 6 Mar. 1740.

34. *Ibid.,* 1 May 1740.

35. *Ibid.,* 25 Aug. 1743 and 21 Mar. 1744. The quotation is from 21 Mar. 1744.

36. Ralph Davis, *The Rise of the English Shipping Industry in the Seventeenth and Eighteenth Centuries* (London, 1962), 77–78; Byron Fairchild, *Messrs. William Pepperrell: Merchants at Piscataqua* (Ithaca, N.Y., 1954), 104; Goldenberg, *Shipbuilding in Colonial America,* 79–80; Middleton, *Tobacco Coast,* 217; Chapelle, *History of American Sailing Ships,* 15–16.

37. Goldenberg, *Shipbuilding in Colonial America,* 80–81; Davis, *Rise of the English Shipping Industry,* 79; Middleton, *Tobacco Coast,* 217.

38. Ford *et al.,* eds., *Mass. House Jours.,* XXI, 28.

39. *Pa. Gaz.,* 8 Aug. 1747.

40. *Ibid.,* 30 Aug. 1744.

41. *Ibid.,* 17 and 24 May 1744.

42. For the small arms normally used by privateers see the entry for 4 Sept. 1741 in the journal of the Newport privateer sloop *Revenge,* commanded by Benjamin Norton, in J. Franklin Jameson, ed., *Privateering and Piracy in the Colonial Period: Illustrative Documents* (New York, 1923), 417.

43. Pearson product-moment correlations (r) were computed to test the relationships of tonnage with crew size, carriage guns, and swivel guns. These tests revealed that all variables were strongly and directly related. The correlation coefficients for British colonial privateers for tonnage with crew size, carriage guns, and swivel guns were, respectively, r=.6909, r=.6948, and r=.7559. All coefficients were significant at the .01 level. Pearson correlations for tonnage with crew size and carriage guns were even stronger for Royal Navy vessels: r=.9677 and r=.9735. Both coefficients were significant at the .01 level. Enemy vessels also exhibited these relationships; correlations for tonnage with crew size and carriage guns were r=.5438 and r=.8957. Both coefficients were significant at the .05 level.

44. An analysis of variance revealed that the differences in the means for crew sizes, carriage guns, and swivel guns for American and French predators were statistically significant at the .01 level.

45. *Pa. Gaz.,* 6 Mar. 1740.

46. *Ibid.,* 6 June 1745.

47. Beekman to John Channing, 1 Sept. 1746, in Philip L. White, ed., *The Beekman Mercantile Papers, 1746–1799* (New York, 1956), I, 7.

48. H.S. Vaughan, ed., *Voyages and Cruises of Commodore Walker* (London, 1928), 2. This anonymous work was originally published in London in 1760.

49. Shepherd and Walton, *Shipping, Maritime Trade,* 196–197.

50. The average duration of 94 cruises conducted by Newport, New York, and Philadelphia privateers was nearly seven months. The Newport data consisted of 47 voyages (average length 6.9 months) contained in officer lists filed with the Newport vice-admiralty court. See Maritime Papers: Colonial Wars, 1723–1760, 82–124, R.I. State Archives, Providence. The New York and Philadelphia data were obtained from dates of departure and arrival for 28 New York privateers (average length 6.5 months) and 19 Philadelphia privateers (average length 6.9 months) reported in the *New-York Weekly Journal, New-York Gazette, New-York Weekly Post-Boy, N.-Y. Eve.-Post,* and the *Pa. Gaz.* Capt. George Walker, the successful Bristol, England, privateer, normally embarked for eight-month cruises. See Vaughan, ed., *Voyages and Cruises of Commodore Walker,* 22, 61, 95, 141.

51. This was the standard ration on the Newport privateer *Revenge* according to the entry for 14 July 1741 in the sloop's journal; see Jameson, ed., *Privateering and Piracy,* 393–394. Massachusetts and Rhode Island coast guard vessels also provided one pound of meat and one pound of bread per man per day along with two quarts of corn or peas per week plus an allowance of rum or beer. See Mass. Archs., LXIV, 181, and John R. Bartlett, ed., *Records of the Colony of Rhode Island and Providence Plantations in New England* (1859; reprint, New York, 1968), V, 91. An entry in the log of the New York privateer *Duke of Cumberland* for 26 Dec. 1758 reveals that "one Pound of Beef per man" per day was still the ration for American privateersmen in the subsequent imperial conflict. Stuyvesant Fish reprinted numerous excerpts from this log in "Privateering in New York under George II, 1758–1760," *New York Historical Society Quarterly Bulletin,* XXIX (1945), 161–171.

52. Fish, "Privateering in New York," *N.Y. Hist. Soc. Qtly. Bulletin,* XXIX (1945), 168.

53. *N.-Y. Wkly. Post-Boy*, 1 Oct. 1744; *Pa. Gaz.*, 11 Oct. 1744.

54. *Pa. Gaz.*, 22 Aug. 1745.

55. Vaughan, ed., *Voyages and Cruises of Commodore Walker*, 96.

56. Sailing instructions to Capt. Nathaniel Ingersoll of the *Despatch*, 27 June 1744, Winslow Papers, Massachusetts Historical Society, Boston.

57. Mass. Archs., LXIII, 578.

58. *Pa. Gaz.*, 20 Aug. 1741, 30 June 1743, 16 Aug., 1 Nov., and 6 Dec. 1744; Ford *et al.*, eds., *Mass. House Jours.*, XXI, 199, 216; Jameson, ed., *Privateering and Piracy*, 359.

59. *Pa. Gaz.*, 27 Mar. 1740.

60. *John Austin* v. *John Dennis and John Colder* (1744), Rhode Island Vice-Admiralty Court Records, Rhode Island Admiralty Papers, II, 53–54, R.I. State Archs.

61. Vernon to the duke of Newcastle and Sir Charles Wager, 30 Aug. 1740, in B.McL. Ranft, ed., *The Vernon Papers* (London, 1958), 125–126.

62. 17 Geo. II, 1744, c. 34, in Danby Pickering, ed., *The Statutes at Large . . .* (Cambridge, 1762–1807), XVIII, 263.

63. Vaughan, ed., *Voyages and Cruises of Commodore Walker*, 132.

64. Hugh F. Rankin, *The Golden Age of Piracy* (New York, 1969).

65. Marcus Rediker, *Between the Devil and the Deep Blue Sea: Merchant Seamen, Pirates, and the Anglo-American Maritime World, 1700–1750* (Cambridge, 1987), 254–287. The quotation is from p. 282.

66. Davis, *Rise of the English Shipping Industry*, 286.

67. Middleton, *Tobacco Coast*, 239; Goldenberg, *Shipbuilding in Colonial America*, 119.

68. Davis, *Rise of the English Shipping Industry*, 280–281.

69. Pringle to Henry and John Brock, 17 Jan. 1745, in Walter B. Edgar, ed., *The Letterbook of Robert Pringle* (Columbia, S.C., 1972), II, 799.

70. Pringle to Livingston, 19 Sept. 1744, *ibid.*, 738.

71. Of the total of 798 British vessels captured by the Spanish and French, 217 listed colonial home ports. The distribution of prize vessel types mentioned above is based on these craft. Unfortunately, 443 British prizes suffered from missing data for home port. It is impossible to say how many of these prizes were American bottoms or to determine their effect on the distribution of the type of vessel.

72. Pringle to Erving, 8 May 1740, in Edgar, ed., *Pringle Letterbook*, I, 195.

73. North, "Productivity Change in Shipping," *Jour. Pol. Econ.*, LXXVI (1968), 959.

74. Shepherd and Walton, *Shipping, Maritime Trade*, 74.

75. Rankin, *Golden Age of Piracy*, 152–158; James G. Lydon, *Pirates, Privateers, and Profits* (Upper Saddle River, N.J., 1970), 57–59; Rediker, *Devil and the Deep Blue Sea*, 281–285.

76. *N.-Y. Eve.-Post*, 6 May 1745.

77. *Ibid.*, 28 July 1746.

78. *Ibid.*, 19 Sept. 1748; *N.-Y. Wkly. Post-Boy*, 15 Aug. 1748; *Pa. Gaz.*, 27 Oct. 1748.

79. See *Pa. Gaz.*, 13 Sept. 1744 and 10 July and 7 Aug. 1746; *Boston News-Letter*, 23 Nov. 1744.

80. Shepherd and Walton, *Shipping, Maritime Trade*, 5.

81. *Ibid.*, 82.

82. Shirley C. Hughson, *The Carolina Pirates and Colonial Commerce* (Baltimore, 1894), quoted in *ibid.*, 84.

83. See chapter 6 for a discussion of the risks to British shipping caused by enemy warships operating on the British North American coast.

84. North, "Productivity Change in Shipping," *Jour. Pol. Econ.*, LXXVI (1968), 953, 967.

NOTES TO CHAPTER 4

1. Journal of the Sloop *Revenge*, in J. Franklin Jameson, ed., *Privateering and Piracy in the Colonial Period: Illustrative Documents* (New York, 1923), 382.

2. *Ibid.*, 382–383.

3. *Ibid.*, 383.

4. *Ibid.*, 383–385.

5. *Ibid.*, 389.

6. *Ibid.*, 390.

7. *Ibid.*, 393.

8. Richard Pares, "The Manning of the Navy in the West Indies, 1702–63," Royal Historical Society, *Transactions*, 4th Ser., XX (1937), 47.

9. Dora Mae Clark, "The Impressment of Seamen in the American Colonies," in *Essays in Colonial History Presented to Charles McLean Andrews by His Students* (New Haven, Conn., 1931), 198–224; Charles M. Andrews, "Vice-Admiralty Courts in the Colonies," introduction to Dorothy S. Towle, ed., *Records of the Vice-Admiralty Court of Rhode Island, 1716–1752* (Washington, D.C., 1936), 25; Richard B. Morris, *Government and Labor in Early America* (1946; reprint, New York, 1965), 247–248.

10. Ralph Davis, *The Rise of the English Shipping Industry in the Seventeenth and Eighteenth Centuries* (London, 1962), 323, 325.

11. Daniel A. Baugh, *British Naval Administration in the Age of Walpole* (Princeton, N.J., 1965), 147, 215–221.

12. Jesse Lemisch, "Jack Tar in the Streets: Merchant Seamen in the Politics of Revolutionary America," *William and Mary Quarterly*, 3d Ser., XXV (1968), 382–383; John Lax and William Pencak, "The Knowles Riot and the Crisis of the 1740s in Massachusetts," *Perspectives in American History*, X (1976), 153–214; Marcus Rediker, *Between the Devil and the Deep Blue Sea: Merchant Seamen, Pirates, and the Anglo-American Maritime World, 1700–1750* (Cambridge, 1987), 238.

13. Baugh, *British Naval Administration*, 229. N.A.M. Rodger and Douglas

Edward Leach have also discussed press-gangs, privateers, and the Royal Navy's manpower shortages. In an almost Panglossian description of life in the Georgian navy, Rodger minimizes the attractiveness of privateering compared with naval service, thus downplaying the hardships impressment caused. See *The Wooden World: An Anatomy of the Georgian Navy* (Annapolis, Md., 1986), 116–117, 126–129, 144, 185–188. On the other hand, Leach sees the friction resulting from impressment as a major cause of the long-term Anglo-American antagonism that ultimately led to the Revolution. See *Roots of Conflict: British Armed Forces and Colonial Americans, 1677–1763* (Chapel Hill, N.C., 1986), 144–156.

14. Baugh, *British Naval Administration*, 205. In *Rise of the English Shipping Industry*, 320–321, Davis says the navy's peak strength was just under 52,000 men in October 1747. The presence of marines and soldiers on the king's ships probably accounts for this discrepancy. Moreover, the number of men *said* to be aboard naval vessels and the number of men *actually* present were frequently different during this period.

15. R. Pringle to A. Pringle, 31 Dec. 1742; Pringle to Partridge, 5 Feb. 1743; Pringle to Dalby, 23 May 1743; Pringle to H. and J. Brock, 12 Dec. 1744; in Walter B. Edgar, ed., *The Letterbook of Robert Pringle* (Columbia, S.C., 1972), II, 471, 496, 557, 777.

16. Laurens to Crokatt, 15 Feb. 1748, in Philip M. Hamer *et al.*, eds., *The Papers of Henry Laurens* (Columbia, S.C., 1968–1985), I, 111.

17. "An additional and explanatory Act, to an Act, entitled, an Act to prevent Mariners and Seamen running into Debt. And to prevent the Desertion of Seamen," published in the *South-Carolina Gazette* (Charles Town), 23 May 1743.

18. *Pennsylvania Gazette* (Philadelphia), 25 Feb. 1746.

19. Morris, *Government and Labor*, 247. For some examples see *Boston Gazette*, 24 Nov. 1747 and 3 May 1748; *S.-C. Gaz.*, 14 May 1744, 10 June 1745, and 25 May 1747.

20. Worthington Chauncey Ford *et al.*, eds., *Journals of the House of Representatives of Massachusetts* (Boston, 1919–1971), XX, 84.

21. *Ibid.*, 98–99; Massachusetts Archives, LXIV, Maritime, 1740–1753, 204–205, Massachusetts State House, Boston.

22. Mass. Archs., LXIV, 209.

23. *Ibid.*, 209–211.

24. Warren to Thomas Corbett, secretary to the Admiralty, 2 June 1746, in Julian Gwyn, ed., *The Royal Navy and North America: The Warren Papers, 1736–1752* (London, 1973), 262.

25. Ford *et al.*, eds., *Mass. House Jours.*, XXI, 209.

26. *Ibid.*, XXII, 12.

27. Warren to Corbett, 8 Sept. 1744, in Gwyn, ed., *The Royal Navy and North America*, 36.

28. Warren to Corbett, 27 Sept. 1744, *ibid.*, 42.

29. Warren to Corbett, 2 June 1746, *ibid.*, 262.

30. *New-York Weekly Journal*, 8 Sept. 1740. For other examples see *Bos. Gaz.*,

10 Feb. 1747, 13 Oct. 1747, and 17 Nov. 1747; *Pa. Gaz.*, 4 Nov. 1742; *Virginia Gazette* (Williamsburg), 2 Nov. 1739; *S.-C. Gaz.*, 3 Jan. 1743, 3 and 10 Oct. 1748.

31. Palmer to Masterson, 2 Aug. 1748, in George E. Reed, ed., *Pennsylvania Archives, Fourth Series: Papers of the Governors* (Harrisburg, Pa., 1900), II, 80.

32. Ford *et al.*, eds., *Mass. House Jours.*, XVIII, 90.

33. Ellis Ames, Abner C. Goodell *et al.*, eds., *The Acts and Resolves, Public and Private, of the Province of the Massachusetts Bay* . . . (Boston, 1869–1922), XIII, 427. This action was taken on 26 Jan. 1745.

34. Ford *et al.*, eds., *Mass. House Jours.*, XXII, 203.

35. *Ibid.*, 115, 121.

36. See, for example, "An Act for equipping the colony sloop, and sending her out to cruise, & c.," enacted Apr. 1741; "An Act for fitting out the colony sloop Tartar, in company with the sloop kept by His Majesty's colony of Connecticut, for guarding the coast," enacted June 1744, in John R. Bartlett, ed., *Records of the Colony of Rhode Island and Providence Plantations in New England* (1859; reprint, New York, 1968), V, 17, 19.

37. *Ibid.*, 253–254. South Carolina also authorized impressment to man its coast guard vessels; see *Boston News-Letter*, 3 Mar. 1748.

38. Shirley to Wanton, 6 June 1745, in Charles H. Lincoln, ed., *Correspondence of William Shirley: Governor of Massachusetts and Military Commander in America, 1731–1760* (New York, 1912), I, 227–228.

39. Willard to Warren, 2 Nov. 1745, in Gwyn, ed., *The Royal Navy and North America*, 185–186.

40. Partridge to Wanton, 18 and 23 July 1745, in Gertrude Selwyn Kimball, ed., *The Correspondence of the Colonial Governors of Rhode Island, 1723–1775* (1902–1903; reprint, Freeport, N.Y., 1969), I, 354, 357–358. The quotation is from Partridge's letter of 18 July.

41. Wanton to Partridge, 26 July 1745, *ibid.*, 367. These themes were reiterated in numerous letters written by Rhode Island's governor or agent; see Bartlett, ed., *Records of Colonial R.I.*, V. 138–140, 148, 154, 183–184. A story in the *New-York Evening-Post*, 22 Apr. 1745, reported that "this little Colony" faced a manpower shortage because of the "great Numbers of People" participating in the Louisbourg expedition.

42. Shirley and Warren to Rhode Island Governor Richard Greene, 4 July 1746, in Lincoln, ed., *Shirley Correspondence*, I, 329–332.

43. Sydney V. James, *Colonial Rhode Island: A History* (New York, 1975), 274–275.

44. Shirley to Newcastle, 31 Dec. 1747, in Lincoln, ed., *Shirley Correspondence*, I, 420–423. The quotation is on 423.

45. *Boston Evening-Post*, 5 Nov. 1739.

46. *Pa. Gaz.*, 6, 14, 18, 25 Dec. 1744, and 1, 8, 15, 29 Jan. 1745.

47. *Ibid.*, 30 Aug., 6 Sept. 1744, 29 Jan. 1745.

48. Beekman to Godfrey Malbone and Samuel Vernon, 23 June 1747, in Philip L.

White, ed., *The Beekman Mercantile Papers, 1746-1799* (New York, 1956), I, 19-20.

49. *Pa. Gaz.,* 21, 28 Jan., 4 Feb. 1746.

50. *Ibid.,* 6 Sept. 1739.

51. *S.-C. Gaz.,* 27 Aug. 1739.

52. H.S. Vaughan, ed., *Voyages and Cruises of Commodore Walker* (London, 1928), 93-94. This anonymous account was originally published in London in 1760.

53. For the popularity of these commanders see *Pa. Gaz.,* 11 Mar. 1740, 20 Aug. 1741, 6 June 1745, 10 Feb. 1747, 9 June and 29 Sept. 1748; *Bos. News-Letter,* 18 Dec. 1746 and 22 Jan. 1747; *New-York Weekly Post-Boy,* 13 June 1748.

54. Mass. Archs., LXIV, 124-125. The records do not reveal the result of Jones's petition.

55. *N.-Y. Wkly. Post-Boy,* 11 June, 3 Sept., 3 Dec. 1744.

56. *Pa. Gaz.,* 17 May 1744.

57. *Ibid.*

58. *Ibid.,* 8 Nov. 1744.

59. *Ibid.,* 24 May 1744 and 18 Apr. 1745.

60. Davis, *Rise of the English Shipping Industry,* 137.

61. *Ibid.,* 165.

62. *Bos. Eve.-Post,* 5 Nov. 1739.

63. Davis, *Rise of the English Shipping Industry,* 137.

64. *Ibid.*

65. Rediker, *Devil and the Deep Blue Sea,* 305.

66. Pringle to H. and J. Brock, 12 Dec. 1744, in Edgar, ed., *Pringle Letterbook,* II, 777.

67. Byron Fairchild, *Messrs. William Pepperrell: Merchants at Piscataqua* (Ithaca, N.Y., 1954), 152.

68. Beekman to Capt. William Collins, 3 Feb. 1748, in White, ed., *Beekman Mercantile Papers,* I, 41. John J. McCusker, *Money and Exchange in Europe and America, 1600-1775: A Handbook* (Chapel Hill, N.C., 1978), 310, 316, 320, provided the sterling exchange rates used in this chapter.

69. Morris, *Government and Labor,* 236, 240-242; Davis, *Rise of the English Shipping Industry,* 140.

70. Christopher Lloyd, *The British Seaman, 1200-1860: A Social Survey* (London, 1968), 248-249; Peter Kemp, *The British Sailor: A Social History of the Lower Deck* (London, 1970), 91; Baugh, *British Naval Administration,* 229; Rodger, *Wooden World,* 125.

71. Lloyd, *The British Seaman,* 235-236; Rodger, *Wooden World,* 125.

72. J.R. Hutchinson, *The Press-Gang Afloat and Ashore* (London, 1913), 44; Pares, "Manning the Navy," Royal Hist. Soc. *Trans.,* 4th Ser., XX (1937), 38; Lemisch, "Jack Tar," *WMQ,* 3d Ser., XXV (1968), 382.

73. For a sharply contrasting view of life in the Royal Navy, see Rodger, *Wooden World.*

74. Ford *et al.,* eds., *Mass. House Jours.,* XXII, 155–156.

75. *Ibid.,* 170–171.

76. *Ibid.,* 203–204, 224–225.

77. *Ibid.,* XXIII, 121.

78. *Ibid.,* 393–394.

79. Kemp, *The British Sailor,* 129.

80. 6 Anne, 1708, c. 37, section II. Parliament reenacted this section in the two prize acts passed during the wars of 1739–1748: 13 Geo. II, 1740, c. 4, and 17 Geo. II, 1744, c. 37, in Danby Pickering, ed., *The Statutes at Large . . .* (Cambridge, 1762–1807), XI, 433–434, XVI, 360, XVIII, 254–255.

81. Arthur P. Middleton, *Tobacco Coast: A Maritime History of Chesapeake Bay in the Colonial Era* (Newport News, Va., 1953), 344–345.

82. Ames *et al.,* eds., *Mass. Acts and Resolves,* XIII, 62.

83. Julian Gwyn, *The Enterprising Admiral: The Personal Fortune of Admiral Sir Peter Warren* (Montreal, 1974), 15.

84. Shirley to Henry Pelham, 27 Sept. 1745, quoted in *ibid.,* 19–20.

85. *Ibid.,* 20.

86. *Pa. Gaz.,* 15 Mar. 1748.

87. Gwyn, *The Enterprising Admiral,* 20.

88. R. Pringle to A. Pringle, 22 Dec. 1744, in Edgar, ed., *Pringle Letterbook,* II, 790.

89. Hutchinson, *The Press-Gang,* 45.

90. *Bos. News-Letter,* 17 Dec. 1741.

91. 13 Geo. II, 1740, c. 4, Pickering, ed., *Statutes at Large,* XVII, 360.

92. *N.-Y. Wkly. Post-Boy,* 3 Dec. 1744; Jameson, ed., *Privateering and Piracy,* 463–464; Howard M. Chapin, *Rhode Island Privateers in King George's War, 1739–1748* (Providence, 1926), 55–56; *Marshall et al.* v. *Ship St. Jacques* (1746), Rhode Island Vice-Admiralty Court Records, Rhode Island Admiralty Papers, IV, 32, Rhode Island State Archives, Providence. The division of prize money for British private men-of-war was apparently less generous for privateersmen since the owners kept half the proceeds instead of one-third. See Richard Pares, *Colonial Blockade and Neutral Rights, 1739–1763* (Oxford, 1938), 8; Rodger, *Wooden World,* 128.

93. *Boston News-Letter,* 7 June and 6 Dec. 1744.

94. *Pa. Gaz.,* 23 May 1745.

95. *Ibid.,* 30 May 1745.

96. For an explanation of these figures and a detailed discussion of privateering's financial rewards, see chapter 7.

97. Lloyd, *The British Seaman,* 239–245.

98. Belcher to Warren, 12 May 1740, Belcher Letterbook, VI, 323, Massachusetts Historical Society, Boston.

99. *Pa. Gaz.*, 12 Mar. 1741.

100. Clark, "Impressment of Seamen," in *Essays in Colonial History*, 199; Pares, "Manning the Navy," Royal Hist. Soc. *Trans.*, 4th Ser., XX (1937), 41–42.

101. Pringle to Erving, 17 May 1740, in Edgar, ed., *Pringle Letterbook*, I, 206.

102. Davis, *Rise of the English Shipping Industry*, 324–325.

103. Pringle to James Hunter & Co., 2 Apr. 1737, in Edgar, ed., *Pringle Letterbook*, I, 10.

104. Pringle to Richard Partridge, 29 Jan. 1742, *ibid.*, II, 491–492.

105. *Bos. Eve.-Post*, 20 Aug. 1739.

106. Ford *et al.*, eds., *Mass. House Jours.*, XXII, 204–205.

107. Franklin to Joseph Galloway, 7 Apr. 1759, quoted in Jesse Lemisch, "Jack Tar v. John Bull: The Role of New York's Seamen in Precipitating the Revolution" (Ph.D. diss., Yale University, 1963), 20.

108. *Bos. Eve.-Post*, 27 Aug. 1739.

109. 6 Anne, c. 37, section IX, in Pickering, ed., *Statutes at Large*, XI, 438.

110. Quoted in Clark, "Impressment of Seamen," in *Essays in Colonial History*, 211.

111. Other scholars have ignored the colonial vice-admiralty records in their discussions of the Sixth of Anne's expiration.

112. Belcher's proclamation appeared in the *Bos. News-Letter*, 16 Aug. 1739.

113. *N.-Y. Wkly. Jour.*, 20 Aug. 1739; *S.-C. Gaz.*, 8 Sept. 1739.

114. Bull's proclamation appeared in the *S.-C. Gaz.*, 15 Sept. 1739.

115. *Bos. Eve.-Post*, 27 Aug. 1739. These excerpts subsequently appeared in the *N.-Y. Wkly. Jour.*, 10 Sept. 1739.

116. *The Journal of the House of Commons*, XXIII, 385.

117. *Ibid.*, 385–409, 427–432, 444–445. *The Journal of the House of Lords*, XXV, 445–451, 453, 487–488; 13 Geo. II, c. 4, in Pickering, ed., *Statutes at Large*, XVIII, 360–370.

118. The Lords Justices to Shirley, 10 Sept. 1741, in Lincoln, ed., *Shirley Correspondence*, I, 73–76.

119. *Pa. Gaz.*, 28 May 1741.

120. Bannister to Hugh Vans, 8 Jan. 1742, John Bannister Copy Book, 1730–1742, 238, Newport Historical Society, Newport, R.I.

121. Bannister to Vans, 8 Jan. 1742, *ibid.*

122. R. Pringle to A. Pringle, 27 Jan. 1742, in Edgar, ed., *Pringle Letterbook*, II, 492.

123. John Osborne to William Pepperrell and Peter Warren, 5 Feb. 1746, in Gwyn, ed., *The Royal Navy and North America*, 211–212.

124. Warren to Clinton, 24 June 1746, *ibid.*, 279.

125. Corbett to the Governors of America, 19 Aug. 1743, in Kimball, ed., *R.I. Gov. Correspondence*, I, 235–237. Corbett included the opinions of the Crown's legal officers that the 1708 Prize Act had lapsed in 1713.

126. Warren to Corbett, 2 June 1746, in Gwyn, ed., *The Royal Navy and North America*, 261.

127. Lords of the Admiralty to the Lords Justices, 26 Oct. 1743. The colonial governors received this letter with another on the same topic from Andrew Stone dated 1 Oct. 1743; see Kimball, ed., *R.I. Gov. Correspondence*, I, 238–241. The text of press warrants issued to Royal Navy captains was also enclosed.

128. *Pa. Gaz.*, 15 and 22 Nov. 1744. The quotation is from the text of the navy's press warrants enclosed in Andrew Stone to the governor of Rhode Island, 1 Oct. 1743, in Kimball, ed., *R.I. Gov. Correspondence*, I, 241–242.

129. *S.-C. Gaz.*, 24 May 1740.

130. *Bos. News-Letter*, 11 and 18 Nov. 1745; *Pa. Gaz.*, 10 Dec. 1745.

131. Ford *et al.*, eds., *Mass. House Jours.*, XXII, 204–205.

132. Morris, *Government and Labor*, 272; Lemisch, "Jack Tar v. John Bull," 48; Clark, "Impressment of Seamen," in *Essays in Colonial History*, 223–224.

133. Ford *et al.*, eds., *Mass. House Jours.*, XIX, 195–199.

134. Shirley to the Lords of Trade, 1 Dec. 1747, in Lincoln, ed., *Shirley Correspondence*, I, 412–419.

135. Rodger, *Wooden World*, 182.

NOTES TO CHAPTER 5

1. Carl Bridenbaugh, ed., *Gentleman's Progress: The Itinerarium of Dr. Alexander Hamilton, 1744* (Chapel Hill, N.C., 1948), 7.

2. *Ibid.*, 17.

3. *Ibid.*, 20.

4. Philadelphia's population was approximately 13,000 in 1743; see Carl Bridenbaugh, *Cities in Revolt: Urban Life in America, 1743–1776*, rev. ed. (New York, 1971), 5.

5. Bridenbaugh, ed., *Gentleman's Progress*, 25.

6. *Ibid.*, 30.

7. *Ibid.*, 37–38.

8. *Ibid.*, 75, 85, 87–88.

9. *Ibid.*, 97.

10. *Ibid.*, 103. Unfortunately, a fire destroyed Malbone's mansion on 7 June 1766. When efforts to check the blaze failed, Malbone, displaying enormous poise, ordered his servants to serve his dinner guests in an outbuilding, commenting, "If I have lost my house, that is no reason why we should lose our dinners." See Bridenbaugh, *Cities in Revolt*, 339; Sydney V. James, *Colonial Rhode Island: A History* (New York, 1975), 243.

11. Bridenbaugh, ed., *Gentleman's Progress*, 136, 141, 145.

12. *Ibid.,* 156.

13. *Ibid.,* 151.

14. *Ibid.,* 172.

15. *Ibid.,* 173.

16. *Ibid.,* 175.

17. The Newport data consisted of 47 voyages (average length 6.9 months) contained in privateer officer lists filed with the Newport vice-admiralty court. See Maritime Papers: Colonial Wars, 1723–1760, 82–124, Rhode Island State Archives, Providence. The New York and Philadelphia data were obtained from dates of departure and arrival for 28 New York privateers (average length 6.5 months) and 19 Philadelphia privateers (average length 6.9 months) reported in the *New-York Weekly Journal, New-York Evening-Post, New-York Weekly Post-Boy,* and *Pennsylvania Gazette* (Philadelphia).

The anonymous account of Capt. George Walker's exploits indicates that the normal duration for cruises commanded by this successful Bristol, England, privateer was eight months. See H.S. Vaughan, ed., *Voyages and Cruises of Commodore Walker* (London, 1928), 22, 61, 95, 141. This work was originally published in London in 1760.

18. See chapter 3.

19. The warships tabulated in Table 5.1 were full-time privateers. Letter of marque vessels are not included. This wartime activity, so popular in the 16th century, was almost extinct by the 1740s; less than 2% of the cases in the data file involved letter of marque vessels.

20. Rhode Island Notary Public Records, IV–V, R.I. Archs.

21. For the various merchants' privateering investments see *ibid.;* William T. Baxter, *The House of Hancock: Business in Boston, 1724–1775* (Cambridge, Mass., 1945), 80–82; James G. Lydon, *Pirates, Privateers and Profits* (Upper Saddle River, N.J., 1970), 274–275; and Robert Pringle to Andrew Pringle, 20 July 1744, in Walter B. Edgar, ed., *The Letterbook of Robert Pringle* (Columbia, S.C., 1972), II, 728. The pattern of ownership for privateers resembled that for merchantmen. Businessmen spread their risks by owning shares in different vessels. See Ralph Davis, *The Rise of the English Shipping Industry in the Seventeenth and Eighteenth Centuries* (London, 1962), chap. 5, 81–109; chapter 7 discusses privateer owners.

22. *Pa. Gaz.,* 18 Apr. 1745.

23. *Boston News-Letter,* 23 Aug. 1739; *N.-Y. Wkly. Jour.,* 23 Aug. 1739.

24. *N.-Y. Wkly. Post-Boy,* 18 June 1744.

25. Boston's dominance is discussed in Carl Bridenbaugh, *Cities in the Wilderness: The First Century of Urban Life in America,* rev. ed. (New York, 1971), 330–333; Jacob M. Price, "Economic Function and the Growth of American Port Towns in the Eighteenth Century," *Perspectives in American History,* VIII (1974), 140–149; and James, *Colonial Rhode Island,* 291–292. For Philadelphia's ascendency over New York see Arthur L. Jensen, *The Maritime Commerce of Colonial Philadelphia* (Madison, Wis., 1963), 82–83.

26. James, *Colonial Rhode Island,* 243; Byron Fairchild, *Messrs. William Pepperrell: Merchants at Piscataqua* (Ithaca, N.Y., 1954), 40.

27. Partridge to Thomas Ramsden, secretary to the Lords of the Regency, 20 July 1745, in Gertrude Selwyn Kimball, ed., *The Correspondence of the Colonial Governors of Rhode Island, 1723–1775* (1902–1903; reprint, Freeport, N.Y., 1969), I, 373.

28. Lydon, *Pirates, Privateers, and Profits,* 38, 60, 64, 72–74, 274–275.

29. Bannister to Samuel Clark, 6 Oct. 1740, John Bannister Copy Book, 1730–1742, 117, Newport Historical Society, Newport, R.I., hereafter cited as Bannister Copy Book.

30. Reynell to Bland, 11 Feb. 1745, John Reynell Letterbook, 29 May–4 Oct. 1745, Historical Society of Pennsylvania, Philadelphia. See also Reynell to Daniel Flexney, 23 Nov. 1744, for Reynell's religious convictions against privateering.

31. Baxter, *House of Hancock,* 80–82; Gary B. Nash, *The Urban Crucible: Social Change, Political Consciousness, and the Origins of the American Revolution* (Cambridge, Mass., 1979), 161–184.

32. Worthington Chauncey Ford *et al.,* eds., *Journals of the House of Representatives of Massachusetts* (Boston, 1919–1971), XXII, 204–205.

33. William Shirley to the duke of Newcastle, 31 Dec. 1747, in Charles H. Lincoln, ed., *Correspondence of William Shirley: Governor of Massachusetts and Military Commander in America, 1731–1760* (New York, 1912), I, 420–423.

34. Ford *et al.,* eds., *Mass. House Jours.,* XXII, 204–205.

35. Robert Dinwiddie to the Board of Trade, 29 Apr. 1740, in Jack P. Greene, ed., *Settlements to Society: 1584–1763* (New York, 1966), 276–277.

36. Pringle to Thomas Burrill, 10 Oct. 1739, in Edgar, ed., *Pringle Letterbook,* I, 139.

37. Pringle to Burrill, 11 June 1740, *ibid.,* I, 218.

38. Pringle to John Erving, 18 Aug. 1744; Pringle to William Cookson and William Welfitt, 15 Jan. 1745, *ibid.,* II, 734, 797.

39. Glen to Lords Commissioners for Trade and Plantations, 1749, quoted in Joseph A. Goldenberg, *Shipbuilding in Colonial America* (Charlottesville, Va., 1976), 120.

40. Summaries from the South Carolina registers are presented in tables 43–45, *ibid.,* 232–236.

41. "Ship Registers in the South Carolina Archives, 1734–1780," comp. R. Nicholas Olsberg, *South Carolina Historical Magazine,* LXXIV (1973), 189–279. Because of its lack of locally owned shipping and dependence on other ports, Jacob M. Price has aptly characterized Charles Town as a "shipping point" ("Growth of American Port Towns," *Perspectives Am. Hist.,* VIII [1974], 162–163). See also Robert M. Weir, *Colonial South Carolina: A History* (Millwood, N.Y., 1983), 171.

42. R. Pringle to A. Pringle, 21 Jan. 1744, in Edgar, ed., *Pringle Letterbook,* II, 636. It would be useful to place the tonnage devoted to privateering in the context of the total shipping of each port, but such a task is impossible. The naval officer lists, the best sources for colonial shipping, are sparse for the 1740s; there are none

for Boston, Newport, or Philadelphia, and the New York lists are lost for half of 1743 and 1748 and for all of 1744–1747. Charles Town's lists are missing for 1742–1748. I am indebted to Lawrence A. Harper of the University of California, Berkeley, and James G. Lydon of Duquesne University for this information.

43. For Charles Town's racial composition see Bridenbaugh, *Cities in the Wilderness*, 249, and Peter H. Wood, *Black Majority: Negroes in Colonial South Carolina from 1670 through the Stono Rebellion* (New York, 1974), 142–155. Wood characterizes the Negro Act as a "noose [that] was being tightened: there would be heavier surveillance of Negro activity" (*ibid.,* 324).

44. R. Pringle to A. Pringle, 31 Dec. 1742; Pringle to Richard Partridge, 5 Feb. 1743; Pringle to Francis Dalby, 23 May 1743; and Pringle to Henry and John Brock, 12 Dec. 1744; in Edgar, ed., *Pringle Letterbook,* II, 471, 496, 557, 777.

45. Laurens to James Crokatt, 15 Feb. 1748, in Philip M. Hamer *et al.,* eds., *The Papers of Henry Laurens* (Columbia, S.C., 1968–1985), I, 111.

46. For West Indian shipping data see Robert Dinwiddie to the Board of Trade, 29 Apr. 1740, in Greene, ed., *Settlements to Society,* 277; Frank Wesley Pitman, *The Development of the British West Indies, 1700–1763* (New Haven, Conn., 1917), 97. Pitman discusses the islands' population on pp. 369–390.

47. Richard S. Dunn, *Sugar and Slaves: The Rise of the Planter Class in the English West Indies, 1624–1713* (Chapel Hill, N.C., 1972); Hugh F. Rankin, *The Golden Age of Piracy* (New York, 1969); James F. Shepherd and Gary M. Walton, *Shipping, Maritime Trade, and the Economic Development of Colonial North America* (Cambridge, 1972), 80–84. Because of their importance to both Britain and the northern colonies, the West Indies attracted thousands of vessels and mariners. For the competition among privateers, the navy, and merchantmen for recruits see Richard Pares, "The Manning of the Navy in the West Indies," 1702–63," Royal Historical Society, *Transactions,* 4th Ser., XX (1937), 31–60.

48. *Pa. Gaz.,* 30 Aug. 1744; *N.-Y. Wkly. Post-Boy,* 3 Sept. 1744.

49. See, for example, *Bos. News-Letter,* 5 and 26 Mar., 16 Apr. 1730; *Pa. Gaz.,* 14 Oct. 1731; *Boston Evening-Post,* 25 July 1737.

50. *Boston Gazette,* 20 Aug. 1739; *Bos. Eve.-Post,* 27 Aug. 1739; *N.-Y. Wkly. Jour.,* 3 Sept. 1739.

51. Bannister to Messrs. Jacobs and Clark, n.d. [Oct. 1739], Bannister Copy Book, 35.

52. Bannister to John Jones, 22 Aug. 1740, *ibid.,* 111.

53. Bannister to Messrs. Jacob and Clark, 11 Jan. 1740, *ibid.,* 50.

54. *Bos. News-Letter,* 28 Mar. 1740. New Yorkers and Philadelphians read about Capt. Hall's exploits in the *N.-Y. Wkly. Jour.,* 5 May 1740, and *Pa. Gaz.,* 10 Apr. 1740.

55. Bannister to Messrs. Sedgwick and Bernard, 21 May 1740, Bannister Copy Book, 74. John J. McCusker, *Money and Exchange in Europe and America, 1600–1775: A Handbook* (Chapel Hill, N.C., 1978), 316, supplied the exchange rates for converting Rhode Island currency into sterling.

56. Bannister to Capt. John Thomlinson, 19 Feb. 1741, Bannister Copy Book, 146.

57. *Pa. Gaz.*, 26 Mar. 1741.

58. Belcher to Malbone, 28 July 1740, Belcher Letterbook, VI, 468, Massachusetts Historical Society, Boston. On the capture of the *Oratava* see *Collingwood* v. *Ship Oratava* (1740), Rhode Island Vice-Admiralty Court Records, Rhode Island Admiralty Papers, I, 3–25, R.I. State Archs.

59. Pringle to Edward and John Mayne and Co., 19 Sept. 1740, in Edgar, ed., *Pringle Letterbook*, I, 248.

60. R. Pringle to A. Pringle, 23 Oct. 1740, *ibid.*, 263; *N.-Y. Wkly. Jour.*, 29 Sept. 1740.

61. Bannister to Thomlinson, 19 Feb. 1741, Bannister Copy Book, 146.

62. Bannister to Hugh Vans, 19 Aug. 1741, *ibid.*, 188.

63. Sir Herbert Richmond discusses the Cartagena expedition in *The Navy in the War of 1739-48* (Cambridge, 1920), I, chap. 6.

64. See the following orders issued by Admiral Vernon: Order to Capt. Douglas of HMS *Falmouth*, 25 Feb. 1741; order to Capt. Cooper of HMS *Dunkirk*, 11 Mar. 1741; order to Capt. Cotterel of HMS *Lyon*, 11 Mar. 1741; and order to Capt. Martyn of HMS *Deptford*, 20 Mar. 1741; see also Vernon to Jamaica Gov. Edward Trelawny, 20 Mar. 1741, in B.McL. Ranft, ed., *The Vernon Papers* (London, 1958), 180–181, 186–187, 194, 196.

65. *N.-Y. Wkly. Post-Boy*, 27 Aug. 1744; *Pa. Gaz.*, 30 Aug. 1744 and 15 Jan. 1745.

66. R. Pringle to A. Pringle, 21 Jan. 1744, in Edgar, ed., *Pringle Letterbook*, II, 636.

67. R. Pringle to A. Pringle, 20 July 1744, *ibid.*, 728.

68. Reynell to Daniel Flexney, 10 Nov. 1744, John Reynell Letterbook, 29 May 1744–4 Oct. 1745.

69. Reynell to Elias Bland, 6 July 1745, and Reynell to Daniel Flexney, 8 July 1745, *ibid.*

70. These French successes upset Adm. Sir. Peter Warren; see Warren to Lord Sandwich, 4 Oct. 1746, and Warren to Capt. Charles Knowles, 6 Oct. 1746, in Julian Gwyn, ed., *The Royal Navy and North America: The Warren Papers, 1736-1752* (London, 1973), 336–337, 339. Richmond and Pares agree that convoys reduced French losses in American waters. See Richmond, *The Navy in the War of 1739-48*, III, 64–66, 122, 148–149, and Richard Pares, *War and Trade in the West Indies, 1739-1763* (Oxford, 1936), 311–325. John Charles Martin Ogelsby has also commented on the successful French convoy system in an informative discussion on the deployment of naval vessels in the Caribbean by Britain, Spain, and France. See "War at Sea in the West Indies, 1739–1748" (Ph.D. diss., University of Washington, 1963), 206–207. The evidence summarized in Table 5.4 supports this view.

71. *Pa. Gaz.*, 26 June 1746.

72. *Ibid.*, 23 July 1747.

73. *Ibid.*, 30 July 1747.

74. *Ibid.*, 13 Aug. and 12 Nov. 1747.

75. *Ibid.,* 28 Aug. 1746. It is unlikely these vessels continued as private men-of-war for their new owners because the data file contains no cases of Virginia privateers after 1746.

76. S. Vernon to Thomas and Adrian Hope, 24 Feb. 1747, Letterbook of Samuel and William Vernon, no. 1, 1738–1759, 29, Newport Hist. Soc., Newport, R.I.

77. Vaughan, ed., *Voyages and Cruises of Commodore Walker,* 196.

78. Table 5.4 includes only those cases in the data file for which the place of action is known. The file contains 939 prize actions involving British colonial privateers. Of this total, 882 (94%) have valid observations for the place of action. Of these, 682 (77%) occurred in the Caribbean, 80 (9%) in northern waters, and 89 (10%) in American waters, but it was impossible to determine if they happened along the continent's coast or in the Caribbean. The remaining 31 (4%) took place in European waters. Table 5.4 includes only the 762 actions that occurred in the Caribbean and along the North American coast. Because the prizes taken during the siege of Louisbourg were captured by the Royal Navy and colonial coast guard vessels, they are not included in Table 5.4.

79. For comparisons of French West Indian and New France commerce see Thomas M. Doerflinger, "The Antilles Trade of the Old Regime: A Statistical Overview," *Journal of Interdisciplinary History,* VI (1976), 401, and Dale Miquelon, *Dugard of Rouen: French Trade to Canada and the West Indies, 1729–1770* (Montreal, 1978), chaps. 6–7. Geoffrey J. Walker demonstrates the importance of Mexican and South American commerce to the Spanish Empire in *Spanish Politics and Imperial Trade, 1700–1789* (Bloomington, Ind., 1979). Because of their trade routes, Mexico and Louisiana have been considered as Caribbean colonies in this analysis.

80. *Pa. Gaz.,* 25 June 1741 and 22 Jan. 1745.

81. *Ibid.,* 26 Feb. 1745.

82. *Ibid.*

83. Charles Gibson, *Spain in America* (New York, 1966), 102–103, 123; Walker, *Spanish Politics and Imperial Trade,* 4–9; J.C.M. Ogelsby, "Spain's Havana Squadron and the Preservation of the Balance of Power in the Caribbean, 1740–1748," *Hispanic American Historical Review,* XLIX (1969), 473–488.

84. *Pa. Gaz.,* 16 and 23 Sept. 1742.

85. *Bos. News-Letter,* 9 and 16 Aug., 27 Sept. 1744. Rouse's exploits received much attention in newspapers throughout British North America. See *Pa. Gaz.,* 16 Aug. and 4 Oct. 1744; *N.-Y. Wkly. Post-Boy,* 17 Sept. 1744; *South-Carolina Gazette* (Charles Town), 1 Oct. and 26 Nov. 1744.

86. For Cartagena see Richmond, *The Navy in the War of 1739–48,* I, chap. 6; Pares, *War and Trade,* 91–92. For the "Gibraltar of the New World" see Howard H. Peckham, *The Colonial Wars, 1689–1762* (Chicago, 1964), 99–106; I.K. Steele, *Guerillas and Grenadiers: The Struggle for Canada, 1689–1760* (Toronto, 1969), 47–50.

87. Table 5.7 includes only those cases in the data file that occurred in North American waters and the Caribbean Sea. Nineteen naval prize actions were excluded because they took place in the New World, but the sources did not indicate a more

specific location. The navy's numerous European prize actions are not included in the table. Two factors may understate the Royal Navy's role in the prize war in American waters. First, the data file is primarily based on the colonial press which may have devoted greater attention to American efforts than it did to the king's ships, though the navy did receive much attention in American newspapers. Second, colonial editors were not always precise in identifying Royal Navy forces. References such as "our Men-of-war" or "the King's Ships" or "Commodore Legge's Cruizers" made correct entry of naval vessels participating in prize actions difficult. In addition, capturing prizes was only one of the navy's objectives. Thus many of the king's vessels, especially ships of the line carrying 70, 80, or 90 guns that were deployed to combat Spanish and French naval forces, were too large to be effective in prize actions. Despite these caveats, Table 5.7 places the roles of private and public men-of-war in perspective. Privateers played an extensive part.

88. Albert Harkness, Jr., estimates that about 3,500 Americans enlisted for the Cartagena expedition ("Americanism and Jenkins' Ear," *Mississippi Valley Historical Review,* XXVII [1950], 70–71). Steele places the number at 3,000 (*Guerillas and Grenadiers,* 49). The Louisbourg assault involved nearly 4,000 colonists; see Nash, *Urban Crucible,* 170–171, and Steele, *Guerillas and Grenadiers,* 49. For the 1746 mobilization see Peckham, *Colonial Wars,* 109.

89. The figures in Table 5.1 indicate privateering berths. Because some mariners made multiple voyages, the number of individual privateersmen was probably smaller than 36,404.

NOTES TO CHAPTER 6

1. Warren to Josiah Burchett, secretary of the Admiralty, 19 Nov. 1739, in Julian Gwyn, ed., *The Royal Navy and North America: The Warren Papers, 1736–1752* (London, 1973), 18.

2. Pringle to Edward and John Mayne, 29 Apr. 1740, in Walter B. Edgar, ed., *The Letterbook of Robert Pringle* (Columbia, S.C., 1972), I, 193.

3. Joyce E. Harman, *Trade and Privateering in Spanish Florida, 1732–1763* (St. Augustine, Fla., 1969), 37–40. For a full report of Capt. Jenkins's misfortunes see *Boston News-Letter,* 14 Oct. 1731.

4. R. Pringle to Andrew Pringle, 10 Mar. 1740, in Edgar, ed., *Pringle Letterbook,* I, 169–170.

5. The expedition is discussed in Trevor R. Reese, *Colonial Georgia: A Study in British Imperial Policy in the Eighteenth Century* (Athens, Ga., 1963), 78–80, and M. Eugene Sirmans, *Colonial South Carolina: A Political History, 1663–1763* (Chapel Hill, N.C., 1966), 210–214. On the Royal Navy's role in the unsuccessful operation see Sir Herbert Richmond, *The Navy in the War of 1739–48* (Cambridge, 1920), I, 50.

6. R. Pringle to A. Pringle, 14 July 1740, in Edgar, ed., *Pringle Letterbook,* I, 230.

7. *South-Carolina Gazette* (Charles Town), 4 June 1741.

8. Pringle to Samuel Saunders, 22 Oct. 1740; R. Pringle to A. Pringle, 31 Oct.

1740; Pringle to John and Thomas Sears & Co., 13 Mar. 1741; in Edgar, ed., *Pringle Letterbook*, I, 260, 265, 302.

9. *S.-C. Gaz.*, 5 Sept., 10 Oct. 1741.

10. Bannister to Capt. John Thomlinson, 1 June 1741, John Bannister Copy Book, 1730–1742, 171, Newport Historical Society, Newport, R.I.

11. *Pennsylvania Gazette* (Philadelphia), 20 Aug. 1741.

12. *Ibid.*, 21 May 1741; *New-York Weekly Journal*, 25 May, 6 July 1741; *Bos. News-Letter*, 28 May 1741.

13. *Pa. Gaz.*, 18 June 1741.

14. *Ibid.*, 23 and 30 July 1741.

15. *Ibid.*, 13 Aug. 1741.

16. *Ibid.*, 20 May 1742; *Bos. News-Letter*, 20 June 1742; *N.-Y. Wkly. Jour.*, 31 May 1742; *S.-C. Gaz.*, 5 July 1742.

17. *Pa. Gaz.*, 1 July 1742.

18. R. Pringle to A. Pringle, 21 June 1742, in Edgar, ed., *Pringle Letterbook*, I, 382. Robert Pringle also knew that Fandino had cut off Jenkins's ear.

19. *Pa. Gaz.*, 1 July 1742.

20. Massachusetts Archives, LXIV, Maritime, 1740–1753, 126, Massachusetts State House, Boston.

21. *Ibid.*, 128–129. See Ellis Ames, Abner C. Goodell *et al.*, eds., *The Acts and Resolves, Public and Private of the Province of the Massachusetts Bay . . .* (Boston, 1869–1922), II, 1085.

22. *Pa. Gaz.*, 28 May 1741. See chapter 4 for the journal of the *Revenge*.

23. *Pa. Gaz.*, 11 June 1741.

24. Message to the assembly, 3 June 1741, in George E. Reed, ed., *Pennsylvania Archives, Fourth Series: Papers of the Governors* (Harrisburg, Pa., 1900), I, 765–766.

25. For apprehensions concerning French entry into the war, see R. Pringle to A. Pringle, 19 Oct. 1743; Pringle to William Cookson and William Welfitt, 7 Nov. 1743; R. Pringle to A. Pringle, 11 June 1744; in Edgar, ed., *Pringle Letterbook,* II, 587–588, 602, 707; Minutes of the Massachusetts Council, 10 Oct. 1743, Mass. Archs., XI, Council Records, July 1741–Dec. 1747, 78; John Reynell to Elias Bland, 18 Apr. 1744, John Reynell Letterbook, 15 Oct.–26 Apr. 1744, Historical Society of Pennsylvania, Philadelphia; Carl Bridenbaugh, ed., *Gentleman's Progress: The Itinerarium of Dr. Alexander Hamilton, 1744* (Chapel Hill, N.C., 1948), 7, 20.

26. Message to the assembly, 31 July 1744, in Reed, ed., *Pa. Archs., Fourth Ser.*, I, 851.

27. Dinwiddie to the Board of Trade, 29 Apr. 1740, in Jack P. Greene, ed., *Settlements to Society: 1584–1763* (New York, 1966), 276.

28. *Ibid.*, 278.

29. Charles Whitworth, *State of the Trade of Great Britain in Its Imports and Exports, Progressively from the Year 1697* (London, 1776), 43.

30. More than four-fifths (83%) of New England's exports and nearly nine-tenths (87%) of New York's, New Jersey's, and Pennsylvania's exports went to destinations outside of Great Britain in 1768–1772; see John J. McCusker and Russel R. Menard, *The Economy of British America, 1607–1789* (Chapel Hill, N.C., 1985), 108 and 199. Most northern colonial cargoes were probably exported to seaports outside Britain in the earlier period as well.

31. *Pa. Gaz.*, 29 Jan. 1745; *Bos. News-Letter*, 3 Jan. 1745; *Virginia Gazette* (Williamsburg), 23 May 1745; *New-York Evening-Post*, 3 June 1745.

32. Dinwiddie to the Board of Trade, 29 Apr. 1740, in Greene, ed., *Settlements to Society*, 278; *Pa. Gaz.*, 11 July and 17 Oct. 1745.

33. *Bos. News-Letter*, 26 June 1746.

34. *Pa. Gaz.*, 4 Sept. 1746.

35. *N.-Y. Eve.-Post*, 1 Dec. 1746.

36. *Bos. News-Letter*, 6 June 1745; *Pa. Gaz.*, 4 Sept. 1746.

37. *N.-Y. Eve.-Post*, 4 Mar. 1745. See also *Va. Gaz.*, 12 Dec. 1745 and *N.-Y. Eve.-Post*, 13 Jan. 1746.

38. *Pa. Gaz.*, 28 Aug. 1746.

39. *Ibid.*, 2 Dec. 1746; *Bos. News-Letter*, 4 Dec. 1746; *S.-C. Gaz.*, 1 Dec. 1746.

40. *Pa. Gaz.*, 30 Apr. and 7 May 1747.

41. *N.-Y. Eve.-Post*, 7 Sept. 1747.

42. Dinwiddie to the Board of Trade, 29 Apr. 1740, in Greene, ed., *Settlements to Society*, 278.

43. For Jamaica's shipping routes see Richard S. Dunn, *Sugar and Slaves: The Rise of the Planter Class in the English West Indies, 1624–1713* (Chapel Hill, N.C., 1972), 164.

44. *N.-Y. Eve.-Post*, 12 Aug. 1745.

45. *Pa. Gaz.*, 29 Aug. 1745.

46. *Ibid.*, 24 Dec. 1745.

47. *Ibid.*, 27 Mar. 1746.

48. *Ibid.*, 3 Apr. 1746.

49. *Bos. News-Letter*, 4 Oct. 1746.

50. *Pa. Gaz.*, 24 Sept. 1747.

51. *Bos. News-Letter*, 29 May 1746.

52. For reports of Royal Navy successes against enemy privateers off Jamaica see *Bos. News-Letter*, 29 May 1746; *Pa. Gaz.*, 22 May and 14 Aug. 1746, 20 Jan. 1747.

53. Seventeen prize actions occurred in North American waters between Maine and Florida. Three more took place south of the Delaware capes; two additional prize actions took place north of the Delaware capes. The more complete data for prize actions fought along the North American coast compared to those in the Caribbean probably result from the North American sources used to construct the data file.

54. *N.-Y. Wkly. Jour.*, 28 Sept. 1741; *Pa. Gaz.*, 16 June 1748; *New-York Weekly Post-Boy*, 20 June 1748.

55. *Pa. Gaz.*, 30 May 1745.

56. *S.-C. Gaz.*, 22 June, 22 July, 9 Sept. 1745.

57. *Ibid.*, 10 Mar. 1746.

58. *Pa. Gaz.*, 30 Oct. 1746.

59. *S.-C. Gaz.*, 22 Sept., 8 Dec. 1746.

60. *Ibid.*, 20 Apr., 24 Aug. 1747; *Pa. Gaz.*, 27 Aug. 1747.

61. *S.-C. Gaz.*, 20 Apr. 1747.

62. *Ibid.*, 24 Aug. 1747.

63. Laurens to James Crokatt, 24 June 1747, in Philip M. Hamer *et al.*, eds., *The Papers of Henry Laurens* (Columbia, S.C., 1968–1985), I, 11.

64. Laurens to Crokatt, 18 Aug. 1747, in *ibid.*, 43; *S.-C. Gaz.*, 25 and 29 June 1747.

65. Laurens to Watson, 7 Nov. 1747, in Hamer *et al.*, eds., *Laurens Papers*, I, 73.

66. Laurens to Thomas Savage, 11 Nov. 1747, in *ibid.*, 82–83.

67. *S.-C. Gaz.*, 6 and 11 Jan., 8 Feb. 1748.

68. *Ibid.*, 28 Mar. 1748.

69. *Ibid.*, 29 Feb., 18 Apr., 16 and 25 May 1748.

70. *Ibid.*, 9 July and 31 Oct. 1748.

71. *Ibid.*, 14 Nov., 12 Dec. 1748.

72. *Pa. Gaz.*, 18 Oct. 1744; *S.-C. Gaz.*, 17 Sept. 1744.

73. *Pa. Gaz.*, 27 June 1745.

74. *Ibid.*, 12 Aug. 1745.

75. *Ibid.*, 8 July 1745.

76. *Ibid.*, 5 Mar. 1745.

77. *Ibid.*, 19 May 1748; *Bos. News-Letter*, 26 May 1748; *N.-Y. Wkly. Post-Boy*, 16 May 1748.

78. *Pa. Gaz.*, 16 June 1748.

79. *Ibid.*, 22 Sept. 1748.

80. *Ibid.*, 7 July 1748.

81. *Sweet* v. *Snow True Briton* (1748), Rhode Island Vice-Admiralty Court Records, Rhode Island Admiralty Papers, VI, 106–122, Rhode Island State Archives, Providence. For the legal deadline for Anglo-French captures, see *Pa. Gaz.*, 29 Sept. 1748.

82. *Pa. Gaz.*, 27 Dec. 1748. The legal deadline for Anglo-Spanish captures appeared in the *Gazette*'s issue for 3 Nov. 1748.

83. *Ibid.*, 11 Oct. 1744; *N.-Y. Wkly. Post-Boy*, 12 Nov. 1744. Leonard Woods Labaree *et al.*, eds, *The Papers of Benjamin Franklin* (New Haven, Conn., 1961), III, 15.

84. *Pa. Gaz.,* 24 Sept. 1747. John Swift, the factor of London merchant John White, informed his superior of these captures. See Swift to White, 20 Sept. 1747, John Swift Letter Book, 30 May 1747–2 May 1751, Hist. Soc. of Pa., Philadelphia, hereafter Swift Letter Book. Swift commented on enemy privateering activity or rumors of such activity throughout the summer of 1747. See Swift to White, 30 May 1747 and 13 July 1747. Philadelphia merchant Samuel Powel also discussed Spanish and French privateering with his correspondents. See Powel to Robert Wheatle, 8 May and 30 May 1747; Powel to Gabriel Manigault, 27 May, 6 June, and 18 July 1747; Powel to David Barclay, 10 June 1747; Samuel Powel Letterbooks, III, 3 Sept. 1746–11 Sept. 1747, 66, 70, 82, 84, 94, Hist. Soc. of Pa., Philadelphia.

85. Palmer to the assembly, 16 Oct. 1747, in Reed, ed., *Pa. Archs., Fourth Ser.,* II, 14–16.

86. Benjamin Franklin to Cadwallader Colden, 27 Nov. 1747, in Labaree *et al.,* eds., *Franklin Papers,* III, 213; John Swift to John White, 29 Nov. 1747, Swift Letter Book.

87. Palmer to Commander-in-Chief at Louisbourg, 5 Mar. 1748, in Reed, ed., *Pa. Archs., Fourth Ser.,* II, 44.

88. Palmer to New York Gov. George Clinton, 8 Mar. 1748; Palmer to Mass. Gov. William Shirley, 8 Mar. 1748; in *ibid.,* 46–48.

89. Palmer to Knowles, 8 Mar. 1748, in *ibid.,* 48–50.

90. *Pa. Gaz.,* 23 Feb. 1748.

91. *Ibid.,* 26 May 1748. Palmer informed the assembly on 17 May 1748 that New York agreed to loan Pennsylvania the cannon. See Reed, ed., *Pa. Archs., Fourth Ser.,* II, 59.

92. Swift to John White, 29 Nov. 1747 and 12 Apr. 1748, Swift Letter Book.

93. Proclamation of the President and Council of the Province of Pennsylvania, 11 Apr. 1748, published in the *Pa. Gaz.,* 21 Apr. 1748.

94. *Pa. Gaz.,* 2 June 1748.

95. *Ibid.,* 19 and 26 May 1748.

96. *Ibid.,* 2 June 1748.

97. *Ibid.,* 26 May and 2 June 1748.

98. Palmer to the assembly, 19 May 1748, in Reed, ed., *Pa. Archs., Fourth Ser.,* II, 60–61.

99. *Pa. Gaz.,* 2 June 1748, published the assembly's reply to Palmer's message.

100. Palmer to Va. Gov. Sir William Gooch, 27 May 1748, in Reed, ed., *Pa. Archs., Fourth Ser.,* II, 61–63. Palmer asked Gooch to send HMS *Hector,* the Virginia station ship, to the Delaware capes.

101. *N.-Y. Wkly. Post-Boy,* 30 May 1748.

102. *Pa. Gaz.,* 2 June 1748.

103. *Ibid.,* 7 July 1748.

104. *Ibid.,* 2 June 1748.

105. *Ibid.*

106. Swift to John White, 10 June 1748, Swift Letter Book.

107. Beekman to Thurston, 19 June 1748, in Philip L. White, ed., *The Beekman Mercantile Papers, 1746–1779* (New York, 1956), I, 48.

108. *Ibid.*

109. Beekman to John Morgan, 4 July 1748, in *ibid.*, 51.

110. *Pa. Gaz.*, 16 June 1748.

111. *Ibid.*, 18 Aug. 1748; John Swift to Joseph Swift, 2 Aug. 1748, Swift Letter Book.

112. Peter H. Wood, *Black Majority: Negroes in Colonial South Carolina from 1670 through the Stono Rebellion* (New York, 1974), 61.

113. Pringle to Thompson, 23 July 1739, in Edgar, ed., *Pringle Letterbook*, I, 117.

114. Pringle to Samuel Saunders, 22 Oct. 1740; R. Pringle to A. Pringle, 23 and 31 Oct. 1740, 15 Feb., 5 Mar., 17 June, and 7 Sept. 1742; Pringle to John Erving, 9 Oct. 1742; in *ibid.*, 260, 264–265, 323, 332, 380, 406–407, 430. Adm. Charles Knowles indicated the importance of fall for Carolina shipping to the duke of Newcastle, 9 July 1746, in Gwyn, ed., *The Royal Navy and North America*, 291.

115. Arthur P. Middleton, *Tobacco Coast: A Maritime History of Chesapeake Bay in the Colonial Era* (Newport News, Va., 1953), 99–101; Ralph Davis, *The Rise of the English Shipping Industry in the Seventeenth and Eighteenth Centuries* (London, 1962), 285. For changes in Chesapeake shipping patterns see Ian K. Steele, *The English Atlantic, 1675–1740: An Exploration of Communication and Community* (New York, 1986), 41–44, 50; Admiral Knowles to the duke of Newcastle, 9 July 1746, in Gwyn, ed., *The Royal Navy and North America*, 291.

116. Middleton, *Tobacco Coast*, 290–293; Jacob M. Price, *France and the Chesapeake: A History of the French Tobacco Monopoly, 1674–1791, and of Its Relationship to the British and American Tobacco Trades* (Ann Arbor, Mich., 1973), I, 93, 177–181.

117. Middleton, *Tobacco Coast*, 297–298; Price, *France and the Chesapeake*, I, 385–386.

118. *Pa. Gaz.*, 7 May 1747.

119. Warren to Burchett, 10 Aug. 1739, in Gwyn, ed., *The Royal Navy and North America*, 13.

120. John R. Bartlett, ed., *Records of the Colony of Rhode Island and Providence Plantations in New England* (1859; reprint, New York, 1968), IV, 584.

121. Mass. Archs. LXIV, 126–129; Ames *et al.*, eds., *Mass. Acts and Resolves*, II, 62; Worthington Chauncey Ford *et al.*, eds., *Journals of the House of Representatives of Massachusetts* (Boston, 1919–1971), XXI, 159.

122. Ford *et al.* eds., *Mass. House Jours.*, XXI, 28.

123. Shirley to Greene, 19 Sept. 1744, in Gertrude Selwyn Kimball, ed., *The Correspondence of the Colonial Governors of Rhode Island, 1723–1775* (1902–1903; reprint, Freeport, N.Y., 1969), I, 271.

Notes to Pages 168 to 174 ‖ 263

124. Bartlett, ed., *Records of Colonial R.I.,* V, 96. Greene to Conn. Gov. Jonathan Law, 21 Sept. 1744, in Kimball, ed., *R.I. Gov. Correspondence,* I, 272–273. The Rhode Island and Connecticut sloops were cruising in consort.

125. Pringle to Erving, 9 Sept. 1740, in Edgar, ed., *Pringle Letterbook,* I, 243.

126. Ames, Goodell *et al.,* eds., *Mass. Acts and Resolves,* XIII, 94, 225, 608, 624, and 655; Bartlett, ed., *Records of Colonial R.I.,* IV, 568, 575; V, 16, 90–92, 101, 167–168, 216, and 246.

127. *Pa. Gaz.,* 30 Aug. 1744, 11 July 1745.

128. Reynell to Henry Sherburne, 26 Mar. 1745, John Reynell Letterbook, 29 May 1744–4 Oct. 1745.

129. Davis, *Rise of the English Shipping Industry,* 279; Richmond, *Navy in the War of 1739–48,* II, 191; Pares, *War and Trade,* 495; Dale Miquelon, *Dugard of Rouen: French Trade to Canada and the West Indies, 1729–1770* (Montreal, 1978), 91; Steele, *English Atlantic,* 25.

130. Richmond, *The Navy in the War of 1739–48,* II, 208–209.

131. Vernon to Harcourt, Oct. 1739, in B.McL. Ranft, ed., *The Vernon Papers* (London, 1958), 27. This volume contains numerous orders to other naval officers to protect British Caribbean commerce.

132. See, for example, the Admiralty's instructions of 14 Aug. 1742 to Capt. Peter Warren to protect Philadelphia commerce from enemy privateers, quoted in Richmond, *The Navy in the War of 1739–48,* III, 276.

133. Pringle to Samuel Saunders, 22 Oct. 1740, in Edgar, ed., *Pringle Letterbook,* I, 260.

134. R. Pringle to A. Pringle, 23 and 31 Oct. 1740, *ibid.,* 264–265.

135. *S.-C. Gaz.,* 23 July 1741.

136. *Pa. Gaz.,* 19 Aug. 1742.

137. R. Pringle to A. Pringle, in Edgar, ed., *Pringle Letterbook,* I, 332.

138. R. Pringle to A. Pringle, 15 Feb. 1742, *ibid.,* 323.

139. R. Pringle to A. Pringle, 17 June 1742, *ibid.,* 380.

140. *N.-Y. Wkly. Jour.,* 6 July 1741.

141. R. Pringle to A. Pringle, 7 Sept. 1742; Pringle to John Erving, 9 Oct. 1742; in Edgar, ed., *Pringle Letterbook,* I, 406–407, 430.

142. E. Lucas to George Lucas, 8 Sept. 1742, in Elise Pinckney, ed., *The Letterbook of Eliza Lucas Pinckney, 1739–1762* (Chapel Hill, N.C., 1972), 55.

143. Bull to George II, 20 Oct. 1742, quoted in W.E. May, "Capt. Charles Hardy on the Carolina Station, 1742–1744," *South Carolina Historical Magazine,* LXX (1969), 8–9.

144. May, "Capt. Hardy," *SCHM,* LXX (1969), 18–19. Joseph A. Devine, Jr., believes South Carolinians criticized Hardy unfairly in this action, and argues that Hardy faced the choice of pursuing the Spaniards to St. Augustine or returning to Charles Town to protect the city from attack. Because Hardy did not know the enemy's whereabouts, he sailed to Charles Town. See Devine, "The British North American Colonies in the War of 1739–1748" (Ph.D. diss., University of Virginia,

1968), 297–298. May offers no opinion on Hardy's conduct in this incident. It seems unlikely, however, that the Spanish forces would have undertaken a new offensive while they retreated from Georgia.

145. Richmond, *The Navy in the War of 1739–48,* III, 269.

146. *Pa. Gaz.,* 18 and 25 Aug. 1743; *N.-Y. Wkly. Jour.,* 21 Nov. 1743.

147. *N.-Y. Wkly. Post-Boy,* 16 Jan. 1744.

148. *Va. Gaz.,* 22 May 1741, quoted in the *Pa. Gaz.,* 11 June 1741.

149. *N.-Y. Wkly. Post-Boy,* 16 Jan. 1744.

150. Partridge to R.I. Gov. Richard Ward, 4 Feb. 1742, in Kimball, ed., *R.I. Gov. Correspondence,* I, 211.

151. *Pa. Gaz.,* 25 Mar., 15 and 22 Apr., and 5 Aug. 1742.

152. *S.-C. Gaz.,* 9 Sept. 1745. This was unfair criticism since the hurricane season normally lasted until the middle of October.

153. Glen to Warren, 23 July 1746, in Gwyn, ed., *The Royal Navy and North America,* 299–300.

154. See, for example, *S.-C. Gaz.,* 24 Aug., 23 Nov., and 28 Dec. 1747 and 25 Jan. and 16 May 1748.

155. Warren to Corbett, 9 and 25 Feb. 1745, in Gwyn, ed., *The Royal Navy and North America,* 51.

156. Reynell to Flexney, 25 Sept. 1746, John Reynell Letterbook 5 Oct. 1745–29 May 1747.

157. Richmond, *The Navy in the War of 1739–48,* III, 66.

158. *Bos. News-Letter,* 15 Sept. 1743.

159. *S.-C. Gaz.,* 24 Sept. 1744.

160. *Ibid.,* 8 June 1747.

161. Warren to Corbett, Feb. 1745, quoted in Richmond, *The Navy in the War of 1739–48,* II, 192.

162. James F. Shepherd and Gary M. Walton, *Shipping, Maritime Trade, and the Economic Development of Colonial North America* (Cambridge, 1972), 80–90; Douglass C. North, "Sources of Productivity Change in Ocean Shipping, 1600–1850," *Journal of Political Economy,* LXXVI (1968), 953–970.

163. Bridenbaugh, ed., *Gentleman's Progress,* 172.

NOTES TO CHAPTER 7

1. The exchange rates used for conversions to sterling throughout this chapter are contained in John J. McCusker, *Money and Exchange in Europe and America, 1600–1775: A Handbook* (Chapel Hill, N.C., 1978), 310, 316, 320.

2. *Pennsylvania Gazette* (Philadelphia), 23 Aug. 1744.

3. *New-York Weekly Post-Boy,* 3 Sept. 1744; *ibid.,* 6 Sept. 1744.

4. *South-Carolina Gazette* (Charles Town), 20 Apr. 1747; *Pa. Gaz.,* 14 May 1747.

5. *Pa. Gaz.*, 29 Mar. 1748.

6. *Boston News-Letter*, 14 July 1748; *Pa. Gaz.*, 21 July 1748.

7. *Pa. Gaz.*, 25 Apr. 1745.

8. *Ibid.*, 25 Sept. 1746.

9. *Ibid.*, 4 Feb. 1746.

10. *Ibid.*, 16 June 1748.

11. Arthur H. Cole, *Wholesale Commodity Prices in the United States, 1700–1861: Statistical Supplement, Actual Wholesale Prices of Various Commodities* (1938; reprint, New York, 1969), 21–31, provided the price data. Twenty-eight cases with quantity breakdowns were discarded because they were too vague or because Cole's work lacked prices for the commodities—quicksilver, gunpowder, and cocoa, for example—or because 1740s price data were unavailable—for coffee, for example. Prices were available, however, for the most commonly captured goods: sugar, indigo, wine, molasses, cotton, beef, and flour. Values for 18th century units of measure (hogheads of sugar, hundredweights of flour, barrels of beef, etc.) are from Cole, *Wholesale Commodity Prices*, ix–x, and James F. Shepherd and Gary M. Walton, *Shipping, Maritime Trade, and the Economic Development of Colonial North America* (Cambridge, 1972), 171–172 and 206.

12. Calculations for the value of prize vessels are based on the estimated cost per measured ton for vessels built in Philadelphia during this period. See John J. McCusker, "Sources of Investment Capital in the Philadelphia Shipping Industry," *Journal of Economic History*, XXXII (1972), 150. The values per measured ton for the prize vessels have been reduced by one-third because they were used craft, not new vessels. The tonnage of all prize vessels has been converted from the tons burden listed in the data file to measured tons according to McCusker's rule of thumb: a vessel's measured tonnage was usually one-third higher than its tons burden. See McCusker, "Colonial Tonnage Measurement: Five Philadelphia Ships as a Sample," and Gary M. Walton, "Colonial Tonnage Measurements: A Comment," *Jour. of Econ. Hist.*, XXVII (1967), 91, 392–397.

13. Thomas M. Doerflinger, "The Antilles Trade of the Old Regime: A Statistical Overview," *Journal of Interdisciplinary History*, VI (1976), 400.

14. *Ibid.*

15. Jean-François Brière, "Granville and the Newfoundland Fisheries in the Eighteenth Century" (Paper delivered at the Annual Meeting of the Canadian Historical Association, Vancouver, B.C., June 1983), 2–3.

16. Jacques Mathieu, "La Balance Commerciale: Nouvelle-France—Antilles au XVIIIᵉ siècle," *Revue d'histoire de l'Amérique française*, XXV (1972), 493.

17. This paragraph is based primarily on Geoffrey J. Walker, *Spanish Politics and Imperial Trade, 1700–1789* (Bloomington, Ind., 1979), 207–216, and Richard Pares, *War and Trade in the West Indies, 1739–1763* (Oxford, 1936), 109–114.

18. John Robert McNeill, *Atlantic Empires of France and Spain: Louisbourg and Havana, 1700–1763* (Chapel Hill, N.C., 1985), 156–158, 164, 191–192.

19. J.C.M. Ogelsby, "Spain's Havana Squadron and the Preservation of the Balance of Power in the Caribbean, 1740–1748," *Hispanic American Historical Review*, XLIX (1969), 479, 483, 485, 488.

20. The number of prizes presented in Table 7.2 (as in Table 7.1) should be viewed as an understatement. Colonial newspapers probably did not report every prize, and some accounts were too vague for inclusion in the data file. The historian of New York's private men-of-war has indicated that Manhattan predators captured 321 prizes worth £617,615. This is a much larger figure than Table 7.2 indicates. On the other hand, the average value for these prizes was only £1,924, a much lower figure than the data presented in this discussion, which suggests that the press concentrated on larger captures. See James G. Lydon, *Pirates, Privateers, and Profits* (Upper Saddle River, N.J., 1970), 271. The paucity of West Indian evidence probably understates the islanders' successes.

21. See chapter 3 concerning the importance of vessel types.

22. Charles Whitworth, *State of the Trade of Great Britain in Its Imports and Exports, Progressively from the Year 1697* (London, 1776), 44–52. Whitworth's statistics have been augmented using Jacob M. Price, "New Time Series for Scotland's and Britain's Trade with the Thirteen Colonies and States, 1740 to 1791," *William and Mary Quarterly*, 3d Ser., XXXII (1975), 322–325.

23. Ralph Davis, *The Rise of the English Shipping Industry in the Seventeenth and Eighteenth Centuries* (London, 1962), 315.

24. Pringle to Thomas Burrill, 10 Oct. 1739, in Walter B. Edgar, ed., *The Letterbook of Robert Pringle* (Columbia, S.C., 1972), I, 139. For other letters expressing this fear, see Pringle to Richard Thompson, 11 Oct. 1739; and Pringle to John Erving, 16 Oct. 1739; *ibid.*, I, 141–143.

25. Pringle to Henry Collins, 19 Oct. 1739, *ibid.*, 145.

26. Pringle to Hubert Guichard, 20 Nov. 1739, *ibid.*, 150.

27. R. Pringle to Andrew Pringle, 27 Dec. 1739, *ibid.*, 163.

28. Pringle to Burrill, 11 June 1740, *ibid.*, 218.

29. Pringle to William Cookson and William Welfitt, 7 Nov. 1743, *ibid.*, II, 602.

30. Pringle to Erving, 18 Aug. 1744, *ibid.*, 734.

31. Pringle to Cookson and Welfitt, 15 Jan. 1745, *ibid.*, 797.

32. Laurens to Richard Grubb, 12 May 1748, in Philip M. Hamer *et al.*, eds., *The Papers of Henry Laurens* (Columbia, S.C., 1968–1985), I, 135. Laurens wrote this letter one week after Britain and France had signed the Treaty of Aix-la-Chapelle.

33. Shepherd and Walton, *Shipping, Maritime Trade*, 191–192.

34. See John M. Hemphill II, "Freight Rates in the Maryland Tobacco Trade, 1705–62," *Maryland Historical Magazine*, LIV (1959), 52–53. See Table 6.1 for Spanish and French privateering activity.

35. Pares, *War and Trade*, 500.

36. *Ibid.*; Davis, *Rise of the English Shipping Industry*, 284.

37. Reynell to Daniel Flexney, 1 Mar. 1740, John Reynell Letterbook, 16 Oct. 1738–15 Oct. 1741, Historical Society of Pennsylvania, Philadelphia.

38. Reynell to Samuel Dicker, 29 Oct. 1740, *ibid.*

39. Reynell to Michael Lee Dicker, 30 July 1744, John Reynell Letterbook, 29 May 1744–4 October 1745.

40. Reynell to Flexney, 3 Sept. 1744, *ibid.*

41. The ensuing discussion is based primarily on A.H. John, "The London Assurance Company and the Marine Insurance Market of the Eighteenth Century," *Economica,* XXV (1958), 126–141.

42. *Ibid.,* 137–138.

43. Lucy S. Sutherland, *A London Merchant, 1695–1774* (1933; reprint, London, 1962), 66–67.

44. Pares, *War and Trade,* 495–496.

45. *Ibid.,* 498.

46. Reynell to Michael Atkins, 1 Mar. 1744, Reynell Letterbook, 15 Oct. 1741–26 April 1744. For a general discussion of insurance in Philadelphia see Arthur L. Jensen, *The Maritime Commerce of Colonial Philadelphia* (Madison, Wis., 1963), 115–116.

47. Reynell to Bland, 18 June 1744, Reynell Letterbook, 29 May 1744–4 Oct. 1745.

48. Reynell to Taylor, 27 Feb. 1745, *ibid.*

49. Powel to Barclay, Samuel Powel Letterbook, 66, Hist. Soc. of Pa., Philadelphia.

50. Reynell to Elias Bland, 2 Mar. 1745, Reynell Letterbook, 29 May 1744–4 Oct. 1745.

51. Dale Miquelon, *Dugard of Rouen: French Trade to Canada and the West Indies, 1729–1770* (Montreal, 1978), 123.

52. *Ibid.*

53. *Ibid.,* 124.

54. *Pa. Gaz.,* 3 Sept. 1747.

55. Miquelon, *Dugard of Rouen,* 114–117.

56. *Ibid.,* 167–170.

57. *Ibid.,* 129.

58. Charles Wright and Ernest C. Fayle, *A History of Lloyd's, from the Founding of Lloyd's Coffee House to the Present Day* (London, 1928), 80–81; John, "The London Assurance Company," *Economica,* XXV (1958), 136–138; Miquelon, *Dugard of Rouen,* 124.

59. *Pa. Gaz.,* 28 Apr. 1747.

60. *Ibid.,* 3 Sept. 1747.

61. Bannister to Handley, 26 May 1748, John Bannister Letter Book, 1748–1750, 18, Newport Historical Society, Newport, R.I.

62. John, "The London Assurance Company," *Economica,* XXV (1958), 136; Wright and Fayle, *History of Lloyd's,* 80.

63. See chapter 4 for a further discussion of rising wage rates for merchant seamen.

64. J. Franklin Jameson, ed., *Privateering and Piracy in the Colonial Period: Illustrative Documents* (New York, 1923), 398.

65. *Ibid.*, 401.

66. *Ibid.*, 403.

67. *Ibid.*, 394.

68. *Pa. Gaz.*, 19 Sept. 1745.

69. H.S. Vaughan, ed., *Voyages and Cruises of Commodore Walker* (London, 1928), 196.

70. Instructions of George II to Captains of Privateers, 30 Nov. 1739, in Jameson, ed., *Privateering and Piracy*, 347–354.

71. *Pa. Gaz.*, 27 Mar. 1740.

72. Jameson, ed., *Privateering and Piracy*, 420–421.

73. For more on this struggle over trade with the enemy, see the work of G.N. Clark, including *The Dutch Alliance and the War Against French Trade, 1688–1697* (Manchester, 1923).

74. Jameson, ed., *Privateering and Piracy*, 375–378.

75. *Flower et al.* v. *Sloop Three Brothers; Flower et al.* v. *Sloop de la Clara; Davidson* v. *Sloop Nooyt Godagt*, Rhode Island Vice-Admiralty Court Records, Rhode Island Admiralty Papers, I, 5–65, Rhode Island State Archives, Providence, hereafter cited as R.I. Adm. Court.

76. See the following cases decided by Judge Leonard Lockman: *Hopkins* v. *Sloop Ufro Sarah* (1743), *Allen and Marshall* v. *Wilhelm Galley* (1745), and *Langdon* v. *Sloop Amity* (1745), in *ibid.*, II, 27–31; III, 28–42 and 85–88. Judge William Strengthfield also condemned neutral vessels: *Helm* v. *Pearl* (1746), *Sweet* v. *Sloop Catharina* (1746), and *Fry and Dunbar* v. *Sloop Endraght* (1747), *ibid.*, IV, 3–14, 77–102, and 122–126. The Newport court did not always condemn neutral vessels. Judge Pemberton ruled against John Bannister's privateer sloop *Victory* in *Power* v. *L'Amiable de Cap* (1742), *ibid.*, I, 34–38. Leonard Lockman acquitted a French vessel taken before the 1744 declaration of war in *White* v. *Schooner Elizabeth* (1744), *ibid.*, II, 46. Strengthfield's decision in *Sweet* v. *Young Johannes* (1747) acquitted a Dutch sloop, *ibid.*, V. 119–124.

77. *Janncey et al.* v. *Ships Arnoldus and Johannes Gally et al.* (1745), Minutes of the Vice-Admiralty Court of the Province of New York, I, 184–198 (photostats), Library of Congress, hereafter cited as N.Y. Adm. Court. *Sibbald* v. *Snow Prince of Orange* (1741), Pennsylvania Vice-Admiralty Court Records, Box 1, 163–183 (photostats), Lib. Cong. *Duthy et al.* v. *Sloop Guffron Angelica* (1747), South Carolina Minutes of the Vice-Admiralty Courts at Charles Town, Box 5, 379–383 (photostats), Lib. Cong., hereafter cited as S.C. Adm. Court.

78. *Pa. Gaz.*, 21 Dec. 1742.

79. Duke of Newcastle to Governor and Company of Rhode Island, 13 Apr. 1743, in Gertrude Selwyn Kimball, ed., *The Correspondence of the Colonial Governors of Rhode Island, 1723–1775* (1902–1903; reprint, Freeport, N.Y., 1969), I, 225–226.

80. *Pa. Gaz.*, 22 May, 5 and 19 June 1746.

81. *Ibid.*, 23 Apr. 1747.

82. Laurens to William Hopton, 27 Dec. 1748, in Hamer *et al.*, eds., *Laurens Papers*, I, 198–199. The Jamaican privateer *Trelawney Galley,* commanded by

Capt. Michael Crispin, captured the *Vrow Dorthea.* See *Goolde et al.* v. *Ship Vrow Dorthea,* S.C. Adm. Court, Box 5, 435–457.

83. *Pa. Gaz.,* 2 Sept. 1742.

84. *New-York Evening-Post,* 22 Oct. 1744; *Pa. Gaz.,* 25 Oct. 1744.

85. *Pa. Gaz.,* 15 Jan. 1745.

86. *Ibid.,* 16 Feb. 1744.

87. *Bos. News-Letter,* 26 Apr. 1744; *Pa. Gaz.,* 3 May 1744.

88. *Pa. Gaz.,* 22 Jan. 1745.

89. *Ibid.,* 11 Aug. 1748.

90. *Ibid.,* 13 Oct. 1748; *S.-C. Gaz.,* 31 Oct. 1748.

91. *Pa. Gaz.,* 26 Mar. 1741.

92. *Bos. News-Letter,* 11 Dec. 1740; *Pa. Gaz.,* 22 Jan. 1741.

93. *Pa. Gaz.,* 12 Feb. 1745.

94. *S.-C. Gaz.,* 17 Nov. 1746; *Pa. Gaz.,* 6 Jan. 1747.

95. *Pa. Gaz.,* 4 Sept. 1740.

96. *Ibid.,* 12 Sept. 1745.

97. *Ibid.,* 3 June 1748.

98. *N.-Y. Eve.-Post,* 1 Aug. 1748; *Pa. Gaz.,* 4 Aug. 1748.

99. *Pa. Gaz.,* 29 Jan. 1741. Fortunately, the privateers escaped the next evening.

100. *Ibid.,* 27 Sept. 1744; K. Malbone to G. Malbone, Jr., quoted in Richard L. Bowen, "Godfrey Malbone's Armorial Silver," *Rhode Island History,* IX (1950), 38.

101. *Bos. News-Letter,* 20 Sept. 1744; *Pa. Gaz.,* 4 Oct. 1744.

102. *Pa. Gaz.,* 10 Mar. 1747.

103. *Ibid.,* 29 Nov. 1744.

104. Jameson, ed., *Privateering and Piracy,* 463–464.

105. *New-York Weekly Journal,* 21 May 1743.

106. *Bos. News-Letter,* 18 Aug. 1744.

107. *Pa. Gaz.,* 11 July 1745.

108. Reynell to Dowers, 19 July 1746, Reynell Letterbook, 5 Oct. 1745–29 May 1747.

109. Beekman to Collins, 5 Feb. 1748, in Philip L. White, ed., *The Beekman Mercantile Papers, 1746–1799* (New York, 1956), I, 43.

110. Davis, *Rise of the English Shipping Industry,* 69; Richard Pares, *Colonial Blockade and Neutral Rights, 1739–1763* (Oxford, 1938), 19–25.

111. These instructions, dated at the Court of St. James's on 3 Jan. 1744, appeared in the *S.-C. Gaz.,* 7 Oct. 1745.

112. Journal of the Newport privateer sloop *Revenge,* 17 Sept. 1744, in Jameson, ed., *Privateering and Piracy,* 420.

113. Bond for a Rhode Island letter of marque, Rhode Island Notary Public Records, IV, 479, R.I. State Archs., hereafter cited as R.I. Notary Rec.

114. *Ibid.,* V, 289. Given the limited extant business records of privateer owners, even an analysis that presumed equal shares is impossible.

115. See Bernard and Lotte Bailyn, *Massachusetts Shipping, 1697–1714: A Statistical Study* (Cambridge, Mass., 1959), 9–12; Davis, *Rise of the English Shipping Industry,* chap. 5, 81–109.

116. *Bos. News-Letter,* 27 Sept., 17 and 4 Oct. 1744; *Pa. Gaz.,* 11 and 18 Oct. 1744.

117. Nearly all investors in Rhode Island privateers listed their occupations as "merchant." Of 89 bonds for letters of marque, only 2 (2%) failed to include merchants. See R.I. Notary Rec., IV–V.

118. K. Malbone to G. Malbone, Jr., 6 Oct. 1745, quoted in Bowen, "Godfrey Malbone's Armorial Silver," *R.I. Hist.,* IX (1950), 88.

119. G. Malbone to G. Malbone, Jr., quoted in *ibid.,* 90.

120. Scott to Malbone, 4 Aug. 1746, quoted in *ibid.,* 91–92.

121. See Bannister to Jacobs and Clark, 5 May 1740; Bannister to Sedgwick and Bernard, 21 May 1740; and Bannister to Capt. John Thomlinson, 19 Feb. 1741; in John Bannister Copy Book, 1730–1742, 67, 74, 146, Newport Hist. Soc., hereafter cited as Bannister Copy Book.

122. Bannister to Samuel Clark, 6 Oct. 1740, *ibid.,* 117.

123. Bannister to Cane, 14 Jan. 1741, *ibid.,* 140.

124. Bannister to Vanburg, 16 Jan. 1741, *ibid.,* 141.

125. Bannister to Vanburg, 19 Oct. 1741, *ibid.,* 211.

126. *Pa. Gaz.,* 30 May and 27 June 1745.

127. *N.-Y. Eve.-Post,* 24 June 1745; *Virginia Gazette* (Williamsburg), 21 Nov. 1745 and 3 July 1746.

128. Pringle to Henderson, 24 Apr. 1745, in Edgar, ed., *Pringle Letterbook,* II, 843. The letterbook ended on 29 Apr. without further comment on this topic.

129. "Journal of Robert Pringle, 1746–1747," annotated by Mabel L. Webber, *South Carolina Historical Magazine,* XXVI (1925), 21–30, 93–112. The quotation is on p. 108.

130. *Ibid.*

131. R.I. Notary Rec., IV, 417.

132. 13 Geo. II, 1740, c. 4, Danby Pickering, ed., *The Statutes at Large . . .* (Cambridge, 1762–1807), XVII, 360.

133. Howard M. Chapin, *Rhode Island Privateers in King George's War, 1739–1748* (Providence, R.I., 1926), 55–56.

134. Jameson, ed., *Privateering and Piracy,* 463–464.

135. *N.-Y. Wkly. Post-Boy,* 3 Dec. 1744.

136. R.I. Adm. Court, IV, 32.

137. See chapter 3.

138. This is a weighted average reflecting the number of yearly privateers. The crew size is based on Table 3.6 in chapter 3.

139. For the costs of Philadelphia vessels see McCusker, "Sources of Investment Capital," *Jour. Econ. Hist.,* XXXII (1972), 150.

140. George E. Reed, ed., *Pennsylvania Archives, Fourth Series: Papers of the Governors* (Harrisburg, Pa., 1900), II, 67–68.

141. The strong, positive correlation between the crew size and the craft's tonnage is the rationale for dividing the vessel's cost by the number of hands. The relationship between crew size and ordnance was also strongly positive. See chapter 3 for a discussion of these relationships.

142. Bannister to Thomas Hall, 18 Dec. 1739, Bannister Copy Book, 43.

143. R. Pringle to A. Pringle, 6 Feb., 20 July, 21 Sept. 1744, in Edgar, ed., *Pringle Letterbook,* II, 639–641, 728, 739–740. Pringle was unsure if the *Recovery,* one of the vessels, was a ship or a snow.

144. This assumes the capital was reinvested and that it earned the same rate for the rest of the year. It is impossible to determine how often these assumptions were valid. For merchants with an investment pattern similar to those listed in Table 7.8, the assumption is probably justified. For investors who risked their capital in a single privateering cruise, the assumption is probably invalid. In any event, returns from privateering were most likely reinvested in other endeavors and not left idle, so the 78% figure would understate annual proceeds.

145. Lydon, *Pirates, Privateers, and Profits,* 253.

146. See chapter 4 for a full discussion of maritime wage rates.

147. *Boston Gazette,* 20 Aug. 1739; *N.-Y. Wkly. Post-Boy,* 17 Sept. 1744.

148. 13 Geo. II, 1740, c. 4, and 17 Geo. II, 1744, c. 34, Pickering, ed., *The Statutes at Large,* XVII, 366–367, XVIII, 258. On the difficulty of collecting bounty money see Mathias Jones to Samuel and William Vernon, 4 Apr. 1748, Wetmore Collection on Rhode Island Commerce, 1706–1754, Massachusetts Historical Society, Boston.

149. Pares, *Colonial Blockade,* 27.

150. Bannister to Roger Moore, 15 Sept. 1741, Bannister Copy Book, 199. Bannister expressed similar sentiments to John Thomlinson in a letter on 23 Sept. 1741.

151. *Pa. Gaz.,* 11 Mar. 1746.

152. *N.-Y. Wkly. Post-Boy,* 13 June 1748.

153. *Bos. News-Letter,* 22 Jan. 1747; *Pa. Gaz.,* 10 Feb. 1747.

154. *Pa. Gaz.,* 10 Mar. 1747.

NOTES TO THE APPENDIX

1. The data file was constructed and analyzed using Norman H. Nie *et al., SPSS: Statistical Package for the Social Sciences,* 2d ed. (New York, 1975).

2. Charles E. Clark and Charles Wetherell, "The Measure of Maturity: The *Pennsylvania Gazette,* 1728–1765," *William and Mary Quarterly,* 3d Ser., XLVI (1989), 279–303, provides a thorough discussion of the *Gazette*'s content, editorial view, and overall quality.

BIBLIOGRAPHY

PRIMARY SOURCES

I. Colonial Newspapers

Boston Evening-Post, 1739.
Boston Gazette, 1739.
Boston News-Letter, 1739–1749.
New-York Evening-Post, 1744–1749.
New-York Gazette, 1744.
New-York Weekly Journal, 1739–1744.
New-York Weekly Post-Boy, 1744–1748.
Pennsylvania Gazette (Philadelphia), 1739–1749.
South-Carolina Gazette (Charles Town), 1739–1749.
Virginia Gazette (Williamsburg), 1739–1746 (no extant issues for 1747–1748).

II. Colonial Vice-Admiralty Court Records

A. Manuscript Materials
Massachusetts Vice-Admiralty Court Records, V, Suffolk County Courthouse, Boston.
Rhode Island Vice-Admiralty Court Records, Rhode Island Admiralty Papers, I–VIII, Rhode Island State Archives, Providence.
Minutes of the Vice-Admiralty Court of the Province of New York, I–II (photostats), Library of Congress.
Pennsylvania Vice-Admiralty Court Records, Boxes 1 and 2 (photostats), Library of Congress.

South Carolina Minutes of the Vice-Admiralty Courts at Charles Town, Boxes 4 and 5 (photostats), Library of Congress.

B. Published Material

List & Index Society, *High Court of Admiralty: Index to Prize Papers, 1739–1748*. London: By Permission of H.M. Stationery Office, 1973.

Towle, Dorothy S., ed. *Records of the Vice-Admiralty Court of Rhode Island, 1716–1752*. Washington, D.C.: American Historical Association, 1936.

III. Correspondence of Merchants, Governors, and Naval Officers

A. Manuscript Materials

John Bannister Copy Book, 1730–1742. Newport Historical Society, Newport, R.I.

John Bannister Letterbook, 1748–1750. Newport Hist. Soc.

Jonathan Belcher Letterbooks. Massachusetts Historical Society, Boston.

Samuel Powel Letterbooks, 1727–1740, 1739–1746, 1746–1747. Historical Society of Pennsylvania, Philadelphia.

John Reynell Letterbooks, 1738–1741, 1741–1744, 1744–1745, 1745–1747. Hist. Soc. Pa.

John Swift Letterbook, 1747–1751. Hist. Soc. Pa.

Samuel and William Vernon Letterbooks, 1738–1748. Newport Hist. Soc.

Wetmore Collection on Rhode Island Commerce, 1706–1754. Mass. Hist. Soc.

Winslow Papers. Mass. Hist. Soc.

B. Published Materials

Edgar, Walter B., ed. *The Letterbook of Robert Pringle*. 2 vols. Columbia: University of South Carolina Press, 1972.

Gwyn, Julian, ed. *The Royal Navy and North America: The Warren Papers, 1736–1752*. London: Navy Record Society, 1973.

Hamer, Philip M. *et al.*, eds. *The Papers of Henry Laurens*. 10 vols. Columbia: University of South Carolina Press, 1968–1985.

"Journal of Robert Pringle, 1746–1747." Annotated by Mabel L. Webber. *South Carolina Historical Magazine*, XXVI (1925), 21–30, 93–112.

Kimball, Gertrude Selwyn, ed. *The Correspondence of the Colonial Governors of Rhode Island, 1723–1775*. 2 vols. 1902–1903. Reprint. Freeport, N.Y.: Books for Libraries Press, 1969.

Lincoln, Charles H., ed. *The Correspondence of William Shirley: Governor of Massachusetts and Military Commander in America, 1731–1760*. 2 vols. New York: Macmillan, 1912.

Pinckney, Elise, ed. *The Letterbook of Eliza Lucas Pinckney, 1739–1762*. Chapel Hill: University of North Carolina Press, 1972.

Ranft, B.McL., ed. *The Vernon Papers*. London: Navy Record Society, 1958.

Reed, George E., ed. *Pennsylvania Archives, Fourth Series: Papers of the Governors*. 12 vols. Harrisburg: State of Pennsylvania, 1900.

White, Philip L., ed. *The Beekman Mercantile Papers, 1746–1799.* 2 vols. New York: New York Historical Society, 1956.

IV. Government Documents

A. Manuscript Materials
Bonds for Rhode Island Letters of Marque. Rhode Island Notary Public Records, IV–V. Rhode Island State Archives, Providence.

Massachusetts Archives, LXIV, Maritime, 1740–1753. Massachusetts State House, Boston.

Mass. Archs., LXXXII, Minutes of the Council, 1733–1753. Mass. State House.

Rhode Island Admiralty Lists. Maritime Papers: Colonial Wars, 1723–1760. R.I. State Archs.

B. Published Materials
Acts and Laws, of His Majesty's Colony of Rhode-Island, and Providence-Plantations, In New-England, In America. Newport, R.I.: Franklin, 1745.

Ames, Ellis, Abner C. Goodell *et al.,* eds. *The Acts and Resolves, Public and Private, of the Province of the Massachusetts Bay. . . .* 21 vols. Boston: Wright & Potter, Printers to the State, 1869–1922.

Bartlett, John R., ed. *Records of the Colony of Rhode Island and Providence Plantations in New England.* 10 vols. 1859. Reprint. New York: AMS Press, 1968.

Ford, Worthington Chauncey *et al.,* eds. *Journals of the House of Representatives of Massachusetts.* 41 vols. Boston: Massachusetts Historical Society, 1919–1971.

Grant, W.L., and J. Munro, eds. *Acts of the Privy Council of England: Colonial Series, 1613–1783.* 6 vols. 1908–1912. Reprint. Nendeln, Liechtenstein: Kraus Reprint, 1966.

O'Callaghan, Edward B., ed. *Documents, Relative to the Colonial History of the State of New York.* 15 vols. Albany, N.Y.: Weed, Parsons and Co., 1853–1887.

Pickering, Danby, ed. *The Statutes at Large. . . .* 46 vols. Cambridge: Cambridge University Press, 1762–1807.

"Ship Registers in the South Carolina Archives, 1734–1780." Compiled by R. Nicholas Olsberg. *South Carolina Historical Magazine,* LXXIV (1973), 189–279.

U.S. Bureau of the Census. *Historical Statistics of the United States, Colonial Times to 1957.* Washington, D.C., 1960.

V. Other Published Materials

Bridenbaugh, Carl, ed. *Gentleman's Progress: The Itinerarium of Dr. Alexander Hamilton, 1744.* Chapel Hill: University of North Carolina Press, 1948.

Greene, Jack P., ed. *Settlements to Society: 1584-1763.* New York: McGraw-Hill, 1966.

Jameson, J. Franklin, ed. *Privateering and Piracy in the Colonial Period: Illustrative Documents.* New York: Macmillan, 1923.

Vaughan, H.S., ed. *Voyages and Cruises of Commodore Walker.* London: Cassell and Company, Ltd., 1928.

Whitworth, Sir Charles. *State of the Trade of Great Britain in Its Imports and Exports, Progressively from the Year 1697.* London, 1776.

SECONDARY SOURCES

I. Books and Articles

Anderson, Fred. "A People's Army: Provincial Military Service in Massachusetts during the Seven Years' War." *William and Mary Quarterly,* 3d Ser., XL (1983), 500-527.

Andrews, Charles M. Introduction to *Records of the Vice-Admiralty Court of Rhode Island, 1716-1752,* edited by Dorothy S. Towle. Washington, D.C.: American Historical Association, 1936.

Andrews, Kenneth R. *Elizabethan Privateering: English Privateering during the Spanish War, 1585-1603.* Cambridge: Cambridge University Press, 1964.

――――. *The Spanish Caribbean: Trade and Plunder, 1530-1630.* New Haven, Conn.: Yale University Press, 1978.

――――. *Trade, Plunder and Settlement: Maritime Enterprise and the Genesis of the British Empire, 1480-1630.* Cambridge: Cambridge University Press, 1984.

Bailyn, Bernard, and Lotte Bailyn. *Massachusetts Shipping, 1697-1714: A Statistical Study.* Cambridge, Mass.: Belknap Press of Harvard University, 1959.

Baugh, Daniel A. *British Naval Administration in the Age of Walpole.* Princeton, N.J.: Princeton University Press, 1965.

Baxter, William T. *The House of Hancock: Business in Boston, 1724-1775.* 1945. Reprint. New York: Russell & Russell, 1965.

Behrens, Betty. "Government and Society." In *The Economic Organization of Early Europe.* Vol. V of *The Cambridge Economic History of Europe,* edited by E.E. Rich and C.H. Wilson, 549-620. Cambridge: Cambridge University Press, 1977.

Blitz, Rudolph C. "Mercantilist Policies and the Pattern of World Trade, 1500-1750." *Journal of Economic History,* XXVII (1967), 39-55.

Bonomi, Patricia U. *A Factious People: Politics and Society in Colonial New York.* New York: Columbia University Press, 1971.

Bowen, Richard L. "Godfrey Manbone's Armorial Silver." *Rhode Island History,* IX (1950).

Bridenbaugh, Carl. *Cities in Revolt: Urban Life in America, 1743-1776.* Rev. ed. New York: Oxford University Press, 1971.

――――. *Cities in the Wilderness: The First Century of Urban Life in America, 1625-1742.* Rev. ed. New York: Oxford University Press, 1971.

Bromley, J.S. "The Channel Island Privateers in the War of the Spanish

Succession." *Transactions for the Year 1949 of La Société Guernesiaise,* XIV (1950), 444–478.

———. "The French Privateering War, 1702–13." In *Historical Essays 1600–1750 Presented to David Ogg,* edited by H.E. Bell and R.L. Ollard, 203–231. London: A. & C. Black, Ltd., 1963.

———. "The Jacobite Privateers in the Nine Years War." In *Statesmen, Scholars, and Merchants: Essays in Eighteenth-Century History Presented to Dame Lucy Sutherland,* edited by Anne Whiteman *et al.,* 17–43. Oxford: The Clarendon Press, 1973.

———. "A New Vocation: Privateering in the Wars of 1689–97 and 1702–13." In *A People of the Sea: The Maritime History of the Channel Islands,* edited by A.G. Jamieson, 109–147. London: Methuen, 1986.

Burg, B.R. *Sodomy and the Perception of Evil: English Sea Rovers in the Seventeenth-Century Caribbean.* New York: New York University Press, 1983.

Chandler, David G., *et al.* "Armies and Navies." In *The Rise of Great Britain and Russia, 1688–1715/25.* Vol. VI of *The New Cambridge Modern History,* edited by J.S. Bromley, 741–833. Cambridge: Cambridge University Press, 1970.

Chapelle, Howard I. *The History of American Sailing Ships.* London: Putnam, 1956.

———. *The Search for Speed under Sail, 1700–1855.* New York: Bonanza Books, 1967.

Chapin, Howard M. *Privateering in King George's War, 1739–1748.* Providence: Rhode Island Historical Society, 1928.

———. *Rhode Island Privateers in King George's War, 1739–1748.* Providence: Rhode Island Historical Society, 1926.

Clark, Charles E., and Charles Wetherell. "The Measure of Maturity: The *Pennsylvania Gazette,* 1728–1765." *William and Mary Quarterly,* 3d Ser., XLVI (1989), 279–303.

Clark, Dora Mae. "The Impressment of Seamen in the American Colonies." In *Essays in Colonial History Presented to Charles McLean Andrews,* 198–224. New Haven, Conn.: Yale University Press, 1931.

Clark, G.N. *The Dutch Alliance and the War Against French Trade, 1688–1697.* Manchester: Manchester University Press, 1923.

Cole, Arthur H. *Wholesale Commodity Prices in the United States, 1700–1861: Statistical Supplement, Actual Wholesale Prices of Various Commodities.* 2 vols. 1938. Reprint (2 vols. in 1). New York: Johnson Reprint Co., 1969.

Coleman, D.C. "Mercantilism Revisited." *Historical Journal,* XXIII (1980), 773–791.

Commission Internationale d'Histoire Maritime. *Course et Piraterie: Études présentées à la Commission Internationale d'Histoire Maritime à l'occasion de son XVe colloque international pendant le XIVe Congrès International des Sciences historiques* (San Francisco, août 1975). 2 vols. Paris: Institut de Recherche et d'Histoire de Textes Edition du Centre National de la Recherche Scientifique, 1975.

Corbett, Julian S. *England in the Seven Years' War: A Study of Combined Strategy.* 2 vols. London: Longmans, Green and Co., 1907.

Craton, Michael. "The Role of the Caribbean Vice Admiralty Courts in British Imperialism." *Caribbean Studies,* XI (1971), 5–20.

Crump, Helen J. *Colonial Admiralty Jurisdiction in the Seventeenth Century.* London: Longmans, Green, 1931.

Cumming, William P. "The Turbulent Life of Captain James Wimble." *North Carolina Historical Review,* XLVI (1969), 1–18.

Davis, Ralph. *The Rise of the English Shipping Industry in the Seventeenth and Eighteenth Centuries.* London: Macmillan, 1962.

De Vries, Jan. *The Economy of Europe in an Age of Crisis, 1600–1750.* Cambridge: Cambridge University Press, 1976.

Doerflinger, Thomas M. "The Antilles Trade of the Old Regime: A Statistical Overview." *Journal of Interdisciplinary History,* VI (1976), 397–415.

Dorn, Walter L. *Competition for Empire, 1740–1763.* New York: Harper & Brothers, 1940.

Duffy, Michael. "The Foundations of British Naval Power." In *The Military Revolution and the State, 1500–1800,* edited by Michael Duffy, 49–85. Exeter, England: Exeter University Studies in History No. 1, 1980.

―――. "Introduction: The Military Revolution and the State, 1500–1800." In *The Military Revolution and the State, 1500–1800,* edited by Michael Duffy, 1–9. Exeter, England: Exeter University Studies in History No. 1, 1980.

Dunn, Richard S. *Sugar and Slaves: The Rise of the Planter Class in the English West Indies, 1624–1713.* Chapel Hill: University of North Carolina Press, 1972.

Edgar, Walter B. "Robert Pringle and His World." *South Carolina Historical Magazine,* LXXVI (1975), 1–11.

Fairchild, Byron. *Messrs. William Pepperrell: Merchants at Piscataqua.* Ithaca, N.Y.: Cornell University Press, 1954.

Finer, Samuel. "State- and Nation-Building in Europe: The Role of the Military." In *The Formation of National States in Western Europe,* edited by Charles Tilly, 84–163. Princeton, N.J.: Princeton University Press, 1975.

Fish, Stuyvesant. "Privateering in New York under George II, 1758–1760." *New York Historical Society Quarterly Bulletin,* XXIX (1945), 161–171.

Garitee, Jerome R. *The Republic's Private Navy: The American Privateering Business as Practiced by Baltimore during the War of 1812.* Middletown, Conn.: Wesleyan University Press, 1977.

Gibson, Charles. *Spain in America.* New York: Harper & Row, Harper Torchbooks, 1966.

Glamann, Kristof. "The Changing Patterns of Trade." In *The Economic Organization of Early Modern Europe.* Vol. V of *The Cambridge Economic History of Europe,* edited by E.E. Rich and C.H. Wilson, 185–289. Cambridge: Cambridge University Press, 1977.

―――. "European Trade 1500–1750." Translated by Geoffrey French. In *The Sixteenth and Seventeenth Centuries.* Vol. II of *The Fontana Economic History of Europe,* edited by Carlo M. Cipolla, 427–526. London: Collins/Fontana Books, 1974.

Goldenberg, Joseph A. *Shipbuilding in Colonial America.* Charlottesville: University Press of Virginia, 1975.

Graham, Gerald S. *Empire of the North Atlantic: The Maritime Struggle for North America.* Toronto: University of Toronto Press, 1950.

Gray, Lewis Cecil. *History of Agriculture in the Southern United States to 1860.* 2 vols. Washington, D.C.: Carnegie Institution of Washington: Publication no. 430, 1933.

Gwyn, Julian. *The Enterprising Admiral: The Personal Fortune of Admiral Sir Peter Warren.* Montreal: McGill-Queen's University Press, 1974.

Harkness, Albert, Jr. "Americanism and Jenkins' Ear." *Mississippi Valley Historical Review,* XXXVII (1950), 61–90.

Harman, Joyce E. *Trade and Privateering in Spanish Florida, 1732–1763.* St. Augustine, Fla.: St. Augustine Historical Society, 1969.

Hemphill, John M. II. "Freight Rates in the Maryland Tobacco Trade, 1705–62." *Maryland Historical Magazine,* LIX (1959), 36–58, 154–187.

Hildner, Ernest G., Jr. "The Rôle of the South Sea Company in the Diplomacy Leading to the War of Jenkins' Ear, 1729–1739." *Hispanic American Historical Review,* XVIII (1938), 322–341.

Hughson, Shirley. *The Carolina Pirates and Colonial Commerce, 1670–1740.* Baltimore: Johns Hopkins University Studies in Historical and Political Science, XII, 1894.

Hutchinson, J.R. *The Press-Gang Afloat and Ashore.* London: G. Bell & Sons, Ltd., 1913.

James, Sydney V. *Colonial Rhode Island: A History.* New York: Charles Scribner's Sons, 1975.

Jamieson, A.G. "The Return to Privateering: Channel Island Privateers, 1739–83." In *A People of the Sea: The Maritime History of the Channel Islands,* edited by A.G. Jamieson, 148–172. London: Methuen, 1986.

Jensen, Arthur L. *The Maritime Commerce of Colonial Philadelphia.* Madison: State Historical Society of Wisconsin, 1963.

John, A.H. "The London Assurance Company and the Marine Assurance Market of the Eighteenth Century." *Economica,* XXV (1958), 126–141.

Johnson, Richard R. "The Imperial Webb: The Thesis of Garrison Government in Early America Considered." *William and Mary Quarterly,* 3d Ser., XLIII (1986), 408–430.

Kammen, Michael. *Empire and Interest: The American Colonies and the Politics of Mercantilism.* Philadelphia: J.B. Lippincott Co., 1970.

Kemp, Peter. *The British Sailor: A Social History of the Lower Deck.* London: J.M. Dent & Sons, 1970.

Konkle, Burton A. *The Life of Alexander Hamilton, 1676–1741: "The Day-Star of the American Revolution."* 1941. Reprint. Freeport, N.Y.: Books for Libraries Press, 1972.

Lax, John, and William Pencak. "The Knowles Riot and the Crisis of the 1740s in Massachusetts." *Perspectives in American History,* X (1976), 153–214.

Leach, Douglas Edward. *Roots of Conflict: British Armed Forces and Colonial Americans, 1677–1763.* Chapel Hill: University of North Carolina Press, 1986.

Lemisch, Jesse. "Jack Tar in the Streets: Merchant Seamen in the Politics of

Revolutionary America." *William and Mary Quarterly,* 3d Ser., XXV (1968), 371–407.

Lloyd, Christopher. *The British Seaman, 1200–1860: A Social History.* London: Collins, 1968.

Lydon, James G. *Pirates, Privateers, and Profits.* Upper Saddle River, N.J.: The Gregg Press, 1970.

McCusker, John J. "Colonial Tonnage Measurement: Five Philadelphia Merchant Ships as a Sample." *Journal of Economic History,* XXVII (1967), 82–91.

―――― . "The Current Value of English Exports, 1697–1800." *William and Mary Quarterly,* 3d Ser., XXVIII (1971), 607–628.

―――― . *Money and Exchange in Europe and America, 1600–1775: A Handbook.* Chapel Hill: University of North Carolina Press, 1978.

―――― . "Sources of Investment Capital in the Colonial Philadelphia Shipping Industry." *Journal of Economic History,* XXXII (1972), 146–157.

McCusker, John J., and Russell R. Menard. *The Economy of British America, 1607–1789.* Chapel Hill: University of North Carolina Press, 1985.

McLachlan, Jean O. *Trade and Peace with Old Spain: A Study of the Influence of Commerce on Anglo-Spanish Diplomacy in the First Half of the Eighteenth Century.* Cambridge: Cambridge University Press, 1940.

Maclay, E.S. *A History of American Privateers.* New York: D. Appleton & Co., 1899.

McNeill, John Robert. *Atlantic Empires of France and Spain: Louisbourg and Havana, 1700–1763.* Chapel Hill: University of North Carolina Press, 1985.

Mahan, Alfred Thayer. *The Influence of Sea Power upon History, 1660–1783.* 1890. Reprint. New York: Hill and Wang, 1957.

Maier, Pauline. "Isaac Sears and the Business of Revolution." In Pauline Maier. *The Old Revolutionaries: Political Ideas in the Age of Samuel Adams,* 51–100. New York: Alfred A. Knopf, 1980.

Mathieu, Jacques. "La ballance commerciale: Nouvelle-France—Antilles au XVIIIe siècle." *Revue d'histoire de l'Amérique française,* XXV (1972), 465-497.

May, W.E. "Captain Charles Hardy on the Carolina Station, 1742–1744." *South Carolina Historical Magazine,* LXX (1969), 1–19.

―――― . "Captain Frankland's *Rose.*" *American Neptune,* XXVI (1966), 37–62.

―――― . "His Majesty's Ships on the Carolina Station." *South Carolina Historical Magazine,* LXXI (1970), 162–169.

Meyer, W.R. "The Channel Island Privateers, 1793–1815." In *A People of the Sea: The Maritime History of the Channel Islands,* edited by A.G. Jamieson, 173–194. London: Methuen, 1986.

―――― . "English Privateering in the War of 1688 to 1697." *Mariner's Mirror,* LXVII (1981), 259–272.

Middleton, Arthur P. *Tobacco Coast: A Maritime History of Chesapeake Bay in the Colonial Era.* Newport News, Va.: Mariners' Museum, 1953.

Minchinton, Walter E., and David J. Starkey. "Characteristics of Privateers Operating from the British Isles Against America, 1777–1783." In *Ships, Seafaring and Society: Essays in Maritime History,* edited by Timothy J. Runyan, 251–274. Detroit: Wayne State University Press, 1987.

Minchinton, Walter E., ed. *Mercantilism: System or Expediency.* Lexington, Mass.: D.C. Heath & Co., 1969.

Miquelon, Dale. *Dugard of Rouen: French Trade to Canada and the West Indies, 1729–1770.* Montreal: McGill-Queen's University Press, 1978.

Morris, Richard B. *Government and Labor in Early America.* 1946. Reprint. New York: Harper & Row, Harper Torchbooks, 1965.

Nash, Gary B. *The Urban Crucible: Social Change, Political Consciousness, and the Origins of the American Revolution.* Cambridge, Mass.: Harvard University Press, 1979.

Nie, Norman H. *et al. SPSS: Statistical Package for the Social Sciences,* 2d ed. New York: McGraw-Hill, 1975.

North, Douglass C. "Sources of Productivity Change in Ocean Shipping, 1600–1850." *Journal of Political Economy,* LXXVI (1968), 953–970.

Ogelsby, J.C.M. "Spain's Havana Squadron and the Preservation of the Balance of Power in the Caribbean, 1740–1748." *Hispanic American Historical Review,* XLIX (1969), 473–488.

Pares, Richard. *Colonial Blockade and Neutral Rights, 1739–1763.* Oxford: The Clarendon Press, 1938.

———. "The Manning of the Navy in the West Indies, 1702–63." Royal Historical Society, *Transactions,* 4th Ser., XX (1937), 31–60.

———. *War and Trade in the West Indies, 1739–1763.* Oxford: Oxford University Press, 1936.

Parker, Geoffrey. *The Military Revolution: Military Innovation and the Rise of the West, 1500–1800* (Cambridge: Cambridge University Press, 1988).

Peckham, Howard H. *The Colonial Wars, 1689–1762.* Chicago: University of Chicago Press, 1964.

Pitman, Frank Wesley. *The Development of the British West Indies, 1700–1763.* New Haven, Conn.: Yale University Press, 1917.

Price, Jacob M. "Economic Function and the Growth of American Port Towns in the Eighteenth Century." *Perspectives in American History,* VIII (1974), 123–186.

———. *France and the Chesapeake: A History of the French Tobacco Monopoly, 1674–1791, and of Its Relationship to the British and American Tobacco Trades.* 2 vols. Ann Arbor: University of Michigan Press, 1973.

———. "New Time Series for Scotland's and Britain's Trade with the Thirteen Colonies and States, 1740 to 1791." *William and Mary Quarterly,* 3d Ser., XXXII (1975), 307–325.

Raban, Peter. "War and Trade in the Mid-Eighteenth Century." *Transactions of La Société Guernesiaise,* XXIV (1986), 131–163.

Rankin, Hugh F. *The Golden Age of Piracy.* New York: Holt, Rinehart and Winston, 1969.

Rediker, Marcus. *Between the Devil and the Deep Blue Sea: Merchant*

Seamen, Pirates, and the Anglo-American Maritime World, 1700–1750. Cambridge: Cambridge University Press, 1987.

────── . " 'Under the Banner of King Death': The Social World of Anglo-American Pirates, 1716–1726." *William and Mary Quarterly,* 3d Ser., XXXVIII (1981), 203–227.

Reese, Trevor R. *Colonial Georgia: A Study in British Imperial Policy in the Eighteenth Century.* Athens: University of Georgia Press, 1963.

Richmond, Sir Herbert. *The Navy in the War of 1739–48.* 3 vols. Cambridge: Cambridge University Press, 1920.

Ritchie, Robert C. *Captain Kid and the War against the Pirates.* Cambridge, Mass.: Harvard University Press, 1986.

Roberts, Michael. "The Military Revolution, 1560–1660." In Michael Roberts. *Essays in Swedish History,* 195–225. Minneapolis: University of Minnesota Press, 1967.

Rodger, N.A.M. *The Wooden World: An Anatomy of the Georgian Navy.* Annapolis, Md.: Naval Institute Press, 1986.

Schutz, John A. *William Shirley: King's Governor of Massachusetts.* Chapel Hill: University of North Carolina Press, 1961.

Shepherd, James F., and Gary M. Walton, *Shipping, Maritime Trade, and the Economic Development of Colonial North America.* Cambridge: Cambridge University Press, 1972.

Sirmans, M. Eugene. *Colonial South Carolina: A Political History, 1663–1763.* Chapel Hill: University of North Carolina Press, 1966.

Speck, W.A. "The International and Imperial Context." In *Colonial British America: Essays in the New History of the Early Modern Era,* edited by Jack P. Greene and J.R. Pole, 384–407. Baltimore: Johns Hopkins University Press, 1984.

Starkey, David J. "The Economic and Military Significance of British Privateering, 1702–83." *Journal of Transport History,* 3d Ser., IX (1988), 50–59.

Steele, Ian K. *The English Atlantic, 1675–1740: An Exploration of Communication and Community.* New York: Oxford University Press, 1986.

────── . "Governors or Generals?: A Note on Martial Law and the Revolution of 1689 in English America." *William and Mary Quarterly,* 3d Ser., XLVI (1989), 304–314.

────── . *Guerillas and Grenadiers: The Struggle for Canada, 1689–1760.* Toronto: Ryerson Press, 1969.

────── . *Politics of Colonial Policy: The Board of Trade in Colonial Administration, 1696–1720.* New York: Oxford University Press, 1968.

Stumpf, Stuart O. "Implications of King George's War for the Charleston Mercantile Community." *South Carolina Historical Magazine,* LXXVII (1976), 161–188.

Sutherland, Lucy S. *A London Merchant, 1695–1774.* 1933. Reprint. London: Frank Cass & Co., Ltd., 1962.

Swanson, Carl E. "American Privateering and Imperial Warfare, 1739–1748." *William and Mary Quarterly,* 3d Ser., XLII (1985), 357–382.

────── . "The Competition for American Seamen during the War of 1739–1748." In *Man and Nature: Proceedings of the Canadian Society for*

Eighteenth-Century Studies, edited by Roger L. Emerson *et al.,* 119–129. London, Ont.: Althouse Press, Faculty of Education, The University of Western Ontario, 1982.

––––––. "Privateering in Early America." *International Journal of Maritime History,* I (1989), 253–278.

––––––. "The Profitability of Privateering: Reflections on British Colonial Privateers during the War of 1739–1748." *American Neptune,* XLII (1982), 36–56.

Symcox, Geoffrey. *The Crisis in French Sea Power, 1688–1697: From the Guerre d'Escadre to the Guerre de Course.* The Hague: Martinus Nijhoff, 1974.

Ubbelohde, Carl. *The Vice-Admiralty Courts and the American Revolution.* Chapel Hill: University of North Carolina Press, 1960.

Walker, Geoffrey J. *Spanish Politics and Imperial Trade, 1700–1789.* Bloomington: Indiana University Press, 1979.

Wallerstein, Immanuel. *The Modern World-System II: Mercantilism and the Consolidation of the European World-Economy, 1600–1750.* New York: Academic Press, 1980.

Walton, Gary M. "Colonial Tonnage Measurement: A Comment." *Journal of Economic History,* XXVII (1967), 393–397.

Weir, Robert M. *Colonial South Carolina: A History.* Millwood, N.Y.: KTO Press, 1983.

Wilson, Charles. " 'Mercantilism': Some Vicissitudes of an Idea." *Economic History Review,* 2d Ser., X (1957), 181–188.

––––––. "Trade, Society and the State." In *The Economy of Expanding Europe in the Sixteenth and Seventeenth Centuries.* Vol. IV of *The Cambridge Economic History of Europe,* edited by E.E. Rich and C.H. Wilson, 487–575. Cambridge: Cambridge University Press, 1967.

Wood, Peter H. *Black Majority: Negroes in Colonial South Carolina from 1670 through the Stono Rebellion.* New York: Alfred A. Knopf, 1974.

Wright, Charles and Ernest C. Fayle. *A History of Lloyd's, from the Founding of Lloyd's Coffee House to the Present Day.* London: Macmillan, 1928.

Wright, J. Leitch, Jr. *Anglo-Spanish Rivalry in North America.* Athens: University of Georgia Press, 1971.

II. Unpublished Materials

Bigelow, Bruce M. "The Commerce of Rhode Island with the West Indies, Before the American Revolution." Ph.D. diss., Brown University, 1930.

Brière, Jean-François R. "Granville and the Newfoundland Fisheries in the Eighteenth Century." Paper presented at the annual meeting of the Canadian Historical Association, Vancouver, B.C., June 1983.

Devine, Joseph A., Jr. "The British North American Colonies in the War of 1739–1748." Ph.D. diss., University of Virginia, 1968.

Johnson, Warren B. "The Content of American Colonial Newspapers Relative to International Affairs, 1704–1763." Ph.D. diss., University of Washington, 1962.

Lemisch, Jesse. "Jack Tar v. John Bull: The Role of New York's Seamen in Precipitating the Revolution." Ph.D. diss., Yale University, 1963.

Lydon, James G. "The Role of New York in Privateering down to 1763." Ph.D. diss., Columbia University, 1956.

Ogelsby, John C.M. "The Maritime Struggle in the West Indies, 1739–1748." Ph.D. diss., University of Washington, 1963.

Rediker, Marcus B. "Society and Culture among Anglo-American Deep Sea Sailors, 1700–1750." Ph.D. diss., University of Pennsylvania, 1982.

Skemp, Sheila L. "A Social and Cultural History of Newport, Rhode Island, 1720–1765." Ph.D. diss., University of Iowa, 1974.

Stumpf, Stuart O. "The Merchants of Colonial Charleston, 1680–1756." Ph.D. diss., Michigan State University, 1971.

Swanson, Carl E. "Predators and Prizes: Privateering in the British Colonies during the War of 1739–1748." Ph.D. thesis, University of Western Ontario, 1979.

Ziebarth, Robert E. "The Role of New York in King George's War, 1739–1748." Ph.D. diss., New York University, 1972.

Index

284